Disaster Response and Recovery: Strategies and Tactics for Resilience

David A. McEntire, Ph.D.
University of North Texas

BICENTENNIAL
1807
⊗WILEY
2007
BICENTENNIAL

Credits

Publisher
Anne Smith

Development Editor
Laura Town

Marketing Manager
Jennifer Slomack

Editorial assistant
Tiara Kelly

Production Manager
Kelly Tavares

Production Assistant
Courtney Leshko

Creative Director
Harry Nolan

Cover designer
Hope Miller

This book was set in Times New Roman, printed and bound by R. R. Donnelley.

The cover was printed by Phoenix Color.

To order books or for customer service please, call 1-800-CALL WILEY (225-5945).

ISBN-13 978-0-471-78974-7

ISBN-10 0-471-78974-7

Printed in the United States of America

10 9 8 7 6 5 4 3 2 1

ABOUT THE AUTHOR

Dr. David A. McEntire is an Associate Professor in the Emergency Administration and Planning Program in the Department of Public Administration at the University of North Texas. Dr. McEntire received his bachelor's degree from Brigham University and his master's and doctorate degrees from the University of Denver. He teaches emergency management courses in both the undergraduate EADP and MPA programs. His academic interests include emergency management theory, international disasters, community preparedness, response coordination, and vulnerability reduction. He has received several Quick Response Grants (funded by the National Science Foundation through the Natural Hazards Center at the University of Colorado) which allowed him to conduct research on disasters in Peru, the Dominican Republic, Texas, New York and California. His research has been published in *Public Administration Review, the Australian Journal of Emergency Management, Disasters, the International Journal of Mass Emergencies and Disasters, Journal of Emergency Management, Journal of the Environment and Sustainable Development, Sustainable Communities Review, International Journal of Emergency Management, Towson Journal of International Affairs, Journal of the American Society of Professional Emergency Planners,* and the *Journal of International and Public Affairs.* His articles in *Disaster Prevention and Management* have received Highly Commended and Outstanding Paper Awards.

Dr. McEntire recently completed an instructor guide for the Federal Emergency Management Agency. He is the editor of a book on interdisciplinary contributions to disaster studies (published by the Federal Emergency Management Agency). He also has forthcoming chapters in books to be published by the ICMA and the Disaster Research Center.

Dr. McEntire has received grants to conduct terrorism response training for FEMA in Arkansas and Oklahoma. He has been a contributing author for a study of Texas Homeland Security Preparedness for the Century Foundation as well as two IQ Reports for the International City/County Management Association. McEntire has presented papers in Mexico and Norway, at the National Science Foundation, at the National Academy of Sciences, and at the Higher Education Conference at FEMA's Emergency Management Institute in Emmitsburg, Maryland. He is a member of Congressman Burgess'

Homeland Security Advisory Board and the Fire Protection Publications Advisory Board. He has reviewed books for Delmar Learning.

Dr. McEntire is a former Coordinator of the EADP program. Prior to coming to the University of North Texas in the Fall of 1999, he attended the Graduate School of International Studies at the University of Denver. While pursuing his degree, he worked for the International and Emergency Services Departments at the American Red Cross.

Contact information:
Emergency Administration and Planning
Department of Public Administration
University of North Texas
P.O. Box 310617
Denton, Tx 76203-0617
(940) 565-2996
mcentire@unt.edu

PREFACE

College classrooms bring together learners from many backgrounds with a variety of aspirations. Although the students are in the same course, they are not necessarily on the same path. This diversity, coupled with the reality that these learners often have jobs, families, and other commitments, requires a flexibility that our nation's higher education system is addressing. Distance learning, shorter course terms, new disciplines, evening courses, and certification programs are some of the approaches that colleges employ to reach as many students as possible and help them clarify and achieve their goals.

Wiley Pathways books, a new line of texts from John Wiley & Sons, Inc., are designed to help you address this diversity and the need for flexibility. These books focus on the fundamentals, identify core competencies and skills, and promote independent learning. The focus on the fundamentals helps students grasp the subject, bringing them all to the same basic understanding. These books use clear, everyday language, presented in an uncluttered format, making the reading experience more pleasurable. The core competencies and skills help students succeed in the classroom and beyond, whether in another course or in a professional setting. A variety of built-in learning resources promote independent learning and help instructors and students gauge students' understanding of the content. These resources enable students to think critically about their new knowledge, and apply their skills in any situation.

Our goal with *Wiley Pathways* books—with its brief, inviting format, clear language, and core competencies and skills focus—is to celebrate the many students in your courses, respect their needs, and help you guide them on their way.

CASE Learning System

To meet the needs of working college students, *Disaster Response and Recovery: Strategies and Tactics for Resilience* uses a four-step process: The CASE Learning System. Based on Bloom's Taxonomy of Learning, CASE presents key emergency management topics in easy-to-follow chapters. The text then prompts analysis, synthesis, and evaluation with a variety of learning aids and assessment tools. Students move efficiently from reviewing what they have learned, to acquiring new information and skills, to applying their new knowledge and skills to real-life scenarios. Each phase of the CASE system is signaled in-text by an icon:

▲ Content
▲ Analysis
▲ Synthesis
▲ Evaluation

Using the CASE Learning System, students not only achieve academic mastery of emergency management *theories*, but they master real-world emergency management *skills*. The CASE Learning System also helps students become independent learners, giving them a distinct advantage whether they are starting out or seek to advance in their careers.

Organization, Depth and Breadth of the Text

Disaster Response and Recovery offers the following:

▲ *Modular format.* Research on college students shows that they access information from textbooks in a non-linear way. Instructors also often wish to reorder textbook content to suit the needs of a particular class. Therefore, although *Disaster Response and Recovery: Strategies and Tactics for Resilience* proceeds logically from the basics to increasingly more challenging material, chapters are further organized into sections (4 to 6 per chapter) that are self-contained for maximum teaching and learning flexibility.

▲ *Numeric system of headings.* *Disaster Response and Recovery: Strategies and Tactics for Resilience* uses a numeric system for headings (for example, 2.3.4 identifies the fourth sub-section of section 3 of chapter 2). With this system, students and teachers can quickly and easily pinpoint topics in the table of contents and the text, keeping class time and study sessions focused.

▲ *Core content.* There is a growing sense among scholars and practitioners that a dramatically greater emphasis needs to be placed on prevention and mitigation activities in the increasingly important profession of emergency management. Recurring hazards, new threats, rising losses and further vulnerability all lead to the inescapable conclusion that a proactive approach to disasters is undeniably warranted.

There is a growing sense among scholars and practitioners that a dramatically greater emphasis needs to be placed on prevention and mitigation activities in the increasingly important profession of emergency management. Recurring hazards, new threats, rising losses and further vulnerability all lead to the inescapable conclusion that a proactive approach to disasters is undeniably warranted.

At the same time, it is also necessary to recognize that response and recovery operations will always be required, to some degree, after earthquakes, hazardous materials spills, or terrorist attacks involving explosives or nuclear, biological or chemical agents. Furthermore, as the activities after Hurricane Katrina illustrate, there is ample room for improvement in how we deal with disasters. At least some of the mistakes made in New Orleans could have been avoided if the extensive disaster literature had been heeded by politicians, public servants, corporations, non-profit agencies and citizens alike. In addition, there is no doubt that post-disaster functions also have an immediate or long-term impact on the protection of life, property and the environment as well as the minimization of social disruption.

For these reasons, *Disaster Response and Recovery: Strategies and Tactics for Resilience,* has been written. Its goal is to integrate the lessons provided by both researchers and professionals, updating the field with current studies and practical guidelines. Rather than address these reactive phases as if they were the only responsibilities of today's emergency managers, this book attempts to illustrate that successful warning, evacuation and other disaster functions require careful implementation as well as advanced preparedness measures. Recovery likewise provides a prime opportunity to implement change, thereby reducing the probability and consequences of future disasters.

Of course, no book can provide sufficient or fail-proof ideas on how to react successfully to the complexities of today's disasters, and the reader should not consider the information in this text to be the best or only way to respond to or recover from deadly, destructive and disruptive events. In spite of this fact, it is hoped that this volume will be of benefit to students, emergency managers and others interested or involved in disaster management.

In order to meet these goals, *Disaster Response and Recovery* provides a thorough review of the challenges confronting emergency managers (and others) after disasters and discusses recommendations for their resolution.

The initial chapter, "Knowing What to Expect," shares background information about disasters, emergency management, types of hazards and their interaction. Chapter 1 likewise discusses the consequences of disasters so you may know what to expect in their aftermath.

Chapter 2, "Understanding the Actors," helps you recognize the large number of individuals and agencies that participate in response and recovery operations. This includes public servants, government departments, private and non-profit organizations, and citizen volunteers.

Chapter 3, "Anticipating Human Behavior in Disasters," covers human behavior in time of collective stress. It challenges widely held views and offers a more accurate view of disasters.

Chapter 4, "Approaching Response and Recovery Operations," identifies two theoretical approaches to the management of disasters. The advantages and disadvantages of the traditional and professional models are also explored.

Chapter 5, "Responding with Initial Measures," mentions how the initial steps of hazard detection, warning, evacuation and sheltering may protect people's lives.

Chapter 6, "Caring for the Injured, Dead and Distraught," discusses several disaster functions including search and rescue, emergency medical care, fatality management, and stress counseling. It enumerates how best to care for those who have been affected by disasters.

Chapter 7, "Managing Media Relations, Donations and Volunteers," explains what can be done to successfully deal with the media, donations and volunteers after a disaster. It will help you know how to manage public relations and community resources.

At this point, the book transitions from response to recovery. Damage assessment, disaster declarations and debris management are the topics covered in Chapter 8, "Moving Beyond Immediate Needs."

In Chapter 9, "Facilitating Recovery and Mitigation," the process of recovery is investigated along with its relation to mitigation. The types of disaster assistance programs are uncovered along with ways to reduce vulnerability.

Typical problems during response and recovery operations are exposed in Chapter 10, "Overcoming Typical Challenges,". The difficulties associated with decision making, transportation, politics, special populations, communication, legal issues, and record keeping are explained to help you fulfill your obligations as an emergency manager.

Chapter 11, "Harnessing Technology and Organization," points out that technology and organization will improve disaster management and coordination among pertinent actors.

Chapter 12, "Dealing with Future Disasters," helps you understand the challenges of the future by looking at the lessons of prior disasters and the nature of emerging threats.

The final chapter, "Promoting Disaster Resilience," focuses on how to develop disaster resilience. It underscores the value of preparedness, improvisation, professionalism and leadership for you as an emergency manager.

Pre-reading Learning Aids

Each chapter of *Disaster Response and Recovery: Strategies and Tactics for Resilience* features the following learning and study aids to activate students' prior knowledge of the topics and orient them to the material.

▲ **Pre-test.** This pre-reading assessment tool in multiple-choice format not only introduces chapter material, but it also helps students anticipate the chapter's learning outcomes. By focusing students' attention on what they do not know, the self-test provides students with a benchmark against which they can measure their own progress. The pre-test is available online at www.wiley.com/college/McEntire.

▲ **What You'll Learn in This Chapter and After Studying This Chapter.** These bulleted lists tell students what they will be learning in the chapter and why it is significant for their careers. They also explain why the chapter is important and how it relates to other chapters in the text. "What You'll Learn . . ." lists focus on the *subject matter* that will be taught (e.g. what emergency planning is). "After Studying This Chapter . . ." lists emphasize *capabilities and skills* students will learn (e.g. how to plan for an emergency).

▲ **Goals and Outcomes.** These lists identify specific student capabilities that will result from reading the chapter. They set students up to synthesize and evaluate the chapter material, and relate it to the real world.

▲ **Figures and Tables.** Line art and photos have been carefully chosen to be truly instructional rather than filler. Tables distill and present information in a way that is easy to identify, access, and understand, enhancing the focus of the text on essential ideas.

Within-text Learning Aids

The following learning aids are designed to encourage analysis and synthesis of the material, and to support the learning process and ensure success during the evaluation phase:

▲ **Introduction.** This section orients the student by introducing the chapter and explaining its practical value and relevance to the book as a whole. Short summaries of chapter sections preview the topics to follow.

▲ **"For Example" Boxes.** Found within each section, these boxes tie section content to real-world organizations, scenarios, and applications.

▲ **Self-Check.** Related to the "What You'll Learn" bullets and found at the end of each section, this battery of short answer questions emphasizes student understanding of concepts and mastery of section content. Though the questions may either be discussed in class or studied by students outside of class, students should not go on before they can answer all questions correctly. Each *Self-Check* question set includes a link to a section of the pre-test for further review and practice.

▲ **Summary.** Each chapter concludes with a summary paragraph that reviews the major concepts in the chapter and links back to the "What you'll learn" list.

▲ **Key Terms and Glossary.** To help students develop a professional vocabulary, key terms are bolded in the introduction, summary and when they first appear in the chapter. A complete list of key terms with brief definitions appears at the end of each chapter and again in a glossary at the end of the book. Knowledge of key terms is assessed by all assessment tools (see below).

Evaluation and Assessment Tools

The evaluation phase of the CASE Learning System consists of a variety of within-chapter and end-of-chapter assessment tools that test how well students have learned the material. These tools also encourage students to extend their learning into different scenarios and higher levels of understanding and thinking. The following assessment tools appear in every chapter of *Disaster Response and Recovery: Strategies and Tactics for Resilience:*

▲ **Summary Questions** help students summarize the chapter's main points by asking a series of multiple choice and true/false questions that emphasize student understanding of concepts and mastery of chapter content. Students should be able to answer all of the Summary Questions correctly before moving on.

▲ **Review Questions** in short answer format review the major points in each chapter, prompting analysis while reinforcing and confirming student understanding of concepts, and encouraging mastery of chapter content. They are somewhat more difficult than the *Self-Check* and *Summary Questions*, and students should be able to answer most of them correctly before moving on.

▲ **Applying This Chapter Questions** drive home key ideas by asking students to synthesize and apply chapter concepts to new, real-life situations and scenarios.

▲ **You Try It Questions** are designed to extend students' thinking, and so are ideal for discussion or writing assignments. Using an open-ended format and sometimes based on Web sources, they encourage students to draw conclusions using chapter material applied to real-world situations, which fosters both mastery and independent learning.

▲ **Post-test** should be taken after students have completed the chapter. It includes all of the questions in the pre-test, so that students can see how their learning has progressed and improved.

Instructor and Student Package

Disaster Response and Recovery: Strategies and Tactics for Resilience is available with the following teaching and learning supplements. All supplements are available online at the text's Book Companion Website, located at *www.wiley.com/college/McEntire*.

▲ **Instructor's Resource Guide.** Provides the following aids and supplements for teaching:

• *Diagnostic Evaluation of Grammar, Mechanics, and Spelling.* A useful tool that instructors may administer to the class at the beginning of the course to determine each student's basic writing skills. The Evaluation is accompanied by an Answer Key and a Marking Key. Instructors are encouraged to use the Marking key when grading students' Evaluations, and to duplicate and distribute it to students with their graded evaluations.

• *Sample syllabus.* A convenient template that instructors may use for creating their own course syllabi.

• *Teaching suggestions.* For each chapter, these include a chapter summary, learning objectives, definitions of key terms, lecture notes, answers to select text question sets, and at least 3 suggestions for classroom activities, such as ideas for speakers to invite, videos to show, and other projects.

▲ **Test Bank.** One test per chapter, as well as a mid-term and a final. Each includes true/false, multiple choice, and open-ended questions. Answers are provided for the true/false and multiple choice questions, and page references for the open-ended questions. Available in Microsoft Word and computerized formats.

▲ **PowerPoints.** Key information is summarized in 10 to 15 PowerPoints per chapter. Instructors may use these in class or choose to share them with students for class presentations or to provide additional study support.

ACKNOWLEDGMENTS

Taken together, the content, pedagogy, and assessment elements of *Disaster Response and Recovery: Strategies and Tactics for Resilience* offer the career-oriented student the most important aspects of the emergency management field as well as ways to develop the skills and capabilities that current and future employers seek in the individuals they hire and promote. Instructors will appreciate its practical focus, conciseness, and real-world emphasis.

Appreciation is expressed to several organizations and individuals that have helped significantly in the development of *Disaster Response and Recovery*. Although I alone am responsible for the content of this book, I am indebted first and foremost to the Federal Emergency Management Agency for a grant that made much of the research for this text possible. Gratitude is also conveyed to Wayne Blanchard, FEMA Higher Education Program Manager, for his ideas and insight regarding the theoretical and practical nature of post-disaster emergency management operations.

Special thanks is warranted for the contributions of Siddik Ekici and Sarah Mathis, two graduate students in the Master of Public Administration Program at the University of North Texas. These dedicated research assistants eagerly assembled additional information and materials that were omitted during the initial literature review search.

I am also thankful for the knowledge and expertise of several scholars that provided useful recommendations on earlier drafts of the book. These reviewers included Danny Peterson (Arizona State University), Phil Politano (Onondaga Community College), James Richardson (San Antonio Community College), William L. Waugh Jr. (Georgia State University), Cherlyn Wilhelmsen (University of Idaho), and Stacy Lynn Willet (University of Akron). The constructive advice of Gregg Dawson, Steve Reddish and other professional emergency managers in Texas is likewise noted.

Finally, Wiley's staff, including Karyn Drews, Laura Town and Jorkill Almanzar, deserve credit for their time-consuming preparation of this manuscript for publication. While every effort has been taken to produce an accurate portrayal of response and recovery activities and to incorporate appropriate citations, it is possible that mistakes or errors remain present. Should this be the case, the reader is encouraged to share thoughts on the book with the author.

David A. McEntire, Ph.D.
Emergency Administration and Planning
Department of Public Administration
University of North Texas
P.O. Box 310617
Denton, Texas 76203-0617
Mcentire@unt.edu

FOREWORD

The attacks of September 11, 2001 and the controversial response to Hurricane Katrina reminded the entire world that even a nation as developed and wealthy as the U.S.A. is vulnerable to catastrophic disaster. No longer could events like the Indian Ocean tsunami (December 26, 2004) or the earthquakes that left over 200,000 dead in the Kashmir region (October 8, 2005) be viewed as tragedies that only happen to people "over there." So it is no wonder that the topic of disaster response and recovery operations has emerged on the public agenda in a way never before seen in this country.

Long before these events, however, a slowly accumulating knowledge base was being constructed by scholars within numerous academic disciplines, especially sociology, geography, political science and public administration. Simultaneously, those charged with the responsibility of preparing for, responding to, recovering from, and mitigating future disasters, began to explicitly recognize the need to transfer this knowledge base into their rapidly emerging profession.

While research based materials had been created decades earlier for those on the front lines of disaster—fire, police, and emergency medical specialists—too often the agency that should have been at the very core of the response team remained invisible, incompetent, or irrelevant.

This book, *Disaster Response and Recovery,* will help change that situation. It provides future, as well as incumbent, emergency managers with a readable, up to date, and scientifically sound foundation. It challenges readers to replace myth with scientific fact. It pushes them to place the budding profession of emergency management into historical context. It gives them specific strategies and tactics for confronting the complex, but essential, function of interagency coordination. Dr. McEntire skillfully moves the reader through both the horizontal layer of community organizations and the vertical nexus of the intergovernmental system of partnerships that link local jurisdictions to the resources of the state and federal government. It is through the entire array of these systems that communities respond to and recover from disaster. With this in-depth but highly readable, presentation of these and related topics, the entire profession may attain a new level of competence, visibility, and legitimacy.

Dr. McEntire directed the highly regarded emergency management program at the University of North Texas for several years. There he successfully blended the methods and theories of the academy with the concerns and needs of people working out in local communities in both private organizations and governmental agencies. Most recently, he has moved beyond this administrative post and now has more time for research and writing. Through his initial doctoral studies at the University of Denver, his superb work at North Texas, and several FEMA funded projects designed to assist other emergency management faculty worldwide, he brought the perfect blend of experiences for the preparation of this text.

It is the first of its kind. It will be an invaluable tool for all who practice this profession. Emergency managers everywhere, like the public whom they seek to involve and protect, will remain indebted to Dr. McEntire for many years because of this unique contribution.

Thomas E. Drabek
John Evans Professor, Emeritus
Department of Sociology and Criminology
University of Denver

BRIEF CONTENTS

CONTENTS

1

KNOWING WHAT TO EXPECT
Hazards and Disasters

Starting Point

Go to www.wiley.com/college/McEntire to assess your knowledge of the basics hazards and disasters
Determine where you need to concentrate your effort.

What You'll Learn in This Chapter

▲ Differences between accidents, emergencies, and disasters
▲ Functions of emergency management
▲ Types of natural and technological civil/conflict hazards
▲ The interaction of hazards
▲ The nature of disasters
▲ The need for response and recovery operations

After Studying This Chapter, You'll Be Able To

▲ Distinguish among the different types of disasters
▲ Examine the overlap between response and recovery
▲ Categorize hazards into different categories
▲ Understand the interaction of hazards and the impact of disasters
▲ Analyze disaster demands to be met

Goals and Outcomes

▲ Compare and contrast the magnitude of different types of disasters
▲ Use basic disaster terminology
▲ Evaluate distinct types of hazards as well as common disaster characteristics
▲ Predict changes resulting from disasters
▲ Assess the importance of response and recovery operations

INTRODUCTION

As an emergency manager, it is crucial that you are aware of important concepts relating to your profession. It is especially imperative that you know the types of events that interact with people produce disasters. For instance, it is vital that you understand natural, technological, and civil/conflict hazards as well as how they interact. Comprehending the impact of disasters and the changes that take place in society when they occur is absolutely necessary. Being aware of the goals pertinent to response and recovery operations will also help you become a successful emergency manager.

1.1 The Occurrence of Disasters

Everyday people around the world are impacted by events that cause death, produce injuries, destroy personal belongings, and interrupt daily activities. These disturbing experiences are known as accidents, crises, emergencies, disasters, calamities, or catastrophes. Such incidents adversely affect individuals, groups, communities, and even nations. Each of these events is similar in that they require action from government officials, businesses, nonprofit organizations, bystanders, and even the victims themselves. However, these occurrences vary dramatically in terms of magnitude and extent of duration. For example, a traffic accident typically can be handled by a few police officers and a tow truck to remove wreckage within minutes. A structural fire may require one or two fire departments, but it can displace the resident or family for months. When a terrorist attack occurs, additional resources are needed to investigate the incident, and the psychological toll of intentional acts could be long lasting. An airplane crash may necessitate the participation of police, fire personnel, and emergency medical service (EMS), as well as corporate employees and government employees such as a coroner or public information officer. If the crash leaves survivors, victims of this ordeal may be permanently disabled. When a major hurricane makes landfall in an urban area, additional personnel will be needed to remove debris, provide relief assistance, and coordinate rebuilding endeavors that could take years. The impact of a minor accident is therefore both quantitatively and qualitatively different from a disaster or uncommon catastrophe (see Table 1-1).

1.1.1 Important Concepts

Disasters are defined as deadly, destructive, and disruptive events that occur when a hazard interacts (or multiple hazards interact) with human vulnerability. The **hazard** is an agent or threat such as earthquakes, industrial explosions, or terrorist attacks. **Vulnerability,** on the other hand, refers to the proneness of people to disasters based on factors such as their geographic location, exposed property, and level of income. The ability of individuals, organizations, and communities to deal with disaster also has a close relation to vulnerability. While hazards are not always controllable, people and organizations do have impact on the

Table 1-1: Comparison of Event Magnitude

	Accidents	Crises	Emergencies/ Disasters	Calamities/ Catastrophes
Injuries	few	many	scores	hundreds/ thousands
Deaths	few	many	scores	hundreds/ thousands
Damage	minor	moderate	major	severe
Disruption	minor	moderate	major	severe
Geographic impact	localized	dispersed	dispersed/ diffuse	diffuse
Availability of resources	abundant	sufficient	limited	scarce
Number of responders	few	many	hundreds	hundreds/ thousands
Time to recover	minutes/hours/ days	days/weeks	months/years	years/decades

degree of their vulnerability to disasters. For this reason, disasters—along with mass emergencies, calamities, and catastrophes—require the knowledge and expertise of professional emergency managers.

Emergency managers are public servants that help jurisdictions reduce the liabilities that lead to disasters. These government employees and other concerned stakeholders also endeavor to build capabilities to deal with them more effectively. Such efforts are commonly described as the four phases of emergency management: mitigation, preparedness, response, and recovery.

▲ **Mitigation** refers to two things, disaster prevention and loss reduction.
▲ **Preparedness** implies efforts to increase readiness for a disaster.
▲ **Response** Activity in the immediate aftermath of a disaster to protect life and property.
▲ **Recovery** Activity to return the affected community to predisaster or, preferably, improved communities.

Mitigation and preparedness should be given the highest priority in the emergency management profession today. For this reason, emergency managers must not be seen solely as an extension of **first responders**—police, fire personnel, and emergency medical personnel. The goals of emergency managers are more proactive and encompassing, even if they do overlap with the objectives and operations of first responders at times.

However, because it is impossible to eliminate all disasters, emergency managers must also be involved in disaster response and recovery operations. Disaster response is action "taken immediately before, during, or directly after an emergency occurs, to save lives [and] minimize damage to property" (Godschalk 1991, p. 136). Examples of disaster-response activities include:

▲ Warning people of severe weather
▲ Evacuating those considered to be at risk
▲ Sheltering the affected population

During response, it is also necessary to provide emergency medical care, relay information to the public, and manage the arrival of donations and volunteers.

Disaster recovery includes actions "to return vital life support systems to minimum operating standards and long-term activity designed to return life to normal or improved levels" (Godschalk 1991, p. 136). This includes efforts to repair homes damaged by disaster and rebuild community infrastructure, such as power lines, roads, and courthouses.

Each of the above phases is closely related to the others (Neal 1997). For instance, it is difficult to separate mitigation from preparedness as both are proactive measures for disaster reduction. Preparedness also has a significant impact on post-disaster management since it enables a community to be ready for the response and recovery periods. In many cases, it is difficult to determine when response ends and recovery begins. For instance, are damage assessment and debris removal part of disaster response or disaster recovery operations? Also, during recovery, it is vitally important that steps be taken to prevent future disasters or minimize their impact. Instead of simply rebuilding homes that have been damaged by a flood or earthquake, it may be necessary to relocate them to safer areas or implement more stringent construction requirements. The word "phases," therefore, may be somewhat misleading. With this in mind, it may be advisable to substitute "phases" with the term "functional areas" or "functional activities." These areas or activities of emergency management do not appear in a neat, linear fashion, so it is difficult to separate them conceptually.

1.1.2 Preview of Disaster Response and Recovery

This book describes strategies and tactics to improve the management of disaster response and recovery operations. This decision is not meant to deny the value of mitigation and preparedness functions. It is instead based on the observation that there is a need for a more current textbook about post-disaster activities. Although there are some great books on this subject, they may lack current information or approach the material from an academic or practical standpoint only. Response and recovery operations have changed significantly over the past decade or two. The informative research generated by disaster scholars over the years also needs to be integrated with the extensive experience of professional emergency managers. In addition, there is a dire need to educate local government leaders in order to avert the repetition of mistakes made after Hurricane Katrina and other disasters. Nevertheless, this book may be of use to incorporate personnel or humanitarian workers who are also involved in response and recovery operations.

In order to meet these goals, *Disaster Response and Recovery* will provide a comprehensive discussion about post-disaster management issues and recommendations for their improvement. Chapter 2 will help you as an emergency manager identify the actors involved in response and recovery operations. This includes government officials and agencies as well as corporations, nonprofit organizations, and even ordinary citizens. Chapter 3 discusses human behavior in times of disaster. It dispels widely held myths and illustrates typical social reactions to collective stress. Chapter 4 compares alternative theoretical stances regarding the management of disasters. It acknowledges the strengths and weaknesses of traditional and professional approaches. Chapter 5 covers initial response measures, and it provides ideas on how to protect people through hazard detection, warning, evacuation, and sheltering. Chapter 6 lists steps that can be taken to care for those who have been adversely affected by a disaster. This chapter shares information about search and rescue, emergency medical care, fatality management, and psychological stress. Chapter 7 gives recommendations on how to manage public relations and community resources. In particular, it discusses how you can effectively manage the media, donations, and volunteers after a disaster. The transition from response to recovery is the subject of Chapter 8. It assesses functions such as damage assessment, disaster declarations, and debris removal. In Chapter 9, disaster assistance programs are discussed along with ways to reduce vulnerability. This chapter provides information on recovery and how this functional activity can be linked to mitigation. The challenges of response and recovery are exposed in Chapter 10. It will help you understand difficulties associated with decision making, transportation, politics, special populations, communication, legal issues, and record keeping. Chapter 11 points out tools that can be used during response and recovery operations. These include technological equipment as well as organizational arrangements (e.g., incident command and emergency operation centers) that will improve coordination. Chapter 12 mentions lessons from prior disasters and identifies new threats and reasons for rising vulnerability. It attempts to help you think critically about the future of emergency management. The final chapter of the book illustrates additional ways to post-disaster operations. Chapter 13 discusses various aspects of disaster preparedness in addition to the importance of improvisation, professionalism, and leadership among emergency managers.

Before proceeding with the outlined direction of the book, the remainder of this initial chapter will provide additional information about hazards and how they interact one with another. It also describes the impact of disasters and what you as an emergency manager can expect in their aftermath.

- What events can occur on a daily basis?
- How are they different from one another?
- What are **disasters** and what are their causes?
- What is **emergency management**?
- How do you define **response?**
- How do you define **recovery?**

1.2 Types of Hazards

As an emergency manager involved in disaster response and recovery, you must understand the nature of hazards if you are to be successful. A hazard is a physical, technological, or intentional agent such as an earthquake, industrial explosion, or terrorist bombing. These hazardous events occur in the United States and around the world. Vehicles collide due to careless drivers or poor weather conditions. Trains derail due to mechanical failure or human error. Floods, tornadoes, and earthquakes occur, leaving buildings in rubble and other property damage. Petrochemical facilities rely heavily upon the use of hazardous materials, sometimes causing an explosion at the industrial complex. Terrorists detonate improvised explosive devices, producing carnage and fear in their wake. Hazards are present for many different reasons. Some hazards naturally occur in the environment, whereas others are the result of human activity, mistakes, or malicious intent.

1.2.1 Natural Hazards

Natural hazards are those events originating from the physical environment, typically because of radiation from the sun, heat flow within the earth, or the force of gravity. Natural hazards occur in and across three arenas of action (Mileti 1999):

▲ The lithosphere (the earth's crust)
▲ The hydrosphere (the earth's water system)
▲ The atmosphere (the air surrounding the earth, which is made up of various gasses)

Natural hazards are classified as being atmospheric, geologic, hydrologic, seismic, volcanic, and wildfire in origin.

1.2.2 Atmospheric Hazards

An **atmospheric hazard** is a hazard agent that is produced in or by the earth's atmosphere. A hurricane is one type of atmospheric hazard. Hurricanes begin as tropical depressions in the Atlantic Ocean and form as low-pressure systems that rotate in a counterclockwise direction due to the warm water that fuels them. In the Indian Ocean these storm systems are known as cyclones, and in the Pacific Ocean they are labeled typhoons. When wind speeds top 74 m.p.h., the tropical depressions become hurricanes. The eye or center of the storm is calm, but it is surrounded by circling cloud bands that produce rain in large amounts. Some hurricanes may have winds in excess of 100 or even 200 m.p.h., and they also may produce a storm surge of up to 24 feet. In the northern hemisphere, hurricanes travel in a west-northwesterly direction. They frequently hit Atlantic states and those along the Gulf Coast. The strength of a hurricane is noted under the Saffir-Simpson Scale. The **Saffir-Simpson Scale** is a descriptive tool to explain the magnitude of a hurricane in terms of wind and storm surge. It includes five categories. Category 1 is the weakest, whereas category 5 is the strongest.

Florida is prone to hurricanes. Hurricane Andrew made landfall on August 24, 1992. Its strong winds devastated the Miami-Dade area. This hurricane produced dozens of deaths and left thousands of people without power and shelter. Weak building codes and poor enforcement resulted in major structural collapses and a debris-management nightmare. Hurricane Andrew's impact on Florida was only surpassed by the four hurricanes and one tropical storm that hit Florida in 2004. This was one of the worst hurricane seasons on record. However, these hurricanes combined did not cause as many deaths as a cyclone that hit Bangladesh. It killed as many as 300,000 people.

A thunderstorm is another atmospheric hazard. Thunderstorms are produced when warm, moist air rises through convection (thermal uplift). They also occur along cold and warm fronts where different air masses collide or when clouds traverse mountain chains (i.e., orographic lifting). When thunderstorm cells form (cumulus and cumulonimbus clouds), air rises and then descends quickly, leading to rain, sometimes in copious amounts.

Depending on weather conditions and temperatures, the vertical movement of air also freezes water droplets that fall to the earth as hail. Most hail is small (pea size), but it can be large at times (baseball or even grapefruit size). Hail can damage the roofs of buildings, destroy car windshields, and even kill those that are struck by it. Some of the most costly natural disasters are hail storms, such as the one that hit Fort Worth, Texas during a 1995 Mayfest celebration. More than 100 people had to be taken to area hospitals after being struck by softball-sized hailstones.

Thunderstorms also result in downdrafts and straight-line winds (wind that travels vertically to the ground and then moves horizontally along the earth's surface). Such winds travel quickly and can bring airplanes down and flatten fences and barns.

Thunderstorms are common around the world. There are 16,000 thunderstorms per year in all locations, excluding the North and South poles. In the United States, strong thunderstorms occur frequently along the Gulf Coast or in the Midwestern states. Such storms also generate lightning, which is the emission of electrical bolts as a result of the interaction of positive and negative charged fields. Lightning bolts are discharged from clouds. They often strike buildings, trees, and the ground. Because the temperature of the bolt is extremely hot (perhaps up to 50,000 degrees Celsius), people can be killed due to burns, respiratory failure, and cardiac arrest. Forests may be ignited with fire also. Approximately 6,000 lightning strikes occur every minute around the world.

Tornadoes are another type of atmospheric hazard. Tornadoes are closely associated with thunderstorms. In fact, the name "tornado" stems from the Spanish name for such storms. As warm, moist air collides against cool, dry air, winds may move in a circular or rotating direction. For reasons not fully understood, one portion of the rotating air shaft drops while the other portion remains or moves upward in a vertical manner. When the resulting funnel reaches the ground, it becomes known as a tornado. The speed of winds moving in opposite directions may start out around 65 m.p.h. Wind speed is the factor used to describe the strength of tornadoes under the Fujita scale. Small tornadoes (e.g., F0 or F1) are very common but possess slower wind speeds. Large tornadoes (e.g., F4 or F5) are infrequent, but their wind speed reaches over 200 mph. At such high speeds, windows are broken, roofs are ripped from walls, and even foundations can be sucked from their moorings. Glass, brick, two by fours, and even cars become missiles and may penetrate other structures.

Tornadoes are very common to the Midwest portion of the United States due to the jet stream and the movement of air from Canada and the Gulf of Mexico. Tornadoes have occurred in many states, including those outside the central portion of the country. In fact, 90% of the world's tornadoes take place in the United States (roughly 500 to 600 per year). Oklahoma has been especially hard hit on occasions, as was the case on May 3-5, 1999. Fifty-nine tornadoes were reported in central Oklahoma, and many of them lasted several minutes in duration and traveled great distances. At least 40 people were killed during the outbreak, and 675 people were injured. More than 10,000 homes were damaged or destroyed. Losses were estimated at $1.2 billion.

Winter storms are atmospheric hazards that occur mainly in December, January, and February in the northern and central United States. However, it is possible for lower states to receive snow periodically, and ice storms are not excluded from places like Louisiana and Texas. Winter storms include snow, sleet and ice, and are associated with extremely cold temperatures. Ice storms are sometimes difficult to distinguish from sleet, although sleet has more water in liquid state than ice. If it is sufficiently cold, sleet will form into ice when it hits the ground.

A very damaging ice storm took place in the northeastern United States and in Canada in January 1998. Ice piled up several times higher than prior records,

FOR EXAMPLE

Heat Wave in France

In August 2003, France experienced some of the highest minimum and maximum daily temperatures recorded in history. Because many families and physicians had taken time off during this typical vacation period, many elderly were left at home or without sufficient care in hospitals and nursing facilities. The lack of air conditioning units in France combined with temperatures up to 104 degrees Fahrenheit and insufficient fluid intake resulted in the death of over 15,000 people. Heat waves such as this one are not always recognized as significant hazards, but their impact can be extensive, as France discovered.

and many power lines and transmission towers collapsed due to the excessive weight. Similar problems occur with excessive snow. On January 28, 1977, Buffalo, New York received 93 inches of snow. This is an amount greater than the average for that area during the entire year. Blizzards are snowstorms with high winds. They can leave several inches or feet of snow on the ground, making transportation difficult. When snow falls on steep slopes, the potential for avalanche may result. Avalanches are quick and violent movements of snow down the mountainside. They are common in Utah and Colorado. Snow characteristics, changing temperatures, wind, skiers, and snowmobiles can trigger avalanches. While snow and avalanches create several challenges, the cold weather also produces hypothermia in individuals who are exposed. In some cases, the heating or lighting of homes during winter storms may lead to fires that cause death and destruction.

A final atmospheric hazard is a heat wave. A heat wave is a prolonged period of high temperatures that may also be coupled with excessive humidity. Heat waves create loss of agricultural crops and also stress humans to the point that they cannot cool their bodies through the normal process of sweating. If relief from the weather or medical care is not given, coma, paralysis, and death will follow. For instance, approximately 700 deaths (mainly among the elderly) resulted in Chicago in July 1995 due to a prolonged heat wave. Such events require constant communication with the public. The heat index predicts the severity of the situation. This index incorporates both the temperature and humidity. It is used to warn people to stay inside and drink lots of water.

1.2.3 Geological Hazards

Geological hazards are those hazard agents associated with the earth's soil and rock. Landslides are the most damaging kind of geological hazards. Landslides occur because of a number of variables, such as slope angle, moisture content of the soil, and rock conditions. The presence or absence of vegetation may also be a reason why landslides occur. Landslides may move swiftly and occur without warning or creep at a slow and perhaps unnoticeable pace. Such events are possible in any hilly or mountainous area but are probably most common in the Rocky Mountain region and along the Pacific Coast. In 1983, a major landslide blocked a major highway in Thistle, Utah. The sediment and rock created an earthen dam that backed up a river and flooded a city. In 2005, a major portion of the mountain separated in La Conchita, California and fell to the valley floor below. It buried 15 homes, damaged 16 others, and killed several individuals.

Besides landslides, there are also subsidence and expansive soil hazards. Subsidence occurs when the water table or underground rivers erode the soil around them and the earth collapses. Another cause of subsidence is mining for coal and ore, or the pumping of ground water out of a certain geographic area. New Orleans and Mexico City are sinking due to this latter activity. Sinkholes are also common in Florida. In contrast to subsidence, expansive soils may actually rise or drop due to the presence or absence of moisture in ground. This hazard is especially prevalent in locations that have clay soils. Although expansive soils are found most often in the South and West, they can be present in many parts of the United States. Expansive soils do not kill individuals but they can create a large amount of property damage.

1.2.4 Hydrologic Hazards

Hydrologic hazards are hazard agents that emanate from the earth's water systems. There are four types of hydrologic hazards, one of them being floods. Floods are the most prevalent of any hazard, natural or otherwise. They are also among the most costly. Episodes of flooding occur when there is too much precipitation or there is an inability for soil to absorb water. Flooding can also result from melting snow pack, ice jams, and dam failures. Soil type, topography, and level of development have a bearing on flooding. For instance, clay soils are more likely to produce runoff in comparison to sandy soils. Hills, valleys, and the use of cement in highly urbanized areas may also contribute to this type of hazard.

The 1993 great Midwestern flood is the most widespread and costly flood in U.S. history. Months of unusually wet weather and the seasonal snowmelt overwhelmed the Mississippi River Basin with water. Dykes, locks, and dams were eventually filled to capacity, and many of them were breached. The water emitted from broken levees only added to the flooding downstream. Thousands of people had to be evacuated, and property losses totaled in the billions of dollars.

Storm surges and coastal erosion may result from hurricanes or other types of phenomena (e.g., low-pressure systems, strong winds, high tides, etc.). A storm surge is a temporary rise in the water level of an ocean or river estuary. Flooding is a product of storm surges, and it can take days and weeks before water recedes after such events. Coastal erosion may also occur as a result of

Figure 1-1

Home destroyed by flood damage.

storm surges, and it often damages roads, bridges, dunes, and beaches. Florida is frequently affected by the storm surges and coastal erosion associated with hurricanes. Losses can amount to millions, or even billions, of dollars.

Droughts are another kind of hydrologic hazard. Low amounts of rainfall and high evaporation rates due to warm or hot temperatures lead to conditions of drought. Drought can have a major negative impact on agricultural output, thereby contributing to widespread famine. In the United States, droughts do not typically result in a shortage of the overall food supply (although the abundance of individual crops may be extremely low). Famines in other countries can be especially deadly. The lack of adequate food intake has resulted in malnourishment and the spread of fatal diseases in Ethiopia in the 1980s and Niger in the mid 2000s. The Great Depression in the United States was triggered in part by severe drought. Dust storms, desertification, and salinization of soil often result from droughts.

1.2.5 Seismic Hazards

Seismic hazards are hazard agents produced by the movement of tectonic plates that float on magma. They are earthquakes that occur along fault lines where landmasses move apart, collide, or slide against each other laterally. Earthquakes produce waves that travel in and on top of the earth. These waves emanate from the geographic origin of the earthquake, known as a focal point. The location on the earth's crust directly above the focal point is the epicenter. Earthquake intensity is measured with the

▲ **Richter scale** measures earthquake intensity by measuring registered shaking amplitudes.
▲ **Mercalli scale** measures earthquake intensity physical observation of damages that result from the movement of the earth's crust (e.g., broken windows, cracked walls, and falling pictures).

Earthquakes occur in every part of the world, although their probability is highest in places such as the ring of fire (locations surrounding the Pacific rim). In the United States, there are major fault lines in California, Utah, Illinois, and South Carolina and in New England. There are also earthquakes along the New Madrid fault that have changed the course of the Mississippi River in the past. Earthquake faults along the Pacific Coast slip frequently and have destroyed gas and water lines, roads and bridges, and homes and other structures. The 1989 Loma Prieta and 1994 Northridge earthquakes killed scores of individuals. Tens of thousands and even hundreds of thousands have perished in earthquakes in China, Mexico City, Russia, India, and Iran. Building codes have been weak in these countries, resulting in additional building collapses and the crushing of their inhabitants.

Tsunamis are associated with recurring submarine landslides and possible asteroid impacts, but they result most often from earthquake hazards. If fault lines slip under the ocean, the seismic waves displace water, which races horizontally across the ocean floor. When these waves reach land, they become amplified on the surface. The resulting harbor waves may appear in a series of waves that travel hundreds of feet to a few miles inland. These waves travel quickly (as fast as 500 mph) and may reach one or two stories in height. They level much of what lies in their path.

Tsunamis result in drownings and sweep their victims out to sea as they recede. Hawaii and the northwestern coast of the United States are prone to tsunamis. One tsunami struck Hilo, Hawaii in 1946, and another affected Alaska in 1964. Several deaths resulted in each event. The most powerful tsunami in history occurred on January 4, 2005. The Sumatra earthquake registered over 7.0 on the Richter scale; it sent tsunami waves to more than 12 countries surrounding the Indian Ocean. More than 300,000 people died from this tragic event.

Volcanic activity is another type of natural hazard, and it is closely related to earthquakes and the movement of magma within the earth's crust. Magma may bubble up through fissures in the earth, creating a cone with a reservoir of lava. Such cones may vent super heated gasses and emit lava flows down the side of the crater. Volcanoes are particularly deadly when they erupt, as was the case with Mt. St. Helens in 1980. A bulge developed on Mt. St. Helens over time, and eventually the pressure gave way in a violent explosion. Tons and tons of soil, lava, and mud were sent down the side of the mountain and into the valley and rivers below. Fifty-seven people were killed in the incident, being vaporized immediately or buried in volcanic debris. The logging industry in this area was severely disrupted, and ash fell on communities around the volcano and even in nearby states. This made some vehicles inoperable and caused a clean-up nightmare. In the United States, volcanic activity is present mainly in the Northwest and Hawaii.

1.2.6 Wildfire Hazards

Wildfires hazards result from lightning strikes, and they can quickly envelop hundreds of acres of forest and brush. Humans may also play a role in the ignition of wildfires due to carelessness with matches, cigarettes, and campfires. Drought conditions, high temperatures, low humidity in the air, and strong winds can spread wildfires rapidly. In some cases, wildfires fires will die out due to topographic conditions (e.g., a gulch or river), weather changes (e.g., rain), and the lack of fuel (e.g., scarcity of trees and undergrowth). There have been major forest fires in Yellowstone National Park and in numerous other forested areas around the country. Increasingly, wildfires threaten development settlements due to the urban-wild land interface. The 1991 Oakland Hills Fire illustrated such a dangerous combination. Over a thousand acres were burned along with hundreds of homes in the area. The fire spread quickly as a result of the dense brush and wood-shingle roofs. Narrow streets and inadequate water supplies hampered firefighting efforts. More than 20 people died in the incident, and millions of dollars were lost as a result.

1.2.7 Biological Hazards

Biological hazards are agents that spread disease or are otherwise poisonous. Such hazards pose a grave threat to humans, and millions of people have died by coming into contact with them. Biological hazards may be broken down into two categories: pathogens and toxins.

- ▲ **Pathogens** are organisms that spread disease and may include anthrax, smallpox, plague, hemorrhagic fever, and rickettsiae.
- ▲ **Toxins** are poisons created by plants and animals. Ricin and botulism are examples of such toxins.

Toxins are not likely to kill many people at a time although they can produce fatalities. However, pathogens could. The 1918 Spanish influenza pandemic killed more people in the United States than had died in combat in World War I. When famines occur and people are malnourished, disease epidemics are especially likely. In recent years, there has been growing public health concerns related to hoof and mouth disease, hantavirus, severe acute respiratory syndrome (SARS), West Nile, and the Avian "bird" flu. Such hazards have created many worries for public health officials, particularly in light of our highly mobile populations and the ease of traveling around the world. Much more needs to be done to prepare for biological hazards.

1.2.8 Environmental Hazards

Pollution, degradation, and overuse of natural resources are types of ecological or environmental hazards. **Environmental hazards** are agents that involve the degradation of the environment, such as pollution, that pose a risk to people's health and well-being. Pollution involves the emission of wastes in the physical environment. This may include the distribution of solid, liquid, and gas wastes into landfills, rivers, and the atmosphere. Such activities harm the soil, contaminate the water, and poison the air. Pollution can hinder farming, spread disease, and lead to other health problems. Other forms of degradation, including desertification and salinization of the soil, are the result of over-farming. This limits the production of agricultural goods and could lead to famines. Furthermore, the emission of pollutants may add to global warming, although there is political controversy about such causes and consequences. Nevertheless, climate change could affect weather patterns and the nature of storms. For instance, flooding could become more severe, and locations that had sufficient water in the past may later find themselves amid drought. The depletion of natural resources is not typically considered an environmental hazard. However, the loss of oil and gas would limit the heating of homes during the winter or the use of air conditioning during summer. This could put many lives in jeopardy.

SELF-CHECK

- What is a natural hazard?
- What are the types of natural hazards?
- Are atmospheric and hydrological hazards related?
- How is a geological hazard different from a seismic hazard?
- What are the effects of biological and environmental hazards?

1.3 Technological Hazards

Technological hazards are hazard agents related to industry, structures, hazardous materials, computers, and transportation systems. These hazards abound in our modern, industrial world, and they range from hazardous material releases to structural failures and beyond.

1.3.1 Industrial Hazards

Industrial hazards are hazard agents produced by the extraction, creation, distribution, storage, use, and disposal of chemicals. Chlorine, benzene, insecticides, plastics, fuel, and other materials are released when regulations are ignored, employees are untrained or careless, and equipment fails. Such materials in solid, liquid, or gas state may be toxic, flammable, explosive, or corrosive. They may react in very complex ways depending on temperature and the presence of water, oxygen, or other chemicals. The release of methyl isocyanate (MIC) in Bhopal, India from the Union Carbide Company is regarded to be the most deadly industrial accident in history. While the cause of this event is under dispute, it is believed that poor maintenance resulted in a chemical release. Forty-five tons of gas was emitted into the city, killing anywhere between 2,500 and 10,000 people. While there is much disagreement about the extent of fatalities resulting from this hazard, the event had a profound impact on hazardous materials regulations in the United States and elsewhere.

1.3.2 Structural Collapse Hazards

The collapse of structures is another potentially deadly hazard. **Structural collapses hazards** occur when gravity and poor engineering result in the failure of buildings, roads or other construction projects. They may include the breaking of dams and dykes or the crashing down of buildings. There have been numerous dam failures throughout the history of the United States, including those in Johnstown, Pennsylvania (1889), Buffalo Creek, West Virginia (1972), and Teton, Idaho (1976). The failure of dykes and retaining devices has also occurred in the 1993 Midwest floods and after Hurricane Katrina in New Orleans. Thousands of lives have been lost due to such hazards.

Structural failures are not limited to water-retaining devices alone, however. Bridges, parking garages, and buildings have also suffered from poor engineering, inadequate construction, or improper use. One of the most notable structural hazards was the Hyatt Skywalk collapse. While a dance was being held in the hotel atrium, the suspended walkway broke loose due to the dynamic load of those dancing on it. The walkway fell to the floor on top of those below. The event killed more than 100 people, injured twice that amount, and posed extreme difficulties for those involved in search-and-rescue activities.

1.3.3 Nuclear Hazards

A **nuclear hazard** is a hazard resulting from the presence of radioactive material. These types of hazards are rare. However, they are extremely disruptive. Nuclear power plants provide electricity for communities, businesses, and individual citizens. Although these facilities produce nuclear wastes that must be disposed of, they pollute less than the power plants running off of coal. Nevertheless, nuclear power plants create health risks because radiation can injure or kill people if it is accidentally released into the environment. This potential was witnessed in 1979 at the Three Mile Island nuclear power plant in Harrisburg, Pennsylvania. Because of a leak in some equipment that purifies the water entering the turbines, a back-up system had to be activated. Unfortunately, an employee had shut this off during maintenance, which caused the system to overheat. A warning light did not activate as it should have, and radioactive material was released into the containment building. An employee finally noticed what was taking place and was able to close a valve to reverse the unfolding chain of events. The public became alarmed at the lack of information during the warning and evacuation process. However, no one was killed in the incident. This was not the case at the Chernobyl reactor in the former Soviet Union. After similar mechanical failures and human mistakes, many of those responding to the hazard died and thousands had to be evacuated. The nearby area is inhabitable, and cancer has appeared in those that failed to leave as requested by the government.

1.3.4 Computer Hazards

Computers have posed a technological hazard in the past and will continue to do so in the future. A **computer hazard** is a disruptive hazard associated with computer hardware and software. The calendaring hazard associated with Y2K created fears that anything run by computers would fail. This included potential failures in plane flight programs, public utility systems, and communications media. After serious attempts to change the dates in computer coding and prepare for any eventuality, the arrival of the new millennium came and went without any substantial disturbance. There have been several situations, however, where ice freezing temperatures, floods, and fires have damaged computers. Such hazards shut down power grids, traffic signals, communications capabilities, and online banking records. Also, there is always a chance that a hacker will enter a secure website to steal information. Hackers can also shut down computer systems. Businesses have had corporate information stolen. The Department of Defense firewalls have been breached. People in other countries have interfered with 911 communication centers in the United States because of the knowledge and skills of today's hackers.

1.3.5 Transportation Hazards

Because of the ease of moving people, goods, and services around the world, we are faced with several transportation hazards. A **transportation hazard** is an accident that occurs on roads or railways, at sea, or in the air. Such incidents may result from adverse meteorological circumstances, human error, or mechanical failure. There may be mass vehicle accidents owing to fog or wet and winter weather. At other times, tired or careless drivers may overturn their tankers, which carry hazardous materials and force the evacuation of neighborhoods and other portions of cities. Train derailments are also common and may result from young drivers trying to beat the safety gates, animals grazing on the tracks, and the expansion or contraction of rails due to heat and freezing temperatures. Train derailments can kill passengers, emit hazardous materials into the environment, and create a clean-up nightmare.

FOR EXAMPLE

Ferry Sinking in Bangladesh

In July 2003, a ferry carrying 500 or more passengers sank, killing hundreds of those on board. Traveling to the southeast from the capital of Dhaka, the vessel encountered turbulent waters where two rivers merge. The boat capsized as a result and quickly took on water. About half of those on the ship were rescued by fishermen or managed to swim to shore about 75 yards away. The over-crowded ferry and strong currents produced one of the deadliest transportation disasters in Bangladesh ever.

Instances of ferries sinking, vessels crashing into docks, or oil tankers hitting jagged rocks and puncturing their hulls are transportation hazards that have occurred in past and more recent years. The sinking of ferries is common in places like the Philippines, where they are often overloaded with people and supplies. Captains have lost control of ships in harbors in New York and Canada. In some cases, extreme environmental damage may result. The most famous oil spill occurred on March 24, 1989 in Prince William Sound, Alaska. When the ship ran aground, more than 240,000 barrels of oil were deposited into the seawater, polluting the beach and killing thousands of animals.

Airplane crashes are less frequent than most other types of transportation accidents, and they may result when pilots overshoot runways, when windshear occurs, when landing strips are wet or icy, and when planes are not meticulously crafted and maintained. Plane crashes can be particularly devastating when they occur. In many cases, all passengers on board will be killed. In November 2001, an Airbus A300-600 broke apart over Queens, New York, due to problems associated with the stress placed on the vertical stabilizer. All 260 passengers and crewmembers were killed, and most of the fuselage landed in a neighborhood, adding to the adverse consequences.

SELF-CHECK

- **What is a technological hazard?**
- **What are the types of technological hazards?**
- **Why do technological hazards occur?**
- **How do industry and commerce influence hazards?**
- **What can be done to prevent them?**

1.4 Civil/Conflict Hazards

There are several types of **civil/conflict hazards**. Mass shootings, panic behavior, riots, terrorism, and war fall into this category.

1.4.1 Mass Shootings

Mass shootings are one example of civil/conflict hazards. Unfortunately, these events have become more common in recent years. The list of shootings at schools and other locations in the late 1990s is disturbing:

- ▲ Pearl, Mississippi (1997)—3 killed
- ▲ Paducah, Kentucky (1997)—3 killed
- ▲ Jonesborough, Arkansas (1998)—5 killed
- ▲ Springfield, Oregon (1998)—5 killed
- ▲ Conyers, Georgia (1999)—4 wounded
- ▲ Atlanta, Georgia (1999)—9 killed
- ▲ Pelham, Alabama (1999)—3 killed

Sniper shootings also occurred over a period of several weeks on the freeways in Ohio and at gas stations in Virginia. Post offices and the workplace have been targets of mass shootings. These violent acts pose serious problems for law enforcement agencies as well as emergency medical technicians. A particularly deadly shooting took place on September 15, 1999 at a church in Fort Worth, Texas. A gunman walked into a youth rally and discharged two weapons into the congregation. Seven people were killed. The shooting provoked a massive investigation, and the injured had to be quickly taken to area hospitals.

1.4.2 Panic Behavior

Panic flight, or the fleeing of many individuals from what appears to be imminent harm, is extremely rare. However, it has led to major emergencies in certain situations. Panic flight is most likely to occur when large crowds gather at concerts, sporting venues, and other events. An example took place on February 20, 2003 in West Warwick, Rhode Island. The rock band Great White was performing at a nightclub. The road manager used pyrotechnics inside the building, causing the ceiling to catch on fire. As the fire spread quickly, the occupants headed for the doors. Because most people exited the same way they entered the building, a bottleneck ensued and many were trampled or became stuck. Approximately 100 people died, and more than 187 were injured. The fire led to a drawn-out debate about who was legally liable. Was it the fault of the city inspectors, the building owner, or the band manager? The tragedy prompted a review of fire exits and sprinkler systems around the nation. Such events are not confined to the United States. In 2005, 841 people were killed and another 323 were injured while attending a religious gathering at a mosque in

Baghdad. While inside, someone reported the presence of a suicide bomber and people began to evacuate the area. Hundreds of people stampeded towards a bridge, which broke and fell into the Tigris River. Panic flight does not occur very often, but it can turn deadly, as these cases suggest.

1.4.3 Riots

Riots are another type of civil/conflict hazard. **Riots** are large disturbances where people engage in antisocial behavior. This conduct includes rock throwing, looting, tipping over vehicles, setting off fires, and attacking law-enforcement personnel. Social protesters and their opponents sometimes spark riots. Riots can also start because of political or economic circumstances and other factors, such as a city's loss to another team in the Superbowl. Riots can disrupt business activities and hurt the economy. They often produce a large number of injuries and even death. There have been several riots in the United States, including the Watts Riot in Los Angeles in 1965. This riot began when an officer pulled over an African-American man for driving erratically. In another racially charged situation, jurors found four police officers innocent of police brutality against Rodney King in Sylmar, California. The incident was caught on tape and many people believed that the police were beating King unnecessarily and in a brutal manner. Others believed the legal system was biased when the verdict was made public. On April 29, 1992, scores of people took to the streets to illustrate their dismay. Fifty people were killed, hundreds were injured, and thousands were arrested. Damage was in the millions of dollars. Another riot occurred in Seattle in 1999 when environmentalists and others protested the policies of the World Trade Organization. During a 4-day period, people marched, broke windows, disabled busses, and heckled police. Law-enforcement agencies in Seattle were not fully prepared. They were caught off guard by the demonstration that turned violent.

1.4.4 Terrorism

Terrorism has been one of the most deadly civil/conflict hazards. **Terrorism** is the threat or use of violence to intimidate someone or a government. The perpetrators usually have ideological motives and a political objective to reach. For instance, terrorists engage in this behavior to seek independence, promote their religion, protest abortions, or protect the environment. Terrorists have used weapons, arson, and other measures, such as cyber-terrorism, to kill and disrupt the activities of others. Their attacks have occurred around the world. Suicide bombings are common in the Middle East, particularly in Israel. Other attacks have occurred in Spain, Germany, Russia, the United Kingdom, and Iraq.

The worst case of terrorism in the United States was on September 11, 2001. Islamic extremists hijacked four planes and used them as missiles against buildings symbolic of U.S. political, military, and economic interests. With the exception of one plane, the hijackers were successful. The World Trade Centers were two of the main targets. The towers collapsed after the ignited jet fuel weakened

> ## FOR EXAMPLE
>
> ### Manchester Bombing
>
> In June 1996, terrorists parked a vehicle near a major intersection in the commercial district of Manchester, England. A local television station received word that a bomb would be detonated. A bomb squad was brought in. The team was not able to dismantle the explosives. However, the city was able to evacuate 80,000 people from the area. No one died in the attack, but it did injure more than 200 people, who were cut by glass, impaled by objects, or otherwise affected by the blast. Several buildings were damaged or destroyed, and many businesses and apartment dwellers lost office space or residences. This intentional disaster cost millions of dollars in direct and indirect losses. It prompted a major emergency response and criminal investigation.

the structure. Thousands of people died, and several buildings in New York were turned into a pile of broken glass, twisted metal, and other dangerous and unhealthy debris. The Pentagon was also struck during the attack, but fewer people died in this building than in the World Trade Centers in New York.

Terrorists may also use nerve, blister, blood, choking, and incapacitating agents in their campaigns of intimidation. Shortly after 9/11, envelopes containing anthrax were sent via mail to the headquarters of a newspaper in Florida and to Congressional leaders in Washington, D.C. This killed a handful of people. A worse attack involved the use of Sarin gas by the Aum Shinrykio cult in Japan. This attack, which occurred in a subway, killed several people. It also created medical care needs for thousands of others. It illustrated the grave potential of biological, chemical, and nuclear weapons of mass destruction (WMD). The threat of terrorism has prompted a significant reorganization of the U.S. government and the establishment of the Department of Homeland Security. Billions of dollars have been poured into first-responder training and public health preparedness.

1.4.5 War

Conflict has occurred throughout history between different tribes, ethnic groups, and nation-states. With the advent of modern weaponry, however, the stakes of fighting have become much higher. Millions of people are killed when negotiations break down. Cities have been also been leveled. Such was the case in World War II when London, Dresden, Hiroshima, and Nagasaki were bombed with conventional or nuclear explosives. During the Cold War, the fear of a nuclear attack from the Soviet Union prompted the United States to invest heavily in civil defense initiatives. The goal was to prepare for such an attack, stockpile supplies, and evacuate and shelter citizens. There is not a great deal of interstate conflict today compared to the past, although there are certainly notable examples. An example of this is the U.S. deposing of the Taliban in Afghanistan. Nonetheless, there has been a great deal of intrastate fighting as in places such as Somalia, Yugoslavia, and Rwanda. These internal wars are known as "complex emergencies." They typically involve ethnic cleansing, a failed government, and economic turmoil combined with natural and environmental hazards and especially famines. Those responding to such events have been targeted by the warring factions. For example, relief workers in Iraq have been kidnapped and killed.

SELF-CHECK

- What is a **civil/conflict hazard?**
- What are the types of civil/conflict hazards?
- What is the role of humans in civil/conflict hazards?
- How is each type of civil/conflict hazards related to the other? Are they different? If so, how?

1.5 The Interaction of Hazards and Impact of Disasters

Although it is useful to classify hazards in order to understand their unique features, it is also important for you to recognize that hazards are not mutually exclusive. In other words, each hazard may interact with others in complicated and perhaps even unpredicted ways. The examples are numerous:

- ▲ An earthquake may break a dam, cause a building to collapse, and produce landslides.
- ▲ Degradation of the environment (e.g., deforestation) could exacerbate flash flooding and mudslides owing to severe storms.
- ▲ Flooding could lead to the spread of certain communicable diseases.
- ▲ Computer failures might lead to hazardous material releases or industrial explosions.
- ▲ A train derailment could result in the spill of dangerous chemicals and harm the natural habitat.
- ▲ Those participating in riots often set fire to nearby structures, which may trigger panic flight behavior.

As an emergency manager, you must appreciate the complex nature of hazards as they can have serious impact on response and recovery operations. In most cases, you will be responding to multiple hazards in any given disaster. This creates serious challenges that you must be ready to deal with.

FOR EXAMPLE

Hurricane Katrina

Hurricane Katrina will long be remembered as a complex disaster. In September 2005, Hurricane Katrina, a category 4 storm, slammed into the coast of Louisiana, Mississippi, and Alabama. All states suffered severe losses. However, it was New Orleans that gained national and international attention. The winds of the hurricane damaged structures in the "Big Easy" and affected power and phone service. The storm surge and heavy rains were most problematic. Lake Pontchartrain rose to historic levels, and the levees set up to keep the waters from inundating the below-sea-level community were breached. New Orleans was flooded homes and businesses were under water. Water, sewer, and gas lines were broken. The contents of numerous petroleum and hazardous chemical tanks were released. Making matters worse, antisocial behavior, including looting and fights, were reported around the city. The local, state, and federal response was slow and inadequate. The response was also hampered further when criminals began firing weapons at rescue helicopters and relief workers. Many evacuees sought shelter in the superdome, where supplies were inadequate and conditions were filthy. Behavior was beginning to turn violent among many disaster victims by the time federal aid arrived at the superdome. The delivery of assistance was delayed as flooding severely affected the transportation system. As the city was evacuated, public health workers feared an outbreak of disease due to the squalid living conditions. Katrina involved natural, environmental, biological, technological, and civil hazards.

1.5.1 The Nature of Disasters

When a hazard or multiple hazards interact with humans and their settlements and possessions, disasters occur. People may be injured or killed as a result. The number of injuries from disasters averages about 100 per week in the United States (Mileti 1999, p. 66). For instance, injuries may include superficial cuts from flying glass in a tornado or serious internal wounds due to the collapse of a building after an earthquake. Deaths are also significant. For instance, "it is estimated that natural hazards [in the United States] killed over 24,000 people between January 1, 1975 and December 31, 1994" (Mileti 1999, p. 66). This may result from burns, drowning, or other hazards. These numbers do not include the toll of disease outbreaks, which have been substantial throughout history.

Property is likewise damaged or destroyed in disasters, costing billions of dollars each year. Homes and belongings can be covered by landslides, fishing vessels are sunk in hurricanes, and businesses are flattened by strong winds. Clothing, computers, and cars are ruined in disasters. Losses average about $1 billion per week in the United States, and these figures are rising exponentially (Mileti 1999, p. 66). Hazardous materials spills, nuclear accidents, and other events can likewise degrade the natural environment, thereby affecting the health and well-being of people over generations.

Disasters also disrupt individuals and society as a whole. Routine activities such as cooking, sleeping, and bathing may be hindered due to the damages of one's appliances, bed, or home. Jobs are also lost, traffic is blocked, and business transactions are inhibited. Disasters are accompanied by building collapses, road closures, and downed power and phone lines. The infrastructure is often severely impacted. Simple tasks such as mailing a letter or having your trash hauled away cannot be performed because the government is also adversely affected. Disasters, including terrorist attacks, can sometimes jeopardize mental health and cause economic troubles. Disasters have even led to political turmoil at times and have changed the direction of policy in the United States (e.g., the creation of the Department of Homeland Security after 9/11). There is no doubt that disasters have a bearing on taxes, insurance rates, and many other aspects of our lives.

1.5.2 Changes Associated With Disasters

During the immediate emergency period of a disaster, several significant changes occur that complicate the job of an emergency manager. Dynes, Quarantelli, and Kreps (1972), three well-known disaster scholars, have identified six of them:

1. **Uncertainty.** In the immediate aftermath of disaster, there is a lack of information about what has happened, why it occurred, the number of injured or dead, the extent of the devastation, and what should be done to deal with these problems.

2. **Urgency.** Seeing needs arise, most citizens and leaders initially agree about the importance of issuing warnings, treating injuries, and clearing roads of debris as quickly as possible.

3. **Emergency Consensus.** Individuals, groups, businesses, government departments, and political leaders generally work together (at least in the immediate aftermath of a disaster) to overcome problems.

4. **Expansion of Citizen Role.** People are not only more willing to cooperate in a disaster, but they are also likely to be involved in searching for neighbors trapped under debris, transporting the wounded to hospitals, and providing relief supplies to charitable organizations.

5. **De-emphasis of contractual relationships.** Because victims' needs must be met as soon as possible, written agreements are not relied on. Verbal arrangements are made instead. Accounts and debts are settled when the situation calms down. It is also likely that supplies will be donated with no thought of reimbursement.

6. **Convergence.** People and material resources will flow to the scene of a disaster. This may include evacuees returning to the location and those wanting information about victims. It may also include volunteers, reporters and researchers, criminals wanting to take advantage of the situation, groups cheering on the emergency workers, and others mourning those who have died in the event (Kendra and Wachtendorf 2003).

These changes can have a dramatic impact on those involved in the management of disasters. Decision making becomes difficult, and post-disaster operations are stressful. Poor communications in disasters complicate the sharing of information. Many agencies and volunteers help to get things done quickly, but the arrival of too many organizations and donations can add to the overwhelming nature of disaster. Resources may be available, but they may not be shipped or tracked in an effective manner. Later on, blame may be placed on those considered to be at fault. Disagreements might arise about recovery policies, particularly in regards to rebuilding priorities. Some of the changes that take place after a disaster have positive features, and others are negative. In most cases, the changes resulting from disasters will provide benefits and drawbacks for those working in emergency management.

1.5.3 The Need for Response and Recovery Operations

Besides understanding the consequences of disasters, you must be aware of the goals of response and recovery operations if you are to be a successful emergency manager. Such objectives include protecting lives, limiting property loss, and overcoming the disruption that disasters cause. There are other aspirations that must be considered as well. You must care for special populations such as those in nursing homes. You must coordinate the efforts of all types of disaster participants. Another desire is to reduce further deterioration of the environment. You may rely on both predetermined organizational arrangements and technology to complete these responsibilities. In most disasters, multiple activities will require your attention and involvement concurrently. Extreme care should be taken to avoid possible lawsuits. It will be important to record what has transpired so you can learn from your successes and shortcomings. Resources should be tracked to help cover expenses.

Your job during response and recovery operations is therefore extremely challenging. There are many demands that have to be addressed, and two of them have been identified by Ronald Perry (1991, p. 201).

▲ **Agent-generated demands** are the needs made evident by the hazard (e.g., problems resulting from the disaster agent itself). These demands appear immediately as the disaster unfolds, and examples include sandbags to fight flooding, shelters to care for those made homeless, and the restoration of electricity owing to power outages.

▲ **Response-generated demands** are the needs that are made evident as individuals, organizations, and communities attempt to meet agent-generated demands. They are visible as people and agencies try to deal with the impact of flooding, earthquakes, and other hazards.

Acquiring sandbags, finding suitable shelter sites, and obtaining portable generators or electricians are examples of response-generated demands. Response-generated demands thus deal with the logistical issues pertaining to the reaction of people and organizations to agent-generated demands.

In addition to these demands, we should recognize that there will be two other expectations placed on you after a disaster:

▲ **Normalcy-generated demands** are the pressures to quickly get things back to pre-disaster conditions. Returning people to their homes and restarting business activity are types of normalcy-generated demands.

▲ **Mitigation-generated demands** are the desires to prevent a recurrence of the disaster. Creating more stringent building codes or relocating residences to less-hazardous areas are examples of mitigation-generated demands.

Normalcy-generated demands sometimes run in opposition to the mitigation-generated demands. People want to return to their homes even when it would be best to remove them permanently from the flood plain. Despite of these conflicts, you must take advantage of the increased public concern disasters provide to promote change during response and recovery. All of these goals and functions are directed toward the goal of disaster **resilience**. You must develop the ability to react effectively and efficiently in time of disaster.

SELF-CHECK

- Do hazards interact with each other?
- What do we call hazards that occur in conjunction with other hazards?
- How are disasters different than hazards?
- What changes occur in society after a disaster?
- Why are response and recovery operations needed?
- What demands do emergency managers face after a disaster?

SUMMARY

As an emergency manager, you should be aware of important concepts such as hazards, disasters, and disaster response and recovery. You must understand what types of hazards may occur, including their natural, technological, and civil/conflict variants. It is also imperative that you comprehend how hazards interact with each other and how this may determine the impact of disasters. Successful emergency managers should know what changes to expect when a disaster occurs and what must be done to deal with the demands they present in an effective manner.

KEY TERMS

Agent-generated demands	The needs made evident by the hazard (e.g., problems resulting from the disaster agent itself).
Atmospheric hazards	A hazard agent that is produced in or by the earth's atmosphere.
Biological hazards	Agents that spread disease or are otherwise poisonous.
Civil/Conflict hazards	Violent events that have the potential to produce mass casualties.
Computer hazards	A disruptive hazard associated with computer hardware and software.
Disasters	Deadly, destructive, and disruptive events that occur when a hazard (or multiple hazards) interact(s) with human vulnerability.
Emergency managers	Public servants that help jurisdictions reduce the liabilities that lead to disasters. They also help build community disaster capabilities.
Environmental hazards	Agents that involve the degradation of the environment, such as pollution, that pose a risk to people's health and well-being.
First responders	Public safety personnel such as police, firefighters, and emergency medical technicians.
Geological hazards	Hazard agents associated with the earth's soil and rock.
Hazard	A physical, technological, or intentional agent such as an earthquake, industrial explosion, or terrorist bombing.
Hydrologic hazards	Hazard agents that occur with the earth's water systems.

Industrial hazards	Hazards produced by the extraction, creation, distribution, storage, use, and disposal of chemicals.
Mercalli scale	A scale to measure earthquakes based on physical observation of damages that result from the movement of the earth's crust (e.g., broken windows, cracked walls, and falling pictures).
Mitigation	Activities that attempt to prevent disasters or reduce potential for loss.
Mitigation-generated demands	The desire to learn from the disaster and avoid making similar mistakes in the future.
Natural hazards	Events originating from the physical environment, typically because of radiation from the sun, heat flow within the earth, or the force of gravity.
Normalcy-generated demands	The pressures to get things back to pre-disaster conditions.
Nuclear hazards	A hazard resulting from the presence of radioactive material.
Pathogens	Organisms that spread disease and may include anthrax, smallpox, plague, hemorrhagic fever, and rickettsiae.
Preparedness	Efforts to increase readiness for disaster response and recovery operations.
Recovery	Activity to return the affected community to pre-disaster or, preferably, improved conditions.
Richter Scale	A measurement of the registered shaking amplitudes of an earthquake.
Resilience	The ability to respond to and recover from a disaster quickly, effectively, and efficiently.
Response	Activity in the immediate aftermath of a disaster to protect life and property.
Response-generated demands	The needs that are made evident as individuals, organizations, and communities attempt to meet agent-generated demands.
Riots	Large disturbances where people engage in anti-social behavior.
Saffir-Simpson Scale	A descriptive tool to explain the magnitude of a hurricane in terms of wind and storm surge.
Seismic hazards	Hazard agents produced by the movement of tectonic plates that float on magma.

Structural collapse hazards   Hazards that occur when gravity and poor engineering result in the failure of buildings, roads, or other construction projects.

Technological hazards   Hazard agents related to industry, structures, hazardous materials, computers, and transportation systems.

Terrorism   The threat or use of violence to intimidate someone or a government.

Toxins   Poisons created by plants and animals.

Transportation hazards   An accident that occurs in the air, on roads or railways, or at sea.

Vulnerability   Proneness to disasters or the inability of individuals, organizations, and communities to prevent them or react effectively.

Wildfire Hazards   Hazards that result from lightning strikes, which can quickly envelop hundreds of acres of forest and brush.

ASSESS YOUR UNDERSTANDING

Go to www.wiley.com/college/McEntire to evaluate your knowledge of the basics of hazards and disasters.
Measure your learning by comparing pretest and post-test results.

Summary Questions

1. A crisis is a much bigger problem than a catastrophe. True or False?

2. A disaster occurs when a hazard interacts with human vulnerability. True or False?

3. Emergency management is a profession that attempts to reduce the probability of disasters or be prepared to respond and recover effectively if they cannot be prevented. True or False?

4. There is no relation or overlap between response and recovery operations. True or False?

5. An earthquake is an example of a geological hazard. True or false?

6. Mass shootings and riots are civil/conflict hazards. True or false?

7. Disasters are not characterized by the disruption they cause to people's daily, routine activities. True or false?

8. A normalcy-generated demand is a desire to prevent the recurrence of a disaster. True or false?

9. A disaster is:
   (a) smaller than an accident
   (b) smaller than a crisis
   (c) larger than an emergency
   (d) larger than a calamity
   (e) larger than a catastrophe.

10. A winter storm is an example of:
    (a) a natural hazard
    (b) a technological hazard
    (c) a civil/conflict hazard
    (d) all of the above
    (e) none of the above

11. Tornadoes may be classified as:
    (a) an atmospheric hazard
    (b) a hydrologic hazard
    (c) a biological hazard

(d) a civil/conflict hazard

(e) none of the above

12. Uncertainty:

(a) is defined as an urgent situation

(b) results from an expansion of the citizen's role

(c) is associated with a lack of information

(d) is equated to a de-emphasis of contractual relationships

(e) a and b

Review Questions

1. Explain the difference between an accident and a catastrophe.
2. Define the term "disaster" and note its relation to hazards and vulnerability.
3. What is an emergency manager and what does he or she do?
4. What are the four phases or functional areas of emergency management?
5. List the major categories of hazards.
6. Provide one or two examples of hazards under each category identified in question 5.
7. What are the major changes an emergency manager can expect after a disaster?
8. What are the goals of disaster response and recovery?
9. What is an agent-generated demand?
10. What is a response-generated demand?
11. What is a normalcy-generated demand?
12. What is a mitigation-generated demand?

Applying This Chapter

1. After responding to a major apartment fire in Boise, Idaho, you become aware of the fact that a sprinkler system would have prevented much of the damage. How can you link recovery activities to the goals of mitigation?
2. Suppose you are expecting the arrival of a hurricane in Charleston, South Carolina. What hazards might be present along the coast, and how would they interact with each other? Give two examples.
3. A terrorist has just blown up a court house in Seattle, Washington. What changes might occur when this takes place? What can you as an emergency manager do to effectively deal with the unique challenges associated with disasters?

4. The mayor and city manager in Birmingham, Alabama are questioning you about the value of your position in the government. Explain what types of disasters could occur in your city and justify the need for response and recovery operations.

5. A flood has destroyed many homes and businesses in Greenville, Mississippi. How can you help your community recovery from disaster while also promoting the necessary changes to prevent a recurrence in the future?

6. As an emergency manager, you are frequently invited to speak to various organizations in your community. While discussing the goals of response and recovery to a group of Boy Scouts, one of those in attendance asks "What is resilience?" How would you define it to the young man and explain why it is necessary to pursue after disaster strikes?

How Can I Get Information About Hazards?

Answer the following questions by providing a list of organizations and their contact information. If you wanted information about hurricanes, who could you contact? If you needed details about the impacts of earthquakes, who could assist you? If you needed to learn more about volcanic hazards, what government agency could assist you? If you needed to understand tornadoes better, who could answer your questions? What if you needed to better comprehend hazardous materials incidents? Who could provide such information? What about terrorism? Who could help you understand terrorist behavior better?

What Would I Do?

Suppose your community was affected by a tornado. What are the possible consequences of this hazard if it interacts with human vulnerability? What would you need to do to respond? What considerations should be brought up for recovery?

The Interaction of Hazards

You are the emergency manager for New Orleans. Hurricane Katrina has just struck your community. What are the hazards? Are the hazards related? If so, how? What are the implications of such hazards?

Disasters and Change

Disasters result in a great deal of change. What are some of the changes you can expect? Are these good or bad? How would they impact your job as an emergency manager? Why is it important to be aware of them?

Meeting Demands

What are the agent-generated demands, response-generated demands, normalcy-generated demands, and mitigation-generated demands? Make a list of the demands placed on you, after a disaster, and categorize them. How do these impact your job as an emergency manager? Do they present difficulties for you? How could you overcome them?

2

UNDERSTANDING THE ACTORS
Roles and Responsibilities of Disaster Participants

Starting Point

Go to www.wiley.com/college/McEntire to assess your knowledge of the basic roles of disaster participants.
Determine where you need to concentrate your effort.

What You'll Learn in This Chapter

▲ Activities of the local, state, and federal government
▲ Roles of businesses and companies
▲ Responsibilities of the nonprofit sector
▲ Involvement of citizens in disasters
▲ How to work with different groups

After Studying This Chapter, You'll Be Able To

▲ Compare and contrast the roles and responsibilities of the public and private sectors
▲ Examine the roles and responsibilities of the nonprofit sector
▲ Differentiate between the responsibilities of the local government after a disaster versus those of the state and federal government
▲ Distinguish how corporations and faith-based organizations can assist with emergency management functions after a disaster
▲ Analyze how citizens form emergent groups to address disaster demands

Goals and Outcomes

▲ Compare and contrast the roles and responsibilities of the public, private, and nonprofit sectors
▲ Evaluate the different services individuals and organizations may provide during post-disaster activities
▲ Assess who can help you fulfill response and recovery operations
▲ Predict challenges of coordination
▲ Determine how groups and individuals interact during disasters

INTRODUCTION

After Hurricane Andrew devastated Miami Dade County, one local emergency manager asked "Where's the cavalry on this one?" This so-called "Calvary" includes many people and organizations. There are numerous individuals, groups, and agencies that are involved in response and recovery operations. By understanding these participants, you will be better able to use their knowledge, skills, and abilities in a disaster. Such actors include individuals and organizations from the public, private, and nonprofit sectors. The **public sector** is segment of society that is made up of government offices, departments, and agencies. The **private sector** is a part of society that includes businesses and corporations. The **nonprofit sector** is the division of society that is comprised of humanitarian, charitable, religious, and voluntary organizations. Citizens also join in disaster response and recovery activities. Understanding the many organizations that are involved in post-disaster operations can help you promote resilience.

2.1 The Public Sector

As an emergency manager, you should be aware of the many participants involved in disaster response and recovery operations from the public sector. The public sector includes government entities at the local, state, and federal levels. No two jurisdictions operate or are organized alike. However, city personnel, state agencies, and federal officials all form part of the public sector.

2.1.1 Local Government

Local governments are the first to react to disasters from the public sector. **Local governments** are city or county organizations that perform important public functions. They employ emergency medical technicians (EMTs), firefighters, police officers, and emergency managers. Other departments and political leaders also play a role in response and recovery at the local level.

EMTs are paramedics who provide emergency medical care to the injured and transport disaster victims to hospitals. They often work as or with firefighters. Firefighters extinguish fires and investigate their causes. Firefighters are also involved in the response to other types of disasters. They perform search and rescue operations after floods, for example. They also clean up hazardous materials spills. Police officers, or law enforcement personnel, join EMTs and firefighters as first responders. Whereas EMTs and firefighters deal with medical and fire suppression issues, police provide traffic control after disasters and close off dangerous areas to the public. Police and other first responders are sent to the scene of a disaster. If local first responders are not able to cope effectively with the disaster demands, mutual aid agreements can be activated. **Mutual aid** is the sharing of personnel, equipment, and facilities. This occurs when local resources are inadequate to meet the needs of the disaster. It may include the sharing of resources among regional, state, and federal governments. A vivid example of this is Hurricane Katrina. New Orleans could not cope without the assistance of nearby but unaffected jurisdictions. Louisiana also needed aid from other states and the federal government to cope with the impact of the hurricane.

Emergency managers are public servants who help communities prevent and prepare for disasters. They issue warnings, oversee evacuation, and communicate with first responders. They also assemble statistics on damages, share disaster knowledge with citizens through the media, and work with those in charge of shelters. Emergency managers also acquire resources. They make sure that departments are working together to address response and recovery challenges. They gather information about expenses. They help determine response and recovery priorities. Their contributions are crucial during post-disaster operations.

A host of other departments play vital roles after disasters. Public Works re-establishes public utilities such as water. They also remove disaster debris. The Department of Transportation assists with evacuation and removes debris from roads. This department makes repairs to signal lights and reconstructs damaged roads and bridges. Parks and Recreation does not have specific responsibilities other than caring for its own facilities. However, it is a great support asset as it loans out personnel as well as equipment and trucks to other departments for debris removal or transportation assistance. Public Health is in charge of caring for victims who have been infected by disease outbreaks or a biological terrorist attack. It interacts frequently with hospitals on patient bed availability. If there is not a Mental Health Department in the city, Public Health also counsels those who have been affected emotionally by the disaster. Public Health also issues orders to isolate patients when diseases spread. The coroner is responsible for gathering, storing, and identifying bodies of the deceased. He or she also processes them for burial or cremation. The Engineering Department inspects buildings to determine if they are habitable or if they should be condemned. This department also promotes strong building codes before reconstruction can begin. The Chamber of Commerce works with businesses to identify the financial impact of the disaster. It helps companies resume normal activities. The Department of Housing tells tenants if homes and apartments have been destroyed. They also facilitate the building of new housing. Development and Redevelopment Agencies may work with Engineering, the Chamber of Commerce, and the Housing Department to make recovery decisions, rebuild urban areas, and implement mitigation measures.

Elected civic leaders are heavily involved in post-disaster operations. Mayors and County Judges or County Commissioners declare emergencies and disasters, which is necessary if outside assistance is required. These politicians work closely with city managers, emergency managers, and public information officers (PIOs) to establish priorities after a disaster, mobilize personnel and resources, and keep the public up to date on post-disaster activities. In some cases, cities and counties take a regional approach to response and recovery operations. They work with officials in councils of government organizations.

Although many cities operate as described above, you must recognize that no two communities are organized exactly alike. Some cities may rely on private ambulance companies. Others may have volunteer firefighters and no emergency manager. In different cities, departments may be organized in other ways and have distinct disaster responsibilities. It is therefore imperative that you understand your city organization and that of nearby jurisdictions.

2.1.2 State Government

Many state agencies are involved in response and recovery. The **state government** is the political unit comprised of numerous cities and counties as well as bureaucratic agencies and politicians. This includes departments similar to those at the local level, but there are some notable differences in states as well.

For instance, the Department of Forestry is in charge of suppressing forest fires. It is like a city fire department, but it is much larger. Also, it typically operates in rural areas instead of cities. The Department of Public Safety or Highway Department acts similar to the local police department by handling traffic control after disasters. The State Emergency Management Agency is like the local emergency management office. It works with all other departments at the state level as well as local emergency management offices.

In addition to these agencies, many departments are involved in response and recovery operations. The Department of Transportation facilitates evacuation and rebuilds freeways. The Health department assists with public and mental health issues. The Housing Department addresses housing shortages made evident after disasters. The Environment Department protects the quality of natural

---

FOR EXAMPLE

Evacuation Before Hurricane Rita

After witnessing several weaknesses in Louisiana's response after Hurricane Katrina, Texas wanted to avoid going through similar problems. The Texas Division of Emergency Management and Department of Public Safety worked closely with local law enforcement officials to evacuate Houston citizens before the arrival of Hurricane Rita. When the northbound side of the freeway became jammed with thousands of motorists, the southbound lanes were reversed. This increased traffic flow but required the coordinated assistance of police, sheriffs, and others from the highway patrol. The state also had to provide gas for vehicles that ran out of fuel. The state worked with north Texas communities to receive evacuees and open shelters. The evacuation was not without problems. However, hundreds of thousands of people were successfully moved from harm's way. (See Figure 2-1 on page 37.)

Figure 2-1

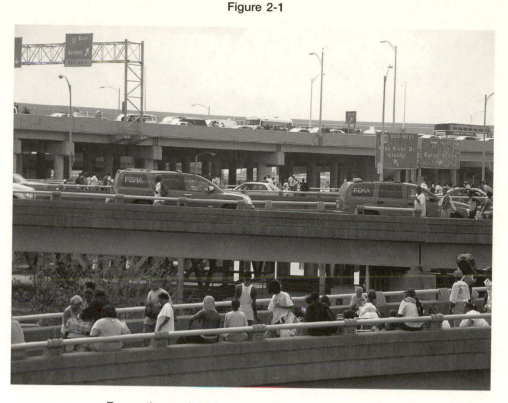

Evacuating a city takes a great deal of coordination.

resources such as soil and water if they are adversely affected by a hazard. The Agriculture Department tries to limit the loss of crops and cattle in disasters. The state Department of Insurance and Department of Commerce may also become involved if there are conflicts regarding claim settlements or price gouging during recovery operations.

The governor declares emergencies and disasters on behalf of the state. If the state is overwhelmed, the governor may seek relief from other states or the federal government. This may include calling up the National Guard to assist law-enforcement personnel, conduct search-and-rescue operations, remove debris, or provide other types of assistance. The **National Guard** is a reserve military unit operated under the direction of the governor. Upon the governor's request, the **Emergency Management Assistance Compact** (EMAC) can also be activated. This is like a local mutual-aid agreement, but it is for states. EMAC is operated under the National Association of Emergency Managers, an emergency management organization for governors and state emergency management agencies. If the resources given by other states are insufficient, the governor may also seek help from other states. For example, Louisiana sought help from Texas during Hurricane Katrina. Texas responded by hosting thousands of evacuees. Even

Figure 2-2

Texas came to the aid of Louisiana when it agreed to take in thousands of evacuees after Hurricane Katrina.

though the Texas effort was generous, it could not meet all of Louisiana's needs (see Figure 2-2). Other states also had to take in evacuees. The significance of this challenge necessitated federal disaster involvement.

2.1.3 Federal Government

The **federal government** is the national political unit, which is composed of many officials and agencies. The federal government includes political leaders who fulfill important roles. For example, if state and local jurisdictions cannot cope with a large disaster, the president may declare a federal disaster and provide national resources. If this is the case, the Department of Homeland Security (DHS) and the Federal Emergency Management Agency (FEMA) become involved.

DHS was created after the September 11, 2001 terrorist attacks. DHS is responsible for public security in the nation. DHS incorporates several directorates such as Management, Science and Technology, Preparedness, and Policy. The main goal of DHS is to prevent terrorist attacks on American soil. It therefore relies heavily on agencies such as the Transportation Security Administration and the U.S. Coast Guard. If a disaster or terrorist attack occurs, FEMA deploys resources to assist local and state governments. FEMA was created in the late 1970s by

President Jimmy Carter to help coordinate the activities of the government. It also helps direct search-and-rescue operations, reimburse local government for certain emergency operations, facilitate debris removal, and assist people with funds for rebuilding. This includes all of the departments that participate in the National Response Plan. The **National Response Plan** is a document that describes what the government will do in catastrophic disasters. Some of these organizations take on primary responsibilities, whereas others perform support functions. Several of these departments and agencies are listed in Table 2-1.

There are many other agencies and individuals that respond to disasters besides those listed in the National Response Plan. Some agencies also explore the causes of disaster. For instance, the Federal Aviation Administration (FAA) controls flight traffic after disasters. The National Transportation and Safety Board (NTSB) investigates transportation accidents such as plane crashes. For example, a few days after 9/11, there was a plane crash in a residential neighborhood in New York. The NTSB traveled to the scene and determined that the accident was caused by turbulence. The Occupational Safety and Health Agency (OSHA) also probes accidents, but they focus on the workplace. Specifically, they determine the cause of industrial explosions that result from safety violations. The Federal Bureau of Investigation (FBI) is another federal agency that is involved in investigations. After the bombing of the Murrah Federal building in Oklahoma in 1995, the FBI was on the scene to determine if it was an act of terrorism. The FBI also pursues and captures terrorists.

Other federal groups are involved in hazard detection and warning, fraud deterrence, and general oversight. U.S. Geological Survey (USGS) is one example. It helps predict volcanic eruptions and determine the location and magnitude of earthquakes. The National Oceanic and Atmospheric Agency (NOAA) tracks hurricanes. The National Weather Service (NWS) deals with thunderstorms, flooding, tornadoes, hail, and other forms of severe weather. The Office of the Inspector General (IG) ensures that federal agencies and disaster victims are not misusing disaster assistance funds.

Besides government agencies, Congressional representatives often become involved in post-disaster activities. They bring visibility to disasters and attempt to get additional resources for victims and affected jurisdictions. After 9/11, for example, New York Senators Hillary Clinton and Charles Schumer gave several interviews on the state of New York City and what assistance was still needed. Congressional representatives also help communities and states resolve problems made evident during response and recovery operations. For example, the politicians from Louisiana are now determining how to improve their state's response capabilities. They are also working on measures that would make New Orleans safer, such as strengthening the levees. Senators and House Representatives may also pass ad-hoc legislation after a disaster to provide funding for disasters. The agencies and officials involved in disaster response and recovery operations indicate that the federal government is a major player in emergency management activities.

Table 2-1: Departments and Their Roles in a Disaster

Department/Agency	Disaster
U.S. Department of Agriculture (USDA)	Suppresses rural and urban fires.
U.S. Department of Commerce (DOC)	Provides information and assists with planning, resource support, communications, and hazardous materials incidents.
U.S. Department of Defense (DOD)	Assists with public works and engineering, flood control, transportation, urban search and rescue, firefighting, mass care, and health and medical services. The DOD may also become involved in the detection and response to hazardous materials spills and weapons of mass destruction.
U.S. Department of Education (DOED)	Collects, processes, and disseminates critical information.
U.S. Department of Energy (DOE)	Restores energy systems and reacts to nuclear power plant emergencies.
U.S. Department of Health and Human Services (HHS)	Supplements local and state public health and medical operations.
U.S. Department of Housing and Urban Development (HUD)	Provides or re-establishes temporary and permanent housing.
U.S. Department of the Interior (DOI)	Supports with information and planning, emergency, communications, firefighting, and hazardous materials functions.
U.S. Department of Justice (DOJ)	Participates in information and planning, urban search and rescue, health and medical, and hazardous materials issues. Also ensures that all laws pertaining to disaster assistance are followed.
U.S. Department of Labor (DOL)	Contributes to public works, engineering, resource support, urban search and rescue, and hazardous materials areas.
U.S. Department of State (DOS)	Takes part in transportation, energy, and hazardous materials services.

Table 2-1 *(continued)*

Department/Agency	Disaster Functions
U.S. Department of Transportation (DOT)	Fulfills transportation, information and planning, energy, and hazardous materials duties after a disaster.
U.S. Department of Treasury (TREAS)	Funds long-term recovery projects and mitigation measures.
U.S. Department of Veterans Affairs (VA)	Seeks assistance for veteran needs after disaster as well as mass care and health and medical services.
U.S. Environmental Protection Agency (EPA)	Responds to and cleans up hazardous materials spills and also works in firefighting, health, and medical services.
Federal Communications Commission (FCC)	Facilitates communications after a disaster.
General Services Administration (GSA)	Aids in transportation, information and planning, mass care, and food distribution.
National Aeronautics and Space Administration (NASA)	Completes urban search and rescue and other functions in reference to satellites and remote sensing.
Nuclear Regulatory Commission (NRC)	Shares expertise in energy and hazardous materials disasters involving nuclear plants.
Office of Planning and Management (OPM)	Advances logistical and resource support to all other federal agencies involved in disaster response or recovery.
Small Business Administration (SBA)	Offers financial assistance to individuals and businesses affected by disasters.
Social Security Administration (SSA)	Supplies mass care, housing, and human services needs.
Tennessee Valley Authority (TVA)	Makes available transportation, public works, engineering, and energy services.
Agency for International Development (AID)	Supplies urban search-and-rescue resources.
U.S. Postal Service (USPS)	Imparts transportation support.

SELF-CHECK

SELF-CHECK

- What are the different sectors that are involved in disaster response and recovery?
- What does the local government do when disaster strikes?
- How can the state help the emergency manager deal with disaster?
- Why is the federal government a major player in recovery operations?
- What are the major agencies involved in the national response plan?

2.2 The Private Sector

As an emergency manager, you may rely heavily on businesses and corporations that make up the private sector. Their first goal is to seek profit through commerce of various types. However, companies play important and varied roles after disasters (McEntire, Robinson, and Weber 2003). The responsibilities of the private sector range from emergency medical care to the reporting and settlement of insurance claims.

2.2.1 Emergency and Long-Term Medical Care

Providing emergency medical care is one of the first things the private sector will do after a disaster. Paramedics from both the public and private sectors will be dispatched to the scene. These paramedics, or EMTs, will assist those injured in the accident or disaster by providing basic first aid and other necessary medical procedures. This may include applying bandages to stop bleeding, treating shock, and setting broken bones. It could also include giving medicines and intravenous fluids. After or while the patient is being stabilized, the paramedics will transport the individual to the hospital by ambulance or helicopter. When several victims are involved in an event, many paramedics and transportation units will arrive. At the hospital, the injured will receive more advanced treatment. This may include x-rays, surgery, and care for burns. The hospital will continue care and rehabilitation until the victim has recovered. If a patient dies, the private sector is involved in mortuary services such as body cremation or preparation for burial and memorial services for the deceased.

2.2.2 Sheltering and Construction

Businesses also shelter individuals who evacuate from hazards such as hurricanes. For example, hotels provide shelter for those who leave the coast when a hurricane approaches. This could amount to thousands or hundreds of thousands of people moving inland to higher and safer ground. Hotels may also house emergency workers as they arrive from outside jurisdictions to serve the affected community. The private sector also shelters others who lose their apartment or home in disasters. Manufacturers may produce tents or mobile homes for temporary or more permanent accommodations. This is especially important when disasters create serious housing shortages. The private sector also helps rebuild roads and bridges. In addition, the private sector helps to construct public facilities such as schools, courthouses, and other city facilities.

2.2.3 Media Reporting

The private sector informs the public about hazards and disasters. For example, it is the meteorologists and news anchors from radio and television stations that convey weather warnings from the National Weather Service and relay information from the Emergency Alert System. When a disaster occurs, the media reports damages, deaths, and injuries. The media also reports on government response and recovery efforts and tells the public where to go for shelter and assistance. They can be an important asset to you as an emergency manager if you work with them closely.

2.2.4 Volunteers and Donations

Companies support disaster response and recovery activities in several other ways. Businesses send volunteers and donations to those in need. This may include cooks and waiters from restaurants to distribute food. It may include sending construction personnel to tarp destroyed roofs. Heavy equipment operators may be dispatched to assist with debris removal. Companies also give supplies to communities and individuals in need. For example, there are several instances of businesses delivering bottled water to hard-hit areas. The private sector may also give or loan cell phones, flashlights, work boots, hard hats, gloves, generators, computers, vehicles, or anything else that is needed after a disaster.

2.2.5 Insurance Settlements

Because disasters result in the loss of life and property, insurance companies send teams of adjusters to the affected areas to settle claims. Their services are needed for several reasons. People are injured and have large medical bills. The bread winner in a family may have died, and future income may be jeopardized. Cars and homes are often destroyed, and other forms of personal property may be lost or rendered unusable. State Farm, All State, and other insurance providers therefore reimburse expenses, replace losses, and help disaster victims begin to recover.

2.2.6 Utility Restoration

Major windstorms, earthquakes, and other hazards often impact utilities. Phone and electrical poles can be downed. Water and gas lines can be severed. Hundreds or millions of people may be left with limited or no services. Utility companies will put their own employees to work or contract with competitors to get lines quickly restored. In many cases, these employees will work around the clock to re-establish utilities. Without their assistance, it would be impossible for the community to resume routine activities. Electricity, for example, is required for response operations (e.g., emergency lighting). It is also essential to rebuild homes and operate businesses.

2.2.7 Business Continuity

Companies help others affected by disasters. But they also take care of themselves because disasters often affect businesses and disrupt activities. For example, a manufacturing plant can be destroyed by an industrial explosion. A bank cannot issue loans if computer records are lost due to a power outage. For this reason, business continuity plans are established. Continuity plans identify ways to re-establish facilities and ensure business transactions can continue when a disaster strikes. Exxon/Mobil, Raytheon, Marriott, Target, and many others have business continuity programs that can be activated in time of disaster. Some of the employees in this area are known as business continuity specialists, risk managers, or even emergency managers.

FOR EXAMPLE

The Role of Businesses After 9/11

Corporations were integral to the response to 9/11. After two planes were intentionally flown into the World Trade Center, businesses facilitated the evacuation of the Twin Towers. They donated office supplies for the makeshift emergency operations center on pier 92 after building number seven was gutted by fire. Companies donated software to help emergency managers track resources. They helped control the perimeter around ground zero with fences. Medical care was performed by private hospitals. The local and national media informed the public of the events and how to seek assistance. As recovery proceeded, many companies worked to restore phone, electric, and gas utilities. Others helped to clean up dust in buildings, remove debris, relocate those who had lost office space, and submit payments for life insurance policies. It is doubtful that response and recovery operations could have taken place as quickly as they did in New York City without the heavy involvement of the private sector.

2.2.8 Transportation

Another role of businesses is transportation. Companies evacuate individuals before or after disasters. The private sector operates or contracts out taxis, rental cars shuttle vans, busses, trains, boats, and airplanes. Transportation companies may also be directly involved in an accident or crash. This could be due to adverse weather conditions, mechanical failure, or human error on land, on rail, at sea, or in the air. If this is the case, employees may be sent to the area to assist passengers and provide information to victims' families. Employees will also have to clean up wreckage, prevent or settle lawsuits, and provide other services to the media. At times, such crashes may result in the emission of hazardous materials. This will require remediation efforts to clean up the environment according to DOT or EPA regulations. Specialized employees are needed to follow such guidelines to prevent the company being fined.

2.2.9 Vending of Goods and Services

Some companies will make a great deal of money from disasters. Sand bags, personal protective equipment, fences, portable sanitation units, and heavy equipment are all needed during response and recovery. Businesses are always willing to assist with these resources. This is especially true when a fee can be charged.

Figure 2-3

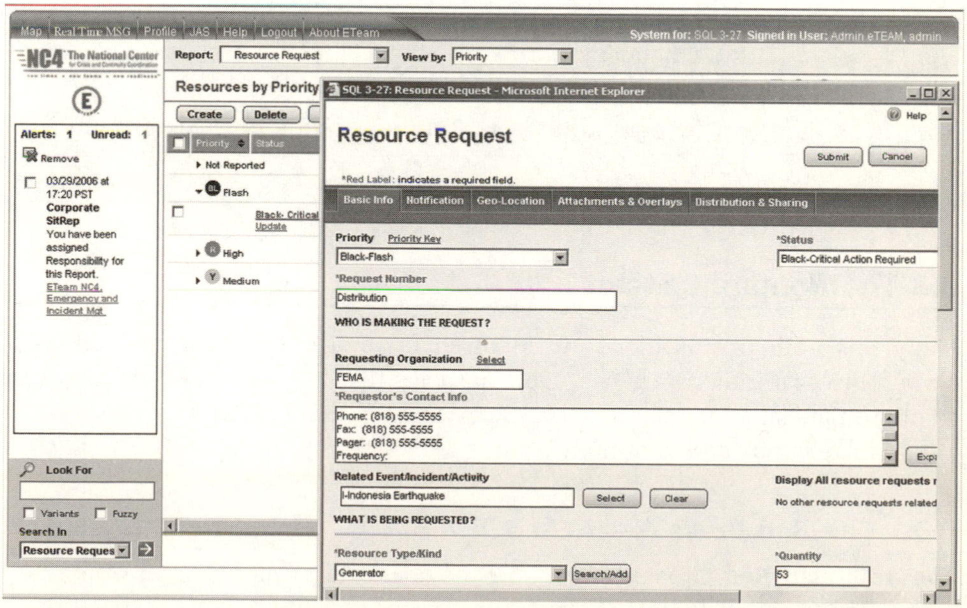

Using NC4's E Team incident management system can help you manage resources in real time. © 2006 NC4 Public Sector, LLC. All rights reserved.

Corporations also seek profits in other ways. There are companies that sell computer programs to communities so they can manage the disaster effectively. One example is Web EOC. Another is E Team as is shown in Figure 2-3. E Team helps emergency managers track resources after a disaster. You can view their website at http://www.eteam.com/index.html. Engineering firms play a role after disaster as they inspect damages to buildings to determine if they are safe for future habitation. Other companies remove debris. If a rail accident or disaster involves hazardous materials, Cura Emergency Services and Hulcher Services Inc. may remove contaminated soil and complete required state and federal paperwork. When water or fire affects a building and its contents, BMS Catastrophe sends employees to the site to pump out unhealthy air, remove mold and soot, and restore vital documents and waterlogged computer equipment. Businesses are therefore vital partners in disaster response and recovery operations.

SELF-CHECK

- Why are businesses involved in disaster response and recovery?
- How can the private sector help with emergency medical care?
- Who can help you manage public relations?
- Could insurance companies provide statistics on homes damaged in disasters and property loss?
- Why would it be necessary to work with utility companies involved in recovery?
- What else can corporations do to help you promote disaster resilience?

2.3 The Nonprofit Sector

Many nonprofit organizations are involved in disaster response and recovery. Nonprofit organizations are charitable agencies that are prohibited by law from gaining financially for their services. They include the Red Cross in addition to a host of religious and community groups.

2.3.1 The Red Cross

The **American Red Cross** is a national member of the International Committee of the Red Cross (ICRC). It is also a member of the International Federation of Red Cross and Red Crescent Societies (IFRCRCS). These organizations were created because of the caring leadership of Henry Dunant. As a young man from

Switzerland, Dunant recognized the need to assist those wounded during an 1859 battle in Solferino, Italy. Thousands of soldiers were injured in the conflict between the Austrian army and the Franco-Sardinian Alliance. Most lay helpless and dying in the battle field. Dunant organized a relief effort among citizens to provide medical care to those in need. He also advocated that prisoners on both sides be treated with respect and dignity. These principles were ratified in 1863 by many European governments in Geneva, Switzerland (now the headquarters of the Red Cross movement). Today, the International Committee of the Red Cross is based on several principles.

- ▲ **Humanity.** The Red Cross has a desire to help those in need.
- ▲ **Impartiality.** The assistance it gives will be provided without discrimination.
- ▲ **Neutrality.** No preference will be shown toward either side involved in hostility.
- ▲ **Independence.** Each society acts autonomously according to the laws of each nation.
- ▲ **Voluntary service.** Volunteers and charitable service motivate actions, not profit.
- ▲ **Unity.** There can be only one Red Cross organization in any particular country.
- ▲ **Universality.** All Red Cross societies are equal; none is more important than the other.

The Red Cross not only deals with conflict-related events, however. Dunant himself thought that anyone in need of medical assistance should be given care, regardless of the cause. From its founding, the Red Cross has been involved in disaster relief activities.

As the Red Cross was being established abroad, Clara Barton (a nurse in the United States) was caring for the soldiers injured the Civil War. She heard about the International Red Cross movement and traveled to Europe to learn more about the fledgling organization. She returned home and in 1881 established the American Association of Red Cross Societies. The American Red Cross as it is known today is a member of the IFRCRCS and serves Dunant's dual aims.

Over time, the American Red Cross was mandated by Congress to address citizen needs in time of disaster. The Red Cross has chapters and branches around the United States to prepare communities for disasters and give assistance after disasters strike. Their services, which are provided by both a small cadre of employees and a large number of volunteers, can be broken down into six areas:

1. **Disaster health services.** Provide first aid, fill prescriptions, and collect and distribute blood for those in need.
2. **Mental health services.** Support the emotional needs of disaster victims through counseling sessions and foster psychological recovery.

FOR EXAMPLE

The Red Cross After Paso Robles Earthquake

A 6.5-magnitude earthquake struck the city of Paso Robles in central California on December 22, 2003. The Red Cross quickly mobilized to assess damages in residential areas. At least 10 teams of inspectors were sent into neighborhoods to determine the extent of destruction on homes and personal property. Their findings were shared with the local government, which facilitated a federal disaster declaration.

3. **Disaster welfare inquiry.** Receive calls from loved ones who are worried about their loved ones, take steps to contact such individuals, and relay information back to the concerned family members.
4. **Family services.** Determine and meet the immediate and long-term needs of people, including clothing, furniture, temporary housing, and even tools for work.
5. **Mass Care.** Feed and establish shelters for emergency workers and the public.
6. **Other Services.** Facilitate and support damage assessment, communications, volunteer management, logistics, interagency liaison, and public affairs.

The Red Cross is an important part of emergency management in this country (see Figure 2-4).

2.3.2 Faith-Based Organizations

Faith-based organizations are nonprofit groups that perform some of the same functions as other nonprofits, but they are associated with religious organizations. One of the most notable is the Salvation Army. This religious movement was founded in England by William Booth in 1852. It was initially called the Hallelujah or Volunteer Army. The goal of the Salvation Army is to preach Christianity and care for the poor and needy. In 1879, this organization gained a foothold in the United States and established its headquarters in Alexandria, Virginia.

Today, the Salvation Army is divided into four geographic areas around the country. It has developed memorandums of understanding to assist local and state governments when disaster strikes. Its 60,000 employees and thousands of volunteers take care of immediate and long-term needs of disaster victims. This includes material, physical, emotional, or spiritual needs. Like the Red Cross, the Salvation Army provides food, water, and sheltering. These organizations are

Figure 2-4

The Red Cross is a nonprofit organization that aids victims of disasters.

different in other respects, however. The Salvation Army has religious motivations, whereas the Red Cross does not.

There are several other faith-based groups that participate in response and recovery efforts. They include the Baptist Men, Catholic Relief Services, Lutheran World Relief, Latter-Day Saint Charities, and United Methodist Committee on Relief. There are also many Muslim groups that help after disasters. These agencies care for the physical needs of disaster victims and provide spiritual and mental health counseling. There are hundreds of similar organizations around the world that respond to disasters in developing nations.

2.3.3 Community Groups

Many community groups are involved in disaster relief. Such groups include the United Way, the Rotary Club, Goodwill Industries, and Boy and Girl Scout chapters, among others. These organizations donate food, water, clothing, and other necessities of life. They provide disaster victims and communities with financial resources and construction supplies. In some cases, these community groups may translate for those who have questions about relief programs or cannot read instructions in English regarding aid applications. They also cover medical expenses that result from disasters. In addition, these groups attend to the long-term needs of victims, including crisis counseling, physical therapy, transportation, and housing. Some groups address the needs of animals that have been adversely affected by disasters. While such organizations are helpful, they may also complicate response and recovery activities. For instance, volunteer groups may start rebuilding neighborhoods before new codes can be passed and enforced. Coordination with and among community groups can be enhanced by the **National Volunteer Organizations Active in Disasters** (NVOAD). This organization brings such agencies together to promote various types of assistance after disasters.

SELF-CHECK

- What are **nonprofit organizations**?
- Who are the most prominent nonprofit organizations that are involved in disasters and what do they do?
- What are **faith-based organizations** and how do they relate to disasters?
- What are the community groups in your community that could help with response and recovery operations?
- How could the National Volunteer Organizations Active in Disasters (NVOAD) assist with coordination?

2.4 Citizen and Emergent Groups

Citizens are also involved in a variety of post-disaster activities ranging from volunteering to contributing donations. Citizens perform other vital functions after disasters. They may be fairly organized or spontaneous in nature. You must be aware that they will be some of the first people that will respond to disasters when they occur.

Some citizens are members of Community Emergency Response Teams (CERTs). A **CERT** is a group of concerned citizens that receive some basic disaster training. This enables them to care for their neighbors and co-workers after a disaster and until formal assistance arrives. CERTs are different from certain types of nonprofit organizations in that they have no paid employees. They also have a greater interest in disasters than many other community groups.

CERTs first appeared in California in 1985. At this time, it was recognized that first responders would not be able to satisfy all of the needs from major earthquakes. Public officials realized that damaged roads, large numbers of victims, and a shortage of trained professionals would prohibit needed care for disaster victims. There was consequently a need to educate citizens and train them to be self-sufficient for at least 72 hours.

CERTs are established by publicizing training opportunities and accepting applications from interested volunteers. They are often located in areas that deserve special attention. This might be a distant neighborhood, a retirement facility, or a community college or university. Participants then undergo training. Training usually consists of several 4-hour classes over a 7- or 8-week period. Classes address types of disasters to be expected, basic preparedness measures, fire suppression, search and rescue operations, disaster medicine, and disaster psychology. There is now more attention on what to do about terrorism in light of the 9/11 attacks.

CERT training is funded by government grants. This funding may also help CERT members obtain basic equipment such as hard hats, gloves, and other supplies that might be useful in time of a disaster. Today, there are hundreds of CERT programs around the nation. The skills of CERTs are increasingly recognized by those involved in emergency management.

Citizens also create and participate in emergent groups. **Emergent groups** are individuals who work together to perform common goals but do not have a formalized organization (Stallings and Quarantelli 1985, p. 84). Put differently, an emergent group is a collection of people that unite for the sole purpose of addressing disaster needs. The people that make up emergent groups are involved in activities that they do not typically perform. Their organization is quickly disbanded once the disaster situation is resolved.

Scholars have long recognized the role of emergent groups in disasters. Samuel Prince, a doctoral student at Columbia University, examined an explosion

FOR EXAMPLE

Public Response to the Loma Prieta Earthquake

On October 17, 1989, a massive earthquake shook the cities of Santa Cruz and San Francisco. The earthquake was a 7.1 on the Richter scale. Research by O'Brien and Mileti (1992) reveals that roughly 65% of citizens in these communities took part in disaster response activities. Nearly 200,000 people donated water and food to victims. 71,000 people supported the victims' emotional needs. Another 31,500 took part in search and rescue operations. Citizens also cared for the wounded, cleared debris, and sheltered those in need. The major lesson from this disaster is that people living in affected or nearby locations are resources that can be utilized to address urgent disaster needs.

that occurred when a French munitioner ran into a Belgian relief ship during World War I in a harbor in Halifax, Canada. His dissertation is the forerunner of modern disaster sociology. It illustrated that strangers, friends, relatives, neighbors, and even the victims themselves interact to care for the injured, gather the dead, and fulfill other important functions.

Since the time of Prince's dissertation, emergent groups and the measures they undertake have been studied extensively. Their unique features and activities have been characterized in a variety of ways (see Drabek and McEntire 2003, p. 98):

▲ **Therapeutic community.** Citizens come together to promote healing and rehabilitation.
▲ **Synthetic community.** People working together to resolve major challenges.
▲ **Mass assault.** A massive response that can be overwhelming.
▲ **Altruistic community.** Selfless acts to help others.
▲ **Utopian community.** Harmonious relations that may exist only right after a disaster.
▲ **Emergence.** The appearance of new organizations in time of crisis.
▲ **Emergent behavior.** The pursuit of tasks that are new and unfamiliar.

Research also reveals that groups are most likely to emerge when there have been insufficient steps for preparedness, when disasters are especially severe, when there is a perception of dire need, and when people place blame for what has happened. Culture, socioeconomic status, and other factors may also determine the formation and purpose of groups. Such determinants may include religion, gender, and race and ethnicity.

Once formed, emergent groups may become involved in search and rescue operations, damage assessment, shelter provision, emotional support for victims, and other relief activities. As a result, these spontaneous organizations are beneficial for disaster response and recovery. They are always the first to arrive at the scene, even arriving before official "first" responders. Emergent groups organize themselves quickly to address the needs made evident by disaster. Emergent groups also provide an impressive number of volunteers, diverse skills, and a deep commitment to the cause.

These groups are not without drawbacks, however. Citizens may have no formal training. They may unintentionally injure those people they are trying to help (e.g., by making mistakes while providing basic first aid). Emergent groups may also get in the way of professional responders as they go about their duties. They may even create unique challenges for emergency managers. For example, after Hurricane Andrew, there were so many donations of food and supplies that it was difficult for organizations to distribute the aid efficiently. Successful response and recovery operations require the harnessing of emergent groups while simultaneously minimizing their negative impact.

SELF-CHECK

- What is a **CERT**?
- How could CERTs help you as an emergency manager?
- What are emergent groups and why do they form after a disaster?
- Are emergent groups beneficial or detrimental? Explain your reasoning.
- How is a "mass assault" different from an "altruistic community?"
- What can be done to utilize emergent groups effectively?

2.5 Working With Different Groups

You must be aware of how each of the individuals and groups interact during disasters. The people involved in disasters can be viewed holistically by means of the well-known disaster organizational typology (Dynes 1970) (See Figure 2-5).

Figure 2-5

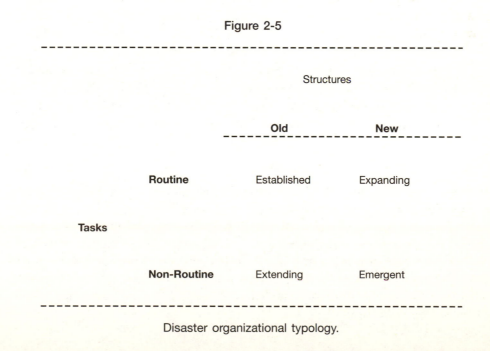

	Structures	
	Old	New
Routine	Established	Expanding
Tasks		
Non-Routine	Extending	Emergent

Disaster organizational typology.

This model was developed by scholars from the famous Disaster Research Center at Ohio State University (now located at the University of Delaware). For this reason, it is called the DRC typology. Its purpose is to help scholars and practitioners comprehend the unique characteristics of organizations that become involved in disasters.

Before developing the DRC typology, Russell Dynes and E.L. Quarantelli interviewed hundreds of people and practitioners who observed disasters or were involved emergency managers (Quarantelli 1966; Dynes 1970). They categorized these reports based on two dimensions and produced a fourfold typology of organizational involvement in disasters. The two dimensions of the model are tasks and structures.

Tasks refer to the activities of the organization. This may include functions that are routine (common to the organization) or nonroutine (unfamiliar to the organization). Structures refer to the organization's relationships and longevity. The organizational structure may be old (implying that it existed before the disaster) or new (implying that it was created after the disaster).

▲ **Established organizations** are groups that perform routine tasks with existing structures. A fire department falls under this category. It was present before the disaster, and it fulfills fire suppression functions on a daily basis.

▲ **Expanding organizations** are groups that perform routine tasks with new structures. The Red Cross falls under this category. Its workers from around the country are sent to a disaster site even though they complete their normal responsibilities.

▲ **Extending organizations** are groups that perform nonroutine tasks with existing structures. A possible example of this type of organization is a church. The pastor and congregation take new duties but were familiar with one another before the disaster.

▲ **Emergent groups** are organizations that perform nonroutine tasks with new structures. Citizens who were strangers before a disaster fall into this category if they are completing search and rescue activities for those injured in an earthquake.

The DRC typology should be considered a useful tool by those involved in response and recovery operations. There are obviously many groups that participate in emergency management activities, and they have distinct backgrounds, different goals, unique experiences, and varying lengths of existence. This complexity hinders coordination and often creates conflicts. Knowing this, you can better recognize potential problems that may occur among different organizations. You will be able to harmonize their interaction based on their unique skills and abilities in disasters.

SELF-CHECK

- What is the **DRC typology**?
- What are **tasks**?
- What are **structures**?
- What is the difference between an established organization and an extending organization?
- Can you give an example of an expanding organization?
- How can the DRC typology assist you in knowing what to expect when a disaster occurs?

SUMMARY

To promote disaster resilience, you must be aware of each of the participants in response and recovery operations. Local government departments and agencies are the first public organizations to respond to disaster. If needed, state and federal governments provide additional disaster assistance. Services, donations, and volunteers are made available by corporations and nonprofit organizations. Citizens—whether part of CERTs or emergent groups—also give their time and energy to help victims affected by disasters. Awareness of the DRC typology can illustrate unique features of the organizations involved in disasters. It is imperative to understand who can help you fill your role as an emergency manager when disasters occur. It is also imperative that you comprehend what types of conflicts may arise as multiple organizations react to disasters.

KEY TERMS

American Red Cross	A national member of the International Committee of the Red Cross (ICRC) and a member of the International Federation of Red Cross and Red Crescent Societies (IFRCRCS).
Community Emergency Response Team (CERT)	A group of concerned citizens who receive some basic disaster training.
Emergency Management Assistance Compact (EMAC)	Similar to a local mutual aid agreement but for states.

Emergent Organizations

Groups of individuals who work together to perform common goals but do not have a formalized organization (Stallings and Quarantelli 1985, 84).

Established Organizations

Groups that perform routine tasks with existing structures.

Expanding Organizations

Groups that perform routine tasks with new structures.

Extending Organizations

Groups that perform nonroutine tasks with existing structures.

Faith-Based Organizations

Nonprofit groups that perform some of the same functions as other nonprofits but are associated with religious organizations.

Federal Emergency Management Agency

Federal agency created in the late 1970s by President Jimmy Carter to help coordinate the activities of the government.

Federal Government

The national political unit that is composed of many agencies and officials.

Local Governments

City or county organizations that perform important public functions.

Mutual Aid

The sharing of personnel, equipment, and facilities. This occurs when local resources are inadequate to meet the needs of the disaster.

National Guard

A reserve military unit operated under the direction of the governor.

National Response Plan

A document that describes what the government will do in catastrophic disasters.

National Volunteer Organizations Active in Disasters (NVOAD)

An organization that brings agencies together to promote various types of assistance after disasters.

Nonprofit Sector

The division of society that is comprised of humanitarian, charitable religious, and voluntary organizations.

Private Sector

A part of society that includes businesses and corporations.

Public Sector

The segment of society that is made up of government offices, departments, and agencies.

State Government

The political unit that is comprised of numerous cities and counties and includes bureaucratic agencies and politicians.

ASSESS YOUR UNDERSTANDING

Go to www.wiley.com/college/McEntire to evaluate your knowledge of the basic roles of disaster participants.

Measure your learning by comparing pretest and post-test results.

Summary Questions

1. The public sector is a subdivision of society made up of ordinary, every-day citizens. True or False?

2. A business would be categorized under the private sector. True or False?

3. An example of a nonprofit organization is a community-based agency that engages in humanitarian and charitable work. True or False?

4. Mutual aid involves the sharing of first responders or necessary supplies. True or False?

5. Mayors and other elected officials are responsible for declaring a disaster at the local level. True or False?

6. State governments will not become involved in disasters but will simply request assistance from the federal government. True or False?

7. The National Guard may help conduct search and rescue missions or remove debris after a disaster. True or False?

8. FEMA is the only organization at the federal level that gets involved in disaster activities. True or False?

9. Companies may provide donations, but they do not have a bearing on sheltering and construction. True or False?

10. The Salvation Army is a faith-based organization. True or False?

11. Which is not included in the public sector?

    (a) A firefighter that is a trained emergency medical technician.

    (b) A company that supplies first responders with flashlights and batteries

    (c) Members of city council

    (d) A local emergency manager

    (e) State and federal emergency management offices

12. What department is most likely to be able to assist you with traffic control issues?

    (a) Public Health

    (b) The Coroner's Office

    (c) Engineering

    (d) The Police Department

    (e) Department of Housing

13. Which person or entity may call up the National Guard?
    (a) The governor
    (b) The emergency manager
    (c) A representative from the Red Cross
    (d) The mayor
    (e) All of the above

14. The directorates of the Department of Homeland Security include:
    (a) Border and Transportation Security
    (b) Science and Technology
    (c) Information Analysis and Infrastructure Protection
    (d) Emergency Preparedness and Response
    (e) All of the above

15. Which federal agency or department may assist with hazardous materials cleanup?
    (a) General Services Administration
    (b) Department of Agriculture
    (c) The Environmental Protection Agency
    (d) Department of Labor
    (e) Tennessee Valley Authority

16. Individuals that help companies recover from disasters are known as:
    (a) Private contractors
    (b) Business continuity specialists
    (c) CERT members
    (d) Members of emergent groups
    (e) None of the above

17. Under the principle of impartiality, the Red Cross tries to:
    (a) Help anyone in need
    (b) Serve out of charity and not for profit
    (c) Act autonomously in each nation
    (d) Provide assistance without discrimination
    (e) Remain neutral in armed conflicts

18. A major role of the Red Cross after disaster is to:
    (a) Remove debris in the roads
    (b) Rebuild damaged infrastructure
    (c) Feed emergency workers
    (d) Shelter victims affected by disaster
    (e) c and d

19. CERT stands for:
    (a) Civilian Emergency Repair Technician
    (b) Community Emergency Response Team
    (c) Civilian Emergency Response Technician
    (d) Community Emergent Recovery Team
    (e) Community Emergent Recovery Technician
20. An emergent group may be defined as:
    (a) The pursuit of tasks that are new and unfamiliar
    (b) Selfless acts of heroism
    (c) An organization that appears after a disaster to care for disaster victims
    (d) A department of the federal government
    (e) A member of the National Volunteer Organizations Active in Disasters
21. An example of an extending organization is:
    (a) A church
    (b) A fire department
    (c) The police department
    (d) The Red Cross
    (e) The local government

Review Questions

1. Explain the difference between the public, private, and nonprofit sectors.
2. What are the responsibilities of the emergency manager?
3. If local resources are limited after a disaster, who could you contact for assistance?
4. How can the State Department of Public Safety help after a disaster?
5. What is the Emergency Management Assistance Compact?
6. What is the National Response Plan, and how can it help you when a disaster occurs?
7. What is the role of the National Weather Service in disaster response?
8. What businesses could you contact in the private sector if you had to evacuate thousands of people from a city?
9. What functions can be performed by the American Red Cross when a disaster occurs?
10. How could a CERT save lives and protect property?
11. Why is it necessary for an emergency manager to be aware of emergent behavior?

12. What is an established organization?
13. How can the DRC typology benefit those working in disaster response and recovery operations?

Applying This Chapter

1. The National Weather Service predicts the arrival of severe weather in Chicago, Illinois. Your mayor is questioning who would be involved in response activities should a disaster occur. What are some of the participating organizations from the public, private, and nonprofit sectors?

2. An earthquake has damaged many of the homes and much of the infrastructure in Corona, California. What businesses from the private sector would logically be involved in the response to this disaster? How could you work with them to facilitate recovery?

3. A tornado has struck your community in the Midwest portion of the United States and left many people homeless. As a result, you have had to open up a shelter at a local church. Who could assist you with feeding and mass care issues?

4. You serve as a volunteer emergency manager in a small, rural community in Montana. Your town has been adversely affected by a major winter snow storm—one that has shattered all of the prior records. Roads are impassible and you are worried about the elderly in your jurisdiction. Could the state government assist you? Could faith-based organizations help? How would you call up their services?

5. Major events such as the Indian Ocean Tsunami generate impressive amounts of volunteerism. What do we call this type of behavior? Is it good or bad? How could you deal with it effectively?

What is a local emergency manager?

Consider the position of an emergency manager. Write a 1- or 2-page paper that addresses the following questions: Where could it be located in local government? Could it fall under the city managers office? Fire department? Police department? What would the local emergency manager be in charge of? Who would he or she work with? What would he or she do on a daily basis? How would this change when a disaster occurs?

The need for mutual aid

A major fire has broken out at an industrial complex in a major metropolitan area near Los Angeles. Local fire-fighting resources are stretched thin, and crews are beginning to tire. What could you do to get more personnel to the scene? What is the name we give to the sharing of such resources among neighboring jurisdictions or states? Why is this necessary?

How can a business help you?

Suppose a major hurricane swept over your community in Florida. The strong winds and storm surge downed power lines, deposited 2 feet of sand on roads, scattered boats blocks from the coast, and damaged thousands of homes. Who could you contact in the private sector to help you resolve these problems created by the disaster?

Have you participated in or witnessed an emergent group?

If a disaster has affected your city or state recently, did you participate in or see citizens respond? What did you or the others do? Did you or others perform a valuable role? What would have happened if you and others were not involved in that function? How important are citizens when a disaster strikes? Do you see any mistakes made or problems resulting from emergency groups?

Consider how organizations interact

A terrorist attack has just occurred in a busy downtown area in Denver, Colorado. The police have cordoned off the area for safety. The Red Cross would like to provide snacks for firefighters, and business men and women would like to return to their buildings to retrieve their belongings. Spontaneous volunteers are arriving in the hundreds to donate blood and help remove debris. Are there any potential conflicts among these organizations? Can they be resolved? If so, how?

3

ANTICIPATING HUMAN BEHAVIOR IN DISASTERS
Myths, Exaggerations, and Realities

Starting Point

Go to www.wiley.com/college/McEntire to assess your knowledge of human behavior during disasters.
Determine where you need to concentrate your effort.

What You'll Learn in This Chapter

▲ The impact of Hollywood and media portrayals about disaster behavior
▲ Research about human responses to disasters
▲ Reasons why researchers must study human behavior
▲ What people actually do in the aftermath of a disaster
▲ The importance of understanding behavior correctly

After Studying This Chapter, You'll Be Able To

▲ Compare and contrast the meaning of the words "myth" and "exaggeration"
▲ Determine what really happens in disaster situations
▲ Examine ways to prevent the spread of incorrect views about human conduct after disasters
▲ Explain how views about behavior affect response and recovery activities

Goals and Outcomes

▲ Evaluate the accuracy of Hollywood films and media broadcasts about disaster behavior
▲ Assess between fact and fiction about disaster behavior
▲ Argue against inaccurate views about disaster response and recovery operations
▲ Predict human behavior in disasters and respond accordingly

INTRODUCTION

In order to respond to a disaster effectively, it is imperative that you understand people's misperceptions about human behavior. Much of this comes from Hollywood films and the mass media. Unfortunately the information presented in movies and by reporters focuses on sensational and unusual stories. For this reason, it is vital that you are aware of the research findings about human behavior in disasters. At the same time, you must also recognize that there is some degree of truth in the public's perception of post-disaster behavior. One way to ensure resilience is to understand exactly how people behave after disasters.

3.1 The Impact of Hollywood and the Media

Most people get their views about human disaster behavior from films and the media (Fischer 1998). Movies are entertaining, of course, and media reports can keep one riveted to a disaster as it unfolds. Unfortunately, the view portrayed by Hollywood and the media are almost always inaccurate. Scholars have labeled these inaccuracies as "myths." A **myth** is defined in many dictionaries as a false belief. It is difficult to counter such incorrect portrayals about disaster behavior that are quickly spread through modern video footage.

3.1.1 Hollywood

Hollywood is one of the major contributors to the public's perceptions about disasters. There are several movies that portray people's behavior in a negative and fictitious light.

Dante's Peak is a good example. This movie relays a ficticious story about a volcanic eruption in the Northwestern United States. After several deaths result from the emission of dangerous gasses from the volcano, community leaders hold a meeting to calm the public. During this gathering, an earthquake occurs and people panic as a result. They run haphazardly out of the building and begin to evacuate in droves as the volcano explodes from the mountain above them. Cars and trucks run into each other as their occupants drive frantically to escape the oozing lava and falling ash. Roads become clogged, and people do all they can to protect themselves while ignoring the needs of others. The movie suggests that when disaster strikes, people behave erratically.

Volcano is another disaster movie. It provides an amusing, but not completely accurate, view of human behavior in extreme events. After workers die in an underground utility tunnel in Los Angeles, a scientist named Dr. Amy Barnes discovers a growing volcanic threat. While investigating the source of deadly gasses below ground, the volcano becomes active. Dr. Barnes climbs out of the hole to save her life. When she arrives on the surface, she takes off her breathing apparatus and sets it down nearby. As she turns around, a bystander grabs her mask and runs off with it. This film gives the impression that theft and looting are common in disasters.

The movie *Asteroid* also provides an interesting portrayal of disasters. Upon learning that an asteroid is about to hit the United States, the government begins a massive evacuation. As people leave the target area, one person becomes irate because of the government's decisions and shoots a FEMA official at an airport hangar. This movie, like many others, presents lawlessness and violence as the norm in disasters.

3.1.2 The Media

News reports, whether they come from television coverage, radio broadcasts, or newspaper articles, also portray human behavior in a dismal fashion. News reports and headlines tend to suggest that victims cannot care for themselves. After Hurricane Carla, several newspapers ran a headline noting "More than 100,000 Persons Flee in Near Panic." This occurred despite the fact that less than 1% of the evacuees were involved in a traffic accident (Quarantelli and Dynes 1982, p. 70). Other stories claim that businesses price-gouge the victims and survivors.

To some extent, such reports are to be expected. The media is interested in abnormal events. For instance, if a dog bites a man, that is not particularly newsworthy. However, if a man bites a dog, this would certainly generate a great deal of publicity! Such unusual stories are the ones the media is infatuated with. They keep the viewers, listeners, and readers interested because of the drama being presented. Media ratings rise as a result.

Nevertheless, the accuracy of such presentations may be in question. Truth is neglected because the media is not providing the full story. The media loves sensational stories. Since the media wants a unique angle on the human

---

FOR EXAMPLE

Media Reports of Disasters

Turn on the television to any news broadcast and you will likely find at least one disaster-related story. News anchors or reporters will describe what occurred and the resulting impact. Chances are, they will also mention something about looting: it is occurring after the disaster, residents are worried about their property being stolen, law-enforcement officials are out in force to discourage looters. The media seems to be obsessed with looting, even though it is not widespread in most disasters.

disaster-related activities, they are not always careful about gathering all of the facts. For example, one study revealed that people sorting through debris after one disaster were not looters but were good Samaritans who were trying to collect belongings so they could be returned to their rightful owners (Fischer 1998). The media, quickly reacting to the appearance of wrongdoing, incorrectly reported that a large group of people was engaging in looting behavior. This is an excellent, but disappointing, example of how people erroneously gain their views about human behavior in a disaster.

SELF-CHECK

- From where do most people get their understanding about disasters?
- How does Hollywood depict human responses to disasters?
- What is the role of the media in providing misrepresentations about disaster behavior?
- Does the media like sensational stories? How does this impact people's perceptions of disasters?

3.2 Research on Myths

Many sociologists have studied human behavior in disasters (see Table 3-1), and a great deal of literature has thus been written about the topic of disaster "myths." As an emergency manager, you should be familiar with this literature. Much of this research is dated, but prior studies reveal "most persons held preconceived notions about disaster behavior that were essentially untrue." (Quarantelli and Dynes 1972, p. 67). In other words, "many common beliefs and perceptions about disaster response and post-impact behavior are not empirically valid" (Wenger, Dykes, and Sebok 1975, p. 33). Recent research continues to reiterate previous findings (Tierney, Lindell, and Perry 2001). New investigations are being undertaken after Hurricane Katrina and should be out shortly.

One of the most widely held myths according to the literature is that people act irrationally in disaster situations. It is believed that people always panic. **Panic** is an inability to think clearly or a tendency to run frantically from buildings or the disaster scene. Another related belief is masses of people evacuating at once.

It is true that many people will leave the scene of a disaster. This need not result in panic, however. Research suggests that "despite the fact that people may

Table 3-1: Respondents' Beliefs About Disaster Response

Statement	Agree	Disagree	Undecided or No Response
A major problem community officials confront when faced with a natural disaster is controlling the panic of people fleeing from the danger area.	83.6% (296 respondents)	10.2% (36 respondents)	6.2% (22 respondents)
Looting rarely occurs after the impact of natural disasters	27.7% (98 respondents)	64.7% (229 respondents)	7.6% (27 respondents)
When warned of an impending disaster, people are willing to cooperate and evacuate the area.	80.2% (284 respondents)	13.6% (48 respondents)	6.2% (22 respondents)
The crime rate of a community usually rises after it has experienced a natural disaster.	50.8% (180 respondents)	34.4% (123 respondents)	14.4% (51 respondents)
Immediately following the impact of a disaster, the disaster victims are in a state of shock and unable to cope with the situation by themselves.	73.7% (261 respondents)	19.2% (68 respondents)	7% (25 respondents)
The news media accurately portray the amount of devastation resulting from a natural disaster.	54.5% (193 respondents)	35.6% (126 respondents)	9.9 (35 respondents)
Martial law has never been instituted in a disaster area in the United States	17.2% (61 respondents)	60.2% (213 respondents)	22.6% (80 respondents)

Adapted from Wenger, Dykes, and Sebok 1975, p. 42.

well be terrified in disaster situations, even to the point of feeling that their lives are in imminent danger, they almost never resort to the kind of highly individualistic, competitive, headlong flight behavior that characterizes true panic" (Tierney 2003, p. 35). Panic flight is rare, occurring only when there is an imminent threat to the well-being of the person or people evacuating.

In addition, not everyone evacuates when requested to do so. Many people will ignore warnings and remain in the area that will be or has been affected by a hazard. This creates the need for dangerous search and rescue missions from police, fire, and military personnel.

A second major myth is in regards to antisocial behavior. This includes at least three aspects. First, people assume that **looting**—people searching debris or damaged homes with the intention to steal others' personal belongings—occurs rampantly after a disaster. Because doors and windows are broken, it is believed that people will automatically enter businesses and homes to steal food, electronic equipment, and other goods. This belief occurs even though much of the property is damaged beyond repair. Second, it is assumed that people will resort to violence to protect their interests. Guns are needed to fight off potential looters. Third, other types of deviant behavior, including price gouging, are viewed as predominant behavioral patterns. People think other individuals or groups will take advantage of victims to make money.

In most disasters, however, there are only reports of antisocial behavior. In other words, people think that looting might be taking place, but they have no evidence to support their assertions. In other cases, people expect there will be looting in disasters because it has occurred in riots and other forms of civil disturbance. Research reveals that this assumption is often erroneous.

Price gouging, or the selling of goods and services at a price higher than the normal market rate, is not a widespread phenomena. Most citizens and businesses recognize that victims have experienced severe trauma. They would not think of adding to their problems. Some scholars even suggest that criminal activity may witness a decrease after a disaster. For instance, "in the month in which Hurricane Betsey struck New Orleans, major crimes in the city fell 26.6 percent below the rate for the corresponding month of the previous year. Burglaries reported to the police fell from 617 to 425. Thefts of over $50 dropped from 303 to 264, and those under $50 fell from 516 to 366" (Quarantelli and Dynes 1972, p. 69). Similar drop in criminal activity may have been noted in Oklahoma City after the bombing of the Murrah Federal Building. There is a possibility that reporting of crime may be inaccurate, however, since police are concerned about bigger issues than petty theft after a disaster.

Another myth relates to people taking advantage of disaster victims to make money. For instance, it is reported that stores sell ice at inflated costs, as people need to keep food cool due to the loss of power to refrigerators. In other cases, it is commonly assumed that convenience stores raise the price of gasoline as people evacuate. Although such behavior does occur, it is probably the exception rather than the norm.

An additional myth is that emergency workers are unreliable in the aftermath of disaster. This is known as **role or post abandonment**. It is believed that police officers, firefighters, and EMTs will not fulfill important disaster functions. They will leave their post when disaster strikes to take care of personal or family needs. Emergency workers are believed to fear the danger they face. Others are expected to quit their jobs to take care of themselves and their families. These views cannot be corroborated in the vast majority of cases.

People also have wrong or incomplete views about disaster victims. Some think that victims will always be in a state of **shock**—a situation of disbelief after disaster, which renders them unable to think or take care of themselves. "The common belief is that shock leaves the victims dazed and disoriented, unable to cope with the immediate task of recovery" (Quarantelli and Dynes 1972, p. 36). Table 3-2 shows common responses to perceived notions of needed aid.

Evidence suggests that victims exhibit shock symptoms in a minority of disaster cases. Most victims do not have long-lasting mental health effects. In addition, the vast majority of people will not require shelter or housing assistance. Typically, "congregate care utilization is likely to be in the range of 5-15 percent" (Tierney, Lindell, and Perry 2001, p. 97).

Table 3-2: Respondents' Beliefs About Effective Personal Aid to Disaster Victims

Respondents were asked to complete this statement: What is the most effective assistance you as a concerned citizen can offer to the victims of natural disasters? Would you:	*Response*
a) send supplies or money to the stricken community?	35.9% (127 respondents)
b) go in person to the community to help?	17.5% (62 respondents)
c) send money to disaster-relief organizations?	38.1% (135 respondents)
d) do nothing?	3.4% (12 respondents)
e) undecided.	5.1% (18 respondents)

Adapted from Wenger, Dykes, and Sebok 1975, 42.

> ## FOR EXAMPLE
>
> ### Alleged Price Gouging
>
> Two scholars traveled to Texas to study the community response to Hurricane Gilbert (Fischer 1999, p. 4). While watching media broadcasts of the event, news reporters claimed that local merchants were arrested for charging high prices for the plywood needed to protect windows from strong winds. The researchers called the police to see if this was accurate. The answer they received was "no." The media should have reported instead that city council had passed an ordinance to prevent such behavior.

There are other myths about disasters that should be mentioned. It is frequently assumed that the media provides an accurate portrayal of the disaster. It is believed that the statistics regarding the number of dead or injured are complete and trustworthy. Because the media focuses excessively on destruction, the viewers are given an inflated impression about the extent of the situation. People therefore believe that a massive amount of aid is needed.

Research also indicates that the initial media reports are almost always inexact. No one, including the media, has a complete and accurate understanding about disasters initially because information is limited, sketchy, and uncorroborated. Estimates regarding those killed and otherwise affected are almost always over or underestimated. Also, in their efforts to help disaster victims or increase interest in the disaster, reporters frequently request donations even though they may not be needed.

A final myth is that martial law must be imposed after disasters. **Martial law** is the replacing of civilian authority with that of the military. It involves the imposition of strict curfews and limitations on people's movement and activity. It is commonly held that the military and National Guard must be mobilized and utilized to maintain social stability when disasters occur. Research shows that martial law may never have been imposed after disasters in the United States. "Press reports of martial law inevitably turn out to be entirely false or incorrect descriptions of limited emergency power usually given to local police by mayors or city councils—usually to bar sightseers. In no way do such actions imply or involve cessation of regular civilian authority in the area" (Quarantelli and Dynes 1972, p. 69).

To summarize, irrational behavior, anti-social behavior, unreliable emergency workers, the helpless state of disaster victims, and other myths are commonly held views about people's behavior in disaster. They do not appear to be correct in most cases.

SELF-CHECK

- What are the commonly held views about panic in disasters?
- Do most people loot after a disaster?
- Do all businesses gouge disaster victims?
- Is it wishful thinking to rely on emergency responders?
- Do communities always require relief assistance after a disaster?
- Is it necessary to implement martial law after disasters occur?

3.3 Evidence of Exaggeration

The above sections raise some interesting questions about human behavior in disasters. Is the portrayal of disasters by Hollywood and the media completely wrong? Is the research literature entirely correct to assert that widely held views about disaster behavior are purely myths? The answer to both of these questions is somewhat complicated, although in both cases it is probably no. There is now research that seems to question our prior understanding on the matter (see Table 3-3 taken from John Handmer 2006).

Films and media reports may have some element of truth, but the word "myth" could be slightly misleading. It might be more realistic, therefore, to alter our choice of words slightly. When speaking about people's perspectives of human behavior, we might want to use the term "exaggeration" instead of myth. An **exaggeration** is a simplistic overstatement about some type of phenomena. This term acknowledges that there could be some element of truth to the impression given by movies and news reports. This should not discount the predominant behaviors exhibited in disasters, however. As an emergency manager, you should be aware of this fine point of distinction.

For instance, people have at times participated in "flight behavior" when a threat requires immediate action. Another example is from the 9/11 terrorist attacks. When the buildings collapsed, people ran down the streets to get out of harm's way. This, of course, may amount to rational behavior to save one's life. But it is often portrayed by Hollywood and the media as panic, regardless of the motive.

There are also several factual reports of a few individuals who have had their property stolen after a disaster. When a computer failed due to the collapse of the World Trade Center, at least 66 people illegally withdrew 15 million dollars from the Municipal Credit Union in New York City (Saulny 2002). There was also a visible degree of looting in New Orleans after Hurricane Katrina, as witnessed in many reports from journalists for local, national, and international media outlets. Although some people failed to adequately prepare for this situation, others did need food and water to sustain life (and may have been justified in caring for their physical needs under such dire circumstances). However, many others ran off with TVs, other electronic equipment, and clothing or shoes that had little to do with immediate needs after the hurricane (see Table 3-3).

Victims and communities may also be taken advantage of in some disasters. Vendors or contractors who get paid in advance will sometimes fail to complete their work. Businesses can also misrepresent their services and goods in advertisements. As an example, a scam promoted by one corporation promised consumers would be reimbursed by FEMA if they purchased air conditioners and purifiers after the 9/11 terrorist attacks. Flyers and websites implied that everyone would be eligible for this special offer. These advertisements did not mention the unique requirements for each grant (Barron 2004). The FBI has also noted that there were several fraudulent websites claiming to collect donations for the Hurricane Katrina victims.

Post abandonment may not be a completely untrue perspective either. Investigation after Hurricane Katrina illustrated that a few police officers did leave their duties unattended. Some were worried about personal protection. Some stopped patrolling the streets during the flooding and went home to care for loved ones. Others even participated in criminal behavior such as looting and lost their jobs as a result. One officer left his post, stole a car, and was arrested a short time later. This is certainly the exception, however, not the rule.

It is also true that a minority of victims can be stunned by the death, property destruction, and social disruption caused by disasters. Victims may be emotionally distraught. Survivors may wander aimlessly around their property, trying to salvage anything worth retrieving. Some may cry and become depressed as a result of lost loved ones. Others may question their future in terms of housing and employment. This negative impact is to be expected. Who would not be overwhelmed initially with the grief and chaos that disasters produce?

Although the need for aid is regarded to be a myth, disasters always require at least some form of outside assistance. In fact, aid from nearby communities or from donors around the country is sometimes essential in major events. Food, water, supplies, emergency workers, and reconstruction specialists are therefore sent in to save lives and help the community recover. However, it is certainly doubtful that affected individuals and jurisdictions need everything. Politicians may overstate need in order to acquire as much free federal disaster assistance as possible.

Finally, disasters may require a heavy law-enforcement and military presence to maintain order. After Hurricane Katrina, lawlessness could be clearly observed in some areas. In addition to the occurrence of looting already

Table 3-3: Disaster Myths, Reality, and New Orleans

"MYTHS" about what happens in a disaster, drawing on the research literature	*"REALITY" as established by research & experience*	*NEW ORLEANS—What seemed to happen*
Widespread looting is expected.	There is no increase in criminal activity and little or no looting.	We all saw "looting," and there were numerous media reports and reports by local officials, people in the streets, blogs, etc. There was evidence of looting by officials. Some reports of looting and criminal behavior have been withdrawn. Looting has been redefined by some commentators to exclude much of the behavior: the hungry were feeding themselves, the drug addicted were raiding hospitals for their needs, and so on. Criminal drug gangs were very active.
Helplessness and abandonment of the weak. Disasters strike randomly.	People help those in need. Differential impacts on the vulnerable.	More than 100,000 people did not have the means to evacuate and became dependent on others to keep them alive. This help was very slow to come and seriously inadequate. Some in nursing homes and private hospitals were abandoned and died. (St. Rita's Nursing Home—pending criminal charges).
Officials experience conflict between their official duties and family demands. Some will hide from the crisis.	Officials will do their job and not abandon their posts because of "role conflict."	Large-scale abandonment of officials' posts and duties. Fifty officers were fired for going AWOL; 228 are still under investigation (Perlstein, 2005). Police were also caught looting department stores. The situation seemed well beyond the capabilities of CEOs at all levels of government. Priority went to security rather than attending to those desperate for food and water and to those dying for want of medical attention. There were no public heroes.

Table 3-3 (continued)

"MYTHS" about what happens in a disaster, drawing on the research literature	"REALITY" as established by research & experience	NEW ORLEANS—What seemed to happen
Large-scale demand for temporary official accommodation.	Little need for official emergency accommodation.	About 200,000 people were being housed through official channels a month and a half after the disaster. About 120,000 needed accommodation on the day. The mass evacuation centers were over-whelmed. (There is a dispute over the actual figure, with much higher numbers occasionally quoted.)
People take advantage of the vulnerable.	Much behavior is altruistic.	There was no shortage of price gouging and people being evicted from private rentals, creating homelessness (Hartman, 2005) and adding to the burden for public authorities. The town of Gretna, across the Mississippi from New Orleans, barricaded itself and at gunpoint prevented refugees from entering the town (Khaleej Times, 2005).
Outside rescue teams save many lives.	People next door do the saving as outside help may take too long.	There are reports of people assisting each other, but the general picture is of an absence of rescue and help by neighbors.

Adapted from Handmer 2005, p. 32.

mentioned, some people broke into hospitals to obtain narcotics for illicit drug use. Weapons were also fired at those trying to prevent crime or rescue victims stranded on rooftops. People, despite of their own responsibility to care for themselves and others, were angry because of the slow federal response. Citizens were also upset with those who were hoarding relief supplies. The city of New Orleans appeared to be under a condition of anarchy for several days after Katrina struck. The situation was so dire that some people called for martial law. This was never carried out, however. Instead, curfews were established and the streets were patrolled to purge them of criminals. This case, as well as the other evidence presented above, indicates that there might be some degree of truth regarding Hollywood movies and media reports. However, "while the

FOR EXAMPLE

Evacuation After Hurricane Rita

Because the entire nation had witnessed the dangers of not evacuating after Hurricane Katrina, hundreds of thousands of people left the Gulf Coast region of Texas when Hurricane Rita neared. Even those in the interior got in their cars and left, even though they were probably far enough inland to avoid major damage from the approaching storm. The presence of so many vehicles on the road clogged the major arteries going away from Galveston and Houston. The situation required that both lanes had to be opened going northbound, a practice known as contra-flow that is common in Florida and other Gulf Coast states. Some people ran out of gas in the stop-and-go traffic, which further exacerbated the situation. This over-response has been labeled the "Katrina effect."

stories may be factually correct, they are not representative" (Quarantelli and Dynes 1972, p. 70). It may be wise for you to label these behaviors as exaggerations instead of myths.

SELF-CHECK

- Have there been any cases of panic flight in disasters?
- Do some people take advantage of disaster victims through looting or price gouging?
- Are emergency workers always selfless during response operations?
- Are some victims incapacitated after a disaster?
- Do major disasters require outside assistance?
- Can a heavy law enforcement or military presence be beneficial for post-disaster operations?

3.4 Realities About Response and Recovery

The previous comments must not discount human behavior research. Studies do provide a dramatically different view than is commonly presented by Hollywood and the media. During and after disasters, people act rationally and altruistically. Workers typically do not neglect their duties, and victims can do much to take care of themselves. Other common perceptions about the media, the need for disaster relief, and the use of martial law are also overstated. In order to react successfully to a disaster, you must understand actual behavior better than anyone else in your community.

Instead of showing extreme panic in disasters, people are generally very rational (Quarantelli 1986, p. 4). People typically respond with logical and calm behavior. They often know what to do to care for themselves and others, and they react accordingly. For instance, while the World Trade Center towers burned out of control on 9/11, people were seen walking calmly out of the building as if they were reacting to a fire drill. Rather than wait for emergency personnel to arrive at the scene, victims will often care for themselves and others.

What is more, the belief about mass evacuation is often overstated. It is true that many people do in fact leave an area when requested to do so. However, it is also likely that some people will not evacuate. These individuals will ignore warnings, potential risks, and requests for evacuation. Such people often require rescue during flooding incidents. Hurricane Katrina illustrated these points clearly. About 100,000 people did not or could not leave New Orleans. Many were rescued by the National Guard and the Coast Guard. Therefore, "it appears that the major problem in an emergency is getting people to move, rather than preventing wild panic and disorderly flight" (Quarantelli and Dynes 1972, pp. 67–68).

If there is looting or antisocial behavior during a disaster, it is typically exhibited only among a small minority of the population. In fact, some studies reveal that deviant behavior actually declines in times of disaster. The vast majority of people illustrate pro-social behavior. They work together to solve mutual problems. For example, co-workers help to evacuate the physically disabled if their building is on fire. Taking this into account, Quarantelli observes, "if disasters unleash anything it is not the criminal in us, but the altruistic" (1986, p. 5).

The assertion that emergency workers will always fail to report to work is ludicrous. Police, firefighters, and medical personnel often go to work or volunteer in times of disaster even when they have not been asked to report for duty. In fact, there are often too many emergency personnel responding to the disaster (Drabek 1986). Emergency workers recognize the dangers inherent in their work, but they do it anyway. For instance, on 9/11, firefighters entered burning buildings to rescue those that were trapped. Furthermore, emergency workers do not always stop working to take care of their own personal or family needs. In contrast, many firefighters left home and arrived at the scene and began to help without reporting to incident commanders. Responders often work too long and often burn themselves out responding to the disaster. Some may fail to perform their assigned duties, but this is certainly the minority.

Although some victims may be overwhelmed or otherwise incapacitated due to the disaster, most are not helpless. Those affected by disaster generally take care of themselves and others (Tierney, Lindell, and Perry 2001). As an example, some may fight fires with extinguishers or garden hoses until firefighters arrive. Others provide basic first aid to the wounded. Victims are creative in how they respond to the needs. For example, people trapped in collapsed buildings eat gum to stay alive and whistle or tap debris (with fingers, hands, rocks, or other debris) to help emergency workers locate them.

Because the expected number of people needing shelters is often overestimated, many responding organizations set up and operate shelters after the disaster. However, most victims will not use them. Evacuees tend to stay in hotels or visit friends and relatives (Quarantelli 1995). They prefer to stay in comfortable accommodations with people they are familiar with. In fact, some people stay in hotels rather than shelters. They are subsequently surprised when they find out the federal government will not reimburse them for their hotel stay.

There is another reality that should be considered. The initial reports by the media are likely to be inaccurate, incomplete, and even misleading (Scanlon 1985). For instance, the number of deaths reported by the media is often blown out of proportion. After the 9/11 terrorist attacks, it was believed that up to 50,000 people could have been killed. The actual number was around 3,000. The number of deaths after Hurricane Katrina was also different than predicted.

Although specific types of assistance may be needed, certain types of relief are frequently unwarranted. Food, clothing, and other supplies are generally available to victims and emergency workers. If aid is not present initially, it is likely that it will be after the media reports the need. In many disasters, there is an overabundance of aid. Such aid may create additional problems because it has to be disposed of or sorted and distributed (Neal 1994).

Finally, major disasters do occasionally require the services of the National Guard and armed forces. The governor or the president may request reservists and active-duty personnel to keep people away from dangerous areas or clean up debris. This is not martial law, however. Although martial law has been imposed in wartime and due to disgruntled employees or workers on strike (see http://www.usconstitution.net/consttop_mlaw.html), "it has never been necessary to declare martial law following any U.S. disaster" (Tierney, Lindell and Perry 2001, p. 110). Even with the social chaos after Hurricane Katrina, martial law was not enacted. Some force was needed at times to reign in criminals toting weapons. But martial law was not imposed even in this dire situation. Americans are extremely hesitant to turn over total control to government officials, police, and the military. For example, President Bush was criticized for wiretapping potential suspects after the 9/11 terrorist attacks.

All of this suggests that people tend to behave in ways that are not always consistent with Hollywood and media portrayals. Research findings on myths may also be questionable in regards to certain situations, although they are generally accurate most of the time. You should be cognizant of actual human behavior after disasters.

FOR EXAMPLE

The Reaction to Hurricane Katrina

Hurricane Katrina illustrated both the worst and best of people in New Orleans. Some people looted and engaged in violent behavior after the disaster. However, many people from inside and outside the community worked tirelessly to respond to victims' needs. The deviant behavior after Hurricane Katrina may be a reflection of the continuities in society rather than a sharp break from daily life. "An orthodoxy discussed more among researchers than practitioners, is that disasters tend to highlight or sometime exacerbate existing trends, that then create entirely new circumstances. Given the 'normal' circumstances in New Orleans, what was seen and the fall out does not seem so surprising" (Handmer 2006, p. 33). The case of New Orleans is somewhat unique. It is also complicated. "Press and agency apologies for exaggerating aspects of the extent of the crisis are emerging, although some evidence suggests that aspects were even worse than reported" (Handmer 2006, p. 29).

SELF-CHECK

- Can fleeing the scene of a disaster be rational?
- Do all people leave when an evacuation request is made?
- Do many crimes decline after a disaster?
- Will emergency workers show up, even when they have not been requested?
- Are most people altruistic after disaster?
- Why do most individuals and families avoid public shelters?

3.5 The Importance of Understanding Behavior Correctly

Does human behavior in disaster really matter? The answer is an emphatic "yes"! You must base your post-disaster decisions and policies on what people are most likely to do. You don't want to implement choices on incorrect or incomplete beliefs. Doing so would unintentionally add to the problems associated with disasters. For example:

▲ The media's reporting of a "panicked evacuation" may make the emergency manager and government look incompetent. It could also postpone necessary evacuations.

▲ Inaccurate beliefs about human behavior may have led to the inability of DHS to create an effective homeland security advisory system for terrorist attacks.

▲ The belief that there will be massive amounts of looting and price gouging may take law-enforcement officials away from more important work after a disaster (e.g., traffic control). Reports of criminal activity and the law-enforcement responses may also prevent victims from returning to their homes to salvage their personal belongings.

▲ The assumption that responders will be unreliable may result in unnecessary communications to make sure emergency workers are doing their jobs. This ties up communication channels and interrupts vital activities.

▲ The assertion that victims cannot help themselves in disasters may also slow down the recovery of the community. This is because it is believed that the government and official disaster organizations must perform all disaster-related tasks.

▲ An overstatement of the disaster's impacts may result in the delivery of unnecessary donations. Volunteers may also show up at the scene when they are not needed.

▲ The perception that martial law will be imposed could cause some potential volunteers to refrain from participating in the response and recovery.

Fortunately, emergency managers are more likely to have accurate perceptions of reality today. Henry Fischer surveyed 54 local emergency managers in Ohio to assess their understanding of actual disaster behavior. His study indicates that education and training have helped emergency managers to gain "an increasingly accurate understanding of the actual behavioral response to disaster" (Fischer 1998, p. 94). Table 3-4 reveals the percentage of respondents that had correct views about human behavior in disasters. Progress has therefore been made over the past two decades. Fewer emergency managers accept the portrayals of Hollywood and the media than a decade ago.

However, inaccurate views of disaster behavior are still prevalent among some emergency managers (particularly on the behavioral statements in the lower half of the chart on p. 70). The public at large has even more room for improvement. Therefore, it is necessary to reiterate that Hollywood and the media frequently do

Table 3-4: Emergency Managers Views About Disaster Behavior

Behavior Statement	Percentage Correct
Emergency workers will not be selfish	98
There will not be volunteer shortage	85
Local leaders will not panic	83
Local citizens will help each other	80
Local citizens do not price gouge	74
Local merchants do not price gouge	72
Local residents refuse to evacuate	68
EMS workers will not leave posts	68
Survivors will not behave selfishly	67
Shelters will often be underused	63
Residents will be looting	61
There will not be too few shelters	54
Citizens will not panic	50
Residents will not behave irrationally	46
Survivors will know what to do	39
Damage estimates not initially accurate	37
Death/injury estimates not accurate	31

Adapted from Fischer 1998, 102.

not accurately portray human behavior in disasters. People tend to act rationally and exhibit a great deal of pro-social behavior. Emergency workers are generally selfless individuals that respond to the needs of disaster-affected communities. Victims are most likely to be proactive and take care of themselves and others. Media reports about disaster impacts are often overstated. Too much aid is frequently sent to the scene. The government has not imposed martial law when disaster strikes. The reality of disaster behavior is thus quite different from the exaggerations that are so commonly believed. Thinking otherwise adversely affects response and recovery operations. Nevertheless, more studies will be needed in the future. As an emergency manager, it is your responsibility to maintain awareness of this research.

FOR EXAMPLE

Volunteers After the Loma Prieta Earthquake

After experiencing the Loma Prieta earthquake in October 17, 1989, relief agencies and citizens immediately began to respond to the disaster. Within 30 minutes, the Local Amateur Radio Group set up communications among its members in the affected area. One of its main goals was to assist the operations of the American Red Cross. Volunteers from the Red Cross reported to headquarters and began to register victims and volunteers, establish shelters, feed victims and emergency workers, and take care of other pressing needs. The Salvation Army also distributed food as well as clothing, blankets, and other supplies to disaster victims. The Local Volunteer Coordination Council met to begin matching volunteers with community needs. According to Neal, "One staff member estimated that for every call that requested a volunteer, five people called to volunteer their services. For example, engineers, plumbers, daycare professionals, and businesses called to offer resources (e.g., personnel, expertise, equipment)" (1990, p. 94). It appears that most organizations and people work diligently and cooperatively to help those affected by disasters.

SELF-CHECK

- Could media reports of panic make response activities look unsuccessful?
- Do reports of looting keep police from other important responsibilities after a disaster?
- Is it necessary for superiors to always check on first responders?
- Do reporters influence the amount of donations that arrive in a disaster-stricken community?
- Can education and training change perspectives about human behavior in disasters?

SUMMARY

Having accurate views of disaster behavior is one of the best ways to promote successful response and recovery operations. Unfortunately, Hollywood films and the media often incorrectly portray human behavior in disasters. People tend to believe these sensational reports, which scholars label as myths. At times, human disaster behavior is less than desirable. But, for the most part, humans do try to assist one another in times of disaster. For this reason, you may wish to consider using the term "exaggeration" instead of "myth." You should also develop a solid understanding of how people actually behave in disasters. Failing to do so could jeopardize post-disaster activities.

KEY TERMS

Exaggeration	A simplistic overstatement about some type of phenomena.
Looting	Stealing others' personal belongings.
Martial law	The replacing of civilian authority with that of the military.
Myth	A false belief.
Panic	People's inability to think clearly or their tendency to run frantically from buildings or the disaster scene.
Price gouging	The selling of goods and services at a price higher than the normal market rate.
Role or post abandonment	Not showing up to work during an emergency.
Shock	A period of disbelief after a disaster that renders people unable to think or take care of themselves.

ASSESS YOUR UNDERSTANDING

Go to www.wiley.com/college/McEntire to evaluate your knowledge of human behavior during disasters.
Measure your learning by comparing pretest and post-test results.

Summary Questions

1. Most people get their understanding of disasters from movies and the media. True or False?

2. News reports often convey the impression that victims can care for themselves. True or False?

3. Anyone sorting through debris is a looter. True or False?

4. Most people panic when warned of an impending hazard. True or False?

5. Price gouging is not a widespread phenomenon. True or False?

6. Emergency workers cannot be counted on to get their jobs done. True or False?

7. Most people will not need some type of public shelter after a disaster. True or False?

8. Media reports may give a biased representation of the extent of the disaster damages. True or False?

9. The president always imposes martial law after disasters. True or False?

10. When the World Trade Center Towers fell, people ran. This is an example of:
    (a) Panic behavior
    (b) Rational behavior
    (c) Irrational behavior
    (d) Panic flight
    (e) a and d

11. Vendors and contractors
    (a) Will always be honest in their dealings with disaster victims
    (b) Will always be dishonest in their dealing with disaster victims
    (c) May sometimes be honest in their dealings with disaster victims
    (d) May sometimes be dishonest in their dealings with disaster victims
    (e) Will complete all work and never cheat the disaster victims

12. After a disaster, we should expect:
    (a) That all goods are sold at a higher price
    (b) That all goods are sold at a lower price
    (c) That some people might be emotionally distraught

(d) That no people will be emotionally distraught

(e) b and d

13. After Hurricane Katrina:

(a) There were no reports of looting.

(b) There were some reports of looting.

(c) There were no reports of violence.

(d) There were some reports of violence.

(e) b and d

14. In a disaster situation:

(a) It is likely that not everyone will evacuate.

(b) It is likely that everyone will evacuate.

(c) It is likely that everyone will panic.

(d) It is likely that all businesses will be involved in unethical behavior.

(e) It is likely that all citizens will be in a state of shock.

15. Rather than stay in public shelters, most people will:

(a) Try to ride out the disaster at home

(b) Try to ride out the disaster on the road

(c) Try to stay with family and friends

(d) Be involved in violent criminal activity

(e) Not be involved in violent criminal activity

Review Questions

1. Do people have erroneous views about disasters? If so, why?

2. What does the research say about disaster myths?

3. Do most people panic after a disaster?

4. What is a bigger challenge—panic or getting people to evacuate?

5. Is looting a common occurrence in every disaster?

6. Will police and fire personnel abandon their posts?

7. Can victims care for themselves after disaster?

8. Are media reports always accurate? Are they always inaccurate?

9. Do all victims need disaster donations?

10. Do disaster victims often require outside relief assistance?

11. Is martial law required after every disaster? Is it required in the vast majority of disasters?

12. Why is it preferable to use the term "exaggeration" instead of "myth"?

13. How do people really behave in disasters?

14. Could incorrect views have a negative impact on response and recovery operations?

15. What can be done to counter common but erroneous beliefs about human behavior in disasters?

16. What should the emergency manager do to make sure myths do not adversely affect response and recovery operations?

Applying This Chapter

1. As a risk manager for a major business, you have just been notified that severe weather is approaching your corporate headquarters. One of the Chief Executive Officers asserts that warning the employees will cause a great deal of panic. How would you deal with this situation?

2. An 6.9 earthquake has just occurred in Salt Lake City, Utah. It has damaged thousands of homes and offices, which will take months to repair. It is now winter and the temperatures are reaching record lows. The mayor has requested that you open up shelters for everyone that has been affected. Is this a good or bad decision? What should you tell this community leader?

3. You are in charge of logistics for the American Red Cross. A major winter storm has just affected your community in Minnesota. The news media is requesting that people outside the area send you donations of coats and blankets. Could these items be useful? Could you get too many of them? How would you deal with this situation?

4. While managing the response to a terrorist attack in the central business district in your city, you have been told that looting is taking place in a nearby neighborhood. Would it be advisable to get additional information about this report from the media? Should you send police officers to the neighborhood? What concerns would you have about sending too many officers to this area?

5. An outbreak of a strange strain of flu has occurred in Boston, Massachusetts. Public health officials are concerned that they will not have sufficient flu shots for citizens in this area. A medical official at a nearby hospital has requested that you implement martial law immediately. Is this a wise decision? What factors would you need to consider before proceeding with this choice?

YOU TRY IT

Debunking Myths

You just saw the movie *Titanic* with a friend. In one scene, an employee of the cruise line calls for order and shoots his gun into the air to get people's attention. Your friend comments that "disasters always bring out the worst in people." Write a four-page paper illustrating how you would deal with this situation. Be sure to discuss the media, Hollywood, disaster research, and actual behavior.

Talking Points

While talking to the media about an upcoming disaster exercise, a reporter states "people always panic when a hurricane approaches the coast." How would you respond as an emergency manager to help him/her understand human behavior accurately?

Educating the Public

As you are engaged in community education about emergency management at a middle school, a students raises his hand and asks "How many firefighters quit their job during disasters?" What would you say to give an accurate view of the situation?

Verifying Sources

While responding to a disaster, the police chief comments that he needs to send some officers to stop looting in one particular neighborhood. The police chief is basing his comments on media reports. How can you ensure that the jurisdiction has sufficient officers to take care of traffic control issues after the disaster?

4

APPROACHING RESPONSE AND RECOVERY OPERATIONS
Alternative Management Theories

Starting Point

Go to www.wiley.com/college/McEntire to assess your knowledge
of response and recovery operations.
Determine where you need to concentrate your effort.

What You'll Learn in This Chapter

▲ The traditional perspective of response and recovery operations
▲ Strengths and weaknesses of the traditional approach
▲ The professional approach to emergency management
▲ Advantages and disadvantages of the professional approach
▲ How the traditional and professional models are similar and distinct

After Studying This Chapter, You'll Be Able To

▲ Distinguish between the traditional and professional approaches to disasters
▲ Examine strengths and weaknesses of the traditional model
▲ Compare and contrast the benefit and drawbacks of the professional approach
▲ Determine which approach is most applicable for any given disaster situation

Goals and Outcomes

▲ Assess the traditional approach to response and recovery
▲ Assess the use of the professional model after disasters
▲ Understand the pros and cons of each approach to disasters
▲ Evaluate when to apply each disaster management model

INTRODUCTION

In order to react effectively to disasters, you must approach response and recovery operations critically. Whether we recognize it or not, our lives are guided by theory. The same is true about disasters. Our notions regarding disasters determine what we will do about them. For instance, in some societies people view disasters as acts of God. Accordingly, repentance or sacrifices are regarded as the means to appeasing a deity. Others equate disasters with the natural hazard agents that trigger them. Therefore, early warning systems and containment devices such as dams are seen as ways to give advanced notification of adverse weather or control rising floodwaters. Others also feel that technology provides a "silver bullet" for all of the disaster problems that confront us. Satellites, communications equipment, and improved engineering are all that are required for preparedness and mitigation. Today, many scholars also argue that disasters are socially constructed. If our values, attitudes, and practices lead to disaster, then these must be changed if we are to prevent them or deal effectively with their adverse consequences. There are also two theoretical approaches that guide our responses to disaster. These include what may be labeled as the traditional and professional models. Each model makes unique assumptions about disasters. Both approaches have respective strengths and weaknesses that you should consider.

4.1 The Traditional Model

As an emergency manager, you should be aware that the **traditional model** has been employed in many disasters in the United States. It is referred to as the civil defense, command and control, bureaucratic, or emergency services perspective (Quarantelli 1987; Dynes 1994; Neal and Phillips 1995; Schneider 1995; Selves 2002; Edwards-Winslow 2002). The traditional model is not the preferred emergency management model among many scholars today, but it still provides useful insights into post-disaster operations. To understand this model, it is necessary to review the evolution of emergency management in the United States.

Federal participation in disaster activities goes back more than 200 years (Drabek 1991). The involvement of the national government in disasters was generally reactive and typically dealt with natural disasters such as floods and hurricanes. Things began to change after World War II, when the world entered a new period of crisis. Political disagreements emerged between the Soviet Union and the United States. The conflict was ideological in nature, with dictatorship and communism in the East pitted against democracy and capitalism in the West. Small skirmishes occurred around the world between these superpowers and their allies, but the biggest concern resulted from the fact that both parties in this dispute acquired nuclear warheads and threatened each other with **mutually assured destruction (MAD).** This implied that the use of these weapons against one's enemy would invite massive retaliation that would result in the annihilation of most major cities in both countries. (see Figure 4-2)

In response to the threat of this "Cold War," emphasis in emergency management shifted toward national security. Civil defense offices appeared in many cities around the United States. **Civil defense** was an effort by government officials to prepare for nuclear war. It included the building of underground shelters and the creation of plans to evacuate targeted urban areas of strategic value. The government thought there would be a great deal of panic on the part of the populous and felt that social order would have to be maintained after a nuclear exchange. Although the distinction between civil defense and natural disaster relief activities created friction among agencies, these efforts were believed to be justified among federal policy makers. It was out of the context of the Cold War and fear of nuclear attack that the traditional model became popular. (see Figure 4-1)

The traditional model has also been prevalent because the first emergency managers typically had military backgrounds. They gave priority to war disasters and accepted the attitudes and structure of military organizations. Civil defense directors were comfortable with the hierarchy of the armed forces, the centralization of decision making, and a reliance on standard operating procedures. They applied this military model towards their disaster response and recovery operations.

First responders also supported the traditional model. In many ways, it is natural that first responders would accept hierarchical organization and adherence to **standard operating procedures (SOPs).** Police and fire departments perform their activities under the direction of chiefs, and subordinates are supposed to respond according to organizational policies for their own safety and that of others. SOPs are rules and guidelines to complete disaster functions effectively and efficiently. They also approach disasters from a mission perspective, focusing on what their organization can do to accomplish the functions it is tasked with.

4.1.1 Features of the Traditional Model

There are four major components of the traditional model:

1. We need to give highest priority to war disasters.
2. Government is the most reliable actor because societal chaos will result in times of disaster.
3. It is best to operate under hierarchy and adhere strictly to standard operating procedures.
4. Emergency management is concerned with first-responder issues only.

Figure 4-1

Civil defense directors worked with communities to prepare them for attacks involving nuclear weapons.

The traditional model assumes nuclear war would be the most devastating type of disaster imaginable. Its principle fear of mutually assured destruction tended to neglect the frequency and impact of other types of disasters. This model mostly considered the role of government in disaster situations (Schneider 1992). Civil defense directors were comfortable with this approach, as it was relevant to the context in which they operated. While it is natural that people view disaster response operations from their own perspective, this sometimes meant that the important roles performed by others were misunderstood and not integrated into the overall management of disasters.

In addition, the departments that responded to disasters were often organized in accordance with a chain of command under this model. For example, fire and police departments have chiefs, captains, lieutenants, and sergeants. Orders are given by superiors, and they are followed by those of lower rank. Disregarding requests made by leaders is not tolerated. The traditional model therefore accepts classical management theory (Britton 1989, p. 10). It assumed that decisions are made rationally by leaders who find solutions to the problem identified. Therefore, the traditional approach simplifies a complex process of policy making in times of disaster. Practitioners employing this model also relied on "clearly defined objectives, a division of labor, a formal structure, and a set of policies and procedures to fulfill disaster operations" (Schneider, 1992). It did not allow people to adapt when performing tasks or functions.

The traditional model was also characterized by numerous other assumptions, which were often incomplete or incorrect:

▲ Emergency management should be located in fire or police departments.
▲ Emergency managers coordinate emergency service operations only.
▲ Politicians are nuisances who get in the way of disaster response.
▲ Information obtained or relayed by non-government personnel and agencies cannot be trusted.
▲ Key leaders and decision makers thought emergency services personnel will neglect their duties in order to look after their own well-being and self-interest (or that of their friends and families).
▲ Laws, policies, and standard operating procedures are always applicable and effective in any and every disaster situation.
▲ Failing to follow bureaucratic guidelines is detrimental to the response operation.
▲ Citizens do not respond to disasters, or cannot do so effectively. Their behavior always involves panic, looting, or other anti-social activities.
▲ The spontaneous involvement of emergent groups hinders governmental response operations.

The suppositions of the traditional model have several significant implications for emergency management (Edwards-Winslow 2002; Selves 2002). For instance, it rejected the need to deal with natural disasters, which have obviously been more frequent throughout history than nuclear attacks. The use of the traditional model also led to a situation where power and decision making became centralized in disaster situations. Bureaucratic expertise and strong government leadership were required to make sense out of the event and decide how best to respond. Other participants in emergency management were therefore excluded from the decision-making process, and important functions such as media relations and resource coordination were consequently overlooked. Hierarchy and top-down communications were needed to limit input or filter information from those in the field. Strict adherence to bureaucratic norms and procedures as outlined in emergency operations plans is valued, along with skepticism for creativity and improvisation (Britton 1989, p. 13). The traditional model advocated a limited and very rigid approach to the management of disaster response and recovery operations. (see Table 4-1)

4.1.2 Strengths of Traditional Model

The traditional model has several strong points. First, it is true that war produces more devastating consequences than many natural and technological disasters. A detonation of a single nuclear weapon could kill millions of people. We must therefore be prepared to respond to acts of aggression.

Another advantage of the model is that it recognizes that the government is a vital participant in disaster response operations. In our current war on terror, the government is responsible to stop terrorists from carrying out attacks. The government is typically involved in issuing warnings and evacuating people from hazardous situations. Public agencies also help to clean up debris and provide financial assistance to the victims of disaster.

A third benefit is in standard operating procedures and hierarchy. Standard operating procedures help responders know what to do in case of a crisis situation. For example, emergency responders are requested to survey the scene of a tanker accident from a distance in order to protect workers from hazardous material spills. SOPs can therefore be valuable in post-disaster activities. Hierarchy and orders are often advantageous. They can protect lives and help accomplish tasks based on the prior experience of commanding officers. As an example, it may be wise for firefighters to wait to enter a burning building until the chief has had enough time to conduct an initial evaluation of the situation. On 9/11, many off-duty first responders arrived at the World Trade Center to help. Instead of checking in with their fire chiefs, they grabbed their gear and entered the Twin Towers. Fire chiefs were not aware of their involvement and had no way of communicating with the off-duty personnel. When it became apparent that the second tower would fall, an evacuation order was given. Ad-hoc responders did not

Table 4-1: Assumptions and Conclusions of the Traditional Model

Assumptions	Implications/Conclusions
War and civil defense disasters are of paramount importance	Other types of disasters are neglected
Emergency management should be located in emergency service departments	Emergency management functions are only related to first responders
Emergency managers coordinate emergency services only	Disaster functions such as media relations are overlooked
Emergency managers need to have control, uniforms, emergency vehicles, and sirens	Turf battles and resentment build among first responders
Politicians are nuisances	Isolation from key leadership and other departments
Disasters result in a great deal of social chaos	The desire to bring order to disaster is natural and to be expected
Government is the main or only responder in times of disaster	Centralization of power and decision making is beneficial during disasters
Information obtained or relayed outside government cannot be trusted	Bureaucratic expertise and top-down communications structures are best
Emergency workers will leave their posts	A strong paramilitary leadership is required
SOPs will be effective in any and every disaster situation	Adherence to SOPs is preferred over creativity and improvisation
Failing to follow SOPs will be detrimental to the response	Same as above
Citizens do not or cannot respond effectively to disasters	Exclusion of others is viewed as the most effective type of response
Victim behavior includes panic, looting, and antisocial behavior	Same as above
Emergent groups hinder response operations	Same as above

receive this message. Had a chain of command been established and the order been heeded, fewer lives would have been lost.

The desire to respond to the disaster in the most efficient manner is another benefit of this model. Disasters are nonroutine social problems that pose significant challenges to responders and the community. Therefore, it is natural that emergency managers want to remedy the situation. They will logically want to effectively manage response personnel and other resources.

4.1.3 Weaknesses of Traditional Model

The traditional model also has several weaknesses. These failures have caused many to disregard it as an effective approach. A major weakness of this approach is unwillingness to appreciate the low probability of war-induced disasters. Natural and technological events are far more likely to occur. In 2005, there were numerous hurricanes that affected the United States. There were no conflict disasters on American soil.

Another weakness of the traditional model is the neglecting of other actors involved in response operations. Emergency managers and government agencies are not the only actors involved in disasters. Volunteers, hospitals, businesses, and nonprofit organizations also play vital roles in search and rescue operations, medical care, utility restoration, and mental health counseling after a disaster. The Red Cross, for example, plays a vital role. Churches and shelters play an important role as well. The traditional approach overlooks the contributions of other people and agencies outside the public sector.

A third weakness of the approach is the reliance on standard operating procedures that do not work in every disaster. Disasters, by their very nature, create challenges that cannot always be predicted and planned for. For instance, an SOP may discuss guidelines about delaying the response to a hazardous materials spill until the chief has conducted his size up of the situation. Would this SOP help an emergency worker know what to do if he or she determines that delaying the response could be dangerous as the spill is draining toward a crowded restaurant or industrial complex? A good example of this is in the response to 9/11. When the Twin Towers collapsed, the Coast Guard allowed more people to evacuate Manhattan on boats than is legally permitted in regulations (Kendra and Wachtendorf 2003). This decision allowed up to 500,000 to leave the island quickly. If regulations had been followed, it is likely that evacuation would be delayed and the response would have been more complicated. Because of its heavy reliance on standard operating procedures, the traditional model may not be able to handle unpredictable or dynamic environments.

A fourth weakness is that the traditional model does not acknowledge that there may be order in situations that appear to be chaotic on the surface (Dynes 1994). While the involvement of numerous actors in post-disaster operations often looks confusing, this does not necessarily mean that there is duplication

> ## FOR EXAMPLE
>
> ### The Role of the Military in Natural Disasters
>
> After Hurricane Katrina devastated New Orleans and flooded the city, many wondered why the military was not there sooner. One reason is that Governor Blanco of Louisiana did not specifically request the military as soon as she could have. The governor has to make this request since the deployment of the military is governed by the Posse Comitatus Act of 1878. Under this act, the military cannot participate in state affairs unless requested by the governor. This is one example where a failure to implement standard operating procedures delayed the arrival of needed resources for disaster-affected communities. The military was eventually deployed under a state declaration of emergency, and the armed forces assisted with evacuation and the maintenance of law and order.

of services or a lack of effectiveness. In fact, the participation of many organizations in the response may be necessary to deal successfully with the scope and nature of the disaster. During Hurricane Katrina, for example, there were hundreds of organizations involved. The federal and state governments were central actors. First responders and the Coast Guard helped with search and rescue missions. Charities, such as the Salvation Army and the Red Cross, assisted with the sheltering of evacuees. The media worked to reunite separated families. Even ordinary citizens took in some of the displaced disaster victims. Therefore, disasters are beyond the control of any single individual, department or agency. In addition, people may behave in certain ways (e.g., donate goods and supplies) regardless of your efforts to promote or discourage those particular activities. During 9/11, for example, thousands of pounds of goods were collected for victims. Blankets, water, and food came by the truckload. More donations came in than were needed. Those donated goods now sit in warehouses in New York, ready to be redistributed for other disasters.

Finally, the traditional model also relies on top-down communications. Unfortunately, organizational leadership may not have sufficient information to make correct decisions about the disaster, or it may take too long to relay problems up and down the chain of command before they can be addressed. For instance, the fire chief may not see an individual who is trapped in the burning building. The firefighter will have to rescue the person immediately, thereby acting before requests are made by his or her commanding officer. The traditional model seems to imply that disaster response operations can be directed in an authoritarian manner. This model can be myopic, rigid, and cumbersome. In some circumstances, it can also be ineffective or inefficient. (see Table 4-2)

Table 4–2: Strengths and Weaknesses of the Traditional Model

Strengths	Weaknesses
War may have the most adverse impacts of any disaster	Natural and technological disasters are more common
Government is an important actor in disaster response operations	Government is not the only actor in disaster response operations
SOPs provide logical guidelines for routine emergency situations	SOPs cannot provide guidance in all types of disaster situations
Hierarchy and orders may save lives and help to get things done	Top-down structures may slow down or hinder the response
The desire to bring order to disaster is natural and to be expected	There may be order in chaos, and it is impossible to control a disaster

SELF-CHECK

- What is the **traditional model** and why did it come about?
- What is **mutually assured destruction**?
- What is **civil defense**?
- What does **SOP** stand for?
- What are the assumptions and conclusions of the traditional model?
- What are the strengths and weaknesses of this approach?

4.2 The Professional Model

As an emergency manager, you should be aware that a different model is now preferred among many scholars as the method for dealing with disasters. The **professional model** is an approach to disasters that is based on interdependent organizational operations. It is known as the all-hazards, networking, collaborative, problem solving, or public administration model (Dynes 1994; Neal and Phillips 1995; Schneider 1995; Selves 2002; Edwards-Winslow 2002). Understanding this model also requires an appreciation of how emergency management has changed in the United States since the civil defense era.

In 1979, President Jimmy Carter created FEMA. The formation of FEMA combined several different civil defense and other disaster-related organizations under one roof. The programs incorporated into the new agency formed the basis for emergency management for local and state governments for the next two decades. One of the major changes associated with FEMA was a recognition that that the threat of nuclear war was diminishing as the end of the Cold War neared. Government officials came to understand that natural and technological disasters were more common than war-time disasters. It was recognized that emergency managers must therefore be concerned about more than just civil defense issues relating to evacuation and sheltering. Emergency management was beginning to formalize new responsibilities.

In addition, the traditional model's seemingly exclusive concentration on military involvement did not always fit in with the new FEMA organization. It was increasingly recognized that departments and agencies from all levels of government as well as nearby or distant communities will respond to disasters. Other organizations from the private and nonprofit sectors will also show up and participate in response and recovery operations when disaster strikes. Proponents of the professional model also emphasized that society does not cease to function after disasters. The findings from disaster sociologists were being incorporated into the field during this period. It was realized that people care for themselves and others and are able to react despite severe societal crises (Dynes 1994). For this reason, horizontal relationships are just as important as vertical relationships.

▲ **Horizontal relationships** are those in which parties communicate across departments and communities.
▲ **Vertical relationships** involve information flow up and down government chains of command.

Those favoring the professional model also began to question the merit of following strict standard operating procedures in disasters. Emergency managers became increasingly aware of the fact that disasters pose unique challenges that require departures from routine methods of dealing with smaller emergencies. While plans serve as guidelines, they will not always be applicable to every disaster situation. Along these lines, laws and regulations may at times slow down response. This can make operations ineffective and/or inefficient. Departing from SOPs began to be favored at times as bureaucratic procedures were seen as being too rigid. The professional model became a more flexible alternative to the traditional approach to disasters.

Finally, scholars and practitioners recognized over the past few decades that emergency management is more than emergency services (Selves 2002). Emergency managers are not first responders, and emergency management includes more than life safety issues. In other words, it is increasingly recognized that disasters require media relations, damage assessment, donations management, and rebuilding among other activities. There are also important measures that emergency managers must pursue in order to mitigate and prepare for disasters. Such proactive approaches may be far different from first-responder activities. Furthermore, emergency managers began to recognize that what one agency does or does not do may affect the ability of another to perform its functions. For instance, EMTs cannot transport the injured to hospitals if public works has not cleared the roads of disaster debris. Another example is the inability of departments to communicate fully after a hurricane. Their ability to talk may be limited until utility companies establish emergency phone lines or repair cell towers. No single group can respond effectively to disasters alone or without the cooperation of others. Disaster functions are almost always interdependent on the activities of others.

4.2.1 Features of the Professional Model

If you are to respond effectively to disasters, it will be imperative that you comprehend the assumptions associated with the professional model. These speculations suggest that:

▲ Emergency managers will likely be confronted by many different types of disasters.

▲ No single individual, group, or organization can respond alone.

▲ Disasters pose serious challenges to society, but people will—more than likely—work together to overcome them.

▲ Emergence cannot be prevented (Neal and Phillips 1995, p. 334). Citizens will respond to disasters whether they are invited to or not.

▲ The public is a resource. Public involvement is not necessarily a problem, although involvement may create challenges for emergency managers (e.g., too many volunteers).

▲ Hierarchical and top-down relations among all responding entities are sometimes impossible when multiple organizations respond to disasters.

▲ Disasters exhibit and exploit the weaknesses of standard operating procedures and foster emergent norms. No emergency plan will account for all types of disaster issues.

▲ A willingness to adapt is often required in disaster situations. Departures from emergency operations plans are to be expected at times and will often prove beneficial.

▲ Emergency managers perform different roles than first responders.

▲ Emergency managers will not be able to get things done if they are isolated from decision makers and other department leaders.

There are several conclusions associated with the professional approach as seen in Table 4-3. Emergency managers now recognize that they must take an all-hazard perspective of the disaster problem. Those in the field must also work with the many actors that are involved in disaster response. In particular, you must maintain close relationships with politicians, other departments, and private, nonprofit, and emergent organizations. Emergency managers continue to recognize the value of planning, but they are now more willing to depart from standard operating procedures if needed. Emergency managers are also aware of the need to see a much larger picture than that of the first responders. The professional view of disaster response and recovery operations is thus different than the traditional perspective.

Table 4-3: Assumptions and Conclusions of the Professional Model

Assumptions	Implications/Conclusions
There are more types of disasters than civil hazards	Take an all-hazards approach to emergency management
Emergency managers cannot deal with disasters alone	Include politicians and the leaders of all departments in response activities
Disasters pose challenges; people will meet the demands	Emergency managers must be ready for a multi-organizational response
Emergence is not an aberration	Same as above
The desire to bring order to disaster is natural and to be expected	Same as above
Emergence cannot be prevented	Same as above
Emergence fills a void	Same as above
The public is a resource, not a liability	Same as above
Standard operating procedures do not always work	Flexibility is needed; departures from standard procedures are okay
No single responder can deal with disaster alone	Hierarchical relationships are not possible; stress horizontal relations
Emergency management is not the same as emergency services	Accept a broader view of the disaster

4.2.2 Strengths of the Professional Model

If you are to work in emergency management, you should recognize that the professional approach to disaster response operations has both strengths and weaknesses. One of the advantages of the professional model is that it takes an all-hazard approach to emergency management. It recognizes the fact that there are more types of disasters than war. What is more, many types of disasters share similar response functions. For example, warning and sheltering may be required for hurricanes and hazardous materials releases alike.

Because so many people and agencies are involved in a (see Figure 4-2) disaster, the professional approach underscores the need to integrate activities. For example, it is advisable that police, fire, and EMS officials collaborate with the media, the coroner's office, and crisis counselors at the scene of a major plane crash. These actors would help seal off the area. They would fight the fire. They would search for the wounded. They would also identify the dead and console relatives. Many functions are applicable to this model.

The professional approach also allows one to adapt during response and recovery operations. Every disaster is at least slightly different. Therefore, standard operating procedures may be incomplete, ineffective, or inefficient. An example of this is trying to evacuate a hotel when the alarm systems or phone lines are not working properly. In normal situations, you could sound an alarm or call each room and ask the guests to leave the building immediately. Firefighters would also show up to take care of the problem. However, if the power is out or the phone lines have been rendered useless due to the fire, and if first responders have not yet arrived, it might be necessary to send individuals to the rooms on each floor (assuming it is safe to do so). If guests are from foreign

Figure 4-2

Many people and organizations work together during times of disasters.

> ### FOR EXAMPLE
>
> #### Winging it for Disaster Victims
>
> DHL, a package shipment company, worked with American soldiers to set up shelter for the hundreds of thousands of victims of the 2005 Pakistan earthquake. One area where they concentrated their relief efforts was Kashmir. The location of this community is remote, mountainous, and does not have many roads or an airport nearby. DHL and the soldiers placed food and other supplies into the red polypropylene bags that DHL has been using for years. They then placed these bags on helicopters that could land in this affected region. In 2 weeks the military delivered 6,000 of these bags that each held enough shelter, food, and water to keep seven people alive for 10 days (*Wall Street Journal*, November 22, 2005, Glenn Simpson, "In Year of Disasters, Experts Bring Order to Chaos of Relief").

countries, additional measures will have to be taken to communicate in their language. The decision is therefore situational. The professional model advocates resolving the situation even if it means departing from SOPs or the plan.

The professional model also sees the big picture. Emergency management is not the same as emergency services. It is true that emergency managers work closely with those of emergency services. However, emergency managers also perform dramatically different functions than first responders. This is evident in response operations as well as in mitigation, preparedness, and recovery. The professional emergency management model recognizes these differences and appreciates their implications regarding disaster prevention or the meeting of all types of demands when they occur.

4.2.3 Weaknesses of Professional Model

You should be aware of the possible weaknesses of the professional model. By focusing on all hazards, the professional approach may become too broad. For example, it may fail to acknowledge the threat of and unique challenges associated with civil defense (or homeland security today). A nuclear attack, for example, could kill and adversely affect vast numbers of people. Responding to a biological or chemical attack may be significantly different than providing medical care in a natural disaster. The intentional spread of disease or hazardous materials could possibly outpace the knowledge and ability of civilian medical personnel. The military may need to be involved in such a situation. This is one of the reasons homeland security tends to accept the traditional model of emergency management today.

Also, by stressing the involvement of others, the professional model inadvertently reduces the importance of the government. This is problematic in that the government has access to a wide variety of human and material resources. This

Table 4-4: Strengths and Weaknesses of the Professional Model

Strengths	Weaknesses
Takes an all-hazard approach	Downplays unique difficulties of war-time disasters
Acknowledges many actors	Downplays the role of government and first responders
Stresses integration of involved parties	Fails to recognize importance of hierarchical leadership
Allows for improvisation	Overlooks benefit of standard operating procedures
Accepts a broad picture of disasters	Fails to see details of field level operations

entity is very capable of fulfilling the diverse set of needs on a long-term basis. The professional model may likewise fail to recognize the need for leadership in disaster situations. A vision of what needs to be accomplished and how it is to be done may help to unify the disparate actors involved in disaster response and recovery.

The professional model also overlooks the importance of following strategies that have been developed in the past and tested over time. There may be no need to change public information operations in a current disaster if the methods were previously effective. Following prior guidelines can save time, ensure safety, and allow for an efficient allocation of resources.

Finally, by approaching disasters from a broader perspective, the professional model may downplay the importance of emergency services. When lives are on the line, it is the police, fire personnel, and EMTs that come to the rescue. Although they cannot respond alone, and even though they are likely to experience inter-organizational rivalry, their vital contributions should not be underestimated in time of disaster. (see Table 4-3)

SELF-CHECK

- What is the **professional approach** to emergency management?
- Why did this model emerge?
- What are the features of the professional model? What conclusions are drawn from the assumptions of this model? What are the strengths of this model?
- What weaknesses are common to the professional model?

4.3 Comparison of the Models

There are both similarities and differences between the two models (Neal and Phillips 1995). A comparison of the two approaches involves examination of their:

▲ Respective goals
▲ Levels of analysis
▲ Assumptions
▲ Recommendations

Without a doubt, both the traditional and professional approaches evolved to foster beneficial outcomes in times of disaster. Each model emerged with an awareness of the adverse effects of disasters. Both models try to identify the problems inherent in emergency response operations. Both approaches attempt to resolve recognized problems quickly. Both models try to overcome these difficulties in the most effective way possible. Despite these similarities, there are significant differences between the models.

For example, the traditional model is most applicable to routine emergencies and the activities of practitioners in the field. In contrast, the professional model is more concerned about disasters and activities regarding the entire response system. One focuses on mission tactics, whereas the other is interested in overall strategy.

The models also have their own unique assumptions and recommendations (Dynes 1994). The traditional model assumes that disasters result in widespread chaos. Society may possibly break down during extreme events, and important functions will be neglected. The traditional model recommends command and control as a way to resolve the situation. Centralized leadership is needed to make correct decisions about the event, and procedures must be implemented per the instructions of the figure or agency in authority.

The professional model has different assumptions and recommendations. This model assumes that society continues to function in time of disaster. People

Table 4-5: Assumptions of the Traditional and Professional Models During Emergency Response.

Traditional Model	Professional Model
Chaos in society	Continuity of society
Command over others	Coordination with others
Control over others	Cooperation with others

Dynes 1994.

FOR EXAMPLE

The Response to 9/11

The response to the terrorist attacks in New York illustrated the need for both the traditional and professional models of emergency management. Police and fire chiefs operated at times under the traditional model because they wanted to maintain contact with subordinates to ensure their safety and well-being. Some first responders failed to follow evacuation orders, and this refusal resulted in their death. Emergency managers operated under the professional approach to emergency management. They recognized the need to work closely with others and established a new EOC (even though this procedure was not described in their plan). Most disasters will exhibit the use of each type of model.

and organizations deal with adverse situations in a logical and expected manner. It recommends coordination and cooperation among responding entities. Individuals and agencies are most likely to resolve problems by communicating and assisting one another rather than telling others what to do.

Thus, goals of the two models may be similar, but there are significant differences that must be recognized as well. You should be aware of both the traditional and professional models. It is imperative that you think critically about which model to use in each particular disaster situation. At times it will be necessary to operate under the traditional approach. In other situations, the professional approach will be desired. Knowing when to rely on each model is one of the keys to successful post-disaster operations. (see Table 4-5)

SELF-CHECK

- How are the traditional and professional models similar?
- How are the models different?
- Why is it necessary to understand the traditional and professional models?
- Would it be beneficial to know when to apply each model? Why?

SUMMARY

Theories guide our lives and disaster response and recovery operations as well. There are two theories that seem to impact emergency management. The traditional approach to emergency management focused on civil defense issues during the Cold War. It gave priority to the military and the government, standard operating procedures, and the activities of first responders. The professional model is more inclusive. It acknowledges the possibility of many different types of hazards. It also recognizes that many different actors will participate in response and recovery operations and that plans and SOPs may not be pertinent in every disaster context. Comparing the strengths and weaknesses of the two models and knowing when it is best to operate under one versus the other will help you deal effectively with disasters when they occur.

KEY TERMS

Civil defense	An effort by government officials to prepare for nuclear war. It included the building of underground shelters and the creation of plans to evacuate targeted urban areas of strategic value.
Horizontal relationships	Relationships in which parties communicate across departments and communities.
Mutually assured destruction (MAD)	The use of nuclear weapons against one's enemy that invites massive retaliation and results in the annihilation of most major cities in both countries.
Traditional model	The civil defense, command and control, bureaucratic, or emergency services perspective of disaster response and recovery operations.
Professional model	The all-hazards, networking, collaborative, problem-solving, or public administration model of disaster response and recovery operations.
Standard operating procedures (SOPs)	Rules and guidelines to complete disaster functions effectively and efficiently.
Vertical relationships	Relationships in which there is information flow up and down chains of command.

ASSESS YOUR UNDERSTANDING

Go to www.wiley.com/college/McEntire to evaluate your knowledge of response and recovery operations.

Measure your learning by comparing pretest and post-test results.

Summary Questions

1. Theory has no bearing on emergency management activities. True or False?
2. The traditional approach to disasters is known as the networking and problem-solving model. True or False?
3. Nuclear war was a major threat during the Cold War. True or False?
4. Civil defense was a government initiative to prepare cities for evacuation in case of a nuclear exchange with the Soviet Union. True or False?
5. The traditional approach to disasters disapproves of hierarchy. True or False?
6. There are no weaknesses associated with the traditional model. True or False?
7. The professional model is also referred to as the collaborative approach to emergency management. True or False?
8. When FEMA was organized, emergency management began to focus less on nuclear war and more on natural and technological hazards. True or False?
9. The professional approach to emergency management recognizes that the government is the only actor involved in response and recovery operations. True or False?
10. MAD stands for:
    (a) Management arrangement delay
    (b) Management alternative decision
    (c) Mutually assured destruction
    (d) Mutually assured devastation
    (e) Mitigation action device
11. SOPs are:
    (a) Flexible and rigid
    (b) Flexible
    (c) Espoused by the professional approach
    (d) Rigid
    (e) Related to improvisation and creativity
12. The professional model:
    (a) Gives highest priority to nuclear war
    (b) Focuses on cooperation with other organizations

(c) Is similar to the emergency services model

(d) Is similar to the public administration model

(e) b and d

13. The professional model:

   (a) Assumes that people will be a useful resource in disasters

   (b) Asserts that the government is not the only actor involved in response operations

   (c) Prefers horizontal relationships rather than a command and control mentality

   (d) All of the above

   (e) None of the above

14. A strength of the professional model is its flexible approach to disasters. A weakness of this model is:

   (a) It approaches disasters from an all hazards perspective.

   (b) It is extremely concerned about nuclear war.

   (c) It is closely aligned with emergency service personnel.

   (d) It cannot relate to private and nonprofit agencies.

   (e) It has no relationship to emergent groups.

Review Questions

1. What are the two models of disaster response and recovery management?

2. Why did the traditional model of emergency management appear?

3. What are the other names of the traditional model?

4. What major assumptions are made by the traditional model?

5. The traditional model has numerous strengths and weaknesses. What are they?

6. How did the end of the Cold War and creation of FEMA lead to the professional approach to emergency management?

7. How is the professional approach different from the traditional model?

8. How does the professional model view hierarchy and SOPs?

9. Do the traditional and professional models overlap in any ways?

10. Which model is related most to homeland security? Why?

Applying This Chapter

1. While responding to a house fire in El Paso, Texas, firefighters recognize characteristics in the home that resemble a methamphetamine lab. How could standard operating procedures help protect firefighters in this situation?

2. While responding to a major fire, the fire chief notices that the media and Red Cross have arrived to film the incident and care for those fleeing the apartment fire. What concerns do you have about their presence at the scene of the disaster? Should you avoid working with them? What are the consequences of failing to communicate with them?

3. A major office building has been bombed in downtown Atlanta. Fire has engulfed many of the lower floors, and the stairwells are filling with smoke. The elevator could be used, but the shaft is filled with dangerous fumes. Forty-seven people are stranded on the roof, waiting to be rescued. Helicopters from the fire department and a nearby military base are hovering overhead. Aviation regulations state that no more than five people should be inside the helicopters at any given time. Should you consider putting seven on the helicopters to speed up the evacuation? What are the dangers of doing so? Who could you talk to in order to see if this would be okay?

4. A major flash flood has affected a small community outside of Cheyenne, Wyoming. What are some of the organizations that might converge on this area? How would victims and bystanders behave? Would it be in your benefit as an emergency manager to consider what they are doing and if they could help you?

5. Suppose you were the emergency manager in Tokyo when the terrorist group Aum Shinrikyo released sarin gas in the subway. Many people died and thousands of people were affected. The event required a major medical mobilization, but it required that other functions be performed (e.g., media relations, mass fatality management, and criminal investigation). In what ways could the traditional approach help you? In what ways could the professional approach assist you?

Working With Others

As a fire chief in Las Vegas, Nevada, you are responsible for property protection and the safety of your crew. How can the traditional approach help you extinguish the fire and protect your firefighters? Are there issues relating to the fire you cannot address alone? Why would it be advantageous to work with other organizations?

Standard Operating Procedures

You are the emergency manager for Oak Ridge, Tennessee. Oak Ridge is home to a nuclear power plant. What standard operating procedures might you have to deal with concerning the leak of nuclear material? Could there be a situation where it would be advisable to deviate from SOPs?

Representing Your Organization

You work in the transportation department and have been assigned to the local emergency operations center during a flood episode. Why would it be important to represent the interests of your organization in the EOC? Can your organization resolve all types of disaster problems alone? Why would it be important to work collaboratively with others? Do other organizations need the information you can provide? How do the priorities of other organizations influence the operations of your organization in times of disaster?

Compare and Contrast the Models

Divide into groups of two and make a list of the pros and cons of both the traditional and professional theories pertinent to emergency management. When you are done, present your findings to the class. Be sure to state your opinion about which model is best suited for disasters.

5

RESPONDING WITH INITIAL MEASURES
Hazard Detection, Warning, Evacuation, and Sheltering

Starting Point

Go to www.wiley.com/college/McEntire to assess your knowledge of the initial response process.
Determine where you need to concentrate your effort.

What You'll Learn in This Chapter

▲ Methods to detect hazards in the initial period of disaster response
▲ The importance of warning systems
▲ Different evacuation methods
▲ Categories of sheltering and housing
▲ Human behavior during evacuation and sheltering

After Studying This Chapter, You'll Be Able To

▲ Detect hazards and implement the community disaster plan
▲ Develop effective warning messages
▲ Compare and contrast alternative means to warn people about impending and ongoing disasters
▲ Examine human behaviors during evacuation and sheltering
▲ Evaluate evacuation and shelter options

Goals and Outcomes

▲ Understand ways to identify hazards
▲ Assess the best way(s) to issue warnings and issue effective warning measures
▲ Implement the community's emergency operations plan
▲ Evaluate and select the appropriate protective action for affected populations
▲ Predict typical human behaviors during evacuation and sheltering
▲ Establish and maintain a shelter

INTRODUCTION

As an emergency manager, you will be required to take a number of immediate steps to respond effectively to a disaster. One of the first things you will need to do is detect the hazard or hazards. This allows you to seeking additional information, notify pertinent leaders, activate the EOC, and initiate the response. As this takes place, you must also warn citizens. Warning is often accompanied by evacuation and sheltering functions to protect people or give them a place to stay. This chapter provides guidelines on how to implement these vital activities.

5.1 Hazard Detection

Before you can respond to a disaster, it is necessary that you detect the hazard or hazards. **Hazard detection** is the process of identifying what hazard is about to occur or has taken place. Each hazard is different and may be detected in divergent and multiple ways. Some detection methods may be specific to the type of hazard. For example, you could learn about impending severe weather with the help of a meteorologist or radar equipment. Some hazards may be detected through many different strategies simultaneously. Storm spotters could give you a call about a possible tornado while you are talking to meteorologists from the National Weather Service. Additional detection methods include the following:

▲ **Senses.** As an emergency manager, you may actually experience the hazard yourself. The ground may shake violently due to an earthquake. Or, you may see a building on fire. A release of hazardous chemicals could lead to a physical reaction to the harmful substances.

▲ **Feedback from field personnel.** You may hear of events that require emergency or disaster response operations. For instance, city personnel could encounter emergency situations. A police officer may become aware of a serious accident or other incident because of unusually heavy traffic conditions or a gathering of people in one spot. Firefighters, emergency service personnel, and anyone with a city uniform or vehicle may also become aware of emergency or disaster situations. These individuals frequently drive around the jurisdiction. Citizens will also seek out uniformed personnel and city employees in marked vehicles if public safety is at stake.

▲ **Dispatch.** Citizens will call 911 to report an emergency. Even major disasters such as the World Trade Center terrorist attacks are often reported by 911 calls. Dispatch will then notify the fire and police chiefs. Once an incident has been reported, the police and/or fire dispatch will notify you and other responders about the incident. Additional units will be asked to report to the scene of the incident (e.g., for traffic control or a three-alarm fire). Dispatch may contact you to advise that the emergency operations center will be needed.

▲ **Increased radio traffic.** As an incident or disasters occurs, dispatch personnel, first responders, and police or fire chiefs will discuss the unfolding response on emergency communications channels. Anyone with a scanner may pick up these conversations (unless they are over secured lines). The police or fire chief may notify you directly, stating that an emergency or disaster is occurring and that assistance will be needed. Others may be called to help them with the incident. For example, the mayor and mutual aid partners may be notified.

▲ **News media.** Reports from the news media will increase dramatically when there is an impending hazard or actual disaster. Regular television programs will broadcast special reports about earthquakes, tornadoes, and other events. Newspaper articles may discuss hurricanes that have formed and are approaching the coast. Radio programs will be interrupted by the emergency alert system (e.g., to notify people of the potential of flash flooding). Internet news websites will also share information about the hazard.

▲ **Volunteers.** Volunteers will stay in contact with you when severe weather threatens. ARES (Amateur Radio Emergency Services) and RACES (Radio Amateur Civil Emergency Services) members will spot tornadoes and relay information to the emergency manager (see Figure 5-1).

▲ **Meteorological services and scientists.** Government agencies and natural scientists may notify emergency managers about impending hazards. The National Hurricane Center monitors the development and movement of hurricanes and will provide daily forecasts and projections of the time and location of landfall. The National Oceanic and Atmospheric Administration (NOAA) also assesses weather conditions. National Weather Service (NWS) employees may contact you when weather advisories have been issued. Volcanologists from the United States Geological Survey (USGS) advise of potential eruptions based on past and current volcano activity (e.g., seismic activity and gas emissions).

▲ **Incident page network.** As an emergency manager, you might subscribe to paging services (see http://www.incidentpage.net). These systems give you real-time information about severe weather, traffic accidents, major fire outbreaks, and other types of hazards.

▲ **Hospitals.** Medical facilities may become aware of unique trends in patient flow. Administrators may notify the emergency manager or public health officials if large numbers of people exhibit similar symptoms. This

Figure 5-1

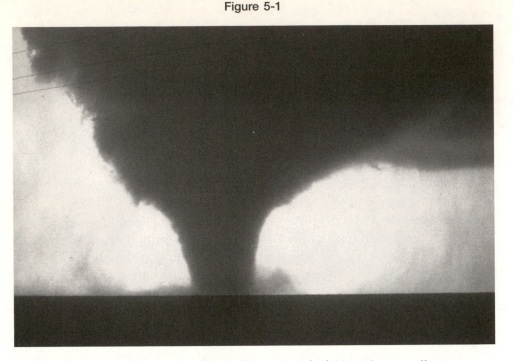

Severe weather can be detected by meteorologists or storm spotters.

is known as **syndromic surveillance**. Hospitals play a crucial role in identifying an attack involving biological weapons.

▲ **Technology.** Modern computers and technology may help detect potential hazards. Satellites provide a birds-eye view of weather systems. Radar is used to detect the formation of tornadoes and the location of rain and hail. For example, buoys monitor the heat and level of the ocean to track surface temperatures and the presence of tsunamis. Seismographs identify where earthquakes occur as well as their magnitude.

Regardless of what means are used, you should constantly monitor hazards in your jurisdiction. There should always someone who is given this responsibility (often on a rotating basis). You may be on call on a 24-hour, 7-day-a-week, 365-days-a-year basis.

5.1.1 Initial Steps

Once a hazard has been identified, it may be necessary to implement the community's emergency operations plan. A **emergency operations plan** is a document that describes how the jurisdiction might respond to a disaster. This typically involves alerting city leadership and uniting them in the emergency

---

FOR EXAMPLE

Detecting Terrorism

New Yorkers woke up on September 11, 2001 to see the World Trade Center covered in smoke after a plane hit the first tower. The event was initially reported as possible pilot error. In retrospect, it seems strange to think that people believed a passenger jet could be so off course that it would smash into a skyscraper. However, the world had never seen terrorists engage in this type of activity before. It was only when the second and third planes hit the other Trade Center tower and the Pentagon that the world realized that America was under attack. As these planes were flown into buildings, several professional and amateur camera operators caught the incident on tape. Workers inside the buildings also called 911 to initiate the emergency response. Many New Yorkers and Americans were unaware of the incident until they saw it on television.

---

operations center. This cadre of department supervisors plays an important role in the initial stages of the response. The department supervisors verify what has happened, determine response priorities, and manage disaster activities.

There are several other functions that you will need to perform, simultaneously in many cases. These include seeking additional information, notifying and communicating with others, initiating the response, and activating the emergency operations center (EOC).

Seeking Additional Information

When a hazard is imminent or occurring, it is always necessary to seek additional information. Having additional details about the hazard or resulting disaster will enable you to initiate an appropriate response. Possible questions to investigate include:

- ▲ What happened?
- ▲ Has the hazard or disaster been verified?
- ▲ What are the consequences?
- ▲ How many people have been killed or injured?
- ▲ Has property been destroyed?
- ▲ What do first responders need?
- ▲ What challenges must be overcome?
- ▲ Can city leaders or departments provide support?

▲ What resources are needed?

▲ Do other individuals and agencies need to be involved?

▲ What can be done to remedy the situation quickly and effectively?

▲ What contingencies need to be planned for?

Notifying and Communicating With Others

It will also be necessary to notify and communicate with others who play important roles in disaster response and recovery operations. This will not only assist in answering the questions posed above but will be required to formulate appropriate priorities. You will need to bring the hazard to the attention of key leaders. This includes mayors, city council members, city managers, department heads, and others. These individuals have a responsibility to act in times of disaster and have authority to mobilize resources and take all necessary actions.

You will also need to maintain communications with those individuals or organizations that notify you about the situation. This may include dispatch, field personnel, and the fire department. These people and groups can provide updated information as it becomes available. You will also want to communicate with others who have or will have details about disaster impacts. This may include meteorologists, flood plain managers, storm spotters, and police officers. These individuals can verify what is happening and provide different perspectives on what is taking place.

Initiating the Response

As information is gathered and leaders communicate with one another, it may be necessary to implement initial response measures. Immediate response measures may include:

▲ Dispatching additional fire units

▲ Seeking mutual aid for mass casualties

▲ Warning the population

▲ Evacuating the population

These measures may be based on increased readiness conditions. **Increased readiness conditions** are sometimes based on numerical numbers (e.g., 1-4) and denote the severity of an event along with appropriate measures to be taken. For instance, a level 4 might imply that a tornado could occur and that department leaders should maintain awareness of weather reports. In contrast, a level 1 may note that a tornado is occurring/has occurred and that all necessary departments should be involved in the response. Thus, the nature and timing of the hazard may determine what readiness level is chosen and acted on.

Activating the Emergency Operations Center (EOC)

As part of the initial response, and in accordance with the information received, the emergency manager, in consultation with the mayor or city manager, may decide to activate the emergency operations center. The **emergency operations center** or **EOC** is a central location where leaders gather information, discuss options, make decisions, disseminate policy, mobilize resources, and communicate with involved parties. EOC activation will help emergency managers plan and coordinate response operations. Activating the EOC may include staffing the EOC, which may be partial or complete.

▲ **Partial activation** may include some individuals, agencies, and functions.

▲ **Full activation** will include all individuals, agencies, and functions.

Partial or full activation will also be determined by the nature of the hazard and impact of the disaster (type, scope, magnitude, etc.).

As the emergency or disaster unfolds, it is important for the emergency manager to understand who participates or should participate in the response. The emergency or disaster will determine who is, will, or should be involved. For example, a small emergency will require fewer people and agencies than a larger disaster. A forest fire could require different personnel than a major flood.

Some agencies will become involved in the EOC automatically (e.g., fire department), whereas others should be notified and asked to participate (e.g., water department). The people and organizations involved in the EOC will not be static but will expand and contract as the response dictates. As an example, information provided by storm spotters is vital before and when a tornado strikes. Their services become less salient after the storm dissipates. However, the American Red Cross plays an increasingly important role as disaster response transitions to disaster recovery.

SELF-CHECK

- Why is it important to detect a hazard, and how does this step impact disaster response operations?
- What are the different ways of detecting hazards?
- What is a **disaster plan**?
- How can communicating with others help disaster response operations?
- Why is it important to activate the **EOC** when a hazard is about to occur?

5.2 Issuing Warnings

One of most important functions you will perform in emergency management is warning the population about an impending hazard or an actual disaster. **Warnings** are advanced notifications that allow people to take measures to protect themselves and their property. Most warnings occur before a hazard has occurred. However, warnings may take place after a disaster to help people to know the best way to respond.

Warnings follow similar patterns. According to Quarantelli, the process typically includes an assessment of the hazard or disaster and a dissemination of a message to encourage some sort of preparatory or protective behavior (1990, p. 1).

▲ The *assessment phase* is when information is gathered, decisions are made, and the message is formulated.

▲ The *dissemination phase* is when information is relayed to those who will issue the warning. It is also the time when it is relayed to, received by, and acted on by the public.

Lindell and Perry (1992) describe the warning process in a series of four steps:

1. Risk identification. Determining if a threat exists.
2. Risk assessment. Determining if protection is needed.
3. Risk reduction. Determining if protection is possible.
4. Protective response. Determining what protective action is best and then taking that action.

To help people prepare for hazards, the National Weather Service uses the terms "watch" and "warning." People may not understand the difference between a watch and a warning, however.

▲ A **watch** indicates that conditions are ripe for a hazard to occur. The severe weather system may produce a tornado or flood.

▲ A warning indicates that the hazard is imminent, is taking place, or has occurred. A tornado warning indicates that the tornado has touched down or that the river is flooding.

People must understand the significance of warnings for their physical well-being. A severe winter weather warning may allow people to buy additional groceries and supplies before the storm hits the area. Hurricane warnings encourage residents to leave low-lying areas. Another example is a tornado warning. When people are given tornado warnings, they should take immediate shelter in a safe room, (a small room in the center of a building on the lowest possible floor).

Warnings provide other vital information, including:

▲ When a hazard/disaster will occur
▲ How long a hazard/disaster will last
▲ What the impact and severity of the hazard/disaster will be
▲ Potential power outages
▲ Closed streets/areas
▲ Projected damages to homes and property

It is important for you to recognize that the warning function is complex. Depending on the type of hazard/disaster, warnings may or may not be possible. Earthquakes or terrorist attacks are extremely difficult to predict and therefore are not typically conducive for warning. For example, the government wasn't able to warn citizens about the 9/11 terrorist attacks. Due to this, the government now issues "security alerts" about possible terrorist activity. The danger here is that the "security alerts" are so frequent that they lose any kind of meaning. The Homeland Security Advisory System also lacks concrete recommendations, leaving you as an emergency manager in a state of confusion. In contrast, severe weather systems can be monitored more effectively and generally allow time for warning. Other hazards/disasters have dramatically different lead times for warning. A hurricane warning can be issued a day or more before landfall. However, a tornado warning may be issued only minutes before touchdown or impact.

When a hazard is imminent or a disaster has occurred, you should take into account several issues to ensure a successful warning. Those issuing the warning should consider what criteria would serve as the basis of the warning decision. For example:

▲ Do you issue a warning when there are signs a tornado may form, or does the tornado have to touch down before a warning is issued?
▲ Do you wait until the fire, accident, or chemical release has been confirmed by an official such as a fire chief, or should you warn others if a citizen has reported the incident?
▲ Is approval from higher sources (e.g., a mayor) needed before a warning can be issued?

There are other factors to consider as well. What are the liabilities (e.g., deaths, property damage, lawsuits) if a warning is issued or not issued? How soon should the warning be made, and is additional information required before a warning can be disseminated? What information should the warning message convey? Will the warning be followed by additional information?

You should also be aware that warnings may come from official and/or unofficial sources. The National Weather Service may issue severe thunderstorm warnings.

A friend may warn others about an approaching ice storm. Emergent groups may assist the fire department in warning others about a nearby forest fire that is approaching the neighborhood. Others also participate in the warning process. Federal government agencies such as the National Oceanic and Atmospheric Administration may issue warnings. State and local emergency management organizations and personnel play a role as well. The media is especially useful since it notifies citizens. Politicians may help you relay warnings also. For example, President Bush, Governor Blanco of Louisiana, and Mayor Nagin of New Orleans all issued warnings about Hurricane Katrina.

Golden and Adams assert (2000, p. 107) that the most important actors involved in tornado warnings include the National Weather Service Office, local emergency managers, and private forecasters/the news media. This group is known as the weather warning partnership.

5.2.1 Types of Warning Systems

Warnings may occur with or without technology. They may include door-to-door notifications. They could be performed in a police cruiser with a bullhorn. Other warnings may rely on computers and modern communications equipment. Also, there are many types of warning systems that are used for specific hazards or in conjunction with multiple hazards. Each type of warning system has strengths and weaknesses. It is important that you are aware of these advantages and disadvantages so you can make the correct decisions when disseminating warnings. This is because the warning system you choose has an impact on the effectiveness of the warning. However, it is true that you may use several warning systems for the same hazard. For instance, outdoor sirens are sounded when a tornado touches down in a residential area. The media is also alerted, and weather radios are activated too. More than one method can therefore be utilized at a time. In fact, it is advisable to use as many means as possible to issue a warning as long as the message is consistent. This increases the chance that most people will receive the warning message.

Sirens

Outdoor mechanical and electronic sirens are used to warn people about severe weather such as tornadoes. Mechanical sirens can warn a large number of people as long as they can hear the siren. People are most likely to be alerted by the siren when they are outside and in close proximity to this warning device. Much like public address (PA) systems, electronic sirens warn a large number people as well. The only difference is that electronic sirens produce numerous tones and allow voice warnings.

The weakness of a mechanical siren is that it produces a single tone, which may not be understood by those who hear it. Both electronic and mechanical sirens are not typically heard by people who are inside buildings. They also break down frequently and may be rendered useless due to lightning strikes or power outages. Sirens also require a significant amount of maintenance.

Media

TV stations issue warnings as part of regular news broadcasts or may interrupt regularly scheduled programming in times of emergency or disaster. Cable stations may issue warnings through scroll text at the bottom of the television screen. Media reports quickly warn a large number of people if they are inside their home watching TV or listening to the radio in the car. Reporters also provide detailed information about the hazard or disaster.

There are weaknesses associated with warnings issued by the media. The problem with media warnings is that people may not be watching TV or listening to the radio. Also, power outages may render some forms of the media useless. The information relayed through the media might also be incorrect because it is often based on initial reports.

Emergency Alert System

The emergency alert system is used for a variety of hazards and may be issued by way of television or radio. It includes an announcement of what is occurring and what should be done for protection. The emergency alert system quickly warns a large number of people. It also provides detailed and accurate information.

The disadvantages of the emergency alert system are largely the same as the weaknesses of the media because the warnings are broadcasted through the television and radio. People may not be watching TV or listening to the radio at the time when warnings are disseminated. Also, power outages can render the television and radio useless.

Reverse 911

Reverse 911 involves a call issued from a single site, which is then transmitted by computer to homes and businesses in a designated jurisdiction. Reverse 911 rapidly warns a large number of people in a specified area. Recorded phone messages can be simple or detailed.

There are drawbacks associated with reverse 911 systems. Hazards and disasters may render phones useless. Some people may not have phones. Also, those answering the call may hang up on or not believe a recorded message.

Intercoms, Teletype Writers, Telephone Devices, and Strobe Lights.

Intercoms, teletype writers, telephone devices, and strobe lights are used to warn people in large buildings and to make the deaf aware of impending hazards.

These systems are good in that they warn people in buildings or those with hearing impairments.

However, these systems warn a limited number of people only. Also devices may not always provide adequate information to those who are notified by them.

Loud Speakers, Door-to-Door Notification, and Weather Radios.

Bullhorns may be used by the police to warn people on a street who could be affected by a chemical release at an industrial complex. Loud speakers are mounted on police cruisers or fire engines. However, loud speakers may not be heard by people who are inside their homes.

Firefighters and police officers may also knock on the doors of nearby residents to encourage evacuation in hotels and apartment buildings. Before Hurricane Katrina, police went door-to-door in the low-lying parts of New Orleans to ask people to evacuate. Door-to-door warnings permit the answering of questions. However, door-to-door warnings require significant manpower and are very time consuming (see Figure 5-2).

Weather radios are set off by the National Weather Service and advise people of what to do in case of severe weather. Weather radios may provide very specific information about hazards in certain geographic areas. However, most people do not have weather radios.

Figure 5-2

Door-to-door warnings are one way of asking people to evacuate or checking on their well being.

5.2.2 Warning Considerations

Besides determining what warning system or systems you will rely on, you should also take the following into account when you issue warnings:

▲ Warnings should be clear and contain accurate information. "The more general a warning is, the less likely it will be perceived as a warning. The more specific a warning is, the more likely it will be heeded" (Quarantelli 1990, p. 4).

▲ Warning messages must be repeated and consistent. If a warning is issued once, or if the message it relays contradicts other warnings, its intended impact on people's behavior will be reduced.

▲ Credible sources must confirm warnings. Quarantelli writes, "Warnings sent via the mass media are more likely to be believed if delivered by governmental officials rather than by private citizens, or by personnel from emergency organizations than by members of other groups. Also, different mass media sources in a community are likely to have different degrees of credibility. Those with the most pre-disaster credibility are most likely to be seen as issuing a disaster warning" (1990, p. 4).

▲ People will perceive warnings differently based on the degree of the threat, prior experience in disasters, and their social interaction with others. If people recognize the severity of the situation, they will most likely heed the warning. If warnings are repeatedly inaccurate, the less the warnings will be heeded (e.g., the hurricane landfall forecasts are incorrect). If people are new to a hurricane-prone area, they might not understand what a hurricane warning means. Also, if someone's friends do not evacuate or take protective action, then they will probably remain home as well.

FOR EXAMPLE

Warning About Hurricane Katrina

Emergency management officials in Louisiana, Mississippi, and Alabama used many different warning systems to warn residents about the destructive impact of Hurricane Katrina. Warnings were given by mayors, governors, and even President Bush. Media reports discussed the damage that would or did occur in an in-depth manner. Evacuation orders were given by all three states, although at different times. Local officials and law enforcement personnel went door-to-door in the most vulnerable areas, asking people to leave. The Emergency Alert System was used, and warnings were issued in different languages. Despite all of the warnings, some people stayed. There are many reasons why people will not evacuate, and these will be discussed in the following section.

SELF-CHECK

- Why is warning a necessary disaster response function?
- What is the difference between a watch and a warning?
- What information make warnings effective?
- What are the different types of warning systems?
- Does each warning system have strengths and weaknesses?
- Why does the source of a warning make a difference to those who receive it?

5.3 Evacuation

In order to respond effectively to a disaster, you must at times evacuate your population. **Evacuation**, or the movement of people away from potential or actual hazards for the purpose of safety, is very common after a warning has been issued or when an emergency or disaster has occurred. The purpose of an evacuation is to reduce the loss of life and the chance for injury.

There are numerous examples of evacuations. A fire in a hotel may require the occupants to leave the building (because of the flames or resulting noxious fumes). An approaching hurricane poses danger to those on the coast, in low-lying areas, and within the projected path. People must leave to avoid being adversely affected by storm surge and high winds.

Those responding to disaster should be aware that there are various types of evacuations.

- ▲ **Horizontal evacuation** is the movement of people away from a hazard.
- ▲ **Vertical evacuation** is the movement of people from low areas to higher areas (moving from lower floors in a building to those above or the roof if there is a fire or flood).

The vast majority of evacuations are horizontal in nature. These may include individuals and families fleeing a burning building. Another example of a horizontal evacuation is people moving inland when a hurricane approaches.

Some evacuations may be vertical. Those in danger move from lower floors in a building to those above if there is a fire or flood (to higher floors or rooftops). However, vertical evacuation may prove deadly if waters continue to rise or if a fire cannot be extinguished (as smoke, flames, and heat rise to the floors above).

Evacuations may be short- or long-term. People may be able to return to their homes or offices within hours or days if the danger has passed or the damage is minor. If buildings are condemned after the disaster or if a geographic area has been contaminated by poisonous chemicals, the evacuation could last weeks or months. Some people who evacuated after Hurricane Katrina may never return home.

5.3.1 Evacuation Considerations

There are several factors that you must consider when contemplating an evacuation. It is often difficult to know if an evacuation should be ordered. It may be wise to shelter in place because evacuations can be dangerous. For example, many people die in floods while evacuating in automobiles (Sorensen and Mileti 1988, p. 205).

It is sometimes difficult to know if an area is or will be at risk. Weather patterns are extremely difficulty to pinpoint. Hurricanes often look menacing and appear to be on a particular path before they change direction. Regardless of the situation, safety should be the first concern. However, it is important to think twice about evacuations because incorrect decisions have negative consequences. "Unnecessary evacuations are expensive, disruptive and unpopular" (Baker 1990, p. 3). The more often people have to evacuate when it isn't necessary, the less likely you will be to evacuate them when it is truly required.

Decisions to evacuate should be based on a number of variables:

▲ Risk/vulnerability. If it appears that people could be injured or killed or property will be damaged or destroyed, it is advisable to evacuate.

▲ The findings of decision aids. Computer software can model hazards and assist with your decisions. HAZ-US identifies vulnerable areas and the potential for damage. CAMEO/ALOHA provides plume models for hazardous chemical releases. SLOSH generates storm surge models and potential inundation areas.

▲ Expert and political opinion. National Weather Service meteorologists predict storm intensity, direction, and speed, which may impact evacuation decisions. Building inspectors identify severely damaged buildings that should not be inhabited after earthquakes. Politicians consider many factors and rely on the input of others, including that of the emergency manager.

▲ Clearance times. It may take hours or even days to evacuate people away from harm. Transportation officials may tell you that roads and highways will become congested with thousands of motorists. You do not want people on the road when a hurricane hits.

5.3.2 Evacuation Procedures

There are routine processes for evacuation. Emergency managers typically follow several steps:

1. Make the decision to evacuate. Fire chiefs, police chiefs, meteorologists, consultants, and politicians talk to the emergency manager to discuss the hazard and identify options to keep people safe.

2. Notify the population at risk that they need to evacuate. Use a warning system or a combination of warning systems described earlier in this chapter to inform people of impending hazards.

3. Provide guidelines, instructions, and directions. People may not understand when to leave, what they should take, what evacuation route is recommended, how long they should be gone, how they will know when to return, etc.

4. Direct traffic to avoid gridlock. Traffic may be unusually heavy during evacuation. Therefore, it may be necessary to open both lanes in one direction for sizable evacuating populations.

5. Ensure compliance and continued safety. Check for stragglers left behind. There is usually a small group of people who refuse to evacuate. These people often have to be rescued (e.g., from rising water) by emergency personnel.

6. Monitor the evacuation and traffic. It is important to make sure everyone who needs to leave is following recommendations to do so. It may be necessary to issue tickets if individuals are violating traffic laws. A heavy police presence will be required when people return as well.

5.3.3 Methods and Means for Evacuation

There are various methods and means that can be utilized for evacuation. Each has respective pros and cons.

▲ **Walking.** Walking is common for hotel and office building evacuations. Walking is frequently a quick way to get people out of harm's way. Pedestrian evacuations may not require large numbers of emergency personnel. It is useful mainly when evacuation distances are short.

▲ **Automobiles.** Cars are useful when evacuation distances are far (e.g., hurricane evacuations). The evacuating traffic may require large numbers of law enforcement personnel, prior planning, and close coordination. The number of evacuees may create serious traffic congestion problems. Some Hurricane Rita evacuees, for example, reported being stuck on the interstate for 12 hours. Evacuating in cars is not an option when roads and bridges are out. (see Figure 5-3)

▲ **Busses.** Busses are useful to move small groups of people short or long distances. Using busses is often a way of taking children away from a school that is at risk. Loading large numbers of people in busses limits traffic congestion problems because each evacuee isn't driving his or her own automobile. Using this method of evacuation requires busses and drivers who may be difficult to obtain or schedule on short notice (e.g., from a school district). As with cars, evacuating by bus is not an option when roads and bridges are out.

Figure 5-3

Some people don't want to evacuate because the return home can be delayed due to the high traffic volume.

▲ **Boats.** Boats aren't an extremely common way to evacuate, but they were used to move people off of Manhattan Island after the 9/11 terrorist attacks. Boats may be used commonly in island areas and flood-ravaged communities. Boats may be one of the only ways to move people who have been isolated by high water. Evacuating this way requires boats and captains who may be difficult to obtain on short notice (e.g., from emergency services, a marina, or transit authority).

▲ **Helicopters/planes.** Helicopters have been used to evacuate people off of burning buildings, and planes have been used to get people off of islands (e.g., volcanic eruption in Monserrat). Evacuating by helicopter or small aircraft may be common to island areas, flood-ravaged communities, or other locations where roads have been damaged or destroyed. Evacuating by helicopter or plane may be one of the only ways to move people who have been cut off due to damaged roads and bridges. Evacuating this way is similar to that of busses and boats. They require helicopters, planes, and pilots that may be difficult to schedule without advanced notice (e.g., from emergency services or an airport).

5.3.4 Evacuation Behavior

One of your concerns as an emergency manager is that people evacuate in a safe and orderly fashion. However, there is typically no or very little panic during evacuation. Some people will evacuate on their own without a recommendation from civil authorities. For example, after witnessing the destruction of Hurricane Katrina, more people voluntarily evacuated during the hurricanes that came later in 2005. This caused some serious problems when Hurricane Rita struck Texas. Others will still only evacuate when ordered to do so. Warnings and evacuation orders from officials are all that it takes for these people to evacuate. Others, as we saw during Hurricane Katrina, do not leave despite a warning.

Why People Do Not Evacuate

There are many reasons why people will refuse to evacuate even when a hazard poses danger to their lives. As an emergency manager, you have to be aware of those reasons to convince people to leave or assist them in their evacuation. The main reasons why people refuse to evacuate are listed below.

- ▲ **Not aware of the risk.** Many of those who do not evacuate are not aware of the request to evacuate. After a fire at a paint store in Ephrata, Pennsylvania in 1990, Fischer reported that 79% of those who were not contacted failed to evacuate (Fischer et al 1995, p. 35).

- ▲ **Do not take the risk seriously.** People downplay risk. Those who do not believe they are in real danger will not evacuate.

- ▲ **Warnings are not clear.** Many do not evacuate because the warning message was unclear. This is why it is so important that the warning issued is well understood.

- ▲ **Fear of looting.** People are often afraid their homes and/or their businesses will be looted if they evacuate.

- ▲ **Age.** The elderly are often unable to evacuate without help from family members, friends, or community officials. Also, the elderly are often tied to their homes emotionally and do not want to leave their familiar surroundings. Some New Orleans residents who did not evacuate before Hurricane Katrina had never left their city before.

- ▲ **Size and make up of family.** Parents with young children are more likely to evacuate, as they view protection of their children from death or injury as their main parental responsibility. People who live alone and who are only risking their own health are less likely to evacuate.

- ▲ **Missing family members and pets.** People who live with elderly parents or sick children that cannot be evacuated will generally not leave their family members. Some people would not evacuate after Hurricane Katrina because shelters would not take their pets.

▲ **Neighbor's behavior.** People who see their neighbors or friends evacuate are much more likely to take the threat seriously and evacuate. The reverse is also true; if neighbors do not leave, you will be less likely to leave also.

▲ **Experience.** Those who are familiar with the possible impact of a hurricane or evacuation orders are more likely to evacuate than others.

▲ **Education.** Those with more education are the most likely to evacuate. Those who have college degrees are more likely to understand the threat and risk of staying behind during the disaster.

▲ **Type of housing.** Mobile home dwellers are more likely to evacuate than any other group. Mobile homes do not survive severe weather well, and the mobile home owners often recognize this.

▲ **Inconvenience.** It is not easy to evacuate. Not only do people have to fight the traffic, but they also have to gather their belongings and face the prospect of living in a public shelter in the short-term or imposing on family members or friends.

▲ **Fear of re-entry delays.** Those who are considering evacuation are often concerned it will be several weeks or months before they can return to their homes and their normal lives.

▲ **Distance from the incident location.** Those who live near the threatened area will be more likely to evacuate; those who live a distance from the threat may believe that they are not at risk.

▲ **Other factors.** Other factors influence people's decisions to evacuate. These include a failure to issue an evacuation order, not being able to leave due to job requirements, a lack of money or car and a belief that there is no place to go.

FOR EXAMPLE

Hurricane Katrina and Pets

Even after Hurricane Katrina devastated Louisiana and the levees gave way, many residents did not want to evacuate. Some people had cats, dogs, or other pets that rescue workers did not want to deal with. In addition, residents knew that the Red Cross does not typically provide shelter for animals. For this reason, many people refused to leave the devastated city of New Orleans. Emergency managers must make accommodations for pets if similar problems are to be avoided in the future.

SELF-CHECK

- Define evacuation.
- What is the difference between horizontal and vertical evacuation?
- What are the various methods used to facilitate evacuation?
- How are evacuations managed?
- Do people panic when they evacuate?
- Will everyone evacuate when warned to do so? Why or why not?

5.4 Sheltering

After you issue warnings and assist with evacuation, people will subsequently be faced with an important decision: where will they go for safety and rest? **Sheltering,** or the location or relocation of evacuees and others to places of refuge, is a function that is frequently required in many disasters. Disaster victims may need sheltering during a short-lived emergency such as a hotel fire, or they may have long-term sheltering needs because they have lost their homes in a hurricane. Those affected by disaster will not be the only ones needing emergency or temporary shelters. Emergency responders, search and rescue teams, state officials, and FEMA employees, may also need a place to stay and rest while they respond to the disaster. For example, after the March 28, 2000 Fort Worth tornado, search and rescue teams stayed at the police and fire training facilities and at the Fort Worth Convention Center.

Emergency managers should remember that sheltering in place may be more advantageous than an evacuation to another area. There are many reasons for this decision. There may not be enough time to evacuate. It may be too dangerous to evacuate. In some cases, such as a hazardous chemical release, sheltering is the best course of action and will protect more lives than an evacuation would. When deciding whether to evacuate or shelter the population after a hazardous materials spill, there are several factors to consider (Hunt 1989, p. 29):

▲ If it is an actual or impending release
▲ The material itself (type/physical or chemical properties)
▲ Location of release
▲ Health/toxicological effects
▲ Atmospheric conditions (wind direction, speed, stability, weather, temperature, dispersion patterns)
▲ Time of day

▲ Numbers and type of population at risk

▲ Estimated duration of release

▲ Emergency response resources and response time

▲ Notification systems

▲ Lead time and elapsed time necessary for evacuation

▲ Evacuation routes and terrain

▲ Ability to shelter in place

▲ Adequacy of shelters relevant to concentration of the release and duration

▲ Deciding to shelter in place should be based on expert opinion

5.4.1 Sheltering Types

If people require sheltering, it is vital that they are aware that there are different patterns for this activity. In an important study, Quarantelli (1995) has identified four ideal types (or examples in pure form) along with their characteristics:

1. **Emergency sheltering.** The first place people go to seek shelter, usually lasting one night only (until more a more desirable shelter can be located). This location may not have many services, at least initially. The Superdome in New Orleans was an emergency shelter during Hurricane Katrina. This shelter was not well staffed or supplied with enough food and water. The emergency management officials did not plan for as many people as they received, and they did not realize that the shelter would be necessary for several days. As a result, there were reports of people dying in the Superdome and of people going hungry.

2. **Temporary sheltering.** Temporary shelters could be second homes, the house of a friend, or a motel. As people left New Orleans, thousands sought refuge in hotels or relatives homes. A temporary shelter often provides basic necessities, such as food and water. Other routine activities may be allowed on a modified basis. For example, bathing may be allowed on a rotating basis. Evacuees might be able to wash their clothes or take their clothing to the laundromat for cleaning.

3. **Temporary housing.** Temporary housing could include mobile homes and rented apartments or homes. After Katrina, FEMA brought in several mobile homes for disaster victims. Temporary housing allows normal household routines, including sleeping, food storage and preparation, dishwashing, waste disposal, and bathing. Temporary housing could extend for months, if not years.

4. **Permanent housing.** Permanent housing is the long-term solution to the housing problem that was created by the disaster. Victims may rebuild their homes or move to new homes. Victims may or may not return to

the city they lived in. After taking temporary shelter in Houston, many Hurricane Katrina evacuees moved to Houston permanently even though they had lived in New Orleans all of their lives. Permanent housing allows all household routines to be re-established. Unfortunately, some people may not obtain permanent housing after a disaster because of their losses, lack of insurance, insufficient federal disaster assistance, or meager incomes.

Also, those who need sheltering do not enter each type of shelter or housing at the same time. A portion of the Hurricane Katrina evacuees, for example, were taking emergency shelter in the Superdome in New Orleans while some evacuees were already in temporary housing, having decided to live with relatives for an extended period of time.

5.4.2 Shelter Use and Characteristics

It is commonly believed that massive numbers of people will require sheltering. The reality is that most people will not use public shelters at all or will use them only as a last resort. They will also stay as briefly as possible. No one likes living with hundreds of strangers in a large shelter. People prefer to stay with friends and family if they can. Hurricane Katrina is an exception to the limited need for shelters in other disasters. The nature of the disaster required that hundreds of thousands be sheltered during and after the event, and in distant locations. This was still only a portion of the population, however.

Emergency managers should also be aware of the fact that shelters will "spring up" automatically and without prior intention as people try to find a safe place to relax and ride out the disaster event. There are other research findings regarding the use of shelters (Mileti, Sorensen, and O'Brien 1992, p. 30-33):

▲ Shelter use in cities will be higher than in rural areas.

▲ Shelter use is highest for hurricanes.

▲ Shelters are more likely to be used when publicized.

▲ The larger the size of the disaster, the larger the relative number of people seeking shelters.

▲ People will be more likely to seek shelter if the disaster strikes at night.

▲ Those from lower socioeconomic groups will be more likely to use shelters than the rich.

▲ Older people are more likely to use public shelters than younger people.

5.4.3 Working With Others to Establish Shelters

Emergency managers will need to work with a number of organizations that participate in sheltering operations. Putting the local government in charge may ensure that sheltering takes place in accordance with municipal priorities in mind. It may also help ensure that official information about the disaster is being given to the disaster victims. However, the local government will already be burdened heavily after a disaster, and sheltering responsibilities will only add to the many functions that it oversees.

In addition to government emergency management agencies, many religious groups are involved in sheltering and housing. According to a congressional mandate, the American Red Cross has been given the primary responsibility for sheltering in the National Response Plan. However, this is not always known or accepted. For example, the Salvation Army is officially in charge of mass care in the state of Texas. Emergency managers must give special consideration to the pros and cons of having the government in charge of sheltering operations or voluntary organizations (such as the American Red Cross or Salvation Army).

Nevertheless, voluntary organizations have expertise in sheltering functions and will reduce the demands placed on the local government. The American Red Cross and Salvation Army have their own method of providing shelter, which may not meet community objectives (e.g., location of shelter or time of closing). Deciding who will operate the shelters is no trivial matter.

The decision of where to open shelters is also important and must include a consideration of potential hazards. Shelters should be opened in geographic areas that are not vulnerable to hazards (e.g., away from the coast, out of the flood plain, far from the fault line, or in a space that has been cleared of flammable vegetation). All too often, shelters will be opened up in churches and schools that may not be located in safe areas. Hurricane Katrina illustrated the dangers associated with placing people in the Superdome for shelter (as the roof was damaged by wind and as it was surrounded by flood waters).

It is not advisable to use trailers or mobile homes for sheltering. These types of shelters are generally not safe places to stay in times of hurricanes or tornadoes. Some people do not accept mobile homes as a temporary place to stay during recovery (because of the stigmatism associated with them) but prefer rental assistance instead (Quarantelli 1995, p. 49). Trailers may pose long-term problems in that people may use them permanently (Bolin and Sanford 1991, p. 31).

There are many potential problems with shelters that must be avoided. These challenges include:

▲ Lack of adequate medical care
▲ Volunteers who aren't properly trained and are unaware of policies and procedures
▲ Uneven distribution of supplies and volunteers within and across shelters
▲ Inconsistent and changing sheltering policies

▲ Lack of record keeping as to who is using the shelter

▲ Disaster victims may not follow shelter rules and obey staff

▲ Conflict among the individuals or groups staying in the shelter (e.g., those of other races, cultures, or neighborhoods)

You can avoid many of the problems listed above. It is imperative that shelters be well stocked with supplies. Some disaster victims died unnecessarily after Hurricane Katrina because the shelter was not adequately stocked with food and water, or sufficient medical care (see Figure 5-4). Successful sheltering operations will result when you:

1. Determine demand by examining the number of people needing shelter (including evacuees, victims, and emergency workers) and comparing it to available shelters and housing stock

2. Identify potential shelters and develop additional shelter agreements (if not already in place)

3. Ensure shelter is located in a safe area and has electricity, adequate water supply, restrooms, parking, etc.

You will need to conduct a brief training session before shelters open to ensure everyone knows how the shelter will be operated. You also need to make sure

Figure 5-4

The New Orleans Superdome was not an adequate shelter after Hurricane Katrina.

the shelter is well publicized, and has sufficient and capable staff that can provide information, medical care, and security. Being able to document the names and numbers of those using the shelters is also necessary.

You should also be aware that shelters may remain open long after a disaster strikes (and longer than anticipated by their operators). Most disaster victims (especially those from the middle class) will desire to leave shelters as soon as possible. Some will take advantage of the free housing and food for extended periods of time. Many people may remain in shelters because they don't have resources to pay rent or they have nowhere else to go. For instance, one shelter in Miami remained opened for a substantial period after Hurricane Andrew; approximately 400 people were slow to leave even 3 or 4 months after the disaster. For this reason, you must work to ensure that temporary shelters do not become permanent. Helping disaster victims find longer-term housing is one way to accomplish this goal. As demand decreases, danger subsides, and recovery proceeds, shelters can be consolidated and shut down.

FOR EXAMPLE

Superdome vs. Astrodome

Hurricane Katrina provided us with two stark examples on the effectiveness of shelter operations. The Superdome in New Orleans was the first emergency shelter that many evacuees went to. The Superdome did not have adequate supplies. People were told to provide for their own needs in some cases, and they had no idea how long they would have to stay in this facility. Consequently, there was not enough food and water for their stay. In addition, the roof of the facility was damaged by the hurricane and the Superdome lost electricity. The restrooms were filthy as the water was not running. Crime was a concern due to inadequate law-enforcement personnel. Also, there was not a sufficient volunteer force. People died in the Superdome due to lack of medical care. The function of sheltering was poorly conceived and implemented, in part because officials thought they would only need to use it for 1 to 2 days instead of 4 to 5 days. Evacuees then went to the Astrodome in Houston. This shelter was well organized. People were checked in, and documentation of their presence was kept. People received medical care and check ups immediately. The shelter had plenty of cots, blankets, food, and water for everyone. There was also a substantial law-enforcement presence. The Red Cross and FEMA also had many people at the shelter working to reunite families and disperse aid. While problems existed, they were addressed in an expedited manner.

SELF-CHECK

- What is **sheltering** and why is it necessary?
- What are the benefits of sheltering in place, and why should it be considered?
- What are the distinct types of sheltering/housing?
- Will most evacuees use shelters? Why or why not?
- How can the nonprofit sector assist with sheltering?
- What are some issues to consider when running a shelter?

SUMMARY

Resilience requires a number of initial response measures. After identifying the hazard, warnings must be issued in a clear and consistent manner. Warnings are typically followed by an evacuation, which helps to protect people from impending hazards. When people leave their homes, they will often need a place to stay. Sheltering will be required in the short term, while efforts may be needed to help victims acquire housing in the future. Performing these functions effectively is the best way to ensure response and recovery operations get off on the right foot.

KEY TERMS

Disaster plan	A document that describes how the jurisdiction might respond to a disaster.
Emergency Operations Center (EOC)	A central location where leaders can gather information, discuss options, make decisions, disseminate policy, mobilize resources, and communicate with involved parties.
Evacuation	The movement of people away from potential or actual hazards for the purpose of safety.
Full activation	The opening of an EOC with all pertinent actors and functions.
Hazard detection	The process of identifying what hazard is about to occur or has taken place.
Horizontal evacuation	The movement of people away from a hazard.

Increased readiness conditions	Rating system that is sometimes based on numerical numbers (e.g., 1-4) and denotes the severity of an event along with appropriate measures to be taken.
Partial activation	The opening of an EOC with some pertinent actors and functions.
Sheltering	The location or relocation of evacuees and others to places of refuge; a function that is frequently required in many disasters.
Syndromic surveillance	Tracking the flow of patients in a hospital or clinic to determine trends and consequences of diseases.
Vertical evacuation	The movement of people from low areas to higher areas (moving from lower floors in a building to those above or the roof if there is a fire or flood).
Warnings	Advanced notifications that allow people to take measures to protect themselves and their property. It indicates that the hazard is imminent, is taking place, or has occurred.
Watch	Notification that conditions are ripe for a hazard to occur.

ASSESS YOUR UNDERSTANDING

Go to www.wiley.com/college/McEntire to evaluate your knowledge of the initial response process.
Measure your learning by comparing pretest and post-test results.

Summary Questions

1. Detecting hazards is one of the first steps for disaster response. True or False?

2. Hazards can be detected by senses but not from increased radio traffic. True or False?

3. ARES and RACES can help you detect a hazard. True or False?

4. A disaster plan is a document that details how a community might respond to a potential disaster. True or False?

5. When activating an EOC, you will need to include all pertinent actors. True or False?

6. According to Quarantelli, warning processes typically include assessment of the hazard and dissemination of the message. True or False?

7. All warnings come from the National Weather Service. True or False?

8. Warnings are likely to be most successful when they are clear, accurate, and consistent. True or False?

9. Horizontal evacuation implies that you move to higher floors. True or False?

10. Fire chiefs, meteorologists, and politicians may have some influence over evacuation decisions. True or False?

11. People can only evacuate by car. True or False?

12. Hazardous material releases may require sheltering in place instead of an evacuation. True or False?

13. Emergency sheltering is likely to include mobile homes and rented apartments. True or False?

14. The incident page network can notify you of:

    (a) Severe weather

    (b) Traffic accidents

    (c) Fires

    (d) All of the above

    (e) Severe weather and fires only

15. Emergency managers:

    (a) Are the only ones that detect hazards

    (b) May be on-call on a 24-hour, 7-day-a-week, 365-day-a-year basis

(c) Do not use technology to detect hazards

(d) Are not able to sense hazards

(e) Do not communicate with hospitals about disease outbreaks

16. If a hazard is about to occur or has occurred, you will:

   (a) Not need to know the consequences

   (b) Not talk to first responders or fire chiefs

   (c) Need to seek additional information

   (d) Need to avoid communication with nonprofit organizations

   (e) Not focus on the number of people killed but those who are still alive

17. EOC stands for:

   (a) Emergent organization coordination

   (b) Emergent operations center

   (c) Emergency organization chart

   (d) Emergency operations center

   (e) Emergency operations chart

18. Risk identification is:

   (a) Determining if a threat exists

   (b) Determining if protection is needed

   (c) Determining if protection is possible

   (d) Determining what protective action is best and then taking that action

   (e) None of the above

19. Warnings provide information about:

   (a) When a hazard will occur only

   (b) When a hazard will occur but not how long it will last

   (c) Potential power outages only

   (d) The impact of the disaster and closed streets

   (e) Projected damages to homes and property only

20. A strength of warning sirens is their ability to warn people outside. A weakness is:

   (a) They are used by reporters to give advanced notice about a tornado.

   (b) They use telephones and computers to issue the warning.

   (c) They break down frequently and may not always be reliable.

   (d) They take up a lot of man power to warn people in apartment complexes.

   (e) They rely on TV stations, which may lose power in a disaster.

21. It may take hours and even days to evacuate people away from peril. This is known as:
    (a) The horizontal decision imperative
    (b) Clearance time
    (c) Evacuation shadow
    (d) Risk
    (e) Cameo/Aloha index

22. People are less likely to evacuate when:
    (a) They do not take risk seriously
    (b) They are elderly
    (c) They live in a mobile home
    (d) They live near the threatened area
    (e) All of the above

23. Staying at a second home or the house of a friend is known as:
    (a) Emergency sheltering
    (b) Disaster sheltering
    (c) Disaster sheltering
    (d) Temporary sheltering
    (e) Temporary housing

24. Shelter use will most likely be highest when:
    (a) There has been a hurricane
    (b) A hazard affects a rural area
    (c) The disaster strikes during the day
    (d) Rich people have been affected
    (e) The disaster is smaller rather than larger

Review Questions

1. What are four ways you could detect a hazard?
2. What types of technology can help you with hazard detection?
3. What are increased readiness conditions?
4. If there is a large apartment complex on fire, who should you invite to the EOC and why?
5. Why is warning a vital disaster function?
6. What criteria do you consider when issuing a warning?
7. How can you ensure that the warning reaches the most people and is acted upon?
8. Why is the media an important partner for warning?

9. What is the difference between a watch and a warning?

10. What steps do you take when you evacuate a population?

11. What can be done to ensure that people with pets evacuate?

12. What are the different types of sheltering/housing?

13. Why is location an important consideration when opening a shelter?

14. Why might medical care, record keeping, and law enforcement be needed when undertaking shelter operations?

Applying This Chapter

1. The media is reporting that a volcano is becoming active on your Hawaiian island. Who could you contact to get more information about this threat? What questions would you ask this person or agency? What steps might you need to implement and why?

2. The National Weather Service has just notified you that a severe weather system (with the possibility of large hail) is moving through the area. A major sporting event is taking place at an outdoor stadium in the community. Who should you alert?

3. A train derailment requires the activation of your EOC in Santa Fe, New Mexico. The cars are spilling hazardous chemicals onto the ground, and they are running into a nearby river. Other tankers are releasing deadly gasses into the air near an industrial area. Who would you communicate with to get more information about the hazardous materials? Who would you invite into the EOC and why? What other steps might you take to deal with this crisis?

4. You are an emergency manager in Iowa. A serious heat wave is affecting your community, and many of the elderly may be severely impacted. The meteorologists on different stations are giving contradictory advice about the need to stay inside. Should you do anything about this? Why is consistent information necessary?

5. The Tsunami warning system has just been activated off of the Washington coast. Expected arrival time is in 30 minutes to 1 hour. If you were the emergency manager in this area, what is the first step you will take to protect people? What could you do as an emergency manager to facilitate their evacuation? What concerns do you have about evacuees as they leave their homes and apartment complexes?

6. You are the emergency manager for Oak Ridge, Tennessee, and you have been told that at the nuclear plant there has been a small release of hazardous nuclear waste in the air. Do you evacuate or shelter in place? Who could help you make this decision? What factors do you consider when making the decision?

Issuing Warnings

You are an emergency manager for Kansas City, and you have been told that an F-4 tornado was spotted and that it will likely hit your city within the next 10 minutes. What warning systems do you use to issue the warning? What instructions do you give residents? How can you increase the likelihood of reaching most people?

Evacuating Miami

You are an emergency manager for Miami, and you have been told that a hurricane will make landfall in 42 hours. How do you evacuate people? What types of transportation can you use? What is the best way to evacuate the elderly? Children? Families? What types, if any, of transportation would not be used?

Reasons not to Evacuate

You are an emergency manager for a small community that is situated in a low-lying valley by the river. Because of excessive rainfall upstream, the river is expected to crest in the next 6 hours. As a first responder, you are preparing to go door to door to tell people to leave. Will everyone want to leave? What might some excuses be for not evacuating? What logic can you use to get the residents to leave the area and move to safer ground?

Shelter

An accident at a nearby nuclear power plant has forced the evacuation of several residents in the surrounding area. More than 75,000 evacuees move 200 miles away from the area in directions away from the predominant wind patterns. What steps do you take to open up shelters? How many do you need? What can be done to ensure the shelters are adequate? What are some of the things that should be considered to help the evacuees?

Anticipating a Disaster

Take 15 mintues to think about the intial measures that must performed before or immediately after a disaster occurs. Make a list of everything that you think you might need to take care of on the first day of a disaster. In three to four paragraphs, discuss how you would meet these demands and who could help you accomplish that.

6

CARING FOR THE INJURED, DEAD, AND DISTRAUGHT
Overcoming Physical and Emotional Impacts

Starting Point

Go to www.wiley.com/college/McEntire to assess your knowledge of caring for the injured, dead, and distraught.
Determine where you need to concentrate your effort.

What You'll Learn in This Chapter

▲ The need for and types of search and rescue operations
▲ Behavior of those participating in search and rescue
▲ Emergency medical care and the ethical debate surrounding triage
▲ The challenges regarding mass fatality incidents
▲ The psychological impact of disasters

After Studying This Chapter, You'll Be Able To

▲ Compare and contrast types of search and rescue operations
▲ Categorize types of human behaviors in search and rescue operations
▲ Examine the need for emergency medical care operations
▲ Determine the steps that can be taken to manage mass fatality incidents effectively
▲ Understand the common signs of Post Traumatic Stress Disorder (PTSD) and Critical Incident Stress (CIS)

Goals and Outcomes

▲ Choose an appropriate search and rescue method
▲ Predict and respond to human behavior in search and rescue operations
▲ Estimate potential injuries in disasters and the type of medical assistance they will require
▲ Manage mass fatality incidents
▲ Evaluate and support victims and personnel who are suffering from PTSD/CIS

INTRODUCTION

To respond effectively to a disaster, you must know that volunteers and professionals will rush to the scene to rescue anyone who is trapped and injured. Emergency medical personnel will also arrive to provide life-saving services. This often requires that difficult choices be made in terms of who will be treated first. At other times, however, the incident is one of mass fatality, and there are several bodies that have to be handled in a sensitive manner. Situations like this can cause post-traumatic stress disorder (PTSD) and critical incident stress (CIS), which are emotional problems that have to be overcome. This chapter will promote resilience by showing variety of ways to handle these situations.

6.1 Types of Search and Rescue

Emergency service personnel often become involved in search and rescue operations in both emergency (routine) and disaster (non-routine) situations. **Search and rescue operations** are response activities undertaken to find disaster victims and remove them from danger or confinement. Search and rescue is necessary so victims may receive urgent treatment such as hydration, basic first aid, or advanced medical care. Search and rescue may include, but is not limited to:

▲ Looking for lost individuals
▲ Determining the whereabouts of disaster victims
▲ Developing and implementing strategies to safely rescue, extract, or set free the person in question
▲ Providing immediate and basic care until further medical assistance is provided
▲ Transporting the individual away from the dangerous area to his or her home or medical facility for further treatment

As an emergency manager, you should be aware that there are at least four types of search and rescue operations. These include:

1. **Rural search and rescue.** This occurs when experienced personnel such as forest department workers enter rugged areas to find missing children or lost campers or hikers.
2. **Swift water rescue.** Firefighters inflate rubber rafts and traverse swollen creeks to access people on top of vehicles or roofs or in trees and bring them back to dry land. For example, this technique might be used to rescue people who are trapped in a car by rising floodwaters.

3. **Air-patrolled search and rescue.** This happens when a small plane is presumed to have crashed in an isolated area along its projected flight path. Civil air patrol members or others from the FAA cover large geographic areas looking for downed aircraft.

4. **Urban search and rescue.** FEMA urban search and rescue teams are dispatched to a large city that has been affected by a major earthquake. For example, multiple individuals and families may need to be extracted from a collapsed apartment building after a resulting collapse. (see Figure 6-1)

There are additional types of search and rescue operations as well. Ski patrol or other skilled individuals look for missing skiers and work to quickly free those trapped in an avalanche. Highway patrol locates automobiles and passengers stuck as a result of major winter storms. Emergency response personnel put on wetsuits and use ropes to rescue people trapped on thin ice or caught in dangerously cold waters.

Figure 6-1

Urban search and rescue often occurs after earthquakes.

SELF-CHECK

- Are first responders involved in search and rescue alone?
- What are the different types of search and rescue?

6.2 Human Behavior in Search and Rescue Operations

As an emergency manager, you must be aware of how humans behave in search and rescue operations. There is a moderate amount of research on this subject. One of the most recent studies is by Aguirre et al (1995). After examining human behavior after a gasoline explosion in Guadalajara, Mexico on April 22, 1992, these scholars recognize many common patterns of activity:

▲ Untrained volunteers are the first to engage in search and rescue operations.

▲ Emergent rescuers will informally or formally assign tasks and create a division of labor during search and rescue.

▲ Spontaneous rescuers will use anything they can find to help them rescue trapped individuals. This may include bare hands, shovels, or other equipment.

▲ These volunteers will give higher preference to rescuing some victims over others, which will impact survival rates. For example, rescuers will first look for their relatives, friends, and neighbors before looking for other possible survivors.

▲ Victims will cooperate with each other while entrapped and with rescuers during extraction.

▲ Professional rescuers may or may not integrate their activities with volunteer efforts. Formal organizations are not always able to use volunteers within their own operation.

6.2.1 Issues to Consider When Carrying Out Search and Rescue Operations

It is imperative that you recognize that search and rescue operations are both vital and dangerous. To ensure success, there are several factors that must be considered. When these issues are considered, search and rescue operations will be move successful.

Tools and Equipment

Adequate and appropriate tools and equipment will be needed for search and rescue operations. The type of tools needed required depends on the situation. For example, after the terrorist attacks of 9/11, cranes were needed to lift debris. After a flood, however, you would need boats, ropes, and life

> ## FOR EXAMPLE
>
> ### Saving Themselves
>
> Many victims actively participate in their own rescue and, by doing so, increase their chances of survival. Aguirre and his colleagues note that victims call attention to their location. "A man and his two nephews are having breakfast in their home. The explosion buries them alive. The man reports experiencing a great amount of difficulty breathing. He can hear his two nephews near him in the rubble. He talks to them and synchronizes their scream for help at his count of three. Eventually, people hear them and save them" (Aguirre et al 1995, 75).

preservers. Regardless of the type of disaster, there are often cases where equipment is insufficient for the massive search and rescue effort. For example, after the earthquake in Bam, Iran that killed 50,000 people, the equipment needed to lift debris was not immediately available.

In all search and rescue operations, it is important to wear safety equipment and clothing appropriate to the task. This equipment includes:

- ▲ Helmets or hardhats
- ▲ Goggles
- ▲ Dust masks (fitted to each responder)
- ▲ Whistles (to alert others if you get trapped)
- ▲ Leather work gloves
- ▲ Steel-toed boots

Situational Awareness

Besides having the necessary gear, rescuers must also be aware of their surroundings. Different types of buildings will have different occupancy levels, which may influence your search and rescue operations. The occupants will also vary in ability and age. Rescuing immobile nursing home residents, for example, will be more difficult than rescuing able-bodied adults.

There will be secondary hazards that may have a bearing on search and rescue operations. For example, those who searched for survivors of the 9/11 terrorist attacks were working in unstable debris piles that could possibly collapse. FEMA advises rescuers to "be alert for hazards, such as sharp objects, dust, hazardous materials, power lines, leaking natural gas, high water, fire hazards, and unstable structures. If water is present, check the depth before entering" (2003, V-4).

Rescuer Needs

Rescuer needs and safety must be ensured. The rescue effort will only be hampered if the well-being of the rescuers is not addressed. Food must be supplied to these first responders, and plenty of fresh water should always be available. Search and rescue work is very demanding. Crews should be rotated to avoid fatigue. This is often difficult to do, as the rescuers will have a personal and emotional attachment to their work. For example, when the firemen were asked to stop searching for their missing co-workers at ground zero after 9/11, a minor scuffle broke out between firefighters and police officers. However appealing it is to keep working so others can be saved, you must remember that many rescuers are injured or killed when they become tired. To maintain an adequate level of safety, FEMA advises rescuers to "always work in pairs, with a third person as a runner" (2003, V-14).

Time

One of the reasons it can be difficult to get rescuers to leave a scene is because it is well known that the chances of finding someone alive diminish with time. The first hour provides the best chance for rescuing people alive, but the next 24 hours are also vital. The injured and trapped have an 80% chance of survival if they are rescued within the first day. After this period, the possibility of survival diminishes rapidly. Search and rescue operations may therefore become search and recovery operations if there is credible information that people have not survived the incident or disaster.

Medical Care

Once the victims are rescued, they will most likely need immediate medical care. Trapped victims often suffer from life-threatening injuries, including the loss of blood and fluids, damage to internal organs, and respiratory failure due to the lack of oxygen. If rescuers are spontaneous volunteers, they often have limited—if any—medical training. It is therefore imperative that victims be handed over to trained medical personnel as soon as possible, even though emergent groups can be extremely helpful.

6.2.2 Professional Urban Search and Rescue (SAR) Teams

Professional urban SAR teams are best able to care for the needs of victims who have been crushed under disaster debris. In 1989, after numerous major disasters resulted in urban structural collapses, the Federal Emergency Management Agency created the National Urban Search and Rescue Response. The **National Urban Search and Rescue Response** is a system made up of 28 FEMA urban SAR Task Forces that are spread throughout the continental United States. These Task Forces are comprised of firefighters, engineers, doctors, paramedics, and canine teams from local communities. Each member of the team must be an emergency medical technician. They must also undergo hundreds of hours of training. Specialties, such as the K-9 unit, have additional hours of preparation. If a disaster receives a presidential declaration, and if the disaster warrants search and rescue, the FEMA urban SAR teams may be activated. The team members will be notified and will unite at the specified location (e.g., an airport). The team members will load their equipment onto military C-130 transport aircraft and then travel to the disaster site. Work will continue until search and rescue services are no longer needed. At this point, the team will be transported home. In some cases, numerous teams will be rotated in and out of the disaster to prevent crew fatigue and allow others to gain experience. Each Task Force has been given 60,000 pounds of equipment (approximately 16,400 pieces) by the Federal Emergency Management Agency. The supplies and equipment for each team is worth more than $1.4 million dollars. This includes medical supplies such as:

▲ Medicines
▲ Intravenous fluids
▲ Blankets
▲ Suture sets
▲ Defibrillators
▲ Burn treatment supplies
▲ Bone saws
▲ Scalpels

It also includes search and rescue machines and supplies like concrete saws, jackhammers, drills, lumber, and rope. Additional gear includes communications and electronic equipment (e.g., radios, cell phones, and laptop computers) or logistic needs (e.g., sleeping bags, cots, food, and water).

It is important that you are cognizant of the many benefits associated with these professional urban SAR teams. The teams are highly trained and fully equipped. The teams have prior SAR experience in major disasters and receive large amounts of funding from the federal government. They can be mobilized to distant disaster sites for long periods.

There are a few significant drawbacks associated with these professional urban SAR teams, however. One of them is their expense. It is very costly to maintain and operate the search and rescue teams. Also, the teams could be inadequate for certain disasters and for multiple ongoing disasters. There are not sufficient professional SAR teams for major or concurrent disasters throughout the country. In addition, professional SAR teams often arrive too late to save significant numbers of victims. They are therefore more involved with search and recovery efforts rather than rescue operations. For example, Pakistan suffered an earthquake that registered 7.6 on the Richter scale on October 8, 2005. Within 1 day, professional SAR teams began to arrive. Although the deployment was very quick, the prime time to find survivors had already passed.

Because of the late arrival and insufficient quantity of professional SAR teams, it will become increasingly necessary that citizens and volunteers engage in search and rescue activities. These individuals and groups are advantageous for disaster response. Citizens and volunteers can perform vital search and rescue services when professional teams are not present or are insufficient in quantity. These people have an advantage as they know or are familiar with the area and the victims. Such individuals and groups may create unintentional problems, however. Volunteer rescuers may unintentionally injure victims or aggravate their injuries to the point of death. Such individuals may be exempt from liability, as many states have Good Samaritan Acts.

The problems associated with citizen SAR teams can be overcome through community education and training (such as FEMA's Community Emergency Response Teams). Efforts can also be made to integrate the activities of professional and volunteer SAR teams at the scene of a disaster. For example, volunteers can perform simple tasks (e.g., basic first aid) so that trained professionals may focus on more difficult rescue operations (e.g., amputations).

6.2.3 Conducting Search and Rescue Operations

An elaborate process must be undertaken to ensure a successful search and rescue operation in urban settings. The Federal Emergency Management Agency asserts there are seven steps in search and rescue operations. Those participating should:

1. **Gather facts.** One of the first things that must be done is to size up the situation. You will need to consider:
   - The number of potential victims.
   - The type and age of construction.
   - The status and potential influence of the weather.
   - The presence of hazards such as sharp objects, downed power lines, and broken gas lines
2. **Assess damage.** Walk around the building and view the structure from different angles. Consider the following general guidelines:

If structural damage is . . .	Then the SAR mission is . . .
Light: Superficial or cosmetic damage, broken windows, fallen plaster, primary damage to contents of structure . . .	to locate, triage, and prioritize removal of victims to designated treatment areas by the medical operation teams.
Moderate: Questionable structural stability; fractures, titling, foundation movement or displacement . . .	to locate, stabilize, and immediately evacuate victims to safe areas while minimizing the number of rescuers inside the building.
Heavy: Obvious structural instability; partial or total wall collapse, ceiling failures . . .	to secure the building perimeter and control access into the structure by untrained but well-intentioned volunteers; seek professional assistance.

3. **Identify and acquire resources.** This may include the availability of and need for personnel, tools, and equipment.

4. **Establish rescue priorities.** Determine the urgency of the situation and verify that it is safe to proceed with the search and rescue operation. You may need to condemn the building to ensure no one else enters the structure. Afterwards, call for additional professional assistance and wait until that help arrives. Easy rescues should be conducted first before proceeding to the rescues that will require additional human or material resources.

5. **Develop a rescue plan.** Determine the following:
   - Who will enter the building
   - How they will enter the building safely
   - What can be done to find and free the trapped individuals
   - How to ensure the safety of both the rescuers and trapped victims

6. **Conduct the search and rescue operation.** Search for people under debris and in voids. This may involve:
   - Calling out (e.g., asking if people can hear you, if they need help, and where they are)
   - Covering the entire building
   - Searching from the bottom-up or top-down
   - Following walls on the right until you complete a search of each floor
   - Looking at debris piles from different angles to fully understand the situations
   - Listening periodically for breathing, whistling, speaking, whispering, tapping, and any noise that indicates someone is alive

7. **Evaluate your progress.** You need to continually monitor the situation not only to see if your plan is working but also to prevent any harm to the rescuers.

While performing search and rescue operations, you may need to use levers, cribbing, and lifting to access the victim. Long pieces of wood (e.g., 2 × 4) may be used as **levers** to lift debris off of people. **Cribbing** is the name given to wood stacked under debris to stabilize it after it has been lifted by a lever. The purpose of cribbing is to increase void space so victim retrieval can occur. The use of levers and cribbing should be done slowly and on a rotating basis (e.g., lift the lever a foot, place cribbing under the debris, and repeat). Lifting debris or victims can be dangerous if not done properly. Be sure to lift in the following way: bend your knees and squat, hold the load close to your body, keep your back straight, and push up with your legs.

After you rescue the victim, you need to move him or her to safety. Have the victim exit the building on his or her own if he or she is able to do so. If needed, assist the victim by supporting, lifting, or dragging him or her to safety. Unless there is immediate danger, people with major head, neck, and back injuries should not be removed until professional medical help arrives. Moving them could aggravate such injuries.

During the search and rescue operation, you will want to mark searched areas with spray paint so the same area isn't searched twice. Use "/" on the door or façade to denote the building is being searched. Use "X" to denote the building has been searched. If needed, you will want to provide additional information near the "X," including searcher initials, time/date, hazards present in the building, and number of victims found or still inside. An "X" placed inside a box denotes "danger, do not enter." This is a useful symbol to keep people away from unstable structures.

SELF-CHECK

- How do people behave in conjunction with search and rescue operations?
- How can worker safety be ensured?
- What equipment do professional teams have?
- What are the steps to performing SAR effectively?

6.3 Emergency Medical Care and Triage

If you are to promote resilience, you should comprehend emergency medical care and triage. Injuries are common to most emergencies and disasters. Some emergency situations may produce a small number of injuries. A collision on the freeway may hurt one or two drivers only. An apartment fire may require that a handful of people (e.g., half a dozen) receive emergency medical care. Other disaster events generate larger numbers of persons who need medical attention. Between 8,000 and 11,000 individuals sought medical care following the 1994 Northridge earthquake (Shoaf et al 1998, 233). It is obvious that disasters create enormous medical challenges. "From 1975 to 1994, natural hazards . . . injured some 100,000 in the United States and its territories" (Mileti 1999, 4).

Injuries resulting from disaster will vary in terms of seriousness. Some wounds will be minor. For example, victims might receive superficial cuts from broken glass. Other injuries will be very serious or even life-threatening. Individuals could be crushed under a collapsed building, damaging vital internal organs. The nature of the injury in a disaster is a result of many factors:

▲ Magnitude of the hazard agent
▲ Location of the victim at the time of the disaster
▲ Availability and performance of protective structures
▲ Age, gender, and prior health status of the disaster victim

It is also important to realize that different types of disasters may produce unique types of injuries. Flooding will produce hypothermia if victims are in water for an excessive amount of time. Earthquakes and tornadoes cause lacerations (from debris) and fractures (from blunt-force trauma). Fires are associated with burns and respiratory problems. A chemical release at a factory may disable one's respiratory or nervous system.

Most disasters will generate a variety of injuries. For example, out of a total of 790 injured victims of the 9/11 terrorist attack, the following problems were treated (Pryor 2003, 9):

Injury	Number	Percentage
Inhalation	387	49
Ocular (eye irritation)	204	26
Sprain or strain	110	14
Laceration	110	14
Contusion	98	12
Fracture	46	6
Burn	39	5
Closed head trauma	14	2
Crush	8	1

Ordinary citizens are not the only ones at risk of injury. Thirty-five percent of the people treated after the World Trade Center collapse included emergency medical technicians, police officers, and firefighters (Pryor 2003, 9). Emergency responders work in very dangerous circumstances; they also require medical attention because of on-the-job injuries.

6.3.1 Treating the Injured

Emergent groups are typically first on the scene to provide emergency medical care to disaster victims (until fire and ambulance services arrive). Emergent groups also provide medical assistance for longer periods of time in large disasters because official medical resources are overstretched. Because disasters recur and produce secondary hazards (e.g., aftershocks, fires, broken glass), anyone involved in disaster response should have basic first aid knowledge and skills. First responders and emergency managers might be put in a situation where they will be required to treat themselves or others. In addition to emergent groups, there are firefighters, emergency medical technicians, nurses, doctors and others who will provide medical care. They must know what to expect in regards to the medical function of disaster response.

For instance, there may be multiple waves of disaster victims. Many people will be injured when the disaster strikes, whereas others will be hurt while response and recovery operations are underway. As mentioned above, victims will be treated by emergent groups first and then by professional medical personnel. Medical personnel will also show up in large quantities or even in overabundance. One hospital employee after 9/11 recalled, "one of our problems was crowd control as so many of our medical professionals gravitated to the emergency department to observe and offer their services" (in Pryor 2003, 14).

In many cases, volunteers and medical personnel will work side by side to meet emergency medical needs. There may be several legal liabilities associated with medical responses to disasters, however. Well-intentioned but untrained volunteers may inadvertently injure or kill victims who require medical treatment. For example, extracting an individual from debris could lead to a more severe back injury for the victim. It is therefore important that the medical function be transferred to knowledgeable and skilled workers as soon as the situation permits.

Because of the chaotic nature of disasters (e.g., many patients and many volunteers), it is difficult to ensure that working professionals who volunteer their medical services have sufficient qualifications. Malpractice lawsuits can result if a victim does not receive necessary medical care or if the treatment proves counterproductive. It is therefore necessary to check the credentials of medical personnel on site or at the hospital. One way to accomplish this is to have emergency medical technicians, nurses, and doctors check in at a specified location. Those verifying credentials will then obtain information about training, education, prior experience, current employment, work record, position/title, and area of specialization. The collected data can be stored and sorted to facilitate selection of needed knowledge and skills. For instance, at St. Vincent's hospital after the 9/11 terrorist attack, "personnel were pooled into ready rooms, one for surgeons, physicians, nurses, etc. When a particular talent was needed, supervisors in these ready rooms were contacted" (Pryor 2003, 13).

The nature of disaster will pose other challenges for medical personnel. Victims will be brought to hospitals by paramedics who discuss the patient's status with the emergency room while en route to this destination. Nevertheless, many patients will be self-referred (walking wounded) or brought in by others without advanced notification. If medical care and transportation are not promptly furnished, many victims will not sit idly by. Instead, they will get themselves or others to the hospital quickly. This may mean that they pass up other hospitals and go to the one that they are most familiar with. As a result, some hospitals may be overwhelmed with patients. This may necessitate that field hospitals be set up to care for victims near the impacted area or outside the hospital. Another issue of concern is that hospitals rarely have an understanding of the scope of the disaster. Paramedics and hospitals should communicate with each other to ensure that the distribution of patients does not overburden any single medical care facility. You may even want to inform hospitals about your understanding of the situation.

Another potential problem is that some hospitals may have to be evacuated during the disaster. A major medical center became flooded in Houston after Tropical Storm Allison. This created several logistical challenges to move the patients to other hospitals (especially those on life-support systems). Hospitals must therefore be ready to evacuate patients, which requires a great deal of foresight as well as trained personnel.

Richard Bievy, Director of the Kansas City Health Department, identified these and other challenges in the medical response when a skywalk (atrium bridge) collapsed in a Hyatt Hotel (see Waugh 1988, 120-121):

▲ "Communication among doctors, paramedics, and ambulance personnel was inadequate because they lacked walkie-talkies, two-way radios, and bullhorns, although some were borrowed from the police and fire units that responded;

▲ Medical supplies, particularly oxygen, splints, and drugs, were in short supply initially, although that problem was solved when supplies arrived from other jurisdictions

▲ Ambulance drivers left their vehicles, slowing down the pickup line of casualties, because the drivers were curious about the conditions in the hotel

▲ Life Flight helicopters were withdrawn before all of the critically injured were transported

▲ Distribution of patients among area hospitals was inefficient and too few casualties were sent to the trauma unit at the Kansas University Medical Center; and,

▲ Ambulance reaction times were too slow because of . . . the problem of establishing the one-way flow to and from the hotel entrance."

6.3.2 Triage

Disasters produce an extremely large number of injuries, and many of them will be life threatening. In many cases, the number of patients will far exceed the number and capacity of medical personnel. For this reason, emergency responders must follow a systematic and efficient approach to emergency medical care. This includes the triage, initial treatment, and transport of injured to hospitals for additional medical care. It may also include handling of victims who have died as a result of their injuries.

Triage is an initial assessment and separation of victims for treatment based on the severity of their injuries. O'Halloran notes (1989, 45) that triage means to "choose," and this term "was originally used as an agricultural system for discarding defective produce." Regardless of its meaning and source, the goal of triage is to do the most good for the largest number of casualties within the confines of limited medical personnel. Mayer states (1997, 2) that the purpose of triage is to "to identify severity of illness and injury . . . so that patients are seen at the right place at the right time to receive the right level of care." He also lists the five functions of triage (Mayer 1997, 3):

1. Identify severity of illness or injury.
2. Provide appropriate stabilizing clinical and nonclinical supportive care.
3. Communicate clinical and nonclinical information to other emergency providers to transition patient care appropriately.
4. Provide the first, best opportunity for customer service to patients, families, and the community.
5. Act as an "ancillary lobby" for the hospital.

Triage is therefore the evaluation, sorting, and treatment of those injured in disasters. As the initial assessment takes place, the medical care provider separates the disaster victims (by attaching the tags) into different groups based on the extent of their injuries. This classification is both categorical and physical. The separation of victims into categories helps paramedics and hospital staff know which patients are in the most need of medical care and which patients can wait to be treated or for additional help to arrive. There are many other classification schemes, and these are summarized below:

Number	Picture	Color	Word
0	Cross	Black	Dead/dying
I	Rabbit	Red	Immediate
II	Turtle	Yellow	Delayed
III	Ambulance with an "X" over it	Green	Minor

Once patients are categorized, they may be physically moved to different locations. In other words, there will be an area (e.g., room, driveway, portion of the

> ## FOR EXAMPLE
>
> ### 9/11 Injuries
>
> Often there are waves of victims in a major emergency or disaster, and 9/11 is an example of this. The first wave resulted from the impact of the aircraft. These victims were in the building and had burns from jet fuel and injuries from the damaged structure. The collapse of the towers caused a second wave of injuries. People had injuries from falling debris or from breathing in chemicals and hazardous contaminated air. The third wave of injuries was visible during the rescue and recovery effort. These injuries continued at a low rate for several months after the attack until bodies and debris were removed.

park, segment of the parking lot) for the dead, immediate, delayed, and others with minor injuries.

The groups are then treated according to their injuries. The dead will not receive any attention until the emergency medical needs of others have been addressed. Those with immediate needs will be treated first and sent to hospitals as soon as possible. Those designated as delayed will receive treatment second. Those labeled as minor will be treated on site. Treatment of minor injuries happens after the immediate and delayed patients have received care. Those with minor injuries may be asked to avoid going to the hospitals.

A commonly made mistake in triage is to send people to the hospital who do not require extra medical care. After the World Trade Center collapse, "of the estimated 1103 survivors that were treated at five hospitals, only 181 (16%) were injured severely enough to be hospitalized" (Pryor 2003, 14). It is therefore important that medical care providers in the field ensure that triage has been performed accurately. "Over triage can cause hospital emergency departments to be over-run with minimally injured patients, consuming resources and potentially delaying care to more severely injured patients" (Pryor 2003, 14).

The Ethics of Triage

Triage is a controversial approach to mass emergency and disaster situations. Some scholars and practitioners regard it to be a very important and necessary procedure. It is regarded by some to be the "keystone" to effective medical care in mass casualty situations (Bowers 1960, 59). Triage is considered by many to be essential for disasters (see Figure 6-2). Ambulance services, hospitals, and FEMA all advocate triage. Others assert that triage is unethical, and they disapprove of it for a variety of reasons.

Figure 6-2

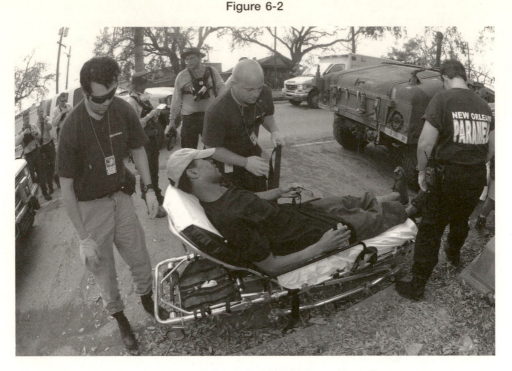

Although triage is controversial, it is still widely used at disaster scenes.

One of the reasons why triage is controversial is because triage decisions can be made by people with limited medical backgrounds. Therefore, some patients may die because of errors and mistakes. Triage may also go against EMT and physician oaths of conduct to minimize suffering, care for the injured, and prevent death. Time spent with a few severely injured patients could deprive many patients with less-severe but life-threatening injuries and deny them of the medical care they need for survival. No responder likes to place a black tag on someone who is dead or expected to die. These points reveal that triage may not be ideal. In many cases, it is an unfortunate necessity after disasters occur.

6.3.3 Disaster Medical Assistance Teams (DMAT)

In major disasters, local resources for medical care and triage will be completely overwhelmed. For this reason, additional well-trained medical professionals will be required. The National Disaster Medical System has instituted a system to help in these circumstances. This system relies heavily on Disaster Medical Assistance Teams (DMAT). According to United States Department of Health and Human Services, a **DMAT** is "a group of professional and paraprofessional medical personnel designed to provide emergency medical care during a disaster or other event." The DMAT concept was generated in 1995 as local and state experts met with the DHHS to discuss the need to improve medical care in disasters. There are now 80 DMATs in the NDMS, which includes more than 7,000 private medical and support personnel.

If local medical resources are stretched beyond limit, a federal emergency or disaster is declared and DMAT members are activated as federal (and, in some cases, state) employees. As such, they are paid as temporary employees of the federal (or state) government. They are also protected by the Federal Tort Claims Act in case of a malpractice claim.

Similar to USAR teams, DMATs are sent out to disasters. DMAT teams are capable of functioning for extended periods of time and in difficult conditions. They have their own supplies that can be replenished by the National Disaster Medical System. DMAT teams also provide their own housing and field hospitals (usually tents), thus allowing them to act independently if the housing stock or hospitals have been depleted or damaged in the disaster.

The team members include doctors, nurses, paramedics, pharmacists, and other health-related professionals. To participate as a team member, these individuals must maintain the proper medical credentials. They must have immunizations, health clearance forms, and other documents to ensure their safety and qualifications. Team members also participate in special drills and exercises to train for medical operations. For example, in July 2000, a disaster medical exercise was conducted in McAllen, Texas. More than 200 U.S. Navy reserves, Texas Army National Guard members, Texas Department of Health workers, and DMAT representatives participated in the 12-day operation. Free medical and dental services were provided to more than 5,600 local residents. The exercise enhanced skills in patient transportation, distribution, and medical care and increased coordination of logistical support.

DMAT team members maintain a 24/7 standby notice. If a disaster occurs and requires deployment, team members will be notified (via phone or page) where to report and at what time. DMAT members will leave for the scene no later than 12 hours after being notified. Once at the disaster site, DMATs will perform medical and nonmedical procedures in accordance with established standards and in conjunction with commanding officer requests.

Every effort is made to allow members to return home as soon as possible. If needed, other teams or members will be deployed and rotated to backfill or meet the demands until emergency medical care is no longer needed. After the 9/11 terrorist attacks in New York, at least five DMATs were activated to care for those injured in the incident. They provided medical services at various clinics within five blocks of the WTC site. These DMATs played an important role in caring for some of the 6,408 injured victims and reducing the burden on local health care providers.

SELF-CHECK

- What types of injuries result from disasters?
- How important are volunteers in emergency medical care?
- What is **triage**?
- Do all scholars and practitioners support triage?
- What medical challenges are faced by hospitals in disasters?
- What is a **DMAT** and how do they operate?

6.4 Mass Fatalities

Mass emergencies and disasters may generate large numbers of fatalities. It is true that fatalities owing to disasters have decreased by 75% over the past 50 years in developed nations (Mileti citing Mitchell 1999). However, hazards and disasters often result in mass fatalities even in the United States. Various hazards (including winter storms, lightning, and hail) produce death, although the number of fatalities is relatively low compared to other types of disasters. Large numbers of people can also die in structural fires or transportation accidents. The toll of major disasters can be staggering—almost beyond comprehension. Some disasters are especially deadly:

▲ Hurricane Katrina produced over 1,300 deaths.
▲ The 9/11 terrorist attacks killed about 3,000 individuals.
▲ The 1995 Kobe, Japan earthquake resulted in 5,000 fatalities.
▲ The Indian Ocean Tsunami left at least 300,000 dead.

In some cases, these disasters show disturbing patterns. Women and children are disproportionately numbered among the dead in various disasters (e.g., Hurricane Katrina in New Orleans). The vulnerability of women and children is attributed to several factors. Unmarried mothers often do not have the financial resources to evacuate. Also, women may not be as physically strong as men to withstand hazard events. Children are not as capable of reacting to hazards as women and men are. In addition, mothers may be at home caring for children while the men are at work, where they are often better protected from disasters as corporate buildings are often stronger than residences.

As an emergency manager, you should be aware of the fact that disasters may produce even more deaths over time. "Some future possible disasters could create victims in the high four or even five figures. Even handling relatively few bodies in most modern societies generates all kinds of problems . . . Future disasters with numerous dead bodies will sharply increase those kinds of disasters" (Quarantelli 1996, 90).

With this in mind, you will need to deal with the consequences of mass fatality incidents. A **mass fatality incident** is any situation where there are more bodies than can be handled using local resources. Mass fatality incidents result in a large number of bodies that stretch the community beyond its resources. Mass fatality incidents often create management problems for those involved in disaster response operations. Well-intentioned citizens may move bodies to various locations, thereby hindering identification. "After the recent earthquake in Kobe [Japan], private citizens brought bodies to the police stations, temples, schools, gymnasia, health and community centers and private companies, where they were laid out on the floor" (Nishimura as cited by Scanlon 1998, 289). This creates problems for those investigating disaster impacts. However, major but localized accidents may witness a very different pattern. "After the 12 December 1985, air crash in Gander, for those example, the area where the crash occurred was quickly sealed off by Royal Canadian Mounted Police and once the fires were out and dangerous objects removed . . . all bodies and body parts were marked and tagged before they were moved" (Scanlon 1998, 289).

Bodies can also be obliterated, as shown by the 9/11 disaster in New York. At ground zero, "Fewer than 300 bodies were intact. Only 12 could be identified purely by sight. Searchers recovered 19,893 separate body parts, including a single tooth. One man [corpse] was found in about 200 pieces" (Hamson and Moore 2003, 1B).

As a result, there may be disputes about the number of deaths in a specific incident or disaster. The actual death count after Hurricane Katrina was much lower than initially anticipated. The final death toll at the World Trade Center is not settled. "On the anniversary, the city counted 2,801 victims. A year later, the city now lists, 2,792 as lost. That figure still varies from databases assembled by the Associated Press (2,775) and USA TODAY (2,784). The exact number killed may never be certain, city officials acknowledge. Evidence could surface of a previously unknown victim—a homeless person, perhaps, or an illegal immigrant. Some DNA samples extracted from bones and tissue do not match any genetic profile submitted by victims' relatives. In the medical examiner's freezers may lie the remains of a victim who was never reported as missing" (Hamson and Moore 2003, 1B).

After many disasters, the identification process cannot occur without the use of modern technology. In New York after 9/11, body identification required samples of DNA. Even then, remains can take years to identify—if they are identified at all. Two years after the World Trade Center attacks, families were still waiting to have their loved ones identified. No trace has been found on 1,268 people. Even when there is a body, the identification process can be very physically and emotionally disturbing as relatives may have to see the bodies of their loved ones burned or in pieces. Identification, however, is important. Friends and family will desire to know the fate of their loved ones and have a proper memorial service.

Those mourning may become frustrated with the procedures of mass fatality management. Some responders may depersonalize the deceased by stacking them up on one another. This aggravates surviving relatives. Mass fatality disasters may also necessitate the cancellation of normal funeral arrangements. However, "in both the Iranian earthquake and the Italian dam disaster, the public authorities had to abandon plans for mass burials due to the strong public outcry when such a disposition of bodies was proposed" (Blanshan and Quarantelli as cited by Scanlon 1998, 290).

Mass fatality incidents necessitate the involvement of several people, including medical examiners, coroners and forensic investigators, morticians, mental health personnel, funeral home directors, hospitals, and even clergy. Private companies also help to recover the dead after disasters.

There are numerous issues to consider when responding to mass fatality incidents:

▲ **Care for investigation/crime scenes.** Accidents, murders, other criminal events and terrorist attacks leading to death require special treatment of bodies so as to not tamper with evidence or hinder ongoing investigations.

▲ **Logistics.** Who will recover bodies (e.g., county coroner's office)? How will they be transported and stored?

▲ **Family assistance.** How will the next of kin be notified? What questions, concerns, and needs might they have, and how can these be addressed?

▲ **Psychological issues.** How will people react to death (both surviving relatives and emergency workers) and what kind of support will they need? What is the best way to communicate with them using tact and sensitivity?

▲ **Cultural and religious issues.** What are the burial customs of different people and groups locally and around the world?

Another recommendation is to avoid removing bodies immediately except in special circumstances. If necessary, a map can be drawn to record the exact location of the deceased. Every body and any personal belongings should be tagged with a unique number. Such record keeping plays an important role in reconstructing the event and identifying the bodies and belongings. Belongings and body parts should be kept near the body or together at all times. In other cases where bodies have been dispersed, efforts should be made to centralize the deceased or maintain meticulous records as to their whereabouts.

After a preliminary investigation has taken place, the deceased should be taken to a central morgue facility. This temporary morgue must be adequate to handle the number of bodies. It should be large enough to store several bodies, be well-ventilated and cold, and have adequate lighting. In addition, the facility should have adequate lighting, sufficient electrical outlets, running water and bathrooms, and furniture for examinations. Clerical, break, and waiting rooms would also be helpful. If no such facilities can be obtained quickly, refrigerated trailers can also be used to store bodies in major mass fatality incidents. However, these trucks should have no visible markings, logos, names, etc. This will help to avoid bad publicity for that particular company.

Mass fatality management includes an effort to determine the cause of death, and victim identification will take place by collecting and analyzing postmortem data. Hooft, Noji, and Van de Voorde (1989, 6) note that:

1. "The bodies are described as they outwardly appear, recording all significant features, mud, clothing and belongings. The same happens for all loose body parts or belongings.

2. Fingerprints should be taken. Photographs should be taken of the clothed body and all relevant external items.

3. The delicate procedures of examining a human body, even if it is dead, are medical acts and should only be performed by a doctor. All relevant marks and signs on the body should be marked. Blood and urine samples or muscle biopsies should be collected for alcohol dosage, blood grouping, and toxicological analysis. As ondontological findings often contribute most to the identification, attention should be given to get complete dental records.

4. If the clothes or any other object are essential for a further investigation or as evidence in court, they should be dried before packing, as wet materials become moldy, change color and disintegrate rapidly, especially in plastic bags.

5. In fire accidents additional airtight blood samples should be taken for the concentration of carboxyhemoglobin and cyanide."

At this point, family members can be brought in to confirm the identification of the deceased. You must ensure that this be done with much care and tact. Will one or multiple families be brought in at a time? Is an escort needed? Will children be allowed to participate? Will the family be required to show personal identification (e.g., drivers license) before being allowed in? These are all important considerations.

FOR EXAMPLE

9/11 Victims

The task of identifying remains at the World Trade Center after 9/11 was especially difficult. Tons of debris had to be sorted through for human remains. There was initial sorting at Ground Zero. Afterwards, heavy equipment moved debris to Staten Island. This caused some victims to complain that their loved ones were placed in a trash heap on Staten Island. Debris was then sorted again to search for victims. Many of the deceased were obliterated and badly burned. Some do not have remains to be recovered. This has been emotionally trying for many of the surviving family members.

Final disposition must also be performed under strict guidelines. Before the body is released, a complete postmortem assessment needs to be completed. Unidentifiable bodies should be buried separately, with the funeral home or coroner keeping a record of their locations.

Other steps to successfully respond to a mass fatality incident include:

▲ Ensuring that those responding to a mass fatality incident know where to report, the best route to get to the scene, what type of equipment they will need, and where the staging areas are

▲ Recognizing that the public is watching how bodies are being handled

▲ Flagging or otherwise marking the location of the deceased

▲ Using grids or pictures of the scene for documentation purposes

▲ Ensuring that the trucks that haul remains have metal floors (as wood may retain odors)

▲ Managing personal belongings and identification records in a careful manner

▲ Communicating effectively with the next of kin and helping them cope with the loss of a loved one

▲ Knowing how to deal with the media to prevent the release of sensational photos of the deceased

▲ Opening family assistance centers to address survivor needs and answer questions about lost loved ones and the mass fatality management process

6.4.1 DMORT

In major disasters, local coroners, morticians, and funeral directors will be overwhelmed, unable to deal with the large numbers of dead. For this reason, it may be necessary to call in Disaster Mortuary Operational Response Teams (DMORT). A **DMORT** is a group of private citizens that is activated under the National Response Plan. A DMORT can be activated in circumstances that do not require utilization of the National Response Plan. State emergency management agencies may request a DMORT (see Figure 6-3).

DMORTs are, in many ways, similar to a USARs and DMATs because they are deployed by the federal government. However, a DMORT is in charge of providing victim identification and mortuary services. They are comprised of several licensed and certified experts. These experts include funeral directors, medical examiners, coroners, pathologists, forensic anthropologists, and medical records technicians and transcribers. Others, such as finger print specialists, forensic ondontologists, dental assistants, x-ray technicians, mental health specialists, computer professionals, administrative support staff, and security and investigative personnel also play an important part in DMORTs.

Once notified and mobilized, DMORT members become federal employees under the Department of Homeland Security. Like USARs or DMATs, DMORTs

Figure 6-3

Members of FEMA's Task Force DMORT team remove a casket from its crypt so it can be reinterred at Bancker Cemetery. The enormous storm surge from Hurricane Rita pushed crypts hundreds of yards from their shallow graves at many cemeteries.

can be sent to any location and are intended to be relatively self-sufficient. Some have Disaster Portable Morgue Units (DPMU), which are complete and mobile morgues with workstations and prepackaged equipment.

DMORTs provide necessary services after mass fatality incidents and operate in a very professional manner. They work with local authorities to process deceased disaster victims. Some of their responsibilities include:

▲ Recovering bodies, body parts, and belongings of the dead
▲ Setting up temporary morgues
▲ Identifying disaster victims
▲ Answering questions from the family of the deceased and providing comfort as needed
▲ Facilitating death certificate issuance
▲ Preparing and disposing of remains

DMORTs can be a great asset to you and to your community in major mass fatality incidents.

6.5 Stress Management

If you are to respond effectively to a disaster, you must recognize that people may succumb to emotional distress and not just physical injuries and death. This psychological harm is commonly referred to as post-traumatic stress disorder (PTSD) or critical incident stress (CIS).

▲ "**Post-traumatic stress disorder (PTSD)** is the clinical diagnosis given by psychiatrists to the development of specific symptoms following a psychologically traumatic event not generally encountered in human experience" (Corneil 1989, 24).

▲ **Critical incident stress (CIS)** is defined as unusual work stress resulting from any trauma, crisis, or event that overwhelms available coping mechanisms of emergency service personnel.

There are multiple reasons why some people experience PTSD or CIS. This may be from the event itself or other stressors in a person's life or work. Disasters, line-of-duty injuries, mass deaths, and the inability to save others from a horrific situation can all lead to PTSD or CIS. Witnessing death or feeling threats to one's life or the lives of friends, families, and co-workers can also lead to PTSD or CIS. For instance, many people in the United States and around the world were deeply distressed when watching news reports of Americans getting killed on 9/11.

In the aftermath of traumatic events, including workplace violence or industrial accidents, citizens and first responders will have to deal with many issues. They may have to grapple with their actions or inaction during the event. Those involved may have no experience in dealing with death and destruction. They could be uncertain of how to act under such circumstances and will often feel depressed wondering whether their efforts were appropriate or sufficient. The community will also be looking to emergency managers to effectively deal with the disaster, which can also take an emotional toll on you.

6.5.1 Vulnerability to PTSD/CIS

Although most individuals who experience a disaster or other traumatic event will not suffer any type of long-term psychological distress, some will have to deal with stressful events. Sixty to seventy percent of all people will experience a traumatic event in their lives (Patterson 2002, 5C). Eight to ten percent of these people will suffer from post-traumatic stress syndrome. Some people will be everyday citizens. Others affected by the disorder will be in emergency services. People in the armed forces as well will suffer from the disorder after witnessing combat. Stress reactions can happen to anyone if the situation is sufficiently disturbing.

Those affected by disaster may experience significant trials, such as the death of family members, friends, and co-workers. They may lose personal property (e.g., home or car). Unemployment may result due to business closures. Disaster victims may also have stressful dealings with insurance claim adjusters or receive what they regard to be insufficient federal or humanitarian relief assistance. For many individuals, disasters will result in a feeling that their dreams have been dashed.

First responders may also become victims of PTSD/CIS. Firefighters, paramedics, and police officers witness many grim realities of their professions. On a daily basis they see gruesome injuries and appalling deaths among those in the community and even within their own departments. Repeated occurrences of traumatic events have a "pile up effect" on rescue workers and can prolong or aggravate PTSD (Harris 1989). For example, a first responder who sees victims of car accidents on a regular basis may develop PTSD after the repeated occurrence of accidents. Rescue workers who see a co-worker die often feel "it could have been me." First responders may have an especially difficult time when they weren't able to rescue victims either due to safety concerns or other factors. If traumatic events occur repeatedly, they also are confronted with other challenges that lead to PTSD/CIS. Rescue workers may have a difficult time expressing emotions, which aggravates the emotional turmoil. In addition to rescue personnel, there are some groups that are at particular risk of mental problems following a disaster:

▲ Those who already have acute stress and those who had a pre-existing psychiatric disorder
▲ Those who have lost a loved one
▲ Those wounded in the disaster
▲ Those who were exposed to the trauma intensely and for a long period of time
▲ Children and the elderly
▲ Those who have a difficult childhood or past traumatic experiences
▲ Those without a strong social support system

6.5.2 Common Signs of PTSD/CIS

There are many possible symptoms of PTSD/CIS. These symptoms include weight loss, anger, depression, alcohol/drug use, guilt, chest pains, headaches, and mood swings. Denial, sleeplessness, withdrawal from friends, flashbacks, and memory loss are also signs of PTSD/CIS.

Many of these symptoms are not readily apparent but may become visible over time. Some symptoms might last for a few weeks or months, whereas others will occasionally endure for years. Some symptoms may be age specific. Young children will resume bedwetting, thumb sucking, and fear of "monsters" and exhibit other behaviors. Older children will rebel and often have poor school performance. Regardless of the length or type of symptoms, the traumatic experience will affect people's personal and professional lives.

6.5.3 Overcoming PTSD and CIS

In light of the psychological problems that result from major emergencies and disasters, it is recommended that post-traumatic stress debriefing/critical incident stress management be implemented by mental health professionals. Critical incident stress debriefing has emanated from military experiences such as combat deaths. According to Jeffrey T. Mitchell (1988a, 47), the two main goals of debriefing are to:

▲ Reduce the impact of distressing critical incidents
▲ Accelerate recovery from those events before harmful stress reactions have a chance to damage personal and professional lives

As an emergency manager or first responder, you can take steps to minimize the risk of critical incident stress. You and the leaders of response organizations should be aware of possible trauma during response. Surprise can be a dangerous psychological element in a field situation, and every effort should be made to cut down on unexpected situations. Frequent breaks for those at the rescue scene will also help as well because people may only be able to work under intense stress before the effects are felt. It is also important to make sure there is plenty of fresh water available. Caffeine and sugar should be avoided because they may magnify a stress reaction.

It is also important for emergency and disaster workers to recognize stress reactions. Change in the behavior of one's personnel is a sign that the event has had a significant psychological impact on them. Decisions on whether a distressed person needs to be removed from service at the scene are usually difficult to make. Hasty decisions will usually not be good ones. It is usually best to offer an extended rest break and see if the person improves. If there is not any improvement, keep the person at the scene but do not assign him or her to other work crews. If the serious distress continues, the worker should be removed from the location.

After the event, defusings can reduce the long-term effects of stress reactions. **Defusings** are short, unstructured meetings that encourage a brief discussion of the events to reduce acute stress. Defusings are done anywhere from 3 to 12 hours after the incident. They often take place at the fire or police station and generally last from 30 minutes to 1 hour. Only those crews most affected are involved; not all emergency responders from the scene need to attend.

Another important activity is to provide ongoing support to those people showing the greatest need and work with their leaders to develop a plan to care for their future emotional needs. Following a crisis, emergency workers are likely to close ranks, preferring to talk with individuals in the unit or participate in small group conversations related to the event. Peer support personnel, including those involved in the incident, may watch for tell-tale signs of distress in their fellow workers: irritability, excessive humor, increased derogatory remarks against one another, significant changes in behavior, or social withdrawal.

Well-run defusings and continued support may eliminate the need for further treatment for PTSD or CIS. However, formal debriefing activities may also be necessary (Mitchell 1988). A **debriefing** is an extensive and possibly recurring discussion about one's feelings regarding a traumatic stress experience such as a disaster. A full formal debriefing can be conducted approximately 3 days after the incident. Debriefings may include a joint session with all types of responders as well as multiple one-on-one sessions a few weeks after the trauma. In debriefings, emergency personnel recount the nature of the disaster and the trauma they experienced on scene. Therapists try to redirect harmful thinking, such as the belief that emergency workers are responsible for the tragedy. Therapists work with survivors to focus on things such as normal reactions to the event, relaxation exercises, and coping strategies. Personnel are given as many practical suggestions for stress management as possible along with an opportunity to ask questions and make comments. The mental-health person assigned to their group remains available to privately discuss the situation or their reactions. Talking to the other mental-health professionals at the debriefing center is also an option. Chaplains may be present at the debriefing center and are available if an emergency person would prefer to discuss something with them. No one is required to talk unless they choose to.

There are seven phases in critical stress debriefings (Mitchell 1988b, 46).

1. In the **introduction,** members of a critical incident stress team (emergency personnel who are training in psychological counseling) state that the material to be discussed is strictly confidential.
2. In the **fact phase,** people are asked to describe what happened at the scene.
3. The **thought phase** of the process usually includes the question, "Can you recall your first thoughts once you stopped functioning in an automatic mode at the scene?" The goal of this question is to help people personalize their experiences.

FOR EXAMPLE

PTSD/CIS Debriefings

Rescue personnel often blame themselves for fatalities on the scene. One useful technique to handle this is to put together a timeline of events to show how quickly people reacted and point out all the things they did right. A fire chief in Hudson, Massachusetts asked his crew to recount their events and recorded them. He said, "by using our radio tape recorder I was able to put together a sequential order of events, and the times they had taken place. I found this to be extremely helpful to the overall effectiveness of the critique because it showed the firefighters how quickly things were done. By the end of the critique the firefighters were openly talking, which made the effects of the incident at least livable" (Garrity 1989, 14).

4. The **reaction phase** is when mental health personnel help victims describe the worst part of the event.

5. The **symptom phase** is when the group or individual is asked to describe stress symptoms felt at different times.

6. The **teaching phase** is when people are taught how to cope with and how to reduce their stress. Education should include material on critical incident stress and how it differs from non-emergency stress. This phase also describes the CISD team and how to utilize it if the need arises. This segment should include specific information on field strategies for stress control during a crisis.

7. The **re-entry phase** is when response personnel may ask whatever questions arise from the session and follow up with each person during the recovery process. Peer supporters may also participate in this phase and assist mental health professionals.

6.5.4 The Merit of Defusings and Debriefings

Research often shows the importance of psychological treatments. Many of these same principles can apply to citizens who have been affected by disasters. For example, it has been reported that "approximately 65 percent of those who received immediate psychological treatment for stress were able to return to combat duties, but less than 40 percent of those who were given delayed treatment in distant areas were able to return to combat" (Mitchell 1988a, 48). Much of this may depend on how the treatment is delivered. According to (Barnett-Queen and Bergmann 1989, 15), effective post-trauma programs seem to require the following four components:

1. **Information.** Personnel who have accurate information about trauma, post-trauma consequences, and productive post-trauma coping skills

seem to make more successful recoveries. Those victims of duty-related trauma who do not have recovery information are less likely to recover. In addition, they tend to use inappropriate coping skills to numb or manage their post-trauma consequences (Barnett-Queen and Bergmann 1989, 15).

2. **Support.** Survivors of trauma tend to feel isolated, distrustful, and detached. Where survivors receive consistent support from their peers and families, they feel more positive about themselves, their efforts to recover, and their prognosis (Barnett-Queen and Bergmann 1989, 15).

3. **Ventilation.** Detailed discussion of the incident with others is an important element of post-trauma recovery. Individuals who can talk about their experiences are more likely to feel supported by the listeners and others involved in the incident. They may learn important details of the event from others or may recall more of their own experiences during the incident, which promotes recovery. Finally, survivors who are able to articulate their experiences are more likely to understand what has happened and how it has changed their lives (Barnett-Queen and Bergmann 1989, 15).

4. **Skills.** The coping skills required for day-to-day living may not be those most helpful for a successful recovery. The use of appropriate coping skills enhances the probability of recovery after a traumatic event (Barnett-Queen and Bergmann 1989, 15).

Despite notable successes, research also reveals that PTSD/CIS treatments may not always be effective. Post-traumatic stress debriefing/critical incident stress debriefing are relatively new techniques to dealing with psychological problems. Emergency medical services organizations began developing psychological support services for staff members in 1972. As a consequence, there are inconsistencies about the benefit of these treatments. Some studies show no relation between critical incident stress management and psychological recovery. For instance, Gibbs et al's study of the AVIANCA air crash illustrates that pre-disaster training on disturbing disaster conditions had no effect on post-disaster symptoms (1996). Barnett-Queen and Bergmann have illustrated that there are at least four difficulties associated with individual counseling after traumatic events (1989, 15):

1. There can be a stigma in seeking psychological help. Other rescue personnel may believe that co-workers getting counseling are not mentally strong enough for their jobs.

2. Emergency workers who are referred to counseling may believe that their feelings are not normal and to be expected. They think they are being singled out because they cannot deal with post-traumatic symptoms (see Figure 6-4).

3. Counseling is expensive. One hour of counseling may cost from $40.00 to $120.00. Debriefing sessions that include multiple individuals at once are more economical.

Figure 6-4

Although anyone can suffer from PTSD/CIS, rescue personnel are particularly vulnerable.

4. Some firefighters hide their true feelings about an incident. If this is the case, some people that need assistance may not receive it.

Post-traumatic or critical incident stress treatments are therefore somewhat controversial. Most scholars agree that critical incident stress management is a complicated matter and that we need more research on the topic. As an emergency manager, you have the responsibility to stay on top of this literature.

SELF-CHECK

- What is **PTSD**? What is **CIS**?
- Why are some people more vulnerable to psychological distress than others?
- What are the symptoms of PTSD or CIS?
- What is the difference between a defusing and a debriefing?
- What are the phases of debriefings?
- Are psychological interventions always advantageous?

SUMMARY

Disasters are associated with injuries, deaths, and even emotional distress. To deal with these challenges successfully, volunteers and first responders must engage in search and rescue operations. Medical care must be given to those who have been physically hurt. When deaths result from a disaster, bodies must be collected, identified, and returned to surviving relatives. Those affected psychologically must be evaluated, treated, and supported through understanding and expressions of concern and hope. Meeting people's physical and emotional needs after disaster is required if resilience is to occur.

KEY TERMS

Cribbing	Wood stacked under debris to stabilize it after it has been lifted by a lever.
Critical incident stress (CIS)	Unusual work stress resulting from any trauma, crisis, or event that overwhelms available coping mechanisms of emergency service personnel.
Debriefing	An extensive discussion about one's feelings regarding a traumatic stress experience such as a disaster.
Defusings	Short, unstructured meetings that encourage a brief discussion of the events to reduce acute stress.
Disaster Medical Assistance Team (DMAT)	A group or team of medical personnel who provide emergency medical care during an extreme event.
Disaster Mortuary Team (DMORT)	A group of private citizens who are activated under the National Response Plan to deal with mass fatality incidents.
Levers	Long pieces of wood (e.g., 2 × 4) used to lift debris off of people.
Mass fatality incident	Any situation where there are more bodies than can be handled using local resources.
National Urban Search and Rescue Response	A system made up of 28 FEMA urban SAR Task Forces that are spread throughout the continental United States.

Post-traumatic stress disorder (PTSD)

A clinical diagnosis that signifies deep stress that is sometimes debilitating resulting from a traumatic event.

Search and rescue operations

Response activities undertaken to find disaster victims and remove them from danger or confinement so they may receive urgent treatment such as hydration, basic first aid, or advanced medical care.

Triage

An initial assessment and separation of victims for treatment based on the severity of their injuries.

ASSESS YOUR UNDERSTANDING

Go to www.wiley.com/college/McEntire to evaluate your knowledge of caring for the injured, dead, and distraught.
Measure your learning by comparing pretest and post-test results.

Summary Questions

1. Search and rescue includes looking for lost individuals but has nothing to do with providing immediate medical assistance. True or False?

2. Emergent groups will use anything they can find to assist them in search and rescue operations. True or False?

3. Those engaged in search and rescue will require sufficient food, water, and rest if they are to be effective and safe. True or False?

4. Before rushing in to conduct search and rescue operations, it is important to assess the situation and determine rescue priorities. True or False?

5. Most hazards will generate the same type of injuries only. True or False?

6. People will only be injured in and not after the hazard occurs. True or False?

7. A purpose of triage is to limit the impact of mass casualty incidents on the hospitals. True or False?

8. Because first responders are well trained, they will never make mistakes regarding triage. True or False?

9. Emergency managers should not expect that people will move the bodies of those who have died in accidents, emergencies, and disasters. True or False?

10. It is vital that temporary morgue sites be large, cold, and have water and electrical outlets. True or False?

11. The public and media have no interest in mass fatality management. True or False?

12. DMORTs are teams that respond to the medical needs of those who are injured in disasters. True or False?

13. DMORTs may help to issue death certificates. True or False?

14. PTSD and CIS are similar but are not exactly the same thing. True or False?

15. Because disasters result in death and destruction of property, some people may become stressed and depressed. True or False?

16. A debriefing occurs in the field right after the accident or disaster. True or False?

17. In the reaction phase, emergency responders engage in search and rescue operations. True or False?

18. Effective post-trauma interventions help disaster victims develop emotional coping skills. True or False?

19. Which type of search and rescue helps to access people and bring them to dry ground?
    (a) Rural search and rescue
    (b) Swift water rescue
    (c) Air patrolled search and rescue
    (d) Urban search and rescue
    (e) Ski patrol search and rescue

20. Professional search and rescue teams:
    (a) Do not have to undergo training because they work as first responders
    (b) Are transported by bus only to avoid plane accidents
    (c) Are located in three cities in the United States only
    (d) Are well equipped with supplies
    (e) Arrive before emergent groups and first responders

21. Cribbing is:
    (a) Used to lift levers
    (b) A device to stop the bleeding on patients
    (c) A process to help victims recover from CIS
    (d) Used to spray paint important information on houses that have been searched
    (e) Used to stabilize debris

22. Self-referred means:
    (a) The dispatch of USAR teams
    (b) The dispatch of DMATs
    (c) The arrival of patients at the hospital without a field diagnosis
    (d) The dispatch of DMORTs
    (e) An acknowledgement that one has been affected by PTSD

23. DMAT stands for:
    (a) Disaster medical assistance team
    (b) Disaster medical advice team
    (c) Disaster mortuary assistance team
    (d) Disaster mortuary advice team
    (e) Disaster memorandum assistance terminology

24. Mass fatality management requires:
    (a) That the outward appearance of bodies be recorded
    (b) That fingerprints be taken
    (c) That evidence be kept for investigation and prosecution

(d) That photographs be avoided to protect privacy

(e) All of the above except d

25. Which of the following are not members of DMORTs:

(a) Funeral directors

(b) Coroners

(c) X-ray technicians

(d) First responders trained to perform search and rescue operations

(e) Administrative support staff

26. Which term is used to describe the impact of disasters on first responders:

(a) Post traumatic stress disorder

(b) Critical incident stress

(c) Defusings

(d) Debriefings

(e) The complex psychoanalysis assumption

27. Which person is most likely to be at risk for mental problems after a disaster:

(a) An emergency manager

(b) A fire chief

(c) Those without strong social support systems

(d) Those individuals who were slightly injured in the disaster

(e) Those who did not have a pre-existing psychiatric disorder

28. Symptoms of PTSD include:

(a) Anger

(b) Guilt

(c) Sleeplessness

(d) Flashbacks

(e) All of the above

Review Questions

1. Why is search and rescue important?
2. How is urban search and rescue different from other types of SAR?
3. What is situational awareness?
4. Explain the characteristics of professional SAR teams?
5. How are SAR missions conducted?
6. What are the determinants of the number and extent of injuries in a disaster?

7. Do disasters produce waves of victims? What does this mean for hospitals?

8. What are the benefits of triage? What are the drawbacks?

9. How are DMAT teams deployed?

10. Should we expect more mass fatality incidents in the future?

11. How can those in mass fatality management deal effectively with the surviving family members?

12. Who is involved in DMORTS?

13. Does everyone become affected by PTSD? Why or why not?

14. Why are first responders affected by CIS?

15. Are the signs of PTSD/CIS physical? Emotional? Behavioral? Cognitive?

16. What can be done to limit CIS?

17. What are the four components of successful PTSD interventions?

Applying This Chapter

1. You are a first responder in a southern California community that has experienced a major mudslide. Many homes are covered with sediment or are damaged extensively. Volunteers are on scene to assist with search and rescure, but time is running out. What concerns do you have and how do you address them?

2. A bus carrying 40 high school students has overturned on a freeway in Oklahoma. Injuries range from minor to major, and some students have died. How can triage be applied in this situation?

3. You are the coroner in a small community in North Dakota. An unexpected storm catches many people off guard in the early summer, and several hikers die from hypothermia as a result. How do you identify the bodies and deal with the next of kin?

4. While responding to a three-alarm fire at an apartment complex, you become worried about the physical and emotional well-being of your crew. What can you do to prevent critical incident stress? If some are affected, how to you help them afterwards?

5. You are a member of a nonprofit organization in a community that has just experienced a major disaster. Hundreds of people have died, and others have lost homes and possessions. Some victims are fighting with insurance companies to settle claims, and others believe the federal government is not providing enough disaster assistance. What are your concerns about people in your area? What can you do to help them cope emotionally? Are there things you can do to prevent symptoms of PTSD?

Volunteer Search and Rescue Teams

You are the emergency manager for your town in the Colorado Rockies, and there has been a terrible avalanche in the area. Hundreds of volunteers and upset parents rush to the local elementary school and begin digging victims out of the snow pile. What concerns do you have about these volunteers? What steps do you take to ensure the volunteers have what they need to be successful and do not injure themselves or others in the process?

Triage

A chemical or nerve agent has been used in a terrorist attack in Phoenix, Arizona. You are a paramedic and have arrived on the scene to help victims. How do you fulfill the five functions of triage?

Mass Fatalities

Write a three-page paper on the following topic: You are the emergency manager for a small town in Ohio when a 747 crashes in a farmer's field, killing everyone on board. What challenges confront emergency responders and others in this a mass fatality incident? What concerns do you have about workers, victims, and relatives of the deceased? What can you do to resolve them?

PTSD/CIS

Many emergency services personnel who worked at the World Trade Center on 9/11 suffered from PTSD/CIS as a result of that disaster. If you were in charge of one of the groups to assist rescue personnel, what steps would you take to prevent PTSD/CIS and to help distraught workers recover? Are there any drawbacks to counseling that you must consider?

7

MANAGING MEDIA RELATIONS, DONATIONS, AND VOLUNTEERS
Expected Challenges and Benefits

Starting Point

Go to www.wiley.com/college/McEntire to assess your knowledge of managing public relations, donations, and volunteers during disasters.
Determine where you need to concentrate your effort.

What You'll Learn in This Chapter

▲ The different types of media and typical media behaviors
▲ The goals of public relations after disasters
▲ Problems associated with donations management
▲ The challenges that volunteers create for first responders and emergency managers

After Studying This Chapter, You'll be Able To

▲ Handle the media effectively after a disaster
▲ Examine donation management difficulties
▲ Prepare for an outpouring of assistance and help from others
▲ Operate closely with volunteer and volunteer associations

Goals and Outcomes

▲ Prepare and provide important disaster information to your community
▲ Enhance your agency's public image
▲ Harness outside generosity for the benefit of disaster victims
▲ Synthesize volunteers into disaster response and recovery operations

INTRODUCTION

One measure of resilience is your ability to deal with the expected reactions of organizations and people to disasters. Members of the media rush to the scene to report on what is taking place. Donations pour in from well-meaning individuals and groups that want to help disaster victims. Volunteers arrive to assist the community recover. Although the media, donations, and volunteers are essential for response and recovery operations, they will present you many challenges. You must comprehend the benefits and drawbacks associated with the media, donations, and volunteers. Managing all three functions effectively will be one of your top priorities in the aftermath of disaster.

7.1 The Media and Disasters

As an emergency manager, you must understand that the media can be your friend or foe during post-disaster operations (Auf der Heide 1987). In the context of emergency management, the **media** includes reporters, camera operators, and news anchors that provide information about disasters to the public. The significance and role of the media cannot be underestimated. The media helps to:

▲ Educate the public on preventive and preparedness measures
▲ Warn the public about an impending hazard
▲ Provide information regarding evacuation and sheltering
▲ Describe what people can do to protect themselves and others
▲ Relay what the government is doing and how they are responding to the disaster
▲ List what organizations are providing relief and how assistance can be given or obtained
▲ Generate support for emergency management personnel and programs

The media may affect emergency management in other ways as well. The media shares communications equipment with responders if needed. They also provide advice to victims on where to go to receive aid. Not every thing that the media does is beneficial for emergency management, however. For instance, the media often points out weaknesses of response and recovery operations and is quick to assign blame. However, this, along with news footage provided by the media, may help you to evaluate and improve response and recovery activities in the future.

7.1.1 Types of Media

To be successful, you must be aware of the different types of media (Scanlon et al 1985). Each represents a different level of society and has a unique audience and objective. For example, local media represents the community. Regional media represents several communities or states. National media represents the entire country. International media brings a global perspective to pertinent issues. The media has different goals based on the segment of society they represent. For example:

▲ Local media will provide very detailed and personal stories, in addition to specific disaster information for victims.

▲ Regional media are somewhat similar to local media, but they also desire to know how multiple cities and the state or states are responding.

▲ National media tend to focus on what the president is doing about the disaster as well as the activities of federal organizations.

▲ International media gives preference to national responses and global impacts (either domestically or abroad).

Just as the media has different types of audiences and goals, it also uses different ways to convey the information based on how the information is delivered (Scanlon et al 1985). The means used by the media often shape their style of reporting. For instance, radio stations want short sound bites from victims, scholars, or public officials. Television/cable/satellite stations prefer interviews as well as pictures and dramatic video footage. Internet and print media seek in-depth coverage and detailed analysis of the situation.

Each of the media organizations and mediums has similar interest in disasters (Scanlon et al 1985). They want to provide those listening, watching, or reading with a human interest stories. Television coverage of disasters is common on any given day and will dominate the news and pre-empt normal programming. They will often include photos of the damage from the disaster because the scenes of destruction are powerful.

Regardless of the type of media, their behavior is generally predictable in normal times as well as in times of disaster. Scanlon and Alldred have identified that the media follows a pattern in reporting disasters (1982):

1. The media will hear of a disaster event.
2. They will immediately report the news of that incident.
3. They will search for additional information via telephone or personal interviews.
4. They will send reporters to the scene. If the event is newsworthy, hundreds of media personnel may descend on the affected area.
5. Once they are there, the media will make demands on local disaster managers. They may pressure you to hold news conferences at specific intervals. The media wants to know the where, when, why, and how of the situation. They will also want numbers—the number of dead, the

number of casualties, the number of destroyed homes, and the number of dollars that will be spent on response and recovery.

6. The media will put their own spin on the story and will make it fit their perception of what has happened or will occur in the future.

In addition, the media tends to rely on official sources of information. Quarantelli wrote, "One Disaster Research Center study found that local governmental officials were cited in 14 percent of radio, 19 percent of television and 24 percent of newspaper stories; police, fire and relief agencies were also frequently cited. In contrast, local emergency management officials were infrequently cited, being mentioned in only 8 percent of radio, 2 percent of television and 3 percent of newspaper stories" (1996, 8).

7.1.2 Challenges Associated With the Media

It is well-known that the media often presents formidable challenges to responders and emergency managers. The problems generated by the media are numerous. Payne (1994) has identified four of the most prevalent problems:

▲ **Inaccurate Reporting.** For instance, it was widely reported during the early days of Hurricane Katrina that there were rapes and murders at the New Orleans Superdome and Convention Center. There were not always witnesses to these crimes, and many of these reports appear to have been rumors. The media later retracted these stories many days later.

▲ **Intrusive Manner.** The press wants first-hand accounts of the situation, and they want to beat their colleagues in getting the best story or getting the story on air first. To do this, they will sometimes stoop to lying. For example, in one disaster, reporters went to a hospital and claimed to be relatives of the victims. They then asked for the victims to recount their stories (Payne, 1994, 26).

▲ **Lack of Sensitivity.** A vivid example of this is when a stampede occurred at a soccer game in England. "In 1989 at Hillsborough, Sheffield, there was live filming of people being crushed to death at the steel barriers. The horror was brought into the homes of the people who were viewing the football match on television. At the ground, a cameraman who moved around the pitch and terraces filming the scenes was sworn at, spat at, cursed and threatened, and not only by the understandably emotional fans. (Later, that cameraman won an award for the best television coverage of the year!)" (Payne 1994, 26).

▲ **Uncooperative Attitude.** The media may stop at nothing to get their scoop, as witnessed after a boating accident in Europe. "When the *Marchioness* pleasure-boat was being lifted from the Thames, the police positioned a number of police launches to screen the area from the intrusive press. The press moved to another less convenient position and covered the salvage operation in full. They claimed they were able to do so tastefully and without causing widespread offence" (Payne 1994, 26).

In addition to these problems, there are at least eight other problems with the media in times of disaster (see Scanlon et al 1985; Auf der Heide 1987).

1. **Convergence at the scene.** The media will show up in massive numbers at the scene of the disaster. As a result, the media can also generate too many volunteers and donations (other problems that will be discussed later on in this chapter).

2. **Additional demands placed on emergency managers and responders.** When a disaster strikes and you are in the middle of response, it is difficult to have sufficient time to deal with the media. Not only do they have an urgent need for complex information, but they may also need security, supplies, and access to facilities. "Many emergency managers have been frustrated when they have had to divert much needed time and resources to address the demands of the media, while at the same time trying to mount a multi-organizational response under conditions of extreme urgency and uncertainty . . . . Their demands may completely tie up any surviving transportation and communication facilities, and local officials may find themselves responding more to the needs of the media than to the disaster situation" (Auf der Heide 1987, Chapter 10, p. 1, p. 5).

3. **Interference with response operations.** A good example of this nuisance is after the 1983 Coalinga, California earthquake, when the media impeded post-disaster activities. "The California Department of Transportation (Caltrans) was called in to help clear earthquake rubble from the streets. Media personnel reportedly contributed to the crowd problems that made it impossible to safely remove the debris. As a result, Caltrans threatened to remove its equipment altogether unless the traffic could be cleared" (Auf der Heide 1987, Chapter 10, p. 8).

4. **Creation of safety problems.** The media often puts their own reporters in danger by asking them to report from cities that are expecting to be hit by hurricanes or affected by earthquake aftershocks. Also, they will arrive at the scene quickly, before security arrangements and procedures can be established. Often there are so many news helicopters in the air at the disaster scene that the chance for mid-air collisions between the rescue helicopters and the media helicopters increases. In the case of conflict disasters, terrorists often want to speak to members of the media. This communication could cause an escalation of violent behavior and hinder law enforcement functions.

5. **Lack of technical understanding.** Media personnel, especially television personalities, were not hired for their scientific expertise. They are intelligent,

communicators, but they are generalists and not specialists. Many media representatives do not understand the technical aspects of stories. They will often incorrectly report details or misinterpret statements from experts.

6. **Misrepresentations and perpetuation of myths.** The media reported rumors of rape and murder in New Orleans during Hurricane Katrina that were never substantiated. Despite the fact that there were not any witnesses and that the story was retracted several days later, many people still believe that people were killed in the New Orleans Superdome and Convention Center. Although looting did occur during Hurricanes Andrew and Katrina, not everyone was engaged in such behavior. Another example of this is the coverage of 9/11. During 9/11, the media reported that the State Department had been bombed. This was not true. The story was corrected hours later. There is always a lack of information in a disaster, and initial details are almost always wrong.

7. **Overstatement of impact.** "Another contention of some disaster researchers is that the media's preoccupation with the dramatic accentuates and exaggerates the destructive magnitude of disasters. This has been labeled the 'Dresden syndrome' (the media make every tornado-stricken community look like Dresden after it was bombed in World War II). News films and photographs focus on scenes of destruction, but not upon surrounding undamaged areas. The audience is often led to believe that the whole community lies in ruins on the basis of intense coverage of damage which may, in reality, be limited to a few buildings or blocks" (Auf der Heide 1987, Chapter 10, p. 6).

8. **Damage to individual or agency reputation.** The media can affect the credibility of leaders and organizations. For example, during Hurricane Katrina, the media was able to report that people had sought shelter in the Convention Center in New Orleans. The media reported on this before FEMA had been notified, making FEMA officials look like they were not as involved as they should have been.

Burkhart summarizes many of these problems: Sensationalizing disasters to build circulation, abusing victims, showing their bias, rushing into print, being less than formal, failing to attribute facts, neglecting to check back with sources, using pseudo experts, omitting important aspects, and failing to admit limitations (Burkhart 1987). These are a few of the challenges the media may create for you after a disaster.

7.1.3 Strategies for Working With the Media

You can take a number of steps to ensure successful media relations. These measures may be taken before, during, and after the disaster (as is the case with any other disaster response and recovery function). You will want to undertake the following activities so you and others can interact with the media effectively when disaster strikes (Scanlon et al 1985; Auf der Heide 1987):

▲ **Appoint a Public Information Officer (PIO).** Public Information Officers are members of a department that have special skills in dealing with the media. Their position could be full-time, or part of their job could include working with the media. This person may answer phone calls or be on-site during disasters to respond to questions from the press. The public information officer should be pleasant, professional, and able to think quickly. This person should be knowledgeable and articulate. In other words, you will want to make sure he or she projects a positive image as a representative of your department. Once appointed, the **PIO** can help you develop policies on how to handle the media. In time of a disaster, you may need to secure additional personnel to field media requests.

▲ **Get to know the media.** You will want to know what media exist and if they are prepared to operate in a disaster. You will also want to know the station manager or owner of the local television stations as well as the publishers of newspapers. "In many communities, media, law enforcement and other emergency service organizations meet regularly to discuss public information issues. These groups often meet bimonthly to discuss how to work together more effectively during complex, major incidents where media is involved (e.g., plane crash). Here it is important to give media personnel some basic understanding of hostage negotiation strategies, the tactical reasons for information dispersement, and other issues that affect media coverage" (Onder 1999, 26). Establishing rapport with the media will go a long way to ease communication during times of crisis.

▲ **Educate the media about disasters.** Explain to the media, for example, how a dispatch center works. They need to know that dispatchers don't have any additional information than what is heard over the scanner. Also teach the media about human behavior in disasters, that panic does not often occur. The media should also be told that any adjustments to carefully worded official statements can change the meaning dramatically and cause problems for you as an emergency manager.

▲ **Know your audience and media market.** You will want to be sure that you reach everyone through the media. If a large part of your population is Hispanic, for example, be sure to work with the Spanish-speaking stations as well.

▲ **Establish agreements.** You can enter into agreements with local wire services and AP and UPI to provide accurate information quickly. In exchange, these services will not bother you as long as they are getting the details they desire.

During response and recovery operations, you also should help the media report the news. But be sure to do so with several points in mind. First, you will need to determine the location of briefings. Will they be at the scene of a disaster or in the emergency operations center (EOC)? Or, will a media staging area be established, preferably one that is accessible to all responding agencies (Onder 1999, 26)? Regardless of the specified location, you can establish rules as a condition of access. This will help to ensure that the media will operate in accordance with your requirements. You will also need to decide how often you will brief them. It is recommended that this take place at least twice a day after a disaster. At times it will be necessary to brief them and answer their questions more often, but do not allow them to dictate your schedule. This will take away from other disaster operations you need to be involved in.

You will also need to ensure the safety of the media and others. Keep close tabs on them in any type of disaster as the location could be extremely dangerous. That last thing that is needed in a disaster is more injuries and deaths. In addition, monitor media activities during criminal or terrorist incidents. Members of the media shouldn't try to negotiate with terrorists or hostage takers. Any piece of information that could compromise the SWAT team members and police tactics should not be broadcasted.

Another step is to recognize what the media is searching for and avoid providing unnecessary information. Obtain the facts before you communicate with the media, and be careful about limiting information. If you do not know the answer to a question, do not hesitate to say, "I don't know." Later on, you can provide the reporter with the correct information. You will likewise want to avoid saying, "no comment." To the media, this implies that you are hiding something. Although you may not disclose everything the media wants to know, be sure you don't give them the impression that that is exactly what you are doing. Also, know that everything you say will likely be reported or published. Nothing is "off-the-record." You will want to present any information you give in simple terms. Avoid using jargon and technical terms to ensure accurate communication. Be sure PIOs are visible and that all department leaders are coordinating to ensure a unified voice.

The final thing you will want to do is to track and periodically evaluate media reporting. Recording interviews can encourage media to be as careful as possible about how they portray your comments. You may also want to review media reports constantly so you can issue any corrections if needed. Recording media reports also helps you evaluate how well your department came across in its public relations efforts and if you need to make any changes to your communications plan in the future. Keeping copies of any positive press you receive may be useful during evaluations and assessments of the organization. If other agencies received good press, you could send them copies with notes thanking them for their contribution.

FOR EXAMPLE

Media Briefings in War

War is a conflict disaster that requires unique coordination with the media. In the past, journalists were not allowed to report on wars. What was largely seen as a public relations move by the Pentagon was the process of "embedding" media with infantry units during the Iraqi war. Members of the media were assigned to a unit. They would ride in the humvees and report on the action they saw. This gave the media immediate access to the front lines on a very timely basis. The safety of the reporters is a big concern, however. Some members of the media lost their lives covering the war. One columnist, Michael Kelly, was killed in Iraq when the humvee he was riding in was trying to evade enemy fire. Another concern of the armed forces is that they do not want the media to broadcast their position or tactics to the enemy. Geraldo Rivera was a journalist who diagrammed troop movement in the sand. He was later removed from the infantry unit. The behavior of reporters in war may have similar implications for disaster response and recovery operations. Safety and content of what is being reported are extremely important to you as an emergency manager.

SELF-CHECK

- Why is the media important to the emergency manager?
- What types of media exist and what type of information or material do they seek?
- What potential problems may result from the media in disasters?
- How can you manage the media in a disaster situation?

7.2 Dealing With Donations

When a disaster occurs, relatives, neighbors, and concerned citizens in other cities, states, and nations will send donations to the affected area. You must understand that this outpouring of donations is owing to several factors. People who have survived disaster feel the pains of those who have lost loved ones or material possessions, and they desire to ease the trials others are going through. Those close to the scene have witnessed the trauma inflicted by the event on individuals, families, and the community as a whole, and they desire to do something about it. Victims, public information officers, politicians, and reporters stress the need to get resources to the affected areas. Others far away from the disaster have seen the devastation on national news broadcasts and have heard the media's request for disaster assistance. Sometimes the request for assistance is not warranted. Kathy Guy, a FEMA donations coordinator, states "The media— particularly television is pretty bad about sticking a microphone in people's faces right after a disaster so they can film them saying 'We need everything'" (Kim 1999a). Although the generosity is heartwarming, the overabundance of donations creates a second disaster for you as an emergency manager.

A variety of donations will arrive in the disaster-affected community, often in very large quantities. Here are some examples of donations in past disasters:

1. Anheuser Busch frequently supplies pallets of canned drinking water to victims and workers after a disaster (Mravcak 1994).
2. There was excessive amounts of ice after a hurricane affected many Northeastern states in 2003.
3. The GM Foundation provided numerous vehicles to those in need after an earthquake in California (Mravcak 1994).
4. After a tornado in Kansas, the Salvation Army received enough clothes to fill a 50-foot warehouse (Kim 1999a).

Another example comes after a tornado struck Fort Worth, Texas on March 28, 2000. It was reported that pizza, hamburgers, fruit, and other food was delivered by local restaurants and grocery stores to the emergency operations center. Home improvement stores also distributed stacks of plywood to victims and owners who needed to make quick repairs to protect homes and office buildings. Cash was donated to the American Red Cross tornado fund. Calls came in from around the world offering additional support (McEntire 2002, 374).

Similar findings were evident after the 9/11 terrorist attacks in New York City. Many of the donations were provided by the private sector. For example, a manager of a sporting goods store allowed first responders to use his store as a shelter when the buildings collapsed. The manager then provided swimming goggles and socks to equip responders so they could continue their life-saving activities. The U.S. Forest Service received containers of coffee from Starbucks for personnel at the staging area near ground zero. Those responding to the terrorist attack donned overalls and other protective equipment provided by various manufacturers. Respirators and mask cartridges were given to search and rescue teams to alleviate breathing problems created by fire, smoke, and unknown particulate matter. Gloves, batteries, and other supplies were sent by private companies to help as well (McEntire, Robinson, and Weber 2003, 452).

Other common donations sent to disaster areas include (see Figure 7-1):

▲ Medicines
▲ Diapers

Figure 7-1

Emergency managers are often overwhelmed with the volume of supplies that are donated in the aftermath of a disaster.

▲ Baby formula

▲ Coats

▲ Shampoo

▲ Soap

▲ Cots

▲ Sleeping bags

▲ Tents

7.2.1 Challenges Resulting From Donations

Donations can prove useful in times of need. However, people's generosity may present several challenges for those involved in disaster response and recovery. Some of the problems may be in regard to the quantity of donations. There are often too many donations. Clothing often falls into this category. An alternative situation is where there may be insufficient donations. There may be a limited number of generators to meet the high demand for electricity when power is out.

Other problems may result from the quality of the donations (McEntire 1997). Most donations are not requested or needed. A pallet of dog food arrived in New York City after 9/11 for the canines involved in body recovery. Unfortunately, the search and rescue dogs have a regimented diet, so the food was not used. Some donations are not helpful for other reasons. Medicines have no labels or are damaged or expired. Other goods are not applicable to the disaster context. Coats are sent to warmer regions of the United States. Donations may not be culturally acceptable to some disaster victims. Followers of certain religions may not eat certain types of food (e.g., pork or other meats). Ethnic groups may prefer their own cuisine, rather than American food.

Excessive and unwanted donations result in additional work (Neal 1994). Donations have to be transported from the donors to the disaster area. Donations also have to be stored until they can be given to disaster victims. After a flood in southwest Texas, a relief organization had to rent a 25,000-square-foot warehouse for donations (Kim 1999c). Donations also need to be sorted by type, size, purpose, etc. After a 1952 tornado in Arkansas, it took 500 volunteers 2 weeks to sort through donations to determine what could be used (Neal 1994, 23).

Donations must finally be distributed to those in need. All of this results in incredible logistical challenges for emergency and relief workers. To illustrate these points, we will look at three important disaster case studies: Hurricane Andrew, the Oklahoma City bombing, and the terrorist attacks of 9/11.

Hurricane Andrew

On August 24, 1992, a major hurricane struck South Florida. The category 4 hurricane, with sustained winds of at least 141 mph and a storm surge of up to

Figure 7-2

Hurricane Andrew devastated Miami in 1992 and donations were used to help those in shelters.

16 feet, pummeled Dade County. The hurricane left 170,000 homes in partial or complete ruin, resulting in 250,000 people being homeless. The storm killed over 40 people and injured hundreds more.

As the extent of the devastation was recognized, a massive donations campaign was undertaken. This proved to be problematic at times, however (Neal 1994). People were encouraged to donate food through food drives that were coordinated by local businesses such as grocery stores and television stations. As a result, too much food was donated. The thousands of cans of food caused distribution, sorting, and cooking problems. For instance, cans of food are difficult to distribute because they are often placed in small boxes without pallets. Then the boxes of food have to be shipped and eventually sorted into logical categories by mass kitchen cooks, which takes a considerable amount of time. Even the process of opening the cans takes valuable amounts of time away from other relief efforts. In disasters where the power is lost, each can has to be opened without the aid of electric can openers.

Whereas these food donations were useful but labor intensive, other donations were not needed and may have been counterproductive. Many winter coats, for example, were donated, but they have little use by Miami residents. Other clothing was sent to Florida on trucks, but the drivers sometimes did not know where to deliver them. In this situation, they would dump them on the side of the road. The heat and the rain rotted the clothes, causing a potential health hazard. Volunteers and city workers had to remove the clothing, which took time away from other recovery activities. Even when clothing got to its desired destination, some of it was dirty and had to be cleaned. Unfortunately, there was a lack of personnel, electricity, and water to clean them in a time-effective manner.

In time, the amount of donations quickly overwhelmed the ability of disaster organizations to deal with them. The Red Cross became so inundated with donations of goods and food that it began asking for cash-only contributions 2 weeks after the incident. The Salvation Army had originally requested diapers, food, and cash, but it also altered its request for financial donations. This option has since become popular among nonprofit organizations involved in disaster response and recovery operations.

The management of donations in Hurricane Andrew also damaged public relations efforts. Neal's research reveals that "news reports and videos throughout the U.S. showing rotting clothing, warehouses overflowing with supplies and bulging trucks full of donations being turned back, created two related images. Reports implied that further donations were not needed. This was not the case. Organizations needed money or specific donations (e.g. institutionalized food) to assist victims. Images of city work crews or the military carting away rotting clothes could imply to viewer that organizations such as the Red Cross or Salvation Army did not appreciate the donations. Simultaneously, organizations continued to request donations (e.g., money)" (Neal 1994, 27). You must learn from the problems of donation management after Hurricane Andrew.

Oklahoma City Bombing

On the morning of Wednesday, April 19, 1995, a disgruntled American used a 24-foot Ryder rental truck to deliver an ammonium nitrate and diesel fuel bomb to the Alfred P. Murrah Federal Building in Oklahoma City, Oklahoma. A detonation cord was used to set off the explosive mixture. The resulting blast destroyed approximately one-third of the building. Major portions of the nine floors crashed on top of one another as they fell to the ground. A pile of rubble and debris was left in its wake. Vehicles in the parking lot and in the street were flipped over and caught on fire. Several nearby buildings received heavy damages. Structural impact was extended over a 48-square-block area.

The bomb also killed 168 people, virtually all of whom were working in or visiting the Murrah Building. Some of the deaths occurred in surrounding buildings, and one emergency worker died when debris fell on a nurse as she was responding to the incident. Out of those 168 people, 19 children were killed (the building had an on-site daycare facility). This news especially affected people around the world.

As the responders worked to locate survivors, remove victims, and process the crime scene, donations began to arrive in the area. Southwestern Bell donated the use of a "cellular-on-wheels" tower, with free-use phone to anyone responding to the incident. Voluntary organizations brought in food to feed emergency workers. The Oklahoma Department of Civil Emergency Management noted how this took place:

> *"The Oklahoma Restaurant Association had just finished their annual conference when the explosion occurred. Subsequently, they quickly established a 24-hour food service operation, at the Myriad Convention Center, to feed all emergency response workers. Eventually, the Myriad was established as a center which met the needs of all personnel responding to the incident"* (ODCEM 1995, 8).

It also observed that:

> *"Donated clothing, food, equipment and supplies were available on a 24-hour basis. Other volunteer and donated services included over-the-counter pharmaceutical and personal hygiene items, hair care, optometric, chiropractic, and podiatric care and massage therapy. AT&T provided free telephone calls home for the US&R Task Forces, complimented by a free mail and parcel delivery service provided by the United Parcel Service"* (ODCEM 1995, 8).

Several efforts were made to coordinate the reception and distribution of donations. The Red Cross made logistical arrangements for donations management from a nearby U.S. Post Office. The Red Cross also established a warehouse at a Coca-Cola plant for donations staging.

The government was also heavily involved in donations management. On April 22, FEMA sent a Donations Coordination Team to the Disaster Field Office.

An In-Kind Donations Coordination Team was established at the Disaster Field Office and included representatives of FEMA, ODCEM, and voluntary organizations. The team's responsibilities were to (ODCEM 1995, 13):

▲ Process information provided by FEMA's toll-free donations hotline
▲ Establish a single, coordinated, unmet needs list
▲ Provide direct communication with the MACC (multi-agency coordination center)
▲ Address the management of spontaneous volunteers
▲ Provide a liaison to the local business community
▲ Share information concerning warehouse space and current inventory (ODCEM 1995, 13)

On April 25, Lt. Governor Mary Fallin participated in the Donation Coordination Team meeting. At this meeting, it was decided that there was no longer a need for mass quantities of goods, and a press release was issued accordingly. On April 26, 1995, a Donations Task Force was identified. Representatives to this task force were state personnel, federal officials, representatives from charities, and members of the local business community. The Donations Task Force was to address items needed by those affected by the blast. They also had to address items needed by individuals and organizations working within the blast area. The task force was not asked to try to meet the long-term needs of victims (ODCEM 1995, 13).

On Saturday, May 6, 1995, the FEMA Donations Team started to return unused goods to original donors. By the middle of May, the donations distribution centers closed down, and an unmet needs committee was formed to deal with long-term disaster assistance issues (see Wedel and Baker 1998). An **unmet needs committee** is a group of government leaders, concerned citizens, business representatives, and nonprofit organizations who join forces to help collect donations to address long-term needs of disaster victims.

The management of donations after the Oklahoma City bombing was regarded to be a successful operation. The responsiveness, teamwork, and caring incurred on the part of all first responders was a big factor. The American Red Cross and other voluntary organizations' responses were immediate. They continued to meet the needs of all of those affected by disaster. Communication support from Cellular One, Southwestern Bell, was superb as they loaned equipment and donated services to the responders. Many officials indicated that city, county, state, and federal response procedures for this incident were a model for future response and recovery operations. Urban Search and Rescue Task Force members commented regularly that they had never been treated so well and that the care and compassion they received had become known as "The Oklahoma Standard." (ODCEM 1995, 18).

Despite the notable successes, there were a few areas where improvement was needed (ODCEM 1995). Those dealing with the massive outpouring did not have an adequate plan in place to identify incoming resources. They could not effectively manage the initial staging area for donations during the first 2 days of the event. Furthermore, it did not appear that there were sufficient personnel to handle the donation challenges this disaster presented. Property accountability at the staging areas and donated goods accountability were virtually nonexistent during the major portion of the incident. In-kind donations management was nonexistent during the initial days of this incident. It was also difficult to send resources to the right place at the right time. You should anticipate these types of problems in most disasters.

9/11 Terrorist Attacks

On the morning of September 11, 2001, several teams of hijackers boarded planes and began the largest and most coordinated terrorist attack on U.S. soil. An American airlines jet headed from Boston to Los Angeles was overtaken by men with box cutters and intentionally crashed into the north tower of the World Trade Center. A short time later, a United Airlines plane, also departing from Boston to Los Angeles, was hijacked and flown into the south tower at the World Trade Center. A third flight went down in Pennsylvania, with the passengers wrestling control away from the hijackers. A fourth plane hit the Pentagon.

Within minutes, hundreds of people were dead. The resulting fires spread throughout the Twin Towers in New York. The massive structures weakened and collapsed as can be seen in Figure 7-3. As the dust settled, the carnage was broadcast on all news networks. World Trade Center employees, firefighters, police officers, and spontaneous volunteers were killed by the hijackings, crashes, fires, and structural failures. Destruction, injury, and death were also seen in Pennsylvania and Virginia.

People were stunned that anyone would desire to perform such a deadly act, and their hearts turned to those who had lost loved ones and the heroic efforts of emergency workers. Over the next few days and months, a large and diverse collection of donations flowed into the area from around the nation and world. The donations included:

▲ A massive blood drive in New York and around the United States for the injured

▲ Food and drinks provided to thousands of emergency personnel

▲ Gear and equipment for search and rescue teams

▲ Computers, phones, fax machines, and other office supplies given to the new emergency operations center in New York (as the established center was destroyed in the collapse)

▲ Fire apparatus, heavy equipment, and cranes sent to replace losses or help with debris removal

Figure 7-3

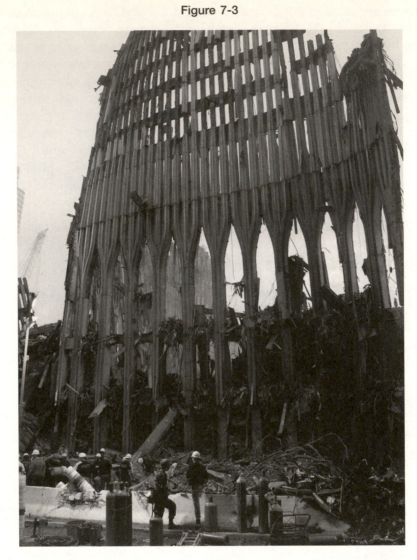

Images of the 9/11 destruction sparked an outpouring of donations.

Recognizing the enormous loss of life and resulting expenses in terms of medical care, funeral costs, and future needs of surviving spouses and children, the American Red Cross welcomed and encouraged financial contributions via cash, check, and credit card donations. The response to the American Red Cross and other charities was overwhelming. According to the Ford Foundation, 58% of all Americans contributed to a fund for the 9/11 victims. Donations to the American Red Cross totaled over $543 million by October 31, 2001. The Red Cross was so overwhelmed that it stopped asking for donations. However, people kept giving. By June of 2002, an additional $424 million was sent to the Red Cross.

There was a total of $1.3 billion for the victims of the 9/11 disasters. This pool of money became known as the "Liberty Fund."

While this large sum of money rolled in, the Red Cross decided to keep some of the donations as a reserve for future disasters. Dr. Bernadine Healy, the chief executive officer of the American Red Cross, announced plans to retain $200 million for potential future terrorist attacks and other disasters. In some ways, the strategy made sense (Harbaugh 2001). Any division of the Liberty Fund would undoubtedly ensure that victims in New York would receive a much larger allotment compared with those affected by other disasters. The victims of the U.S. Embassy bombings in Tanzania and Kenya, for example, did not receive nearly the amount of money that the 9/11 survivors did. Nor did the survivors of the Oklahoma City Bombing. Also, resources are always tight for this disaster relief organization. A reserve fund could ensure operations well into the future.

Nonetheless, there was an immediate outcry regarding the decision of the Red Cross. The media quickly publicized the organization's position about the donations. Donors and victims decried the plan as a misuse of funds. Lawmakers also criticized the misleading of donors and requested that all of the funds be used for the victims of 9/11.

Because of the negative press and pressure to utilize the funds as intended by the donors, the Red Cross immediately changed its position. It promised to spend half of the funds on cash grants for the affected families by December 31, 2001. The Red Cross would cover up to 1 year's worth of living expenses for those in need. The remaining funds would be used to hire 200 caseworkers to assist the disaster victims and their surviving families. The Red Cross also agreed to develop a database with other charitable organizations to oversee the distribution of all of the remaining money.

The American Red Cross learned a difficult lesson from the experience. Under significant public scrutiny, Dr. Healy resigned her leadership position. The agency was accused of "using the September 11 tragedies to address long-term fund-raising goals and of siphoning tens of millions of dollars from widows and children" (Henriques and Barstow 2001). The reputation of the American Red Cross had been tarnished. This resulted in fund-raising problems for several months after the 9/11 disasters. The Red Cross realized that it had to be upfront with its intentions to use donations and make sure that its plans were in conformity with public opinion.

7.2.2 Recommendations for Donations Management

As can be seen, donations are not always easy to deal with when a disaster occurs. For this reason, you will need to give extra attention to donations management. **Donations management** is the receipt, sorting, storing, and distribution of goods and monies for the benefit of victims in response and recovery operations. One of the best ways to increase the chance of a successful donations management campaign is to conduct a very thorough needs assessment so that your requests for donations will be accurate. A **needs assessment** is an evaluation of what supplies or services are required in the aftermath of a disaster. Such assessments will help you request those items that will be most beneficial. The U.S. Army Corps of Engineers has models of what will be needed in the way of water and food after hurricanes of various sizes. The model also discusses how to set up distribution sites, which can help streamline relief operations after disasters (see http://www.englink.usace.army.mil/igp/commodities.htm).

Another major recommendation is to expect and be prepared to deal with massive quantities of both requested and unrequested donations. You will probably get most of what you ask for and even more when you work through the media. The best thing you can do is avoid asking for too many in-kind donations. Cash donations are preferred instead because they allow the most flexibility and can permit you to purchase needed resources locally (and thereby promote the affected economy).

▲ **In-kind donations** are physical items such as supplies, equipment, food, etc.
▲ **Cash donations** are financial contributions to disaster organizations or the victims themselves.

It is also vital that you ensure that donors know and agree with your plans for donations. This will help you avoid the public relations problems that confronted the American Red Cross after the 9/11 terrorist attacks.

One of the most important steps is to work closely with the nonprofit sector. They often have unique skills and knowledge to deal with in-kind or monetary donations. Businesses may also provide supplies and equipment in bulk, thereby eliminating the need to seek donations from the general public. Regardless of who you are working with, be sure to hold meetings to coordinate the receipt, storage, distribution, disposal, or return of donations. These can include regular gatherings at warehouses, EOCs, or among local, state, and federal donations committees.

It is also advisable that you have forms or computer programs to track donation needs, donor contact information, donation quantities, drop off/pick up

FOR EXAMPLE

9/11 Donations From Around the World

The 9/11 terrorist attacks touched people in every corner of the word. The Masai tribe in Kenya donated 14 cows to the victims in New York. Cows are the most cherished possession for the people of Masai as they are sacred animals. The American government initially rejected the donation, not knowing what to do with 14 cows. They later formed a plan and accepted the cows. They were shipped to the Bronx zoo, where they can be enjoyed by adults and children alike. This situation is unusual, but emergency managers should always expect the unexpected.

locations, etc. Having adequately trained individuals to receive phone inquiries will also be of great assistance. Make sure that they can create shipping agreements, locate storage facilities, operate fort lifts, organize warehouses, etc. It is imperative that donations get to the right place at the right time and in the right quantities. If you are involved in donations management, you must pay attention to detail.

SELF-CHECK

- Why are so many donations sent to the site of a disaster?
- What donations are likely to be given in a disaster?
- Why do donations create problems for emergency managers?
- What lessons are learned from case studies on donations?
- What is **donations management** and how can it be performed successfully?

7.3 Volunteer Management

As an emergency manager, you must expect that people want to donate their time and services when a disaster occurs. Ordinary citizens become involved in post-disaster operations to assist you, first responders, and victims. As with donations, there are many positive outcomes. There are also challenges associated with the incorporation of volunteers in disaster response and recovery operations. This process of including volunteers in post-disaster operations in such a way as to harness their contributions and avoid their negative impact is known as **volunteer management.**

When a disaster strikes, there will likely be hundreds if not thousands of people rushing to the scene to assist in response and recovery activities. Some of these people are referred to as spontaneous or unaffiliated volunteers. **Spontaneous or unaffiliated volunteers** are people who engage in response and recovery efforts with no thought of payment; their efforts are directed toward the benefit of victims, first responders, emergency managers, and the community at large (Lowe and Fothergill 2003). Such volunteers may have specific skills that can be extremely useful in response and recovery operations. For example, off-duty policemen, doctors, translators, and counselors all rushed to the World Trade Center to help after the terrorist attacks. These professionals had specific knowledge and abilities that could be utilized immediately. Others may not possess skills that can be used in disaster operations, but they have a desire to help nonetheless. Most of these people will come from the impacted or surrounding areas. Other individuals and groups may not be residents of the area. For instance, even celebrities such as Sean Penn, Jamie Foxx, John Travolta, and Harry Connick Jr. arrived at the scene of Hurricane Katrina to bring attention to their plight.

There are also large numbers of volunteers who are affiliated with organizations such as the Red Cross, churches, and the Salvation Army. Volunteers who are affiliated with organizations may have common characteristics, may have been involved in post-disaster operations before, and may become involved in all aspects of post-disaster operations. For instance, many will be women or retired persons. They worked with disaster, charitable, or faith-based organizations in the past. Such volunteers help firefighters, public officials, and disaster victims in various response and recovery functions.

Regardless of their background and activities, volunteers have a strong desire to assist in the response and recovery effort. For instance, regarding the 9/11 terrorist attacks, scholars discovered:

> *"87% of Americans thought it was the 'most tragic event in their life-time'"* (Kendra and Wachtendorf 2003, 98).
>
> *"Volunteers were emotionally impacted by the disaster and personalized the attacks as members of the community affected, which appeared to have contributed to their heightened feelings of victimization. Many of them explained that when they saw the destruction they knew that they had to do something—they needed to help"* (Lowe and Fothergill 2003, 298).
>
> *"The primary motivation for volunteering was a compelling need to help in some way, particularly a need to assist victims, and a desire—even obsession—to 'do something' in order to contribute something positive and find something meaningful in the midst of disaster characterized by cruelty and terror"* (Lowe and Fothergill 2003, 298).

Therefore, volunteering gives ordinary citizens a sense of "interconnection, healing, and empowerment" after a disaster (Lowe and Fothergill 2003, 303).

There are significant advantages resulting from the integration of volunteers into disaster response and recovery operations. Volunteers can fulfill many functions after a disaster (see Figure 7-4). Here is a partial list that shows the variety of tasks volunteers have participated in:

▲ Sandbagging in case of flooding
▲ Cleaning up the scene
▲ Staffing shelters
▲ Keeping records of who is in shelters
▲ Handing out water and other supplies to victims
▲ Providing healthcare services
▲ Counseling victims
▲ Preparing food
▲ Making beds for emergency workers

Figure 7-4

Emergency managers are often overwhelmed with the number of volunteers who arrive at a disaster site.

▲ Setting up websites
▲ Working with affected businesses to help them resume activity
▲ Working with collection drives
▲ Sorting donations

Volunteers are crucial to any disaster response and recovery operation. FEMA said this about volunteers: they are involved in all phases of disasters, first to arrive and last to leave, trusted by the public, community based, flexible, innovative, resourceful, and a complement to government services (1999, 1.5-1.8).

7.3.1 Difficulties Associated With Volunteers

As noted above, volunteers can be very helpful to you as well as victims, first responders, and the community as a whole. However, volunteers are not without potential drawbacks. The challenges they bring to response and recovery operations include:

▲ **Lack of skills.** Volunteers may lack the necessary training or skills that are needed for a particular disaster. Some may be willing to help, but they are not able to operate heavy equipment, drive donations to warehouses, or perform data entry on distinct types of computer programs.

▲ **Number.** The sheer number of volunteers can be overwhelming to manage. For example, 2.5 weeks after 9/11, the Red Cross had 22,000 people volunteer (Lowe and Fothergill 2003, 294). Each volunteer may be required to complete an application that has to be reviewed and matched up with the needs. Processing the quantity of applications takes a lot of human resources.

▲ **Safety.** As with the media, volunteers create additional concerns about safety. Volunteers can put themselves in danger, especially if they rush to a site of a disaster immediately. A volunteer could also claim to have skills that he or she does not have and thereby put the victims at risk. Also, a terrorist could pose as a volunteer and kill more people.

▲ **Frustration.** Volunteers often get frustrated if they cannot help. Part of this may be due to their lack of skills, their excessive numbers, or restrictions based on safety concerns. Volunteers become offended if they see a need, are willing to sacrifice their time, and cannot be successfully incorporated into the response process. Volunteers may then complain to the media about their skills not being used, and this will cause poor public relations. Also, in New York after 9/11, "the spontaneous volunteers . . . described frustrations of long lines, uncoordinated leadership, disorganized lists, and unclear information about what to do immediately after the attacks" (Lowe and Fothergill 2003, 300). In some cases, volunteers cut in line or walked into relief centers without authorization because they didn't want to wait and they knew their skills were needed as a translator (Lowe and Fothergill 2003, 301). Even if they are incorporated into the response process, volunteers may not be given sufficient direction or supervision. This can further exacerbate a feeling of frustration on their part or for you as an emergency manager.

7.3.2 Strategies for Volunteer Management

The problems associated with volunteers are challenging but not insurmountable. You can increase the chances for successful volunteer management before and after a disaster. To do this, you need to rely on the expertise of nonprofit organizations, register and care for volunteers, match their skills with disaster needs, and evaluate your progress.

Rely on the Expertise of Nonprofit Organizations and Others

When a disaster occurs, it is important that you work closely with potential partners and volunteer sources. These partners may include your local Red Cross and Salvation Army chapters, churches, the medical staff at hospitals, and other local nonprofit organizations. You should harness their extensive experience in volunteer management, determine what capabilities they have, and identify what skill sets their volunteers offer. You can also create a public campaign with your partners and let citizens know what you may need in terms of volunteers. You will also want to communicate with the media to notify them about the measures that volunteers can take to help you and the disaster victims and to thank them for their service. If used correctly, the media can be another great asset for volunteer management.

Register and Care for Volunteers

To manage volunteers successfully, you will need to implement a logical strategy to incorporate them into the response and recovery process. You should consider setting up a toll-free, dedicated line for volunteers to call in and inquire about what they can do to help. You will also want to set up a volunteer reception center that is visible, accessible, and close to the disaster site. This on-site registration center should be staffed by experienced employees or volunteers. It may therefore be wise to set up a volunteer coordination team to help the volunteers through the process of registration. During registration, you will want to screen volunteers to learn about their potential contributions and ensure you don't have any criminals take advantage of the situation (e.g., put a sexual offender in charge of a child's day care group). The database of volunteers you create can be used in response and recovery operations as well as in other disasters. If needed, you should provide mental health counseling or healthcare services to volunteers participating in response and recovery operations. You may also need to provide them food, water, and shelter.

Match Their Skills With Disaster Needs

Be sure you develop key documents that include all instructions for volunteers as well as policies and procedures. The Volunteer Management Committee recommends that you "develop streamlined registration, screening, and interviewing procedures for unaffiliated volunteers that include: databases that catalogs needed skills, information about individual volunteers (for example: skills, interests, availability, geographic location), contact information for voluntary organizations, tasks, roles and time commitment requirements for individuals and groups of volunteers, approximate number of volunteers needed to perform tasks, compatibility of relevant computer systems, back-up plan for power failures and portability" (2003, 7). Such documents can help you match the skills of volunteers to the needs made evident in the disaster.

Evaluate Progress

As with donations management, you will want to review volunteer activities periodically and determine what is being done correctly and what could be improved on. Be sure to use feedback from organizations and volunteers as they might have special insight into what is taking place. While managing volunteers, you will want to document all important facts about them. For example, you will want to record how many volunteers you had, how many hours they served, what functions they performed, and then assign some kind of dollar figure as to the value of services provided by volunteers. This is especially important as there is a chance your community might be reimbursed for such activities under federal disaster assistance programs. When post-disaster operations conclude, you will also want to write up an after-action report. An **after-action report** is a document that describes what went right and what adjustments you will need to make in the future.

7.3.3 Advantages of Volunteer Management

If you are able to manage volunteers effectively, your community will receive many benefits. The Points of Light Foundation has recognized numerous advantages of effective disaster volunteer management. For instance:

▲ "First responders can fulfill their duties without the added responsibility of managing volunteers.

▲ Experienced volunteer coordinators can manage volunteers, to ensure meaningful and quality experiences. As a result, volunteers are more inclined to seek future community service opportunities . . .

▲ Communities will know how to effectively engage citizens as volunteers in all phases of disasters.

▲ Communities can respond to and heal from disasters more effectively when volunteer efforts are well managed" (Points of Light 2002, 4).

For these and other reasons, "our society can ill afford to ignore the potential capacity of its citizens to help improve conditions in their communities, especially in times of disaster" (Points of Light 2002, 3).

SELF-CHECK

- Why are people willing to serve after a disaster?
- What is **volunteer management?**
- Do volunteers pose any problems in emergency management?
- What recommendations can help with volunteer management?
- What are the benefits of integrating volunteers into response and recovery operations?

FOR EXAMPLE

Red Cross and Hurricane Katrina

The American Red Cross worked closely with thousands of volunteers after Hurricane Katrina. Although the Red Cross was criticized for not meeting the needs of people in a timely manner, the Red Cross had to screen and train thousands of volunteers. It also processed 35,000 requests for aid per day. Here are some additional statistics regarding the services they provided:

▲ Estimated number of Hurricane Katrina victims dispersed across the country: 750,000

▲ Number of surviving families provided Red Cross financial assistance: 929,000

▲ Number of Red Cross shelters open to hurricane victims: 1,150

▲ Number of hurricane victims still provided Red Cross housing at shelters and hotels: 483,000

▲ Amount paid out in Red Cross emergency financial assistance to hurricane survivors: $854 million

▲ Amount Red Cross has spent to date on Hurricane Katrina relief efforts: $1.3 billion

▲ Amount in gifts and pledges received by the Red Cross for hurricane relief: $1.1 billion

▲ Amount the Red Cross expects to need for hurricane relief efforts: $2 billion

▲ Number of Red Cross relief workers mobilized in response to Hurricane Katrina: 177,600

▲ Estimated number of people left homeless in Hancock County, Mississippi due to Hurricane Katrina: 30,000 (source: Hancock County Emergency Operations Center)

▲ Population of Hancock County, Mississippi: 46,000 (source: U.S. Census Bureau)

Source: The American Red Cross, except as noted; all data as of Oct. 5, 2005.

SUMMARY

After a disaster, you will be faced with many challenges. The media will arrive to report on the disaster, and they will want to interview you and others in your community. Citizens and organizations will send tons of donations, which you will have to sort and distribute. Thousands of volunteers will arrive at the disaster to offer their services, and they expect to be put to work. By doing your best to manage public information, donations, and volunteers, you will increase the effectiveness of response and speed of recovery. These steps are keys to resilience.

KEY TERMS

After-action report	A document that describes what went right and what adjustments you will need to make in the future.
Cash donations	Financial contributions to disaster organizations or the victims themselves.
Donations management	The receipt, sorting, storing, and distribution of goods and monies for the benefit of victims during response and recovery operations.
In-kind donations	Physical items such as supplies, equipment, and food.
Media	People and news organizations that provide information about disasters to the public.
Needs assessment	An evaluation of what supplies or services are required in the aftermath of a disaster.
Public Information Officers	Members of a department that have special skills in dealing with the media.
Spontaneous or unaffiliated volunteers	People who engage in response and recovery efforts with no thought of payment; their efforts are directed toward the benefit of victims, first responders, emergency managers, and the community at large.
Unmet needs committee	A group of government leaders, concerned citizens, business representatives, and nonprofit organizations who join forces to help collect donations to address long-term needs of disaster victims.
Volunteer management	The process of including volunteers in post-disaster operations in such a way as to harness their contributions and avoid their negative impact.

ASSESS YOUR UNDERSTANDING

Go to www.wiley.com/college/McEntire to evaluate your knowledge of the basics of managing public relations, donations, and volunteers during disasters. *Measure your learning by comparing pretest and post-test results.*

Summary Questions

1. The media includes reporters, camera operators, and new anchors that provide information to the public. True or False?

2. The local media will focus more than other media on what the president does after a disaster. True or False?

3. The media tends to react to most disasters in the same way. True or False?

4. The media is always sensitive to disaster victims. True or False?

5. It is vital that you know your audience and media market. True or False?

6. People donate supplies because they are eager to help those affected by a disaster. True or False?

7. Baby formula and coats are atypical disaster donations. True or False?

8. The donation of clothing caused major problems after Hurricane Andrew. True or False?

9. Donations management was fairly successful in Oklahoma after the bombing of the Murrah Building. True or False?

10. It is generally advisable that people donate cash instead of in-kind supplies. True or False?

11. Spontaneous volunteers are always related to nonprofit organizations such as the Red Cross. True or False?

12. Volunteers can help with sandbagging but not with food preparation. True or False?

13. Some volunteers may not have skills that can be utilized after a disaster. True or False?

14. To manage volunteers successfully, you will need to match their skills with the needs made evident in the disaster. True or False?

15. Television coverage of disasters includes:

    (a) Interviews only

    (b) Extensive examination of the issues most of the time

    (c) Footage of the disaster scene and what people are doing as a result

    (d) Reporters but not the comments of politicians

    (e) None of the above

16. According to Payne (1994), what are common problems created by the media?
    (a) Intrusive manner
    (b) Lack of sensitivity
    (c) Uncooperative attitude
    (d) Inaccurate reporting
    (e) All of the above

17. As an emergency manager, you should know that the media might:
    (a) Create safety problems for themselves and others
    (b) Fully understand technical information
    (c) Underestimate impact almost all of the time
    (d) Improve your agency's reputation in most cases
    (e) All of the above

18. It is okay to tell the media:
    (a) I don't know
    (b) I don't know, but I'll find out for you as soon as I can
    (c) I won't comment on that
    (d) That is off the record
    (e) c and d

19. After disasters, people have donated:
    (a) Vehicles
    (b) Canned drinking water
    (c) Diapers
    (d) All of the above
    (e) b and c

20. The goal of an unmet needs committee is to:
    (a) Collect donations and address long-term needs of disaster victims
    (b) Find volunteers to offer crisis counseling only
    (c) Assist with media relations
    (d) Assess hazards and their potential impact
    (e) Warn people of impending hazards

21. The money raised after the 9/11 terrorist attack was known as:
    (a) The Victims' Account
    (b) The WTC Memorial
    (c) The Freedom Fund
    (d) The Liberty Fund
    (e) The Mutual Fund

22. Supplies, equipment, and food are known best as:
    (a) In-kind donations
    (b) Cash donations
    (c) Donations management
    (d) Disaster relief
    (e) Recovery functions
23. Affiliated volunteers might be associated with:
    (a) The American Red Cross
    (b) The Salvation Army
    (c) Churches
    (d) Nonprofit organizations
    (e) All of the above
24. Difficulties of managing volunteers include:
    (a) Useful skills
    (b) Their large numbers
    (c) Safety
    (d) b and c
    (e) None of the above
25. When managing volunteers, it is advisable that you:
    (a) Rely on the expertise of nonprofit organizations
    (b) Register and care for victims
    (c) Ignore their skills and put them to work anywhere
    (d) a and b
    (e) b and c

Review Questions

1. Is the media a friend or foe of the emergency manager?
2. What types of media exist in your community, and what do they want?
3. How do the media operate in times of disaster?
4. What challenges do the media create for the emergency manager?
5. How can you improve public relations in times of disaster?
6. Why do people donate goods and supplies after a disaster?
7. What are common challenges associated with donations?
8. What does 9/11 teach us about donations management?
9. What is a needs assessment?
10. Why are cash donations often preferred over in-kind donations?

11. What is volunteer management?

12. Why did people want to volunteer after the 9/11 terrorist attacks?

13. Do volunteers become frustrated after disasters? Why or why not?

14. What steps can you take to manage volunteers effectively?

Applying This Chapter

1. On Saturday, September 13, a tropical depression develops in the Atlantic Ocean—nearly 2,000 miles away from the Southeastern shores of the United States. Meteorologists at the National Hurricane Center assert that it is far too early to determine the path of this weather system. You know that it will be vital to get information to the public so they can respond effectively. What steps do you take to handle the media? How will you use the media after the hurricane makes landfall?

2. A school has just burnt down in your community. The school district has found a temporary location to hold classes. They need desks and other school supplies. You have been assigned to relay these needs to the media. What concerns do you have? How can you overcome them?

3. You are the emergency manager for a town that just suffered an industrial explosion. The event killed fewer than 60 people and destroyed many homes and businesses. People are suffering from PTSD, and there is a great deal of debris in the roads. What are some of your immediate needs, and what skills are you looking for in volunteers?

4. A volcano has erupted in Alaska. It has left a great deal of mud and ash on roads. People in the continental United States are sending you canned food, brooms, gloves, lawn mowers, and heavy equipment. Volunteers have arrived to help. What of these items are useful to you? How can you avoid getting unwanted items? Can the volunteers help you? How would you put them to work?

YOU TRY IT

Managing the Media

Divide up into groups of five students. Discuss the following scenario: On Thursday, September 18, the tropic depression is upgraded to a hurricane with sustained winds of more than 82 mph. The location of the storm is 13.0° North and 45.4° East. It continues to travel westward at about 23 mph. Forecasters are still unable to predict the destination of Hurricane Cassey. Leaders in Hollywood, Florida decide to put the emergency operations center on alert. Identify what questions you should be prepared to answer from the media. Also mention how you might answer them effectively.

Donating Equipment and Supplies

You work for Home Depot. A tornado has just ripped through your community, leaving many homes exposed to the elements. What donations could your company provide to help disaster victims? Are there donations that might not be needed? How can you find out what donations are useful and what ones are not?

Handling Donations

You are Director of the Red Cross. A bomb has just been detonated in St. Louis. It has killed at least 250 people and injured many others at the movie theater. People are starting to donate medical supplies, caskets, and money. What can you do to make sure you help disaster victims? What should you do to avoid offending donors?

Registering Volunteers

You are the leader of the most important nonprofit organization in your community. A train has derailed outside of your jurisdiction, and the passengers who did not sustain major injuries need a place to stay for the night. You will need to open a shelter for approximately 75 people. How can you ensure you have people who can help set up the shelter? Provide food? Provide security? Address the needs of infants and children?

8

MOVING BEYOND IMMEDIATE NEEDS
Damage Assessment, Disaster Declarations, and Debris Removal

Starting Point

Go to www.wiley.com/college/McEntire to assess your knowledge of damage assessment, disaster declarations, and debris removal.
Determine where you need to concentrate your effort.

What You'll Learn in This Chapter

▲ The importance of damage assessment
▲ Challenges of assessing damages
▲ Procedures for conducting damage assessment
▲ The benefit of federal disaster declarations
▲ The difficulty of dealing with disaster debris
▲ Methods to manage debris effectively
▲ Regulations governing debris management

After Studying This Chapter, You'll Be Able To

▲ Compare the different types of damage assessments
▲ Categorize the distinct methods for assessing damages after a disaster
▲ Examine ways to protect those involved in damage assessment
▲ Initiate the process for seeking federal disaster declarations
▲ Explain why debris management is so important after a disaster
▲ Compare the types of debris produced in disasters
▲ Illustrate the steps that can be taken to manage debris effectively

Goals and Outcomes

▲ Predict typical challenges facing those assessing damages
▲ Formulate damage assessments successfully and safely
▲ Assess the importance of federal disaster declarations for disaster recovery
▲ Request a federal disaster declaration
▲ Declare how to deal with debris management problems
▲ Manage debris operations in accordance with federal regulations

INTRODUCTION

To promote disaster resilience, you will not only have to address immediate response needs but you must begin to think about recovery issues. One of the most important things you must do is to assess the damages disasters leave behind. You must overcome the challenges of completing damage assessments and follow procedures meticulously to determine the impact of the event in an accurate manner. Knowing the extent of destruction will then determine whether you declare a disaster at the local and state levels and receive outside assistance from the federal government. Besides understanding how federal declarations are given, you should also comprehend the incredible challenges presented by disaster debris. You must anticipate similar and distinct types of debris in various disasters and consider ways to remove debris quickly and efficiently. Assessing damages, declaring disasters, and removing debris are vital if you are to start on the road to recovery.

8.1 Assessing Damages

As an emergency manager, your actions are guided in large measure by the damages and impact of disasters. Therefore, one of the most important functions to be performed during response and recovery operations is damage assessment. **Damage assessment** is a process of identifying the extent of destruction, including individual impact as well as overall economic losses in the community. Damage assessment helps to steer response activities and facilitates the acquisition of outside disaster assistance (McEntire 2002; McEntire and Cope 2004). Damage assessment begins immediately after a disaster and continues into recovery operations. This function:

- ▲ Helps identify the immediate needs of disaster victims. For example, post-disaster evaluations may reveal that victims require emergency medical care or sheltering.
- ▲ Enables first responders and emergency managers to recognize what material and financial resources they need along with where they should be deployed. For example, the assessment after Hurricane Katrina led to efforts to shore up the broken levees with sandbags.
- ▲ Is necessary before federal relief is to be given to disaster-stricken communities. Without damage assessments, outside assistance will be limited and unwarranted.
- ▲ Determines if a structure is habitable. For example, damage assessments determine whether victims can return to their homes. Residences may look safe but could be structurally unsound.

> ## FOR EXAMPLE
>
> ### Additional Information on Damage Assessment
>
> If your community was affected by a major earthquake, you would need to assess damages immediately. Should you be unfamiliar with the nature of this function, you should seek recommendations from experts who have knowledge in this area. Useful documents on damage assessment can be ordered from the Applied Technology Council at www.atcouncil.org. Engineers and economists may also help provide valuable information about damage assessments.

▲ May assist in the designation of hazardous areas and identification of factors such as poor construction that augment disaster vulnerability.

> *In short, "After disasters, the damage assessment process is fundamental to relief and reconstruction as it triggers the beginning of formalized disaster relief and recovery aid, beginning with governmental disaster declarations"* (Oaks 1990, p. 6).

8.1.1 Types of Damage Assessment

Not all damage assessments are the same. There are three types of damage assessments. These are known as rapid, preliminary, and technical damage assessments.

▲ A **rapid assessment** is the initial survey of the disaster damages.

▲ A **preliminary assessment** is a detailed assessment required if federal disaster assistance is sought.

▲ A **technical assessment** is used to determine the cost and method for rebuilding structures or the infrastructure.

A rapid or initial assessment is conducted immediately by city personnel and others (e.g., Red Cross) when a disaster occurs. The purpose of a rapid evaluation is to gain quick comprehension of deaths, injuries, victim needs, and overall scope of the disaster. It is worth noting that rapid evaluations can be widely inaccurate. For example, the deaths resulting from the 9/11 terrorist attacks were significantly lower than first feared. Nevertheless, rapid damage assessments play a vital role in getting additional resources for the affected community. This may include securing mutual aid agreements from neighboring jurisdictions or requesting additional damage evaluators from nearby areas. When the levies broke after Hurricane Katrina, the rapid evaluation illustrated the need to shelter thousands of disaster victims.

A preliminary damage or detailed assessment (PDA) is performed by governmental officials within days or weeks after the disaster. The goal of this type of evaluation is to determine the extent of the disaster and the need for outside assistance. It is required before a disaster can be declared by the president and federal disaster assistance is made available to your jurisdiction. In obvious cases where federal assets are warranted, the declaration can precede the disaster. However, this type of damage assessment must still be performed as soon as possible to comply with laws and justify expenses.

A technical or engineering assessment is performed days, weeks, or months after the disaster. The goal of this evaluation is to determine the exact value of losses and figure out what will be needed for rebuilding. This type of assessment is conducted by engineers, insurance agents, and FEMA employees and contractors. It is a necessary step if buildings are to be repaired or completely rebuilt.

Put differently, "A rapid or initial damage assessment is undertaken to quickly comprehend the scope of the devastation. This usually involves the collection of data regarding deaths and injuries as well as the number of buildings destroyed or partially damaged. A preliminary damage assessment (PDA) is completed with state and federal emergency management officials for the purpose of obtaining a presidential disaster declaration. This assessment examines the extent of losses and determines the status of property in terms of safety, sanitation and security concerns. A technical damage assessment is performed on structures and infrastructure to view engineering in an in-depth manner. It is conducted to estimate or verify the costs of the disaster and recommend the best approach for repairs, demolition and reconstruction" (McEntire 2002a, p. 9).

8.1.2 Methods of Conducting Damage Assessment

After a disaster you will assess damages in different ways (McEntire and Cope 2004; McEntire 2002a). There are three common methods for conducting damage assessments. They are known as windshield, aerial, and walkthrough assessments. Each is common in major disasters.

- ▲ **Windshield or drive-through assessments** are performed immediately after a disaster and are completed without leaving the vehicle. This assessment allows you to gain a visual of the damages on the ground and from a distance. This type of assessment is useful in the initial stages of a disaster to determine response priorities and needs.

- ▲ **Aerial assessments** are conducted in helicopters or planes. The aerial assessment is especially useful when roads are blocked or flooding is widespread. You have probably seen images from an aerial assessment because the media often shows aerial footage of the damage caused by hurricanes or earthquakes on the news. As an example, after Hurricane Katrina, President Bush first surveyed the damage from Air Force One as he was flying over the area on a trip from California to Washington, D.C. This method

Figure 8-1

Engineers and FEMA employees are often involved in walkthrough assessments.

of assessment is popular among politicians and key decision makers as it gives them a better understanding of the scope of the disaster.

▲ **Walkthroughs or site visits** are tours of the damaged areas by foot. The walkthrough helps you determine the amount and type of disaster assistance households, businesses, and the government needs (see Figure 8-1). This method of assessment may require knowledge about demolition and construction. "The technical assessment may include a site visit to the affected home, business, road, school or other public building. It is used to verify damage and fill out extensive reports about losses and/or needed repairs" (McEntire 2002a, p. 9).

SELF-CHECK

- What is **damage assessment**?
- What benefits result from assessing damages?
- What are the different types of damage assessment?
- What methods are used to assess damages?

8.2 Challenges in Damage Assessment

There are several problems or difficulties you will face when involved in damage assessment (McEntire and Cope 2004). These include accuracy, working with others, and access and safety.

8.2.1 Accuracy

There are many reasons damage assessments are often inaccurate. Some of the damages may not be readily visible or may not be reported immediately. After Hurricane Katrina made landfall, the news headlines reported that New Orleans was spared. This is because the levee failure had not yet been detected. Once the levees gave way, the city was flooded and the disaster was much worse than initially anticipated. It is also difficult at times to detect the damage to buildings. For example, in the case of a flash flood disaster, buildings may look structurally sound on the outside, but there could be significant damage to the foundation of the building. Another example is from the 2003 San Simeon earthquake. "Many people were out of town and were only able to report damages when they returned after the holidays. There were also a significant number of vacation homes in rural areas that could not be assessed until the owners came back to inspect them" (McEntire and Cope 2004, p. 8).

Damages may also be missed or double counted due to human error. For example, after a tornado roared through downtown Fort Worth, Texas in March 2000, the numbers from the Red Cross and FEMA did not initially match. Later on, it was determined that one of the organizations miscounted some duplexes, which led to the discrepancy. In addition to damages being missed or counted twice, it is also difficult to know how to identify the monetary value of damages (McEntire and Cope 2004, p. 10). Should damages be recorded based on purchase price, replacement value, or going market rate? This is an important question you will need to answer.

Another reason for inaccuracy is due to the fact that damage assessments are performed repeatedly after disasters. The Loma Prieta earthquake in San Francisco provides a clear indication of this. "Buildings were reassessed and re-evaluated as changing geologic processes and weather affected the damaged structures, and as city officials tried to balance people's needs for food, fuel, and shelter with safety. Significant factors affecting the damage assessment process included aftershocks, continued ground failure, and secondary hazards, such as the exposure of asbestos in earthquake damage buildings. Significant social, economic and legal concerns also influenced the building evaluation process" (Oaks 1990, p. 10).

There are also many types of damages, losses, and impacts that may get overlooked in the damage assessment process (French 1990, p. 18):

▲ Physical and economic damage to the infrastructure, including road, water, sewer, gas, and electric systems
▲ Loss of historical buildings

▲ Diminished ability to carry out emergency response activities

▲ Inconvenience and lost economic revenues due to service interruption

▲ Longer term economic losses due to limits on recovery

▲ Loss of life

▲ Environmental damages

For this reason, damage assessments should consider not only damages but other anticipated losses and needs as well.

8.2.2 Working With Others

Another challenge related to damage assessment pertains to the large number of organizations involved in this post-disaster function. It will be difficult for you to harmonize the activities of everyone who participates in damage assessment. This includes private and public engineers, the Red Cross, local emergency managers, and others from the state and federal government.

Complicating this matter, each organization has divergent purposes for conducting damage assessments. For instance, the Red Cross is involved in assessing residential damages. The Chamber of Commerce may be interested in business losses. City and state officials may want to know how government buildings fared in the disaster. FEMA might look at damage to public infrastructure such as roads.

Furthermore, each organization may use different forms for damage assessments. These distinct documents do not always allow quick and easy integration or summary of the damages. Those evaluating damages may also rely on different coding techniques for the assessment. After the earthquake in Paso Robles, California, some assessors utilized lot numbers whereas others noted the complete street address of the damaged structure (McEntire and Cope 2004, p. 10). This creates additional confusion when trying to compile data or visit the site again. A county emergency management official stated that this presented many challenges when he was compiling the preliminary damage assessment numbers after the earthquake (McEntire and Cope 2004, p. 10).

8.2.3 Access and Safety

Because of the widespread destruction associated with disasters, it can be quite difficult to travel to an affected area to complete a damage assessment. Floods, debris, and missing streets signs may make travel to the damaged area difficult or impossible. For example, the effects of a 1993 Midwest flood was so widespread that those assessing damages could not reach each site. Some areas had so much water that damage assessments had to be postponed for days, weeks, or even longer.

In addition to inaccessibility, damage assessment can be dangerous. Because of the potential for building collapses and fires after disasters, damage assessors can be confronted with various hazards. For example, aftershocks from earthquakes

---

FOR EXAMPLE

Damage Assessment and Businesses

People will often become frustrated with the damage assessment process. Tenants, merchants, business owners, and landlords may be disappointed with damage assessment results. Their buildings may be condemned. Others will want to return as soon as possible to retrieve their belongings, but the hazardous situation will not permit it. Business owners facing this situation will be unable to resume their normal operations. Emergency managers should expect that people will be unhappy with damage assessment even though it may be for their own safety.

---

pose serious risks to the damage assessment teams trying to evaluate the integrity of structures. Additional building collapses are common when aftershocks occur after the initial earthquake.

Damage assessments are dangerous activities, but they do promote a safer environment for the public and those who are involved in demolition or reconstruction. The situation after an earthquake in Paso Robles, California is illustrative of this point. "When the fire department arrived at the area in Paso Robles with the greatest concentration of damages, the dangerous situation of many buildings was taken into consideration. Roofs and upper floors had collapsed to the ground level. Eves and awnings above the sidewalks had fully or partially separated from numerous edifices. Walls had crumbled, and bricks and concrete were hanging precariously from building facades. Firefighters therefore used yellow tape to cordon off the areas that were regarded to be the most dangerous. The goal was to keep the public out of harms way. Over the next few days, the fire and police chiefs met with other city leaders to discuss post-disaster policies. Safety became the number one priority. Anyone entering the area had to have proper safety equipment and had to be accompanied by a firefighter. Fences were brought in and a perimeter was placed around the damaged buildings in the downtown district. Police officers were stationed in the area to prevent people from entering unsafe areas and buildings (and as a symbolic gesture to discourage possible—but improbable—looting). As the inspections continued, those offices deemed safe were opened to building owners and merchant tenants. Other buildings had to have debris removed, receive shoring, and then be assessed again before access could be granted. Condemned buildings remained closed to the public, although there was at least one report of a building occupant disregarding the fences and entering a damaged structure to gather personal belongings. Nonetheless, damage assessment did play a role in limiting the number of injuries and deaths associated with this disaster" (McEntire and Cope 2004, p. 5-6).

SELF-CHECK

- What difficulties face those who assess damages?
- Why is accuracy of damage assessments challenging?
- What organizations are involved in damage assessment?
- Is damage assessment dangerous?

8.3 Damage Assessment Procedures

You must take a number of steps to conduct an effective assessment of damages. Some of these activities will need to be pursued right before the assessment, whereas others may take place during the evaluation of damages.

8.3.1 Preassessment Activities

To effectively assess damages, you will need to meet with others and distribute route assignments.

▲ **Hold meetings.** After a disaster occurs, all of those involved in damage assessment should meet to discuss various issues. During this meeting, you will need to identify the process for conducting the assessment. You will also need to make participants aware of how to correctly and completely fill out the forms. Key distribution (if that is an issue) should be discussed so inspectors can enter buildings. Individuals and teams should know who they should report to and how to communicate concerns or questions. The deadline and location for turning in the assessment should be announced. You will want to make clear the dangers of the job and admonish that people use extreme care. You may need to make arrangements for firefighters to participate in damage assessment in case someone becomes injured.

▲ **Plan routes.** During the meeting, it will be necessary that you identify access routes and locations of responsibility. To avoid gaps or duplication in counting, you will want to divide the affected area into geographic districts. The areas should be divided up in an equal manner and clearly assigned to individuals or teams. Maps may be useful when planning route assignments.

8.3.2 Assessment Activities

When you conduct damage assessments, it is imperative that you follow all instructions and evaluation methodologies. This will help you create as accurate a picture of the damages as possible. Be sure to note damages on forms, post results on buildings, cordon off dangerous areas, and educate the public about assessment codes. Many assessment codes use a popular color scheme:

▲ Green—the building is habitable and residents and businesses are allowed to return.

▲ Yellow—the building should only be entered by trained evaluators to continue assessing damages.

▲ Red—the building is unsafe and is therefore condemned.

You will also need to rely on experts when completing your damage assessment. This may include Red Cross employees and trained volunteers for residential areas or structural engineers for public buildings and businesses. When assessing road damage, you will need the assistance of civil engineers. You will need to work with other specialists to assess water treatment plants, power plants, and phone lines, etc.

Besides working with experts, you may also need to use technology in completing your damage assessments. You will want to use remote sensing for flooded areas, taking aerial pictures from satellites or fixed wing aircraft. Engineers will often place small cameras in water systems (pipes) to see if they are damaged. Computer programs may help you to track damage totals and the locations with the most damage. These tools will help you ensure that data is collected accurately.

As information on damages becomes available, you will need to collect and ensure the accuracy of damage assessment forms and numbers. Once you have complete and accurate data, you can use this information to determine your next actions. Inform the city and county leaders of the damage to identify response and recovery priorities. Give information as required to state and federal officials to open up the possibility of outside disaster assistance. Be sure to shore up, repair, demolish, and/or rebuild structures in accordance with prior codes or new emergency permit requirements.

SELF-CHECK

- What can be done before you complete damage assessment to increase the possibility of success?
- Why is it advisable to plan routes for those assessing damages?
- What are the popular assessment color schemes?
- How can experts assist you in the damage assessment function?
- How can technology facilitate damage assessment?

FOR EXAMPLE

A Successful Case of Damage Assessment

Damage assessment was effectively performed after an earthquake in 2003. "As volunteer engineers and architects arrived in Paso Robles, they were told to check in at the gazebo at the park in front of City Hall. These experts were then divided into teams (comprised of at least one firefighter, an architect and an engineer), assigned geographic areas, given keys to the buildings that were collected from local businesses, and briefed about dangerous conditions and the goals and methods of the assessment. Many people commented about how individuals worked together harmoniously to assess the damages. Another major strength made evident during damage assessment was the widespread knowledge of standard operating procedures. Firefighters spray painted symbols common to the search and rescue community on buildings to denote who evaluated the safety of the structures, when this was done, and what the results were. The Building Department also utilized California's damage codes to track destroyed areas and educate building owners and occupants about their meaning and status. The shift rotation of the Emergency Operations Center appears to have been very smooth, with periodic briefings about the damage assessment function when leadership duties changed. Modern technology such as specialized cameras were utilized to detect damages to the city's water treatment facilities, and Geographic Information Systems helped to track the extent of all types of damages throughout the county" (McEntire and Cope 2004, p. 10-11).

8.4 Disaster Declaration

Once damages, impacts, and needs have been assessed, you will need to share those findings with state and federal officials in the hopes of obtaining a Presidential disaster declaration. A **disaster declaration** is a statement that the community or state cannot respond effectively without outside assistance. To receive a Presidential or federal disaster declaration (see Figure 8-2), the following events and actions must occur (see Robert T. Stafford Act at http://www.fema.gov/library/stafact.shtm):

1. The disaster takes place. City and county initiate response operations. They will assess damages and other negative consequences.
2. If the municipal and county governments determine that the disaster is beyond their capabilities, then a disaster is declared at the local level.
3. If a disaster is declared by city and county officials, the state sends personnel to the scene to evaluate the impact. The state also begins its response to the disaster.

Figure 8-2

President Bush declared areas of Louisiana, Mississippi, and Alabama disaster areas before Hurricane Katrina made landfall.

4. Should state personnel determine that the impact is so severe that additional outside help will be needed, the governor will declare an emergency or disaster. The governor will then request help from the FEMA region responsible for that particular state. At this point, FEMA personnel will be deployed for the preliminary damage assessment. If damages warrant a federal declaration, a request will be made through the FEMA regional office, FEMA headquarters, and the Department of Homeland Security.

5. If warranted, the president will declare a federal disaster and resources will be dedicated to the jurisdiction(s) in question. If damages do not necessitate a declaration, officials at FEMA and/or the Department of Homeland Security will deny the declaration request. The president does not decline the disaster request (to avoid blame and the political fallout from that decision).

8.4.1 Difficulties Associated With the Process

This process of disaster declarations, and what can go wrong with them, can be examined in the aftermath of Hurricane Andrew in 1992. When Andrew made landfall, local and state governments did the best they could to respond to the event on their own. They addressed immediate medical needs and started to determine what else needed to be done for disaster victims. However, it soon became apparent that the affected communities and the state of Florida would not be able to handle the devastation and debris alone.

The day after Andrew hit, President George H.W. Bush promised storm victims that "help was on the way." But local and state officials claimed that the federal government was not responding quickly. Governor Chiles complained that urgent requests for federal assistance had been delayed or hopelessly lost because of bureaucratic red tape and confusion. Kate Hale, director of Dade County's Emergency Office, stated "we have appealed through the state to the federal government. We've had a lot of people down here for press conferences. But [in the end] it is Dade County on its own." (Schneider 1995, p. 95).

FEMA eventually deployed additional personnel and resources to South Florida. However, it could not provide assistance until the damage assessment numbers and a formal request for aid came from the state. The federal government asserts that local and state officials asked for everything but failed to follow damage assessment and disaster declaration requirements. Local and state leaders claim they were overwhelmed and FEMA was too rigid with its standard operating procedures. Regardless of the cause, the mistake or inability of not being specific about needs resulted in delay outside disaster assistance.

8.4.2 Factors Determining Declarations

There are both objective and subjective factors that determine whether a disaster is declared or not. According to the Texas Division of Emergency Management ftp://ftp.txdps.state.ts.us/dem/recovery/recoverymanual.pdf, these factors include, among other things:

▲ The number of homes destroyed or sustaining major damage

▲ The number of homes sustaining minor damage

▲ The extent to which the damage is concentrated or dispersed

▲ The estimated costs of repairing the damage

▲ The demographics of the affected areas including income levels, unemployment, and concentrations of the elderly

▲ The extent to which the damage is covered by insurance

▲ The extent to which the disaster area is traumatized

▲ The extent of disaster-related unemployment

▲ The level of assistance available from other federal agencies such as loans from the Small Business Administration

▲ The state and local governments' capabilities for dealing with the disaster

▲ The level of assistance available from charities

▲ The availability of rental housing

▲ The extent of health and safety problems

▲ The extent of damage to facilities providing essential services such as hospitals and utility companies

8.4.3 Other Unique Requirements

Emergency managers should be aware of the special requisites pertinent to disaster declarations. For instance, requests for declarations typically include letters and other supporting documents that outline what happened and the resources that are needed. In some cases, phone calls to higher levels of government may initiate the declaration process. For example, a conversation may be enough to request a declaration if there is an obvious need due to the readily apparent magnitude of certain disasters. The U.S. Code of Federal Regulations 44 clarifies when this type of exception may occur: "The requirement for a joint PDA may be waived for those incidents of unusual severity and magnitude that do not require field damage assessment to determine the need for supplemental federal assistance under the Act, or in such other instances determined by the Regional Director upon consultation with the State" (Office of the Federal Registrar 2001, p. 400).

Most federal declarations, if they are given, are issued after a hazard has occurred. However, some declarations can be made before the hazard affects the community or state in question. Advanced declarations can be given if it appears that the hazard is inevitable and if steps can be taken to mitigate damages. If this occurs, FEMA can mobilize staff and resources before a hurricane makes landfall. Prepositioning resources can reduce deployment time and increase response effectiveness. Of course, prepositioning personnel and supplies should be pursued only if it is safe to do so.

There are different types of presidential/federal declarations:

▲ An **emergency declaration** is issued by the president for national security situations.

▲ A **disaster declaration** is initiated by the local and state governments but is approved or rejected by the federal government in accordance with the Stafford Act.

An "emergency declaration" may be issued by the president at any time to mobilize federal resources. This does not require local, state, or FEMA involvement. This is most often used for national security purposes. It is also often used when an incident does not qualify under the definition of a major disaster in the Stafford Act. Emergency declarations may entail "more limited assistance aimed at saving lives and protecting property, public health, and safety" (May 1985, p. 110).

A "disaster declaration" may be issued by the President under more stringent guidelines. This always requires local, state, and FEMA requests and involvement. This may be given for many different types of natural, technological, and civil

FOR EXAMPLE

Politics and Presidential Disaster Declarations

Politics can play a role in presidential disaster declarations. The President may declare disasters as a way to obtain votes during campaigning and election years. For instance, "during his four years in office, President George H.W. Bush averaged 39 disaster declarations annually. The seven years of the Clinton presidency that Reeves studied averaged 72 disasters per year. When he focused on the presidential election years of 1992 and 1996, Reeves found that President Clinton was about 60 percent more likely than President Bush to declare a disaster in a pivotal, electorally important state" (Tarcey 2004).

disasters. It also "makes available, as necessary, federal grant and loan programs for individuals and public entities" (May 1985, p. 110).

Most requests for federal disaster declarations are denied because the damages do not meet minimum threshold requirements. Such requests do not result in federal funding because it is believed that the local and state governments can handle the situation without outside involvement. If a disaster declaration request is denied, the emergency manager should not give up hope. An appeal can be made with additional supporting evidence. Denials can be overturned if federal disaster assistance is warranted. In most cases, however, you will be responsible for dealing with the disaster without federal help.

SELF-CHECK

- What is a **disaster declaration**?
- How do disaster declarations take place?
- What problems are inherent to disaster declarations?
- What factors determine whether a declaration is made or not?
- When are most disaster declarations issued?

8.5 Debris Produced by Disasters

As an emergency manager, you must be cognizant of the enormous amount of debris that is generated in disasters (see Table 8-1). Debris produced by a hazard

Table 8-1: Volume of Debris Generated by Various Disasters (Taken from EPA 1995, p. 2)

Community	Disaster	Date	Volume of Debris
Metro-Dade County, FL	Hurricane Andrew	August 1992	43 million cubic yards of disaster debris in Metro-Dade County alone
Los Angeles, CA	Northridge Earthquake	January 1994	7 million cubic yards of disaster debris
Kauai, HI	Hurricane Iniki	September 1992	5 million cubic yards of disaster debris
Mecklenburg County, NC	Hurricane Hugo	September 1989	2 million cubic yards of green waste

may be "eight times the usual amount of trash needed to be picked up" (Wright 2004). Consider the following examples:

▲ 18,000 mobile homes were destroyed in North Carolina by Hurricane Floyd. Floyd also produced over 1,500 tons of animal carcasses.

▲ When a series of tornadoes affected Oklahoma, it was estimated that 500,000 cubic yards of debris was collected.

▲ After the Northridge earthquake, 95,100 tons of debris had to be disposed of.

8.5.1 Types of Debris

Debris produced in disasters ranges from broken tree limbs, mud and sediment, and hazardous wastes to broken plywood, twisted metal, shattered glass, and dead animal carcasses. However, certain disasters may have specific types of debris. For example, hurricanes may destroy buildings due to storm surge and strong winds. They may also move sand, dirt, and rock on top of roads and parking lots. Moreover, these hazards break tree limbs and damage cars, boats, and household contents.

The violent shaking associated with earthquakes results in structural failures, collapsed brick buildings, broken glass, and sediment from landslides. Earthquakes likewise damage personal belongings that fall to the ground and break. This hazard produces ash and charred wood from fires that result from gas line ruptures.

Other hazards are similarly destructive. The severe winds associated with tornadoes pulls trees out of the soil, breaks limbs off of trees, and creates missiles out of lawnmowers, sheds, computers, couches, microwaves, televisions, etc.

Table 8-2: Type of Debris Generated by Various Disasters (Taken from EPA 1995, p. 3)

	Damaged Buildings	Sediments	Green Waste	Personal Property	Ash and Charred Wood
Hurricanes	x	x	x	x	
Earthquakes	x	x	x	x	x
Tornadoes	x		x	x	
Floods	x	x	x	x	
Fires	x			x	x
Ice Storms	x		x	x	

Adapted from EPA 1995, p. 3.

Flash floods may rip buildings from their foundations as well as carry rock, mud, and tree trunks far downstream. Slow rising waters ruin carpets, furniture, electrical appliances, sheet rock, etc. Fires burn buildings and property, leaving charred debris and ash. Ice storms may break tree limbs and create damage to homes and personal property.

The excessive amount and types of debris generated by disasters must be dealt with by the emergency manager. This is known as debris management. **Debris management** is the collection, sorting, storage, transportation, and disposal or recycling of rubble, destroyed materials, and other wastes associated with a disaster. It also incorporates long-term measures to dispose of debris in an environmentally sound manner. Debris management is closely related to damage assessment and disaster declarations. For example, the clearing of debris may help people reach their destinations so they can assess damages. Debris management expenses may be paid in part by the federal government if a disaster declaration is given.

FOR EXAMPLE

Debris Is Not Always From Disasters

There are also other types of debris that do not result directly from the physical hazard. Debris is also produced indirectly in and after the disaster. For example, there could be spoiled food or excessive donations. Debris may also include wastes created by the response itself. Examples include sand bags to fight flooding and water bottles used to hydrate emergency workers.

8.5.2 Debris Management Challenges

Because of the large amounts and types of debris generated in disasters, you should be aware of its significance to you as an emergency manager. The presence and removal of debris have a bearing on the effectiveness of response and recovery operations. For example, police, ambulance, and fire vehicles will get flat tires if glass and splintered wood is not removed from streets and thoroughfares. Conversely, immediate efforts to clear roads of debris will ensure that response organizations may pass without unnecessary delay.

The presence of debris also leads to concerns about mental well-being, safety, public health, and the environment. Debris creates an eyesore for those in the disaster-affected community. For example, after the 2004 hurricanes passed over Pensacola, Florida, one citizen commented, "It's still kind of depressing to drive around with all of this debris" (Thomas 2004). After a March 2000 tornado in Fort Worth, Texas, those assigned to clean up broken glass were threatened by window panes falling out of office buildings. Residents living near some disposal sites have had trouble breathing because of the ash emitted by debris furnaces (Mariano 2004). Debris and debris management can adversely affect our natural resources. Burning debris may pollute the air, whereas burying disaster rubble may adversely effect soil and water conditions. Some people in Palm Beach, Florida became very upset when public land dedicated as an environmentally protected area was used as a dump site (Modzelewski 2004).

Debris management is also very expensive. "Debris cleanup costs in four states and two territories exceeded $310,000,000 following Hurricane Georges in 1998" (Swan 2000, p. 222). The removal of debris from Hurricane Andrew cost $585 million. In most disasters, total debris costs may range from 15% to 33% of FEMA disaster expenditures. "Generally, FEMA pays 100 percent of all debris removal costs in the 72 hours following natural disasters. After that, it's agency policy to pay 75 percent of the costs borne by local governments" (Curran 2004). But the local share is often sizable. And there is no guarantee that every disaster will be declared and permit outside governmental assistance.

Debris management can likewise be very time consuming. After the 2004 hurricanes that affected Florida, some city crews worked 7 days a week for extended periods of time (Wright 2004). Other disasters may require ongoing debris management operations for weeks and even months at a time. People often take advantage of disasters to unload unwanted items such as old sinks, couches, mattresses, refrigerators, car doors, and tires. The presence of such debris at the curbside complicates the debris management process for you as an emergency manager.

Oversight of debris management is difficult as there may be no organization that has clear and sole responsibility for this activity (see Figure 8-3). Citizens will place debris near the curb waiting for someone to pick it up and carry it away. The transportation, public works, and park and recreations departments may be involved in cleaning up roads and the rubble from damaged government buildings. Private contractors are utilized to collect debris for some communities. In federally declared

Figure 8-3

Volunteers can be a valuable asset in debris management activities as long as they understand the importance of following recommended safety precautions.

disasters, FEMA officials oversee costs and the reimbursement of funds. The EPA ensures that debris management takes environmental protection into account.

Debris and debris management may create other problems for you as well. Debris or debris storage may attract rodents that have to be dealt with. Also, the removal and transportation of debris may create dust and noise and annoy citizens. Roads can also be ruined if they are not able to support the weight of heavily loaded trucks. Some of the impacts of disasters, including the loss of livestock, may also pose special debris management challenges. What should be done when hundreds or thousands of animals are killed in major flooding episodes? These are all important issues that you must address after disasters.

SELF-CHECK

- Can disasters generate a great deal of debris?
- What types of debris are produced in disasters?
- What is **debris management**?
- What are the challenges associated with debris management?

8.6 Dealing With Debris Effectively

Several steps can be taken to overcome the typical problems associated with debris management. Because disaster-generated debris may quickly overwhelm a community, it is imperative that the quantity be reduced as much as possible. Reducing debris can be accomplished after the debris is sorted. Damaged materials may be classified as vegetative, aggregate, and construction/demolition debris.

▲ **Vegetative debris** includes broken tree limbs, tree stumps, brush, leaves, and yard waste.

▲ **Aggregate debris** includes asphalt and concrete from damaged roads and bridges.

▲ **Construction and demolition debris** results from damaged homes, commercial property, and various other types of structures (e.g., barns). This may include wood, metal, wiring, insulation, tar or clay shingles, and other types of materials.

There are at least three ways to reduce the volume of such debris:

1. Vegetative debris can be chipped. This may reduce up to 75% of the total debris volume from certain disasters. The resulting product can be used as mulch for gardens and flower beds.

2. Aggregates can be crushed and later used as road base. Asphalt and concrete can in some cases be reused as well.

3. Construction and demolition debris may be recycled in some cases. Broken 2 × 4s and sheets of plywood can be made into pressboard.

Another way to reduce debris is to burn as much debris as possible to reduce the amount sent to community landfills. This will require that special attention be given to the environment, however. For instance, the temperature of burning debris may determine the amount of pollution it produces. Recycling and burying debris also has enormous impact on the quality of air, water, and soil.

To facilitate oversight of debris management, it is recommended that someone be put in charge of this function and that organizations are made aware of each others' roles in this area. Successful debris management operations are often determined by:

▲ Knowing what equipment is available or needed for debris management

▲ Recognizing the capabilities and limits of departments in the public sector

▲ Being able to communicate to all parties involved after a disaster, including contractors from the private sector

▲ Having the legal department review contracts, "right-of-entry permits, community liability, condemnation of buildings, land acquisition for temporary staging and reduction sites" (Swan 2000, p. 224).

> ## FOR EXAMPLE
>
> ### Debris Management and Dangerous Crime Scenes
>
> Debris removal was a very difficult task in the aftermath of the 9/11 terrorist attacks on the World Trade Center. The site was not safe because there were fires smoldering among the debris. The air was also unhealthy and filled with dust from the debris. There was a desire to clean up the site as soon as possible as it was psychologically difficult to view the destruction. However, care had to be taken as the site was also a crime scene. Sifting the debris had to be done in such a way as to look for evidence and separate out human remains. The families of victims were very adamant that their loved ones not be placed in trash dumps. It took over 8 months for all of the debris to be removed from the World Trade Center site and be sorted for evidence and remains.

Individuals and organizations involved in debris removal activities should also understand how debris management activities change over time (Swan 2000, p. 222). Immediately before and after a disaster, communities should increase readiness by confirming staffing assignments for debris management. This is a great time to remind personnel about proper debris management techniques. During the response phase, attention should be shifted to the removal and storage of debris. Once recovery is underway, debris can be sorted, recycled, burned, or buried.

8.6.1 Storage Locations and the Environment

To reduce the problems associated with debris management, you should identify the sites for temporary and permanent storage as well as final disposal. "A listing of potential temporary debris management sites should be investigated and evaluated before a major disaster. Public lands should be used first to avoid costly leases. Consider locations with respect to noise, traffic and the environment. Avoid locating near residential areas, schools, churches, hospitals, and other environmentally sensitive areas. Ensure that sites have good ingress/egress to accommodate heavy truck traffic. Sites should be between 50 and 100 acres in size based on the forecasted quantity of debris" (Swan 2000, p. 223). In some cases, these staging areas may need to be as large as 100 acres (Mariano 2004). Some communities have used fairgrounds and even county airports for this purpose (Moskovitz 2004).

Protection of the environment can be enhanced during debris management if an environmental specialist or organizations are involved in operations. Experts can provide advice on the methods to dispose of debris in an environmentally sound manner. The public can be made aware of how to assist in debris management by communicating public policies and strategies to media organizations.

For instance, NASA and FEMA officials repeatedly advised citizens to stay away from debris laden with hazardous materials after the Columbia Space Shuttle broke up upon re-entry. People can likewise be told to cut tree limbs into sections no longer than 4-feet long and stack them in a way as to not obstruct roads, utilities, and culverts (Ferrante 2004).

8.6.2 EPA Recommendations for Improving Debris Management

The EPA has similar and additional recommendations to improve debris management (see EPA 1995, p. 8-10):

▲ **Consider mutual aid arrangements.** Developing compacts with nearby communities may help jurisdictions find needed personnel and expertise and reduce costs associated with purchasing and maintaining equipment.

▲ **Implement recycling program.** It is easier to recycle debris if a waste recycling program has been established before a disaster strikes.

▲ **Develop a communication strategy.** Government officials must tell citizens about special instructions for reporting and sorting disaster debris, as well as when regular trash collection will resume.

▲ **Anticipate increased outreach and enforcement staffing needs.** Additional personnel should be hired after a disaster to answer telephone calls about disaster debris and assist in the removal of disaster-produced rubble.

▲ **Obtain equipment and supplies.** Cell phones, chain saws, portable generators, flashlights, batteries, vehicle repair kits (for flat tires), extra work clothing, water, and other materials for debris management personnel should be readily obtained after disaster strikes.

▲ **Select collection and storage sites.** Identifying locations for collection, staging, storage, sorting, recycling, land filling, and burning of debris in advance will eliminate unwanted noise and road damage and increase efficiency of debris management operations.

▲ **Determine management options and goals.** Communities should anticipate what types of debris will be produced in a disaster and identify the objectives and methods to appropriately deal with them.

▲ **Segregate hazardous waste.** Ensure that everyone involved in debris management understands how to deal with hazardous materials (so it is not mixed with other disaster debris to produce further environmental degradation).

▲ **Prepare contracts.** Work with the private sector to seek request for proposals (RFP) to collect, store, sort, process, and dispose of disaster debris.

▲ **Plan for FEMA and state reimbursement.** Hire staff to record debris management costs, and file reimbursement in accordance with the rules provided by the Federal Emergency Management Agency.

SELF-CHECK

- How can you sort disaster debris?
- Is it important to reduce the volume of disaster debris?
- What are the characteristics of effective debris management?
- Where should you store disaster debris?
- What recommendations does the EPA have for debris management?

8.7 Regulations and Other Considerations

Successful debris management requires that emergency managers are familiar with federal legislation pertaining to this function. There are a host of regulations that pertain to debris management and the reimbursement of debris removal costs. These guidelines suggest that debris expenses may be reimbursed if:

▲ It is a direct result of the disaster
▲ It is found in the designated disaster area
▲ It will minimize threats to lives and public health
▲ It will reduce additional damage to public or private property
▲ It will help the economic recovery of the area

Debris must also be removed and disposed of within a definite time period—typically within 180 days after a disaster. Regulations also note that eligible removal expenses are associated with the clearing of debris from roads and also protect people and the environment from hazardous materials.

FOR EXAMPLE

FEMA and Trash Pickup Rules

As an emergency manager, you should be aware that "some of the rules relating to the federal government's reimbursement for trash pickup can be confusing, even for FEMA Representatives" (Bierschenk 2004). Differences of opinion regarding debris regulations have led to serious disagreements and even legal actions in some cases (Curran 2004). Rules may be different for various federal agencies, and some of the laws may be changed in specific disasters. In Alabama, after Hurricane Ivan, "The Federal Emergency Management Agency decided to only pay those communities that entered into contracts with the U.S. Army Corps of engineers" (Curran 2004). In other cases, the federal government has paid all debris management costs—even the local and state portions.

Examples of ineligible debris reimbursements include removal of:

▲ Trees and trunks from unaffected forest areas
▲ Sediment from channels that is not a result of the disaster. For example, this would include natural build up of sand and rock in a river basin.
▲ Debris from private road and gated communities
▲ Extra tree trimmings or trees cut up by contractors
▲ Yard waste coming from unmaintained lots
▲ Construction debris created as a result of contractor demolition and repairs

8.7.1 Reducing Expenses

To reduce the exorbitant expense of debris management, several measures can be taken. For instance, contracts with the private sector can be developed. These contracts may be based on lump sum, unit price, or time and materials agreements.

▲ **Lump sum contracts** provide payment for completion of a well-defined scope of work (e.g., when debris is concentrated) (Swan 2000, p. 224).
▲ **Unit price contracts** are based on truck load sizes and are most common in disasters when the exact quantity of debris is unknown (Swan 2000, p. 224).
▲ **Time and material contracts** are based on labor and equipment costs and are suitable for rights-of-way clearance and should not exceed 70 hours according to FEMA regulations for reimbursement (Swan 2000, p. 224).

Human and equipment resources can be creatively acquired for debris management, and expenses must always be carefully tracked. One community utilized prison crews to help them meet their debris management demands (Niesse 2004). Most communities will assign someone the specific duty of recording employee hours, trucks utilized, money spent on fuel, etc. This is crucial because federal reimbursement policies must be followed in a meticulous fashion. Payments will be made in most disasters according to established laws only. Opportunities for reimbursement may be missed if people are not aware of proper methods to complete and submit paperwork.

8.7.2 Preventing Fraud

There are other ways that precious resources can be lost during debris management. This post-disaster function is sometimes associated with scams by public officials and private contractors. "The high dollar value of debris operations can entice Federal officials, local government officials, contractors, and others to step over the line of legal activity in an effort to benefit financially from disaster recovery operations" (FEMA 2003). Some people intentionally try to include non-disaster-related debris for removal. This may include those clearing land of trees and others demolishing or gutting homes to increase debris quantities for reimbursement (Bierschenk 2004).

Such fraud can be eliminated by working aggressively to stop it. Those participating in debris management should be on the lookout for:

▲ The hauling of ineligible debris (e.g., tree stumps)

▲ Excessive water placed in the bottom of dump trucks to increase weight

▲ Inaccurately specified truck-load capacities

▲ Double-counting of personnel and equipment

▲ Trucks re-entering disposal sites

Taking photographs of debris management activities is another way to discourage would-be criminals. "Monitoring can [also] be accomplished using local government employees or separate contractors. Costs associated with hiring outside contractors to provide monitors are eligible for reimbursement by FEMA . . . . Contract monitors must be trained before being placed in the field to observe contractor operations. They must have knowledge of techniques that can be used to inflate debris quantities. Moreover, there must be a reporting procedure in place that identifies questionable activities. Documentation should consist of written reports, photographs, and sketches of questionable contractor activities" (Swan 2000, p. 224). Regulations, expenses, and fraud are important concerns to those involved in debris management. The federal government takes its responsibility to monitor fraud seriously. After the 2004 hurricanes in Florida, "the government agencies . . . have monitors riding along with the trucks to try to ensure people don't take unfair advantage of the free service" (Bierschenk 2004). In other cases, the federal government will send Office of the Inspector General personnel to investigate potential scams, make arrests, and prosecute as necessary.

SELF-CHECK

- Is it important for the emergency manager to know debris management regulations?
- What types of debris are eligible or ineligible for reimbursement?
- What types of contracts are used to pay debris removal contractors?
- Is fraud a problem in debris management?

SUMMARY

The promotion of resilience after disaster requires several additional steps after initial emergency management needs are met. Damages must be calculated to determine what additional steps will be required for response and recovery. You will face several challenges regarding accuracy and safety, but these can be overcome if you follow damage assessment protocols. Once you have a good understanding of the impact, you may seek outside assistance by requesting a federal disaster declaration (if damages warrant that). It will also be necessary that you understand the types of debris that are produced in disasters and take steps to reduce or dispose of them correctly. Each of these functions must be performed in accordance with established regulations if you are to be successful as an emergency manager.

KEY TERMS

Aerial assessment	Review of damage conducted in helicopters or planes. Especially useful when roads are blocked or flooding is widespread.
Aggregate debris	Trash that includes asphalt and concrete from damaged roads and bridges.
Construction and demolition debris	Trash that includes wood, metal, wiring, insulation, tar or clay shingles, and other types of materials.
Damage assessment	A process of identifying the extent of destruction, including individual impact as well as overall economic losses in the community.
Debris management	The collection, sorting, storage, transportation and disposal or recycling of rubble, destroyed materials, and other wastes associated with a disaster. It also incorporates long-term measures to dispose of debris in an environmentally sound manner.
Disaster declaration	A statement that the community or state cannot respond effectively without outside assistance.
Emergency declaration	A statement issued by the president for national security situations.
Lump sum contracts	Contracts that provide payment for completion of a well-defined scope of work (when debris is concentrated) (Swan 2000, p. 224).

Preliminary or detailed assessment   Review of damage that is performed within days or weeks after the disaster and seeks to determine the need for outside assistance.

Rapid or initial assessment   Review of damage that is conducted immediately when a disaster occurs and seeks to gain a quick comprehension of deaths, injuries, victim needs, and overall scope of the disaster.

Technical or engineering assessment   Review of damage that is performed days, weeks, or months after the disaster to determine the exact value of losses and requirements for rebuilding.

Time and material contracts   Agreements that are based on labor and equipment costs and are suitable for rights-of-way clearance and should not exceed 70 hours according to FEMA regulations for reimbursement (Swan 2000, p. 224).

Unit price contracts   Agreements that are based on truck load sizes and are most common in disasters when the exact quantity of debris is unknown (Swan 2000, p. 224).

Vegetative debris   Trash that includes broken tree limbs, tree stumps, brush, leaves, and yard waste.

Walkthrough or site visit   A tour of the damaged areas by foot to determine the amount and type of disaster assistance households, businesses, and the government need.

Windshield or drive-through assessment   An evaluation performed in a vehicle and completed without leaving the vehicle.

ASSESS YOUR UNDERSTANDING

Go to www.wiley.com/college/McEntire to evaluate your knowledge of damage assessment, disaster declarations, and debris removal.
Measure your learning by comparing pretest and post-test results.

Summary Questions

1. Damage assessment looks at destroyed buildings but not economic losses. True or False?

2. A preliminary damage assessment is the first type of damage assessment. True or False?

3. Public officials often view damages from a helicopter or plane. True or False?

4. Buildings may look structurally sound, but they could be unsafe. True or False?

5. The Red Cross often assesses damages associated with homes and apartments. True or False?

6. People may become upset with the damage assessment process or results. True or False?

7. A green paper attached to a house means the house is condemned. True or False?

8. States should declare a disaster only when they cannot respond to the event without outside help. True or False?

9. The number of destroyed homes has a bearing on disaster declarations but unemployment does not. True or False?

10. A disaster can never be declared before the hazard occurs. True or False?

11. Common debris produced by a disaster may include broken tree limbs, sediment, and broken plywood. True or False?

12. Debris management is not concerned with environmental issues. True or False?

13. Debris management is one of the most expensive post-disaster functions. True or False?

14. Brush, leaves, and yard waste are examples of construction and demolition debris. True or False?

15. A major consideration in debris management is the location of storage and disposal sites. True or False?

16. What is/are the benefits of damage assessment?
    (a) It helps to identify needs of disaster victims.
    (b) It is required before outside assistance can be given.
    (c) It determines if structures are habitable.

(d) It identifies areas that might need to be avoided during rebuilding.

(e) All of the above.

17. A rapid or initial assessment:

(a) Is performed weeks after the disaster

(b) Is performed by engineers, insurance agents and FEMA contractors

(c) Helps to gain a quick understanding of the scope of the event

(d) Is the only assessment required for disaster declarations

(e) Recommends approach for repairs and reconstruction

18. A windshield or drive-through assessment:

(a) Is performed in a vehicle

(b) Is common in the initial stages of disaster response

(c) Requires extensive knowledge about engineering and construction

(d) a and b

(e) b and c

19. Reasons why damage assessments are inaccurate include:

(a) The appearance of buildings can be deceiving.

(b) Damages may be missed or double counted.

(c) They are performed repeatedly after a disaster.

(d) Some types of damages and impacts may be overlooked after a disaster.

(e) All of the above.

20. Earthquakes pose serious risks to damage assessors because:

(a) There is a potential for building collapses.

(b) Fires may result from broken power lines.

(c) Aftershocks will not occur.

(d) a and b

(e) None of the above.

21. Holding a meeting before conducting damage assessment operations is advisable because:

(a) The flooding will not destroy street signs.

(b) You might need to distribute keys to those involved.

(c) Route identification is not important.

(d) Yellow-coded buildings are completely safe.

(e) Forms do not need to be given to those involved.

22. What steps are required for a federal disaster declaration?

(a) Local government is affected by a disaster and can't respond alone.

(b) State government requests outside disaster assistance.

(c) The FEMA region relays information to headquarters.

(d) The president agrees that damages warrant federal funding.

(e) All of the above.

23. Factors determining federal declarations include:

(a) The number of homes with minor damage only

(b) Estimated costs of repairing the damages

(c) The extent to which damage is covered by insurance but not unemployment

(d) The concentration of damages but not cost associated with them

(e) All of the above

24. An emergency declaration:

(a) Is the same as a disaster declaration

(b) Requires local and state requests for assistance

(c) Is used when the definition of a disaster does not fall under Stafford Act guidelines

(d) Is never used for national security emergencies

(e) All of the above

25. Disasters may produce what type(s) of debris?

(a) Ash and charred wood

(b) Green waste

(c) Bricks from damaged buildings

(d) Sediment

(e) All of the above

26. Debris management:

(a) Is not very expensive

(b) Is not very time consuming

(c) Is performed by a single agency only

(d) Must be performed in accordance to federal regulations

(e) Is not related to crime scenes in any way

27. Aggregate debris includes:

(a) Tree stumps

(b) Asphalt and concrete

(c) Asphalt but not concrete

(d) Metal and wiring

(e) Metal and wiring but not wood

28. The EPA recommends:

(a) The mutual aid agreements be used in debris management operations

(b) The recycling of debris

    (c) That you have chain saws and vehicle repair kits

    (d) All of the above

    (e) a and c only

29. Which debris is ineligible for reimbursement?

    (a) Debris that is a direct result of the disaster

    (b) Debris that is found within the designated disaster area

    (c) Debris that minimizes threats to lives and property

    (d) Tree trimmings cut up by contractors

    (e) Construction debris only

30. A time and material contract:

    (a) Is based on labor and equipment costs

    (b) Is for well-defined projects

    (c) Can exceed 70 hours

    (d) Is useful for concentrated debris

    (e) Is based on truck loads

Review Questions

1. Why is damage assessment important?
2. What are the different types of damage assessment?
3. What methods are used to conduct damage assessments?
4. What challenges can an emergency manager expect with the damage assessment function?
5. What can be done to perform damage assessment successfully?
6. What is a disaster declaration?
7. What factors determine whether a disaster is declared by the president?
8. What are the different types of federal declarations?
9. What type of debris do disasters generate?
10. What is debris management?
11. What are the common problems associated with debris management?
12. What measures can be taken to deal with debris effectively?
13. What regulations need to be followed when performing debris management activities?

Applying This Chapter

1. You are an emergency manager living near the New Madrid fault. An earthquake has just occurred. How would this hazard affect damage

assessment? Suppose your community was affected by flooding. How does this impact damage assessment? Do other hazards create different concerns for damage assessment teams? Why?

2. Different types of disasters produce different types of debris. Can you provide examples that support this statement? Why is it important to know this?

3. You are an emergency manager in the Northwest, and your community has been devastated by a tsunami generated from an earthquake in the Pacific Ocean. Tons of debris has been generated from destroyed homes and businesses. You will have to sort and remove the debris. Why is debris management important, and what considerations should you think about as you implement this post-disaster function?

4. News reports reveal that the declaration process for Hurricane Katrina witnessed similar problems to that of Hurricane Andrew. What were these and how can they be avoided in the future?

5. A flash flood has destroyed many buildings in a rural area and left animal carcasses strewn about the area. The area is well known for its pristine waters and beautiful scenery. What concerns do you have as the emergency manager for this area? How can you ensure debris management is performed successfully?

6. You are the local emergency manager for a community that was devastated by a major tornado. You need to convince officials to declare your jurisdiction a disaster area. What types of facts do you present them with?

7. You are the local emergency manager for a community in Idaho that was adversely affected by landslide. Many homes sustained minor damage, and there is a great deal of vegetative debris as a result also. What scams might be employed by contractors, and how can you prevent them?

PreAssessment Procedures

Write a two-page paper on the following subject: You are the local emergency manager for a community that has been affected by a volcanic hazard. You now must assess damages quickly. You have called a meeting with those who will assist. What steps do you take to ensure the safety of those involved in this function? What other things should you make them aware of?

Assessing Damages

You are the local emergency manager for a community that was severely affected by a major ice storm. You need to assess the impact and damages. How is this different from assessing damage from an earthquake? Who might be involved in this type of assessment?

Types of Debris

Your community in Arizona has been affected by a major wildfire. Many neighborhoods and small businesses have been ravished in the event. What type of debris will you have to deal with? How does this differ from the debris produced by a hurricane? What concerns do you have about debris management that are common to any type of hazard?

9

FACILITATING RECOVERY AND MITIGATION
Disaster Assistance and Vulnerability Reduction

Starting Point

Go to www.wiley.com/college/McEntire to assess your knowledge of recovery and mitigation.
Determine where you need to concentrate your effort.

What You'll Learn in This Chapter

▲ The purpose and types of individual assistance
▲ How victims may obtain individual assistance
▲ The categories of public assistance
▲ The steps to obtain recovery resources for your community
▲ The potential for disagreement during recovery
▲ The special issues that accompany recovery, including fraud, preservations of historic buildings, and protection of the environment
▲ How to reduce vulnerability after a disaster

After Studying This Chapter, You'll Be Able To

▲ Examine the goals and categories of public assistance
▲ Help eligible applicants seek federal disaster relief
▲ Distinguish between emergency and permanent assistance
▲ Establish a Disaster Recovery Center
▲ Determine possible conflicts could occur among the actors involved in recovery
▲ Analyze your community's vulnerability to fraud, the loss of historic buildings, and damage to the environment from hazards
▲ Examine what measures can be taken to decrease future losses

Goals and Outcomes

▲ Evaluate the process through which individual assistance may be obtained
▲ Compare and contrast categories of public assistance
▲ Synthesize the procedures for obtaining public assistance
▲ Predict conflict during recovery among internal and external actors
▲ Argue for greater resources for emergency management using windows of opportunity
▲ Assess special issues during recovery including ways to minimize fraud, preserve historic buildings, and protect the environment
▲ Evaluate whether rebuilding or relocating is most appropriate during recovery

INTRODUCTION

As an emergency manager, it is your responsibility to help promote resilience during recovery. Victims of a disaster sustain significant losses after disasters and struggle to take care of their immediate and long-term needs. Governments must focus on rebuilding the community and think about ways to reduce future disasters. For this reason, you must help victims understand individual assistance programs and ways they can apply for such help. You will also need to educate public officials about emergency and permanent public assistance as well as the process for applying these programs. While seeking federal relief after disasters, it will be necessary that you brace yourself for disagreement about recovery policies. You should also endeavor to avoid fraud, protect the environment and historic buildings, and work closely with others. You should do all you can to minimize vulnerability during the window of opportunity disasters provide.

9.1 Types of Individual Assistance

Imagine for a moment that you are the victim of a devastating hurricane. You lose your home in this disaster. You lose all your possessions and personal belongings. Your company's office building was destroyed, and you become unemployed. Your family might even suffer the loss of loved ones. Would recovery be difficult? What resources and help would you need? Not only will you need money, but you might also require a host of services such as crisis counseling and unemployment assistance.

As an emergency manager, you must understand victim needs as well as what programs and resources are available to assist them with recovery. Hopefully, individuals will have insurance they can rely on and the nonprofit sector will assist those with long-standing needs. In some cases, the national government may also provide assistance to affected victims. Federal involvement begins after damages and needs have been assessed and if the president has declared a disaster. Such declarations open up the possibility for federal disaster assistance. The resources available from the federal government can be of great benefit to disaster victims.

There are two distinct federal disaster assistance programs:

▲ **Individual assistance** provides relief to citizens, businesses, and others affected by a disaster. Individual assistance is also known as IA.
▲ **Public assistance** makes available recovery aid for government entities. Public assistance is also known as PA.

Based on the extent of disaster impacts, a community may receive neither, one, or both types of disaster assistance. A FEMA handbook regarding disaster assistance states, "While a wide range of Federal programs are available to aid disaster victims, it should not be assumed that all of them will be activated. The determination as to which programs will be provided is made based on actual needs found during the damage assessment and/or on the basis of subsequent information" (FEMA 1997, p. 1–10).

As noted above, individual assistance is geared towards individuals, families, and owners of small businesses. IA helps these people and organizations recover from the effects of a disaster. IA may also reimburse nonprofit agencies that provide assistance after a disaster. There are different types of individual assistance. Some of these are administered by the federal government, whereas others are managed by each state. Because each state is unique, you should expect that these programs may be implemented through different departments and agencies. Regardless, the federal government provides the bulk of the funds for such programs.

9.1.1 Loans and Grants

Individual assistance is largely comprised of loans and grants.

▲ **Loan programs** lend money to individuals, families, and businesses that have sustained losses in disasters. Although interest rates are generally lower than the market average, loan rates and repayment schedules are determined by the ability of the recipient to repay.

▲ **Grants** are gift funds that do not need to be repaid.

There are six types of loans and grant programs for disaster victims seeking individual assistance.

1. **Disaster loans for homes and individuals.** There are loans available for families and individuals who have sustained losses from disasters. These include home/personal property physical disaster loans. Such loans are for homeowners and renters who lose homes and property. Loans of up to $200,000 can be given for primary residences (secondary residences are not eligible). Loans of up to $40,000 can also be provided to replace personal property lost in the primary residence. In addition, loans can be increased by 20% to implement mitigation measures for future disasters. An example of mitigation measures that can be incorporated while rebuilding is improved engineering so the structure can resist hurricane-force winds. The Small Business Administration (SBA) handles these disaster loan programs.

2. **Disaster loans for businesses.** There are loans available for businesses that have sustained losses from disasters. Business physical disaster loans are for small businesses that have been adversely affected by disasters. Loans of up to $1,500,000 are provided to repair or replace structures and machinery. These loans can also be increased by 20% if recovery incorporates mitigation considerations. They are also administered by the SBA. Figure 9-1 shows people seeking aid from the SBA.

Figure 9-1

Victims seeking public assistance from the Small Business Administration.

3. **Economic injury disaster loans.** These loans are for businesses and farming cooperatives that have suffered financial losses or hardship due to the disaster. Loans of up to $1,500,000 may be given to help a business or farm recover. This type of disaster loan is also managed by the Small Business Administration.

4. **Farm service agency loans.** This program provides loans for farmers who lose crops or equipment due to a disaster and/or require resources to continue operations. There is also an emergency conservation program to allocate funds to replace fencing, remove debris, and grade and rehabilitate farmland. A haying and grazing program allows the use of conservation reserve land if this is justified. These disaster relief programs are operated under the direction of the U.S. Department of Agriculture.

5. **Individual and households program (IHP).** This program was formerly known as Individual and Family Grant Program. It provides up to $27,200 for those people who lack homeowners insurance and have uninhabitable homes. The program has two components.

   • The **Disaster Housing** portion is for homes that may be uninhabitable due to unsafe, unsanitary, or insecure conditions. This grant is also used by the government to provide mobile homes or help with minor home repairs, hotel/ motel stays, and rental/mortgage payments. The Disaster Housing program is administered by FEMA and is 100% federally funded. This program was formerly known as Temporary Housing Assistance.

- **Other Needs Assistance (ONA)** is another program under IHP. It is specifically for those without insurance coverage. ONA makes available grants for home repair, replacement of personal property, and other disaster-related expenses for funeral, medical/dental care, and transportation. This program is administered by the state with a 75%-25% federal-state cost share. The maximum funds for IHP may change annually based on current market adjustments.

6. **Tax assistance.** This program allows for the deduction of uninsured losses if they total more than 10% of income. In this case, the Internal Revenue Service provides refunds or tax breaks for victims of disaster.

9.1.2 Services

Disaster victims have other needs besides financial ones. **Services** are government programs that address unique issues or needs made evident in the disaster. For example, victims may need crisis counseling to cope with their losses. Another example relates to the rebuilding of homes. As fraud could be present after disaster situations, homeowners may need consumer services. Examples of services available are described below.

1. **Aging services.** This program provides transportation so disaster victims can meet with government officials and obtain answers to questions about all types of disaster assistance. It is administered by the state Department of Aging.

2. **Consumer services.** Under this program, counseling is given to those people dealing with consumer problems such as the lack of products and services after disasters, price gouging, fraud, and questionable business ethics. It is administered by the state Attorney's Office.

3. **Crisis counseling.** This program reimburses mental health centers and Red Cross counselors that provide stress debriefing for emergency responders and disaster victims. This is 100% federally funded. It is administered by the Mental Health Department in each state.

4. **Emergency services.** This program reimburses voluntary organizations for their post-disaster relief expenses. Examples of organizations are the American Red Cross and the Salvation Army. Emergency services provide food, clothing, shelter, medical care, medicines, glasses, home repair, or replacement of other essential items.

5. **Insurance services.** This program helps individuals file and settle claims with insurance agencies. It also helps victims acquire federal flood

---

FOR EXAMPLE

Where is the help?

Although the federal government offers assistance in many forms, help is not guaranteed. Furthermore, individual assistance is not immediately given to the victims due to the required application process. The FEMA handbook reads, "Individuals and families will need to plan to use their own resources and financial reserves until Federal funds can be released. An application process must be completed before assistance becomes available. Often, it takes several weeks for the Federal government to review requests for financial assistance and to issue funds to those who meet eligibility requirements. Most Federal assistance is in the form of a loan that must be repaid rather than an outright grant" (FEMA 1997).

---

insurance coverage or payments. It is administered by the State Department of Insurance and the National Flood Insurance Program.

6. **Legal services.** This program includes free legal counseling for people dealing with disaster-related legal documents, titles, contract problems, and insurance. The consulting services are provided by the Young Lawyers Division of the American Bar Association.

9.1.3 Benefits

The government also helps people receive or increase benefits that are needed after the disaster. **Benefits** are government welfare programs that can be extended to disaster victims.

1. **Food Stamps.** This program assists in the distribution of groceries after a disaster through food stamps. It is controlled by state Human Services Departments.

2. **Unemployment Assistance.** This program provides income for up to 26 weeks for people who have lost their job due to the disaster. This program is 100% federally funded. It is administered by state Workforce Commissions or Employment Agencies.

3. **Social Security.** This program helps disaster victims complete applications for disability, death, and survivor benefits. It is run by the Social Security Administration.

4. **Veterans Benefits.** This program helps retired military personnel obtain answers to questions and process changes regarding Veterans Administration-insured mortgages as well as death, pension, and insurance benefits. The Veterans Administration oversees this program.

SELF-CHECK

- Do all states operate IA similarly?
- What loans are available to disaster victims?
- What are **grants** and how are they different from disaster loans?
- What services are available to those who have been affected by disaster?
- What are the benefits available to disaster victims?

9.2 Obtaining Individual Assistance

It is necessary that you understand that the process of obtaining assistance can be frustrating for victims. The application process can take time, it can be confusing, and it may take several phone calls or discussions to resolve questions or get the assistance that is needed. If an individual, family, or business has been affected by disaster, they may complete applications for individual assistance by logging on to the FEMA website, calling the National Processing Service Center, or visiting a Disaster Recovery Center.

9.2.1 National Processing Service Center

Because of technological advances, people can register for individual assistance online at http://www. fema.gov/assistance/register.shtm. However, because power and Internet lines may not function after disasters, victims can also call a National Processing Service Center at a publicized toll-free number: (800) 621-FEMA or TTY (800) 462-7585. The **National Processing Service Center (NPSC)** is a location where victims call to apply for government disaster assistance. There are four permanent National Processing Service Centers around the country. They are located in:

▲ Denton, Texas
▲ Berryville, Virginia
▲ Mt. Weather, Virginia
▲ Hyattsville, Maryland

If a disaster warrants additional processing centers, they may be opened on a temporary basis. Some of these may be located in or near the affected area. NPSCs may offer services in a variety of languages, including Spanish, as is the case in Puerto Rico.

At the NPSC, FEMA representatives use a computer program called **National Emergency Management Information System (NEMIS).** This allows FEMA representatives to record personal information about the disaster victim as well as damages, losses, needs, etc. This computer program—along with FEMA employees in the field—determines what types of disaster assistance programs the victim is eligible for. The computer notes if assistance is available after FEMA employees verify damages to property in the declared disaster area. Within days or weeks, financial assistance in the form of a check is sent to the disaster victim. In other cases victims are told how to access other types of assistance.

The use of National Processing Service Centers is an increasingly preferred method for taking disaster assistance applications. In this case, disaster victims only have to log onto the Internet or pick up the phone. They can get the help they need quickly, and FEMA's travel expenses are thereby reduced because fewer personnel are needed in the field. The application process associated with NPSC increases the speed of assistance delivery. A drawback is that National Processing Service Center employees may not always answer detailed questions about each Federal Agency's disaster assistance programs. Phone lines may also be down in the affected community.

9.2.2 Disaster Recovery Center

Because disasters may render personal phone lines inoperable for a long period of time, victims may need to seek assistance in other ways. If this is the case, those

Figure 9-2

Disaster Recovery Centers such as this one in Baton Rouge, Louisiana should be large enough to process the many applicants that seek federal disaster assistance.

affected by a disaster may visit a Disaster Recovery Center (formerly a Disaster Application Center). A **Disaster Recovery Center** is a location where victims go to meet with FEMA representatives and other relief providers to discuss assistance programs and application requirements. A Disaster Recovery Center is generally set up in the hardest hit vicinities in a declared disaster area. In large disasters, there may be multiple DRCs. Disaster Recovery Centers are staffed by state, federal, and nonprofit agencies, which permit easy access to diverse disaster assistance programs and agencies. At the DRC, victims may ask questions and fill out forms. Representatives from FEMA, the SBA, the American Red Cross, and other disaster assistance organizations provide detailed answers to technical questions. DRCs often have working phones so victims can call the National Processing Service Center. There are even mobile DRCs that can be driven to affected neighborhoods. These have satellite communication capabilities that link victims with NPSC representatives.

The selection of the DRC site is often (but not always) a local and state responsibility. You may be assigned the task of identifying a possible location, and you should ensure the DRC has the following characteristics:

▲ The building should be sufficiently large. For example, it should be at least 4,500 square feet.

▲ It should have 25 to 50 tables and 150 to 250 chairs available.

▲ Air, heating, electricity, water, and restrooms must be available.

▲ The facility should have adequate communications equipment and capability. This includes phones and fax machines.

▲ It must have general office supplies, such as paper, pencils, computers, photocopiers, and printers.

▲ The location should allow for adequate parking.

In addition, it is also important that you or other city personnel be present to help answer questions for victims and FEMA officials. You may want to provide transportation arrangements for those who need it as well as custodial, medical, security, bilingual, and childcare services. You must likewise ensure that the location of the DRC be publicized frequently by the media.

Regardless of whether victims apply for disaster assistance over the Internet, on the phone, or in person at the DRC, they must go through a four-step process. Victims must:

1. Rely on personal insurance and go through nonprofit agencies first.
2. Apply for FEMA housing assistance. They must do this even if it is not needed or required.
3. Apply for Small Business Administration loans even if they do not anticipate or desire receiving one.
4. Seek unmet needs assistance from additional community-based organizations if federal assistance is insufficient.

FOR EXAMPLE

Insurance Needs

Because federal disaster programs are available, it is tempting for some people to go without insurance. The FEMA handbook states, "Individuals, families and businesses should all carry adequate insurance to meet their needs in the event of a disaster. It is not the purpose of Federal assistance to duplicate protection available through insurance plans. Federal assistance is provided to address only the most basic disaster-related needs not covered by other means. Besides, most disaster events are not presidentially declared disasters, so Federal disaster assistance is often not available. Disaster assistance may be granted in the form of a loan rather than as an outright cash award. For geographically areas subject to floods . . . the Federal government ensures that residents of participating communities can receive appropriate insurance coverage through its National Flood Insurance Program (NFIP). In addition, flood insurance coverage is required as a condition to receiving Federal disaster aid for permanent repair or reconstruction within an identified floodplain. You may wish to contact your local emergency preparedness office, the local building or zoning official, or your insurance agent to find out whether your local community is a participant" (FEMA 1997).

Only when all of these conditions are met will the federal and state governments provide disaster assistance (assuming it is warranted).

SELF-CHECK

- What does a **National Processing Service Center** do?
- What does NEMIS stand for?
- Why is a **Disaster Recovery Center** needed after a disaster?
- What issues must be considered when setting up a DRC?
- What issues must be considered when operating a DRC?

9.3 Categories of Public Assistance

Local and state governments, just like private citizens or businesses, may require disaster assistance. For this reason, you should be familiar with the Public Assistance program. PA is directed toward governments, organizations, and nonprofits with the purpose of helping them react to and recover from a disaster. Eligible public entities include:

1. **Local governments**. This includes city, township, and regional governments.
2. **State government agencies**. These agencies consist of the Department of Transportation, Environmental Protection Departments, and so on.
3. **Indian tribes and related organizations**. This includes reservations and other Indian operated property and facilities.
4. **Private nonprofit organizations**. This covers critical facilities such as hospitals and schools. It may also encompass utility companies, custodial care centers, zoos, museums, community centers, homeless shelters, and so on. These organizations must have tax-exempt status and must provide services to the general public.

Public assistance is divided into emergency assistance and permanent assistance categories.

▲ **Emergency assistance** is financial or other types of assistance to help local and state governments deal with the immediate impacts of disasters.
▲ **Permanent assistance** is financial payments or reimbursements to local and state governments for long-term rebuilding activities.

Each of these will be described below.

9.3.1 Emergency Assistance

If a disaster is declared at the federal level, emergency assistance is given to communities as soon as possible to help them deal with the immediate impact of disasters. This helps them take care of debris removal and other protective measures.

Debris Removal

Debris removal assistance pays to clear disaster-related debris. For example, building rubble or broken tree limbs would need to be cleared from public property. If debris is posing a threat to the public, the federal government may also pay to have it removed from private property if permission is granted by the owner. The removal of certain debris such as tree stumps will not be reimbursed by the federal government because the cost is very high and it is a nonessential activity. To ensure a debris removal activity is eligible for federal assistance, it is vital that you check with all applicable regulations.

Protective Measures

Protective measures are a reimbursement category that has the purpose of reducing losses or eliminating threats to life, public health, and safety. It may include sandbagging to limit property damage in a flood. Another example is shoring up buildings immediately after an earthquake. Creating a backfire to prevent additional loss of property is another form of a protective measure. The goal of protective measures is to limit further injury, death, and destruction after the disaster occurs.

9.3.2 Permanent Assistance

Permanent assistance may also be given to local and state governments after a disaster has been declared at the federal level. This includes assistance to repair road systems, water control systems, public buildings/equipment, public utility systems, and other facilities.

Road Systems

Road systems assistance repays expenses associated with the rebuilding or repairing of bridges, lights, and culverts. Damages must be directly related to disaster (i.e., not pre-existing). Repair will conform to current standards and will match current market costs.

Water Control

Water control assistance deals with repairs to rivers, dikes, levees, and dams. Repairs must fall under U.S. Army Corps of Engineers or Natural Resource Conservation System specifications. Drainage channels will be restored to preflood capacity—assuming there is evidence of prior maintenance. Debris in natural streams will be removed only if there is a threat to public safety. Payment for seeding is used to stabilize slopes only—not for cosmetic purposes.

Public Buildings/Equipment

Public buildings/equipment assistance is given to repair or replace buildings, supplies, and vehicles. Private or self-insurance must cover all applicable payments before any federal reimbursements are to be made. Payment for rebuilding will conform to pre-existing capacity and standards. Buildings and equipment must have been in use before the disaster. Office furniture is replaced with used items only. Trees on public lands are not eligible for reimbursement.

Public Utility

Public utility assistance includes water, gas, and sewage system repairs. There must be evidence that the disaster caused the damages. Loss of revenue while these systems are down is not eligible for federal reimbursement.

Other Assistance

Other assistance is for the repair of parks, airports, and recreational facilities. Damages must be in a designated disaster-declared area. Seeding is only covered for stabilization purposes, and trees/plants are not eligible for reimbursement. Expenses for beach repair will be granted if there has been evidence of ongoing maintenance.

SELF-CHECK

- **What is public assistance?**
- **Who is public assistance for?**
- **What are the types of emergency assistance?**
- **What are the types of permanent assistance?**
- **How does permanent assistance facilitate recovery?**

9.4 Obtaining Public Assistance

As a local emergency manager, you will receive many questions about how your city or other organizations can obtain public assistance. To acquire public assistance, the affected government entity or organization will need to be aware of the process to obtain disaster recovery assistance. Although the process may vary somewhat in each state, it must conform to federal guidelines.

After an area has been approved for public assistance (e.g., a presidential declaration has been issued), a briefing will be held. A **briefing** is a meeting that reviews all aspects of federal programs and requirements to give local officials an overview of the entire recovery process. It includes local officials and the State Coordinating Officer. The briefing is often arranged by the state emergency management personnel in charge of recovery. A kickoff meeting will then be held with the individuals mentioned above as well as the Federal Coordinating Officer. A **kickoff meeting** covers federal disaster assistance programs and policies in an in-depth manner. This meeting will:

- ▲ Introduce the public assistance coordinator
- ▲ Explain the process of applying for and receiving aid
- ▲ Hand out appropriate forms
- ▲ Discuss damages and applicant needs
- ▲ Answer any questions that may arise
- ▲ Address concerns about mitigation, historical sites, and environmental protection

At this point, the government affected by the disaster is now able to make a formal request for federal disaster assistance. This must be completed within 30 days after the presidential disaster declaration. Applicants must submit:

1. Notice of Interest and Request for Public Assistance forms. These documents show the need for assistance and list damages by category.
2. A Designation of Applicant's Agent form. This document notes the point of contact for the government entity seeking federal assistance.
3. A Project Worksheet for each category of public assistance. This document helps to initiate and record emergency and permanent assistance activities.

Unlike emergency assistance, applications and record keeping for permanent assistance are classified according to one of four types of projects.

▲ **Small projects** are a type of permanent assistance that is typically paid in advance by the federal government. Small projects are those costing less than $48,899. A small project worksheet may combine many projects together (up to the specified amount).

▲ **Large projects** are permanent assistance activities requiring payment over $48,900.

▲ **Improved projects** are assistance programs that make repairs beyond the initial design or expand the building. This may include adding a wing to a building or implementing mitigation measures to prevent a similar occurrence in the future.

▲ **Alternate projects** include permanent projects that require abandonment of an old facility and building in a completely different area. An example of this is demolishing a court house in the flood plain and moving it to higher ground.

Once these application materials are received, FEMA/state officials will complete a **Damage Survey Report (DSR)** for each type of assistance being requested to determine the need and validity of the requests. This information is sent to federal employees to ensure accuracy. These officials are located in the Joint Field Office (formerly known as the Disaster Field Office). A **Joint Field Office (JFO)** is the location where FEMA representatives manage recovery. Local and state representatives may also be housed in the JFO at times. However, the location of the JFO is not announced to the public and should not be confused with the DRC.

At this point, FEMA sends approved DSRs to the state emergency management department/agency. The state then meets with the applicant(s) to discuss program requirements further, and the clean up and rebuilding is officially started. Upon completion, a Project Completion Form will be filled out so local and state governments can seek reimbursement. Any disagreements about projects

> ### FOR EXAMPLE
>
> ### Role of Local Government
>
> Despite the many federal programs available after a disaster, the local government plays one of the largest roles in response and recovery operations. The FEMA handbook states, "The local government is primarily responsible for preparing for disasters that might affect a community and helping residents recover from such events. The great majority of disasters are handled successfully at the local level. State and Federal resources are intended to assist the community only when the community's own resources are not sufficient" (FEMA 1997).

and payment amounts need to be appealed within 60 days. FEMA officials will determine what adjustments, if any, need to be made. Thus, after a declaration has been issued and orientations about the programs have taken place, the city begins the long process of recovery. The state oversees much of the paperwork, and FEMA funds approximately 75% of the costs. The entire process can take months or years, depending on the extent of the disaster losses.

SELF-CHECK

- What is a **briefing** and how is it different from a **kickoff meeting**?
- What forms should be filled out to obtain public assistance?
- What are the types of projects listed under public assistance?
- What is a **Disaster Survey Report** and why is it needed?
- What is a **Disaster Field Office** and who is located there?*

9.5 Important Issues for Recovery

As you begin in earnest the process of recovery, there are four issues that you must consider. These include the minimization of fraudulent activity, environmental protection, historic preservation, and the mitigation of future disasters.

9.5.1 Minimizing Fraud

Because there may be millions of federal dollars pouring in to disaster-affected communities, it is imperative that those working in recovery be vigilant of fraud, waste, and abuse. People have filed individual assistance disaster applications even though they have not been affected by a disaster. For example, there have been instances where criminals have sought individual assistance from unaffected jail cells! Others have requested government relief even though they do not own the piece of property in question. Public officials have also engaged in fraudulent practices. Some city leaders have filed erroneous paperwork to bring additional monies to their communities or themselves. At other times, contractors will attempt to get more reimbursement than they are entitled to by misrepresenting their work on federal documents. You should be aware of these potential scams and work closely with the Office of the Inspector General in the Department of Homeland Security to ensure that this behavior is averted or prosecuted. You may need to notify the public through the media about where to report fraudulent activity. You may also need to monitor government paperwork and contractor recovery activities carefully. FEMA has also set up a toll-free number for you to report fraud. It is (800) 323-8603.

9.5.2 Protecting the Environment

Before large recovery projects can begin, the federal government requires an environmental impact statement. Therefore, the first thing you have to do before rebuilding is complete an assessment of how your actions will affect the air, soil, and water in that area. Environmental impact statements will obviously require the skills and expertise of professionals and scholars who understand the physical environment and human interaction with rivers, plant and animal life, and other natural resources. The goal of this requirement is to ensure that recovery does not harm the environment.

9.5.3 Preserving Historic Buildings

There are thousands of historic buildings in the United States, and these can be adversely affected by disasters. They are especially vulnerable because they are old and not built to current code and regulations. Because these buildings carry a legacy of history, there will be many individuals and groups that will oppose of their demolition. There is consequently a dilemma between historical preservation on the one hand and recovery and future mitigation on the other. You must therefore assess the impact of the disaster on the building and determine what can be done, if anything, to maintain the heritage of the structure. Novel approaches can be undertaken. After an earthquake in Santa Cruz, California, the façade of a 19th-century bank was retained with city redevelopment funds and then attached to a completely new building. In other words, the structure was rebuilt to code, and the original front of the building was reattached. This maintained aesthetic charm but ensured future seismic safety.

9.5.4 Mitigating Future Disasters

Recovery is an excellent time to implement more stringent mitigation measures (Public Entity Risk Institute 2006). In the immediate aftermath of a disaster, interest in mitigation is at an all-time high. You will probably have less resistance against mitigation now than ever before. The city council is likely to be more receptive to change when a disaster occurs. However, this interest does not always stay at this level. Over the next few weeks and months, interest wanes because people want to speed up recovery and resume their normal daily activities as soon as possible. Therefore, it is imperative that you are prepared to implement mitigation measures as soon as a disaster strikes. This may require that a mitigation action plan be written before or after the disaster occurs. A **mitigation action plan** is a document that describes the vulnerabilities of the community and what should be done to correct them in the future. It may also require proposals for improved warning systems, new building codes, or property buy-out programs for low-lying areas be drafted in advance so they can be used when needed. Regarding land-use decisions after disasters, Mileti and Passarini (1996) have noted that there are three options for relocation. These include relocation to a new site, intra-urban relocation, and rebuilding in the same area.

Relocate to a New Site

An example of relocation to a new site occurred in 1964, when the strongest recorded earthquake to ever hit North America struck Valdez, Alaska. The earthquake measured 8.4 to 8.6 on the Richter scale, causing the entire town of Valdez to be severely damaged. Shortly thereafter, a tsunami produced by the earthquake caused additional devastation. During damage assessment, it was determined that the ground under Valdez was unstable and at risk of further losses. The federal government would provide financial assistance to the city only if it would relocate to a safer area. The Army Corps of Engineers decided to move the entire town to the delta of Mineral Creek, which was much safer. It took about 4 years for the new Valdez to become home to all of the old Valdez residents. Sixty-two buildings were moved from the old town to the new site. Public facilities were replaced by the government, and homeowners rebuilt their residences. The advantage of relocating to a new site is a reduction in the vulnerability of the community to disaster. Response and recovery costs associated with future disasters could be minimized. There is also increased employment from relocation after a disaster. However, relocation is very costly, and it does disrupt society a great deal.

Intra-Urban Relocation

The 6.9 earthquake that shook northwestern Armenia on December 7, 1988 provides an example of intra-urban relocation. This earthquake, and an aftershock that followed 4 minutes later, killed 25,000 people. The city of Leninakan, which had a population of 250,000, was destroyed, and other smaller towns were adversely affected as well. Many factors contributed to the disaster, including soil conditions and inadequate building design and construction. In addition to the human losses, many medical facilities were destroyed and the medical profession lost capacity as a result. This devastating loss contributed to a difficult rescue and response operation.

After the earthquake, the Armenian government made some modest changes. They altered how the land was used and restricted the rebuilding of certain structures, such as hospitals, in dangerous areas. In addition, a central planning committee decided to modify where replacement housing could be built. An advantage of intra-urban relocation is the possibility of increased employment. Intra-urban relocation is not as costly as relocating to a new site and does not disrupt society as much either. Intra-urban relocation does reduce the vulnerability of the community to disaster, but not to the same extent as relocation to a completely different site.

Rebuild in the Same Area

A good case of rebuilding in the same area comes from the Whittier Narrows earthquake, which struck the San Gabriel Valley in 1987. This disaster resulted in $358 million dollars in damages, but the community chose to rebuild in the same area nonetheless. Not only did the citizens and businesses rebuild, but they even expanded and constructed more buildings in dangerous areas.

Mileti and Passarini (1996) illustrate that there are many reasons why people wanted to build in the same areas:

▲ **Politics:** Politicians want to rebuild as soon as possible to overcome the negative impact of disasters. Their constituents also want to return to "normal" and have things the way "they used to be."

▲ **Culture:** People have ties to their community and its way of life. Change is socially disruptive, and moving is difficult for most people. Relocation may seem impossible, and there may not be a clear plan of how that is to be achieved.

▲ **Economics:** Massive federal funding enables communities to rebuild in the same areas. Rebuilding also brings in jobs and income for residents living in the area. The poor are affected most but receive less aid and find it difficult to move. Demolition of damaged structures reduces opportunities for cheap housing elsewhere. Many small businesses cannot handle the shock of relocation either.

▲ **Psychological:** People naturally want to return to their lives as they knew them, and they don't want to feel "beaten" by a disaster. They may be stressed and have a hard time coping with the disaster. Moving would disrupt them even further and cause them to lose their social networks.

Rebuilding in the same area has low immediate costs, but it often increases vulnerability. Unfortunately, rebuilding is the most common practice for communities to take after a disaster.

FOR EXAMPLE

Change and Disasters

Disasters do not always spur change in a community. In 1961, Centralia, Pennsylvania city officials were getting ready for a parade. They noticed a lot of trash in a certain area that led to an eyesore, odors, insects, and vermin. They decided to burn the trash and did not consult anyone about their desire. The trash just so happened to be located on an excavation site of an abandoned coalmine. This area had a rich deposit of anthracite coal underneath. The fire spread to the coal and expanded throughout the mine shafts. Because anthracite burns hot and long, smoke was still rising a year after this incident took place. Carbon monoxide rose into people's basements and foundations (at fatal levels). The heat created massive cracks in the earth above it. Sinkholes appeared and swallowed buildings as the land gave way beneath.

A geological team was brought in to inspect the damage. They determined that there were 40 million tons of anthracite coal remaining to be burnt. From 1962 to 1978, the state and federal government spend $3.3 million to control the fire. An additional $10.8 million was spent in 1994, but the results were unsuccessful. Those responding to the incident tried to pump water into mine shafts, but the fire spread over 450 acres. The water created dangerous steam and also polluted local rivers, streams, and lakes. The sludge that resulted was poisoned with lye and acid. By 1980, the Federal government funded a relocation project through the Office of Surface Mining. Route 61 was cut off from the road system and disappeared from the maps. In 1961, there were over 1,200 inhabitants. To date, most residents have moved out of the area. The fire still burns to this day. The Office of Surface Mining determined another $663 million would be needed to extinguish it. Most cases do illustrate a better possibility of change after a disaster.

SELF-CHECK

- Why should you be aware of fraudulent activities?
- How can you protect the environment during recovery?
- Why is historic preservation important to some individuals and groups?
- What are the options for rebuilding after a disaster?
- What is a mitigation action plan?

9.6 The Potential for Disagreement

Because recovery is characterized by the involvement of many different people and priorities, you should be aware of the potential for disagreement about what needs to be done. Bates and Peacock (1989) have identified several modes associated with disaster recovery. Some of these processes are internal to the community, whereas others are external.

Internal recovery processes are labeled as indigenous or independent. There are three paths that fall under this category.

▲ The **individualistic self-help** mode occurs when the community provides its own labor and supplies for recovery. A community operating under this mode also takes sole responsibility for the management of recovery processes.

▲ The **collective or cooperative** mode is characterized by victims working together to achieve a common goal. In this situation, agreement is reached about what to do during recovery.

▲ The **bureaucratized paternalistic** mode suggests that a person or agency inside the community controls recovery with no input from others. Victims may have little influence over what happens to their damaged homes and community rebuilding.

The exogenous or dependent processes are initiated from outside the disaster-affected community. This category also has three distinct paths.

▲ The **independent beneficiary** mode occurs when resources are sent into the affected community. However, the affected people must still provide their own labor and manage recovery operations.

▲ The **collaborative partnership** mode takes place when outsiders and victims work together to facilitate disaster recovery. It is characterized by a great deal of cooperation.

▲ The **bureaucratized external paternalism** mode features an outside agency that controls all decisions and recovery activities. Victims seem to have no input on what happens to their community.

Bates and Peacock admit that "the recovery mode usually is mixed with some resources coming from both sources. Nevertheless, the recovery process for a particular social unit in a particular disaster may be dominated by one mode or the other. It is also true that one mode of adaptation may be employed for one type of unit while a different mode is employed by another in the same disaster. For example, households experiencing a given disaster may receive outside assistance, while in the same disaster organizations (businesses) may be forced to recover on their own. Or, isolated communities may be left to their own devices, while urban centers receive massive outside aid" (1989, p. 359). For this reason, you should view these modes as ideal types that may occur simultaneously rather than being

> ## FOR EXAMPLE
>
> ### Research About Disaster Recovery
>
> Disaster researchers have illustrated that most people work together to resolve mutual disaster problems. However, studies also reveal that citizens, businesses, and politicians may disagree about recovery priorities. For instance, a heated debate about what to do with the World Trade Center site occurred once debris was removed from ground zero. Some wanted to erect new business towers, whereas others desired a permanent memorial for victims of the 9/11 terrorist attacks. Scholars have also shown that outside assistance is both appreciated and feared. Disaster victims may want federal resources, but they do not like others telling them what to do during recovery. Disagreement about what should be done exists to this day.

isolated from one another. Nevertheless, this research is useful because it helps you recognize the possibility of conflicts during the recovery process. Attention should be given to integrate efforts rather than work alone or against one another.

SELF-CHECK

- Is disaster recovery an internal or external process?
- What is the **individual self-help** mode and how is it different than the **independent beneficiary mode**?
- Why are the collective and collaborative partnership modes beneficial?
- What are the problems associated with the bureaucratized paternalistic mode?
- Is the bureaucratized external paternalism mode advantageous or disadvantageous?

9.7 Pressing for Change

Although there are often divergent opinions about what should be done after disasters, local government officials should do their best to implement all types of measures to reduce their community's vulnerability. As the local emergency manager, it is imperative that you take advantage of the "window of opportunity" disasters provide. To examine the affects of a disaster on the community, let's review the changes made after the Loma Prieta earthquake in 1998.

On October 17, 1989 a 7.1 earthquake shook San Francisco. It killed 67, injured 2,435, and caused $5.6 billion in damages. Researchers Olson, Olson, and Gawronski (1998) investigated the policy changes before and after the earthquake.

In the mid 1970s, the federal and state government pushed for mitigation activities. However, the City of Oakland rarely considered the need for such legislation. In fact, from 1954 to 1989, earthquake issues appeared only 17 times in the city council meetings. The researchers also determined:

1. No city meetings discussed unreinforced masonry (URM) buildings.
2. Building inspectors were given no attention and resources.
3. Ordinance SB 547, which was aimed at reducing seismic hazards in existing buildings, was considered another annoying law.
4. The major issues being discussed and addressed were crime and economic development.

However, after the event (from 1989 to 1995), things changed dramatically. The window of opportunity created by the disaster led to the following changes:

▲ Earthquake issues were mentioned 178 times in city agendas.
▲ There were seven laws passed that were related to damage from the event.
▲ Two laws were passed that focused on unreinforced masonry buildings and the reduction of future risk. These were ordinance 11173 and ordinance 11217.
   • Ordinance 11173 was an emergency order to deal with damaged buildings. It allowed building officials to assess buildings after the disaster and determine whether they posed a risk of collapse or falling objects. This ordinance also recommended that all buildings be upgraded to code. There were some waivers for historic buildings, however.
   • Ordinance 11217 was an act that made the temporary law (Ordinance 11173) more permanent. It limited the maximum code for rebuilding. It was also less forceful in wording (e.g., "shall substantially comply") and allowed a way out of compliance if alternative procedures for rebuilding could be found. However, in no case could design specifications be 25% below code. Ordinance 11217 brought other changes as well. It made it unlawful to eliminate historic buildings. The code set priority levels based on building location, stories, traffic, use, number of occupants, and complexity of rebuilding. It recommended that walls be attached to the foundation and the roof to reduce vulnerability.

9.7.1 Lessons From the Loma Prieta Earthquake

As an emergency manager, you can learn a great deal from the Loma Prieta earthquake. Before the Loma Prieta earthquake, building code inspectors and seismic safety advocates were self-suppressed. They recognized their inferior position and did not feel empowered to make changes or suggest them. After the earthquake, this "Seismic Safety" group gained power and took advantage of the situation. One person involved in recovery stated "The earthquake gave us a window, if

---

FOR EXAMPLE

Mitigation Measures for All Disasters

Mitigation measures can protect a community from more than one hazard (Schwab 1998). In Plainfield, Illinois, a tornado struck late in the season (August 28, 1990). It was an F-5 on the Fujita scale, destroying some homes located in the DePage floodway. The city decided to relocate the homes, which cost $180,500. The rebuilding of required building 2 feet above 100-year plain. In 1996, a major flood hit Plainfield. Although some sustained damages, all homes remain standing. Recovery from the tornado linked rebuilding to mitigation for another disaster.

---

we could use it skillfully, to review the entire city approach to building safety in a seismically active area." The seismic safety group educated realtors, business owners, and preservationists about earthquakes. They also brought all parties together to hammer out an agreement about what should be done to reduce future vulnerability (Olson, Olson, and Gawronski 1988).

There are a number of additional lessons from this disaster:

▲ Education is key. Make sure everyone understands the logic behind and need for additional mitigation measures.

▲ Acknowledge different viewpoints. People have divergent opinions about what should be done. For example, real estate and property owners will argue that there is no danger inherent to current building codes. As an emergency manager, you will desire more stringent building codes and adherence to such regulations. Historic preservationists, on the other hand, will want to protect the buildings from demolition. Find a way to compromise among these groups as it increases the possibility of compliance.

▲ Mitigation is as much political as technical. Information about the science behind mitigation is necessary, but the art of persuasion and political acumen will also be needed to implement change after disasters.

SELF-CHECK

- Why did public officials not consider mitigation before the Loma Prieta earthquake?
- Did attitudes in city council change after the disaster?
- Do some groups oppose mitigation activities?
- How did the emergency management group promote change?

SUMMARY

As an emergency manager, you must be aware of federal disaster assistance programs. You should know what types of individual assistance are available and how people can apply for them. In addition, you ought to understand the categories of public assistance and how they can be obtained. Your knowledge about NPSCs, DRCs, NEMIS, JFOs, and required paperwork can help you bring federal assistance to victims and the local government in your community. During recovery, you should avoid fraud, protect the environment, safeguard old structures, and pursue additional mitigation measures. Knowing how to work closely with others inside and outside of your community and take advantage of windows of opportunity disasters provide are also required for resilience.

KEY TERMS

Alternate projects	Permanent projects that require abandonment of an old facility and building in a completely different area.
Benefits	Government welfare programs that can be extended to disaster victims.
Briefing	A meeting that reviews all aspects of federal programs and requirements to give local officials an overview of the entire recovery process.
Bureaucratized external paternalism mode	A way of operating where an outside agency controls all decisions and recovery activities.
Bureaucratized paternalistic mode	A way of operating where a person or agency inside the community controls recovery with no victim input.
Collaborative partnership mode	A way of operating that takes place when outsiders and victims work together to facilitate disaster recovery.
Collective or cooperative mode	A way of operating that is characterized by victims working together to achieve a common goal.
Damage Survey Report (DSR)	A document that verifies the need and validity of the local and state requests for public assistance.
Disaster housing	A government program that helps people find housing for homes that may be uninhabitable due to unsafe, unsanitary, or insecure conditions.

Disaster Recovery Center (DRC)	The location where victims go to meet with FEMA representatives and other relief providers to discuss assistance programs and application requirements.
Emergency assistance	Financial or other types of assistance to help local and state governments deal with the immediate impacts of disasters.
Grants	Relief funds that do not need to be repaid.
Improved projects	Assistance programs that make repairs beyond the initial design or expand the building.
Independent beneficiary mode	A way of operating that occurs when resources are sent into the affected community.
Individual assistance (IA)	A relief program for citizens, businesses, and others affected by a disaster.
Individualistic self-help mode	A way of operating that occurs when the community provides its own labor and supplies for recovery.
Joint Field Office (JFO)	The location where FEMA representatives manage recovery.
Kickoff meeting	A meeting that covers federal disaster assistance programs and policies in an in-depth manner.
Large projects	Permanent assistance activities requiring payment over $48,900.
Loan programs	Funds loaned to individuals, families, and businesses that have sustained losses from disasters.
Mitigation action plan	A document that describes the vulnerabilities of the community and what should be done to correct them in the future.
National Processing Service Center (NPSC)	A location that victims call to apply for government disaster assistance.
National Emergency Management Information System (NEMIS)	A computer program that allows FEMA representatives to record personal information about the disaster victim as well as damages, losses, needs, etc. It is an automated system that helps to distribute relief to those in need.
Other assistance	Category of public assistance funds for the repair of parks, airports, and recreational facilities.

Other Needs Assistance — A government program that provides grants for home repair, replacement of personal property, and other disaster-related expenses for funeral, medical/dental care, and transportation.

Permanent assistance — Financial payments or reimbursements to local and state governments for long-term rebuilding activities.

Protective measures — A reimbursement category that has the purpose of reducing losses or eliminating threats to life, public health, and safety.

Public assistance (PA) — A relief program for government entities.

Public buildings/equipment assistance — Funds to repair or replace buildings, supplies, and vehicles.

Public utility assistance — Funds for water, gas, and sewage system repairs.

Road systems assistance — Funds that repay expenses associated with the rebuilding or repairing of bridges, lights, and culverts.

Services — Government programs that address unique issues or needs made evident in the disaster.

Small projects — A type of permanent assistance that is typically paid in advance by the federal government and costs less than $48,899.

Water control assistance — Funds for repairs to rivers, dikes, levees, and dams.

ASSESSING YOUR UNDERSTANDING

Go to www.wiley.com/college/McEntire to evaluate your knowledge of the basics of recovery and mitigation.
Measure your learning by comparing pretest and post-test results.

Summary Questions

1. Individual assistance is for individuals but not for families or businesses. True or False?

2. The federal government may provide loans, grants, services, and benefits to disaster victims. True or False?

3. To apply for assistance, you must log on to the FEMA's website on the Internet. True or False?

4. The Disaster Recovery Center is the place where federal officials manage the disaster. True or False?

5. There may be more than one DRC in a major disaster. True or False?

6. Indian tribes are not eligible for public assistance. True or False?

7. Sandbagging is an example of a protective measure. True or False?

8. Permanent assistance deals with road and water systems but not public utilities. True or False?

9. A briefing is a meeting where federal programs are reviewed by local and state officials. True or False?

10. During recovery, you should be concerned about fraud, environmental protection, historic building preservation, and mitigation. True or False?

11. Some people will not want to relocate after a disaster because of their cultural ties to the community. True or False?

12. The collective or cooperative mode is characterized by external control. True or False?

13. A window of opportunity to promote mitigation often occurs after disasters, but it is not long-lasting. True or False?

14. Assistance given to local governments is known as:
    (a) Individual assistance
    (b) Public assistance
    (c) Private assistance
    (d) Self-insured assistance
    (e) None of the above

15. Types of individual assistance include:
    (a) Disaster loans for businesses
    (b) Other Needs Assistance

(c) Tax assistance

(d) Economic injury loans

(e) All of the above

16. Services provided after disasters include:

(a) Crisis counseling

(b) Food stamps

(c) Social Security

(d) Veterans benefits

(e) All of the above

17. DRC stands for:

(a) Disaster response category

(b) Disaster response crisis

(c) Disaster recovery center

(d) Disaster resilience change

(e) Damage reporting category

18. Which is an example of emergency assistance:

(a) Road systems

(b) Water systems

(c) Public utility

(d) Debris removal

(e) Other Needs Assistance

19. Types of projects for public assistance include:

(a) Small

(b) Large

(c) Improved

(d) Alternate

(e) All of the above

20. Intra-urban relocation:

(a) Implies rebuilding in the same location

(b) Implies moving to a different and safer area

(c) Implies moving to a safer area within your community

(d) Does not reduce vulnerability as much as relocation

(e) c and d

21. Which of the following is characterized by a person controlling recovery within the community?

(a) Individualistic self-help

(b) Bureaucratized paternalism

(c) Bureaucratized external paternalism

(d) Independent beneficiary

(e) Collaborative partnership

Review Questions

1. Why do individuals and businesses require assistance at times after disasters?
2. What is individual assistance?
3. How are loan programs different from grants?
4. What services are available to disaster victims, and why are they beneficial?
5. How can food stamps or unemployment services help disaster victims?
6. What is a National Processing Service Center, and how does one apply for individual disaster assistance?
7. What is a Disaster Recovery Center used for?
8. What steps should be taken to open an DRC?
9. Who is eligible for public assistance?
10. How is emergency assistance different from permanent assistance?
11. What are the types of permanent assistance?
12. What is a briefing? What is a kickoff meeting? Why are they helpful to the emergency manager?
13. What are the types of projects pertaining to permanent assistance?
14. Who is located at a Disaster Field Office and what do they do?
15. What issues should you consider as you promote recovery?
16. What is a mitigation action plan, and why are they useful?
17. What are the different modes for disaster recovery?
18. Why is it important to push for change after disasters?
19. What does Loma Prieta tell us about "windows of opportunities"?

Applying This Chapter

1. You are the local emergency manager for a town near the Mississippi River. A flood has just devastated the area. Many homes have been affected. There are thousands of people who need to file applications for federal assistance. How does this take place? Can you do anything to help the disaster victims in this process?

2. You are the local emergency manager for a community that has just experience a major hurricane. A great deal of public property has been destroyed as a result. What types of assistance can be obtained for your community? What can you do to help your jurisdiction obtain federal assistance?

3. You are the local emergency manager for a city that was hit by a tornado. Many businesses were destroyed. What advice do you give to businesses in terms of the assistance they are eligible for? What measures can you recommend to reduce their vulnerability to future disasters?

4. Your community has just experienced a major riot. Leaders and community groups are protesting the decisions of civic leaders concerning immigration issues. A great deal of public property has been destroyed by fire and acts of vandalism. What do you need to do to help restore public facilities? Is there a way you could get the different parties to work together to solve mutual problems? If so, how?

5. You are the local emergency manager for New Orleans. The area has just been devastated by Hurricane Katrina. In particular, the low-lying areas of the 9th ward were hit hard as they were completely flooded. What options do you have to reduce the vulnerability of these areas to future disasters?

Types of Recovery Assistance

Write a two-page paper on the following topic: You are the local emergency manager for Los Angeles. An earthquake has just devastated the area. What types of individual and public assistance could be available, and how do you get the help you need?

Disaster Recovery Center

You are the local emergency manager for a community in Tennessee. You have experienced a major flood, and you need to set up a disaster recovery center. What things should you consider when opening up and running a disaster recovery center?

Window of Opportunity

A chemical plant has emitted hazardous materials, forcing the evacuation of hundreds of residents. How can you use the disaster to promote mitigation policies? Why will officials be more receptive to policy changes after this major disaster? Will others oppose more stringent policies? Why or why not? What can be done to get people to comply?

10

OVERCOMING TYPICAL CHALLENGES
Other Anticipated Problems After Disaster

Starting Point

Go to www.wiley.com/college/McEntire to assess your knowledge of post-disaster problems.
Determine where you need to concentrate your effort.

What You'll Learn in This Chapter

▲ Challenges of making decisions during a disaster
▲ Typical transportation considerations
▲ Potential political concerns
▲ Types of special populations
▲ Methods to assist those who are most vulnerable
▲ Importance of communication and coordination
▲ Legal issues facing emergency managers
▲ The need for record keeping after disasters

After Studying This Chapter, You'll Be Able To

▲ Apply decision-making skills that enable you to overcome disaster challenges
▲ Illustrate the need for public transit in response operations
▲ Interpret the causes of political conflict after disasters
▲ Examine the needs of special populations
▲ Differentiate those who are most vulnerable after a disaster
▲ Assess the importance of working collaboratively with other agencies
▲ Distinguish how to consult with the legal representative of the jurisdiction
▲ Demonstrate how to record expenses accurately

Goals and Outcomes

▲ Design ways to avert decision making mistakes
▲ Formulate ways to use transportation resources wisely after a disaster
▲ Assess how to protect yourself against blame after a disaster
▲ Predict who will require additional assistance after a disaster
▲ Select how to best meet the needs of special populations
▲ Appraise how to successfully communicate and coordinate with others
▲ Propose ways to reduce your legal liability
▲ Choose strategies to maintain accurate records

INTRODUCTION

Ensuring resilience requires that you are aware of the numerous problems that become evident when disaster strikes. Decision making is often difficult because of incomplete and ever-changing information. Transportation systems become disrupted, which complicates response and recovery operations. Organizations don't see eye to eye, and blame is placed on those whom are regarded to be responsible for failed operations. Numerous people have unique needs after a disaster, and these must be met in an effective and expeditious manner. Communication is difficult due to technological and human factors, and coordination suffers as a result. Lawsuits may be witnessed as people express anger for the loss of life and property. Record keeping is problematic because of the many activities taking place or because the disaster results in their loss. If you are to overcome these challenges after a disaster, it is imperative that you fully comprehend their causes and what can be done about them.

10.1 Decision Making

Decision making can be extremely challenging—even in routine or normal situations. In their daily activities, people and organizations typically try to make rational choices when they are confronted with problems. **Rational decision making** implies a search for alternative solutions and selection of the one that is deemed most appropriate. This model is not typically applicable to disasters. Disasters rarely, if ever, allow rational decision making. Decision making in disasters exhibits, at best, "bounded rationality." **Bounded Rationality** implies that the attempt to be rational is never fully achieved because of the constraints disasters present to the decision maker.

Yehezkel Dror has identified several reasons why rational decision making under disaster conditions is difficult (1988).

▲ **Facing adversity.** Disasters are characterized by injury, death, and destruction. They will demand the immediate attention of you as an emergency manager. In the aftermath of a disaster, functions to be performed include fire suppression, search and rescue, emergency medical care, damage assessment, and public information. Not only are there many things to do, but the consequences of failure to fulfill duties are very serious. For instance, a failure to sound the siren during severe weather may result in the death of numerous citizens. The sheer number and importance of things to address will be overwhelming to you after a disaster.

▲ **Image production.** During a disaster, information acquired by you may come from the media, first responders, or other sources. The perception relayed or received may be inaccurate. News organizations may show pictures from one area and not show the impact of another neighborhood. The advice of representatives in the field may lead to an over-or-under commitment of resources. Interpretations of radio traffic may also be inaccurate when you are working in emergency management positions.

▲ **Compressed time.** Because people's lives and well-being are at stake in a disaster, there is incredible pressure for decision makers to act quickly and even prematurely. Failure to quickly dispatch the fire department may result in the destruction of a building or even multiple structures in that particular geographical area. Acting early can be dangerous, however. This is because responders and others may be put in harm's way if the accident or disaster is not well-understood. Acting early can also create other problems in response. For example, requesting donations without considering the best way to obtain them could create additional challenges for you as an emergency manager.

▲ **Tragic choice.** Disasters are often accompanied by situations where there are drawbacks to nearly every decision that needs to be made. Helping one person by following medical triage procedures may result in the death of another. Connecting electricity to one neighborhood may result in the delay of assistance to another. It is difficult for you to resolve all disaster problems at any given time.

▲ **Fuzzy gambling.** Decision making during response operations is challenging as uncertainty is an expected correlate of disasters. The full extent of a disaster may not be known for hours, days, or even weeks. There may be too much information, a lack of information, or both. Disaster events unfold in unpredictable ways, hindering decisions and the development of future policies.

▲ **Strain and stress.** The physical and emotional demands placed on you and others involved in response and recovery are so excessive that they impair decision making. Post-disaster operations require long hours and tiresome work. The trauma and pressure may result in impaired judgment and overwhelm you, city leaders, and others involved in response and recovery operations.

▲ **Group processes.** The interaction of individuals and organizations in the decision-making process often leads to suboptimal results. Failure to come to an agreement delays required response and recovery operations. Coming to an agreement to appease elected leaders or go along with the crowd may have negative consequences. For instance, a decision by one organization may undermine the goals of another. Disregarding the need for traffic control may hurt the ability of firefighters to rescue those affected by an earthquake.

10.1.1 Overcoming Decision Errors

Because there is such a great probability of making poor choices during disaster response and recovery operations, you must do all you can to overcome decision errors. Dror (1988) has identified two methods.

The first method is to "design preferable models." This strategy is similar to the rational model. **Designing preferable models** entails studying the situation or problem in detail, determining the gap that exists between the goal and reality, and intervening to adapt the process to the desired outcome. This is not easy. There will be many factors you must consider during a disaster. An example of this is spending sufficient time and resources to determine the best routes for evacuation before a hurricane approaches. This is difficult under the best circumstances; it is nearly impossible under conditions of disasters. There would not be time to conduct a major study about evacuation if it is not completed before the hurricane reaches the coast.

The second method is "debugging." **Debugging** is a method that includes a keen observation of the decision process to correct potential weaknesses and mistakes as the situation unfolds. For instance, if one person in the EOC observes that the request from the fire chief is not being given sufficient attention, he or she may wish to state that there is a need to reconsider the appeal. Another example is a mayor who makes decisions based on political and not practical objectives. In this case, you might ask him or her to review recovery priorities again.

There are additional steps that can be taken to improve decision making:

▲ Increase situational awareness. **Situational awareness** suggests a need to be vigilant of circumstances to understand the context of what is taking place. Look for clues and signals in the disaster as well as options and alternatives.

▲ Listen to the information provided by others and pay extra attention to the tone of voice when they communicate. Rely on your gut instincts, modern technology, and other support systems to help you make choices.

▲ Determine if your perception is accurate and if you comprehend the events of the disaster correctly as it unfolds.

▲ Examine the disaster from different viewpoints. Ask yourself or others periodically if you have made any mistakes or if you have addressed all current and future contingencies.

▲ Take care of physical needs. Getting sufficient rest and adequate nutrients can help improve the level of alertness and mental sharpness. Be aware that some food and drink can be detrimental to your performance. For example, sugars, carbonated drinks, and caffeine inhibit physical abilities.

▲ Accept the need to adapt and be creative. There is a tendency in disasters to follow plans, established guidelines, and widely accepted norms so closely to the detriment of response and recovery operations.

In short, you will need to think critically during response and recovery operations. People often fail to "think outside the box." Ask yourself or others if the policy, decision, or course of action has any negative consequences. Seek fresh thinking from outside the organization. Determine if there are other options that

> ### FOR EXAMPLE
>
> ### Instructions From the World Trade Center Tower
>
> Poor decisions can have fatal consequences. After the North tower of the World Trade Center was hit by a hijacked airplane, someone using the public announcement system in the South tower advised that everyone should stay in the building and not evacuate. Although it is unknown who gave this order, the person or persons may have been under the impression that the first plane was an accident and therefore saw no reason for people to leave the building. In hindsight, the order to evacuate should have been given immediately to protect additional lives.

have not yet been considered. Find an alternate way of viewing or addressing the problem, and assess its feasibility and desirability. Laws and rules are there to protect the decision maker, limit liability, and ensure safety, effectiveness, and efficiency. However, there are other times when flexibility is what is needed to get the job done. Disasters will always throw curves at you and other decision makers.

SELF-CHECK

- Why is decision making difficult in disasters?
- How is bounded rationality different from rationality?
- What can be done to improve decision making in disasters?
- What is a "preferable model?"
- What is **debugging**?
- What is **situational awareness** and how does it relate to decision making?

10.2 Transportation Issues

Another common challenge you will face in disasters relates to transportation. Transportation systems can be severely disrupted in disasters. For example, the collapse of the World Trade Center on 9/11 affected subway operations and tunnel traffic in New York. Another example is the 1995 Kobe earthquake in Japan. Roads were blocked by debris, which inhibited the movement of firefighters and their equipment. There are other problems related to transportation. For instance, one of the failures in the response to Hurricane Katrina in New Orleans was the lack of public transportation for those who were not able to evacuate on their own. During Hurricane Rita, there were too many commuters leaving the Houston area. Roads were jammed. Fuel stations ran out of gas because of the unusually high demand. In other cases, it is difficult to keep people out of unsafe areas or ship needed supplies to affected areas because of logistical challenges.

10.2.1 Dealing With Transportation Problems

If transportation systems and resources are severely disrupted, alternate means for travel can be found. For instance, roads might be blocked. If so, planes and boats might come in handy to move people and supplies around. You should also use other available systems and resources effectively after disasters. Transit companies and "school buses are called on for . . . service especially in smaller communities where they may be the only form of mass transportation" (Scanlon 2003, p. 431). If needed, you should ensure that sufficient fuel is available when people evacuate from hurricanes or other disasters. This requires communication with the private sector.

You should also be aware that drivers, vehicles, and transportation systems can help with other disaster response and recovery functions. In Fort Worth, Texas, police officers controlled access to the downtown area affected by the March 2000 tornado. The police department, public works, and transit authorities also worked jointly to keep people out of the ground zero area and ensure the continued movement of traffic after the 9/11 disasters.

Mass transit is especially useful for evacuation. The most dramatic example of this was the evacuation of Manhattan during the terrorist attacks of 9/11. "In 2001, it was estimated that 2.2 million commuters were in New York City on a normal working day. With the collapse of the second World Trade Center tower on 9/11, hundreds of thousands of such commuters, as well as other workers, residents and transients in the impact zone were mostly blocked off from leaving by the usual land route. Streets around the impact area were debris-clogged and public transportation had ceased operations . . . . At around 11 a.m. there began a massive evacuation [possibly up to 500,000], by a large number of boats and vessels that had converged on the sea walls and few docks in the area. The everyday ferries, tour and dinner boats and pleasure craft that normally carry passengers, were joined by far more numerous vessels such as tugs, outboard runabouts, pilot boats, and oil spill response vessels, a Coast Guard cutter and even a retired fire boat, that were never intended to carry passengers" (Kendra et al 2002 in Scanlon 2003, p. 432). Of course, everything in your power should be done to inform residents where transportation will be available in case of a disaster.

The response from transportation companies is often ad hoc in nature. However, the companies that react to disasters are generally very effective. There are several reasons transportation companies are so responsive in disaster situations. "The first is that transportation companies are always dealing with minor problems that disrupt their schedules, such as those caused by traffic accidents, spills and,

FOR EXAMPLE

Transportation Systems Can Be the Site of Disasters

As we saw with 9/11, the Madrid train attacks, and the London subway bombings, the transportation system is rapidly becoming the target of choice for terrorists. This leads to an increased need for training for transportation workers on what suspicious activity to look for and report and what actions to take in an emergency.

most important, weather. Second, most such companies have experience with special events. . . . Disasters create the same kind of demands: thus the required response is a familiar one even though the timing is unexpected. Third, most transportation companies operate during two peak periods: if the demand for assistance comes at any other time, they have staff and equipment available. Fourth, it would appear that transportation systems treat requests for emergency assistance as a priority, and are willing to adjust their regular service if this is required. Perhaps more important, when transportation systems are called on to provide help in an emergency, they are doing, for the most part, what they normally do, taking persons from one place to another" (Scanlon 2003, p. 436).

Transportation issues therefore have a close relation to disasters as well as response and recovery operations. This is because transportation systems commonly deal with unexpected changes, special events, and severe weather. They carry vital personnel and supplies from far around the world or country to the scene of a disaster to help with recovery. For example, food and equipment were delivered from all over the world during the earthquakes in Pakistan in 2005. Many transportation companies will offer their services to emergency managers voluntarily. They will also contract with you or nonprofit organizations to deliver water, food, ice, or other supplies to affected areas.

SELF-CHECK

- How can transportation be affected by disasters?
- What problems are evident in evacuation? Traffic control? Service delivery?
- Is transportation important to the emergency manager?
- What can be done to overcome transportation problems?
- How vital is the mass transit system or the private sector in disasters?

10.3 Politics

We all saw that in Hurricane Katrina, the needs of many disaster victims were not met. The disturbing footage of people stuck in shelters or on the interstate without any food or water angered many Americans. Hurricane Katrina quickly became a hot-button political issue. Some argued that the needs of certain individuals and groups were not met because of racism. Others argued that the government was just inept or that people need to do a better job of caring for their own needs. Regardless of the cause, these cases show that disasters are undoubtedly a political phenomenon. Politics are exhibited in disaster response operations in at least three distinct ways. Political turmoil or favoritism may be seen in interorganizational conflict, blame, and disaster declarations and assistance delivery.

When disaster strikes and the response begins, you should not be surprised if there is some or a significant degree of interorganizational conflict. There may be disagreement about several issues pertaining to the response. For instance, who will be given authority over the incident? Which organizations will be assigned menial or less-visible tasks? Which organizations will be given additional resources and responsibilities? Who will get credit for their role in the event?

Some organizations will limit their interaction or stop working with others simply because interorganizational rivalries exist. For example, police and fire departments often exhibit this type of competition. An example is a discussion about whether to close a freeway to care for victims of a major traffic accident. The firefighters may want to protect their workers, but the police officers want to keep traffic flowing. In other cases, different departments or levels of government may not agree on response and recovery priorities.

You should also expect that someone or a group will be blamed after a disaster (see Neal 1984). For instance, there was a significant amount of discussion about who was at fault for the 2001 terrorist attacks (9/11 Commission Report 2004). Some claimed that President Clinton did not do enough to respond to terrorist bombings of the embassies in Africa and attack on the USS Cole. Others suggested that President Bush was too concerned about China. He failed to notice the growing threat of terrorism from non-state actors. Fingers have also been pointed to several other organizations for a variety of reasons:

▲ Why did the CIA and FBI fail to integrate clues about an imminent attack from various intelligence reports?

▲ How did the terrorists manage to get into the country past customs and border patrol agents?

▲ Did the aviation schools fail to adequately report suspicious terrorist behavior?

▲ How did airport screeners miss the weapons smuggled on board by terrorists?

▲ Why was communication between the police and fire departments inadequate?

▲ Who issued contradictory evacuation orders in the South Tower?

▲ Why did the Trade Center structures collapse, and could this have been prevented by architects, engineers, and building inspectors?

At the local level, you may receive excessive and undue blame for the impact of disasters or subsequent response and recovery operations. There is a very large chance that you will be seen as the "scapegoat" after disasters. Politicians will often do this because they are interested in protecting their image in the media and popularity among citizens. Many emergency managers have lost their jobs for both justified and unjustified reasons after disasters.

Politics are also prevalent when disasters are declared and when relief assistance is distributed. Local and state officials may exaggerate damages to obtain additional federal assistance. The president may provide disaster relief without going through the regular declaration process (Sylves 1996). There may be disagreement about who should get help first. Politicians may assist major corporations and wealthy neighborhoods initially to gain votes in upcoming elections. They may do this instead of helping smaller businesses and poorer communities because of their lack of political power. Even if there is no intentional malfeasance, some individuals and groups will complain that preference is being given no matter what is taking place. This may be simply because they do not understand that there are limited resources and excessive needs that must be met. Regardless, politics will certainly be a concern for you as an emergency manager.

10.3.1 Overcoming Political Problems

You should not feel powerless in light of the political forces at work in disasters. Steps can be taken to overcome interorganizational conflict, limit blame, and use politics to one's advantage. To reduce interorganizational conflict, you can do several things both before and after a disaster strikes. Get to know departmental leaders in the city and those of all other organizations. Try to develop a rapport with them and encourage them to do the same with others. Work together and clarify responsibilities before disaster strikes. It is much easier to find consensus during normal, routine times rather than resolve disagreements after a disaster occurs. Reason with organizations. Show the merit of collaboration. Illustrate how their involvement and assistance will help disaster victims and speed up response and recovery operations. Go to the political figure for assistance. If all else fails, ask the mayor or county commissioner to settle differences or enforce decisions.

You can also reduce the amount of blame you could receive and protect your career by:

▲ **Keeping records.** Tracking the policy and budget proposals you submit to the mayor and city council and noting the degree of support given or withheld by such decision makers can help you in the long run. For instance, record in a journal that funding for a new warning system was denied by city officials. File the proposal for later retrieval if needed. This could be helpful if warning is seen as problematic in future disasters.

▲ **Monitoring progress.** Review the progress of the response, make adjustments as required, record successes, and work swiftly to correct mistakes in the after-action report. Communicate accomplishments of response operations to key political leaders and work swiftly and diligently to resolve problems evident in the management of the disaster.

▲ **Going to the media if needed.** As a last resort, you can try to keep your job by expressing your viewpoint with the press. Note that this could create even more animosity toward you or it may help you retain employment. Therefore, this should be a last resort and should be approached with extreme caution.

Emergency managers can also use politics to their advantage after a disaster. Disasters generate an incredible amount of interest on the part of the media, citizens, and politicians. Disasters are unique "focusing events" that can determine the policy agenda in this issue area (Birkland 1996). You should harness the interest in disasters to improve the ongoing response, seek recovery aid, and promote additional mitigation and preparedness activities.

FOR EXAMPLE

Hurricane Katrina and the Blame Game

The anger and disappointment that many Americans felt about the response to Hurricane Katrina encouraged politicians to place blame. Local and state politicians argued that the federal government did not respond quickly enough. National politicians asserted that the state and local governments were not prepared to deal with such an obvious risk. In reality, all three levels of government made mistakes that were compounded by a failure to integrate decisions and policies among them. The head of FEMA, Michael Brown, lost his job because of the poor response. This occurred even though some believe that the Department of Homeland Security had set the organization up for failure. Too many changes had been made to the national emergency management system that appeared to work effectively before 9/11.

SELF-CHECK

- Do emergency managers need to be concerned about the politics of disasters?
- What political problems face the emergency manager?
- How can the emergency manager overcome interorganizational conflict and the politics of declarations?
- What can be done to reduce blame after disasters?
- Are disaster declarations and post-disaster activities political?
- What is a focusing event?

10.4 Special Populations

Different people have varying capacities to cope with disasters. For example, some are more likely than others to be affected by disasters. This is because of the location of their home, the construction of their residence, the nature of their employment, their socioeconomic status, their cultural attitudes and practices, and so on. They may not be able to react quickly or effectively to (or after) a disaster because of physical, mental, emotional, economic, and other reasons.

Those persons who are susceptible to disasters and those who are least able to deal with their impact are known as "**special populations**" (Picket and Block 1991, p. 287). A special population is a group of individuals that are prone to become victims of disasters. They also lack capability to respond alone and/or have requirements for additional assistance to fully recover. Special populations may also be known as special-needs groups or vulnerable populations.

A special population is comprised of people who have limited self-sufficiency after a disaster strikes. They require extra or unique aid, resources, care, and attention from others. Although all people may be vulnerable to some degree, some people are especially susceptible to disasters. They are also the least resilient in the aftermath of the event. It is vitally important that you and first responders know who may be regarded as a special population. You must then take steps to ensure that their needs are met after a disaster (see Figure 10-1).

Research literature has devoted a great deal of attention to women, ethnic groups, and the poor. Less is known about others who comprise special populations. We will examine each group.

Figure 10-1

Special populations may require sheltering, as was the case in New Orleans after Hurricane Katrina. Vulnerable individuals and groups may also require evacuation assistance, medical care, and other types of relief after disasters.

10.4.1 Women

Women may, in some cases, be seen as a special-needs group. Women are regarded to be special populations at times for many reasons, including:

▲ **Socioeconomic status.** Women, single women, and single mothers often have a lower socioeconomic status than men. This often places women at risk. "Women in public housing are especially at risk. While projects vary in the degree to which they are safely located, retrofitted, or maintained, on balance the rising maintenance costs in aging structures have resulted in deterioration of the nation's public housing stock" (DeParle 1996, p. 43).

▲ **Their roles as mothers.** Women will often protect their children in time of disaster. Women put their children's needs first, which jeopardizes their own safety. Childcare can also require staying indoors, which is dangerous in some disasters such as earthquakes (Fothergill 1996).

▲ **The likelihood of suffering from post traumatic stress disorder.** Female caregivers have higher incidents of stress and fatigue than other people after disasters (Fothergill 1996).

▲ **Domestic violence after disasters.** Research shows that domestic violence increases in times of disasters. Women are most likely to be the target of such attacks.

▲ **Poorly designed government relief programs.** "Government-provided temporary housing communities were not designed around the needs of women and children. During their long stays in temporary trailers, women's day-to-day efforts to cook, clean, and care for their families, often in combination with paid jobs and unpaid community work, were complicated by the physical limitations of temporary accommodations, e.g., lack of privacy, few play spaces for children or activities for teens, insufficient laundry facilities, and social isolation" (Enarson 1999, p. 48).

10.4.2 Ethnic Groups

The proportion of ethnic groups in the United States is on the rise. Demographers estimate that within 30 years, one-third of the population will be comprised of ethnic and racial minorities. Ethnic groups may have additional disaster needs and are therefore special populations. Ethnic groups are vulnerable in light of several factors.

▲ **Housing in risk-prone groups.** In the United States, many ethnic members live in old apartment buildings and unreinforced masonry structures, which are the most susceptible to damage in a disaster (Fothergill et al 1999, p. 161).

▲ **Risk perception.** Ethnic groups are not as sensitive to risks as most caucasions are. This may be due to cultural factors or socioeconomic constraints that limit their ability to protect themselves.

▲ **Response actions.** Ethnic groups, including Mexican-Americans and African-Americans, are less likely to evacuate than whites (Fothergill et al 1999, p. 160). At times, this may be due to distrust in government authorities.

▲ **Discriminatory practices.** It is believed that some African Americans and Hispanics may receive less aid than whites after a disaster. Undocumented workers will be reluctant to apply for aid for fear of deportation. Ethnic groups are also less likely to receive government loans. This is because of qualification requirements. "Members of racial and ethnic minorities are less likely to qualify and receive various types of aid, including Small Business Administration (SBA) loans, and to have trouble with the housing process" (Fothergill 1999, p. 167).

▲ **Language barriers.** Disaster-related agencies may have little or insufficient bilingual staff. Warnings are often not repeated correctly in other languages. Research also shows problems with translation. For example, in one disaster, the radio operator used the phrase "aviso de tornado." "The operator's use of 'aviso' probably was not correct, for the word means to give news, advice or information. The technical meaning of the word 'warning,' representing a materialized, impending disaster, has no direct translation into Spanish and its meaning is not conveyed by 'aviso'" (Aguirre 1988, p. 72). In addition, relief information for some disasters is provided in English only. This happened after Hurricane Andrew.

▲ **Cultural sensitivities.** "In Miami, immigrants from countries with a history of political repression, such as El Salvador and Guatemala, were averse to getting help (Enarson and Morrow 1997). In California, some residents of Central American origin found the National Guard tents and fences to be reminders of death camps in their native countries and refused to use them (Phillips 1993)" (Fothergill et. al. 1999, p. 166).

▲ **Higher rates of PTSD.** Ethnic groups also have higher rates of PTSD. They have a harder time recovering emotionally from disasters. "Green et al (1990) performed a . . . study on . . . the dam collapse and found that more blacks had delayed post-traumatic stress disorder (PTSD) than whites" (Fothergill 1999, p. 162-163). This may be a result of ethnic groups being located in more hazard-prone areas. It may also result from a lack of insurance, financial reserves, and ability to qualify for loans.

▲ **Other factors.** Undocumented aliens are likely to live in substandard housing. They may not seek or receive federal disaster assistance due to their illegal entry into the United States. Beggs, Haines, and Hurlbert illustrate that some people do not have sufficient social networks so they are unable to tap into formal disaster-assistance programs (1996).

In summary, "many minorities had greater difficulties recovering due to lower incomes, fewer savings, greater unemployment, less insurance and less access to communication channels and information" (Fothergill et al 1999, p. 164).

10.4.3 The Poor

The poor are vulnerable to disasters because they have few resources. The poor are more likely to live in dilapidated buildings or homes that do not meet current building code requirements. It is more difficult for the poor and the homeless to find suitable housing solutions after a disaster. The poor will also have trouble working through the government system and filling out forms because many will lack education. Without help maneuvering the bureaucratic system, the poor will receive less government aid. They will lack insurance, savings, and discretionary spending money. The homeless are especially vulnerable as they have the least resources of any group.

10.4.4 Tourists

Tourists are vulnerable to disasters. The main reason is because many tourist destinations are located in vulnerable areas. For example, coastlines with beautiful beaches are vulnerable to hurricanes and tsunamis. Mountain resorts are vulnerable to landslides or forest fires. Tourists are also unfamiliar with these new surroundings and therefore do not know how to take actions to protect themselves. At times, they may not speak the local language either.

10.4.5 The Elderly

The elderly are more likely than others to be injured because of their frail bodies. In disasters, the proportion of the injured among the 65- to 74-year-old age group is higher than for other segments of the population. Not only will their injuries be greater, but heat and cold temperatures will affect the elderly more as their immune systems are weakened. In addition, disasters can restrict access to medications that the elderly need (Eldar 1992). The elderly may not be able to drive and will need assistance with evacuation. They may also lack financial resources due to limited retirement incomes.

10.4.6 Children

Children are more likely to be injured than most adults, and they may suffer intensely from the emotional strain of disasters. Children will therefore need extra attention to ensure that they do not suffer from post-traumatic stress disorder. Children also have higher casualty rates in disasters. Because they are young, they may not be able to make and implement proper decisions to protect themselves when disasters occur.

10.4.7 The Disabled

The disabled (physically and/or mentally) are vulnerable to disasters. The percentage of people with a disability has increased over time. They now comprise one-quarter of the country's entire population (Rahimi 1993, p. 59). There are many buildings and spaces that are difficult for the disabled to navigate, even during normal times. This is complicated in disasters when buildings collapse. Wheelchair-bound people have an especially difficult time evacuating when the elevators do not work in times of emergency. In these cases, wheelchair-bound people have to rely on their co-workers or rescue workers to carry them down the stairs to safety. The blind, hearing impaired, and others have similar needs others may need additional help to understand warnings and evacuate safely.

10.4.8 Other Special Needs Groups

There are many other special groups who are vulnerable to disasters. Some of these people include:

▲ **Prisoners.** Prisoners may require extra attention for warning and evacuation. This is due to their numbers, confinement, and inaccessible locations. It is also due to the requirement for law-enforcement supervision.

▲ **Hospital and nursing home patients.** Hospital and nursing patients necessitate special attention. This is a result of their lack of mobility, need for medications, importance of medical care, requirement of power supply for life support, etc.

▲ **Homebound.** Those who are homebound may not be able to protect themselves or evacuate to safer areas. They may have to remain at home for physical, mental, emotional, or other reasons.

▲ **Migrant workers.** Migrant workers may live in temporary housing in hazardous areas and be least able to cope with disaster due to poverty and language barriers.

▲ **People with pets.** Individuals and families may not want to evacuate without their pets. Accommodations must also be made when sheltering these people.

▲ **Farmers/ranchers.** People living in secluded areas may be overlooked by emergency management personnel. Farm animals may also have unique needs in a disaster (e.g., food or rescue from flood waters).

You should recognize that certain populations may have compounded needs because they fall into several of the above categories. For instance, a black minority woman might be poor, elderly, and disabled.

FOR EXAMPLE

Hurricane Katrina and Special Populations

If there ever was a disaster that illustrated the challenges of dealing with special populations, it was Hurricane Katrina. A great number of deaths were reported among women and children. They were in many cases unable to escape from the rising flood waters. Most of those seeking shelters were poor African Americans. They did not have their own vehicles to leave New Orleans. The elderly and patients in hospitals and nursing homes would not or could not evacuate when warned. This created enormous problems for health care providers. Prisoners were sent by bus to various cities, including Dallas, Texas. Little or no coordination allowed some of them to escape during the evacuation. Some people would not leave their homes or enter designated shelters. They did not want to leave their pets. Each of these problems illustrates the importance of addressing special population needs during disasters.

SELF-CHECK

- What is a special population?
- Why are ethnic minorities and the poor particularly vulnerable to disasters?
- Why are tourists considered special populations?
- Why are the elderly the most likely to die or be injured in disasters?
- What are the unique needs of the disabled in disasters?
- How do pets impact their owners and emergency managers during response and recovery operations?

10.5 Meeting the Needs of Special Populations

As can be imagined, you should take several steps to ensure that the needs of special populations are met in disasters. Recommended actions are as follows:

1. Identify the special populations that exist in the community and understand the demands they place on emergency response organizations.
2. Recognize the need to promote further social and economic equality in society.
3. Approach the disaster with special populations in mind. Considering the needs of women, ethnic groups, and the poor is essential. The same could be said for all special groups.

FOR EXAMPLE

Poverty and Disasters

In times of relative wealth for the United States, poverty is not in many people's consciousness. When Hurricane Katrina hit New Orleans, it was clear that the majority of the victims were poor. The hurricane raised the economic status of disaster victims as a national issue. Since Hurricane Katrina, there have been many discussions about how to combat poverty and help the poor. Some argue that a culture of entitlement to welfare programs needs to be changed. Others assert that society exploits poor and powerless individuals. Regardless of the cause, it is clear that poverty exacerbated Hurricane Katrina. It remains to be seen if any new federal or state programs will be proposed to address the issue, but there is a growing realization that emergency managers cannot ignore poverty in the future.

4. Seek resources as needed to effectively respond to the needs of special populations. For example, you will probably need to work with bilingual employees or volunteers.

5. Ensure responders and the community are aware of special populations. For example, you will want to ensure disaster personnel are providing appropriate assistance to the elderly (Eldar 1992). You could also contact hotel personnel to make them aware of the procedures they should take after a disaster to help tourists (Burby and Wagner 1996).

6. Address the needs of special populations when disaster strikes. A good way to ensure that this occurs is by communicating with special needs groups and nonprofit disaster-relief organizations.

SELF-CHECK

- What is a special population?
- Why are some people more vulnerable than others?
- What are special or vulnerable populations?
- Can people's situation compound their vulnerability?
- What is the implication of special populations for emergency managers?
- What can be done to assist special populations after disasters?

10.6 Communications and Coordination

Two of the most important activities in disasters are communication and coordination. Ironically, there is no widely accepted definition of what communication and coordination mean.

▲ **Communication** is the process of relaying vital information that has a bearing on the effectiveness of disaster response and recovery operations. This sharing of information can be relayed through verbal, written, and other forms (body language).

▲ **Coordination** is the harmonization of activities among diverse actors in emergency management with the purpose of overcoming the challenges inherent in disasters. It helps emergency managers work with others to reach and attain goals.

Communication and coordination need to occur among all levels of government and with the private and nonprofit sectors. They are two common and closely related activities in response and recovery operations.

In a disaster, communication is needed to understand the impact of the event. Emergency managers must talk among themselves and others so that the needs of the community and disaster victims can be met. For instance, response operations cannot take place unless information has been relayed and received about the location of the incident, the impact of the hazard, and what needs to be done to care for victims.

There is a close link between communication and coordination. Communication is required if individuals and groups are to be made aware of the need to coordinate. Coordination determines who will respond and how this will be accomplished. In other words, if one group is aware of a certain challenge or cannot meet disaster demands alone, they will need to relay this information to others. Personnel and agencies will then need to determine role assignments for response and recovery operations. Agreement is hopefully reached and organizations work jointly to accomplish such tasks.

Everyone involved in response and recovery should communicate and coordinate with other individuals and groups. It is especially important among certain groups such as dispatch, first responders, fire and police chiefs, EOC personnel, neighboring communities, different levels of government, and pertinent actors in the private and nonprofit sectors.

10.6.1 Benefits of Communication and Coordination

Communicating and working with others is crucial in a disaster. Only by sharing information and working with others can you identify the needs of victims and those involved in post-disaster activities. You can inform others about needs, contingencies, goals, and operations by having the lines of communication open. Others can also make you aware of unfolding events, objectives, and response and recovery activities. It is important that you are able to work collaboratively with others to address the demands made evident in a disaster. (see Figure 10-2).

A good example is the exchange of information and harmonization of activity relating to emergency medical personnel and hospitals. "To muster their resources, hospitals need to have advanced warning that they will be receiving patients and timely estimates of the types, numbers, and severities of casualties to be expected. This information must come from those at the disaster scene. In addition, hospitals are at the mercy of those at the scene to see that casualties are equitably distributed, so that no one hospital receives an inordinate number" (Auf der Heide 1989, 5.6).

In contrast, the lack of communication and coordination may result in "an inability to determine priorities, misunderstandings among organizations, failure to fully utilize equipment and personnel, overly-taxed organizations, delays in

Figure 10-2

EOCs like this one in Louisiana are vital for the effective management of disasters. They are vital locations where emergency management personnel meet to discuss priorities, determine policy, and carry out important post-disaster functions.

service, omission of essential tasks, duplication of effort, safety problems, and counterproductive activity among other things" (McEntire 2003).

10.6.2 Communication and Coordination Barriers

Communication is often difficult during disasters for several reasons. Equipment and facilities needed for communication may be disabled or overloaded (Auf der Heide 1989, p. 49-50). After the terrorist attacks on the World Trade Center, police and fire could not communicate. This was due to limited channel capacity and the failure of repeaters. In addition, first-responder radios were unable to penetrate walls, stairwells, and floors. In other disasters, one piece of equipment may not be compatible with others. Disasters often topple antennas and interrupt electrical power. They may lead to the loss of cell towers. Broadcast stations and radio networks may also be adversely affected. This would prevent messages from being relayed to the public.

These problems are real. However, not every communication problem can be blamed on the disaster conditions or equipment. "Some communications problems are 'people problems,' rather than 'equipment problems'" (Auf der Heide 1989, 5.3). These people problems are numerous. Individuals tend to give information to their organizations first. This is regardless of whether or not it makes sense for the response effort. The post-disaster needs of other organizations are not widely understood. Someone may have information that another organization requires and not know it. There is often no agreement for who in the response effort is responsible for collecting and distributing information. Too much information, breakdown in communication networks, and cross checking to confirm others' messages may also hurt communications (Drabek 1985, p. 88). Interorganizational rivalry also hinders communication. Dwyer and Flynn (2005, p. 60) discovered that attempts for interoperability were never acted on or resolved in many cases.

There are several reasons why coordination is likewise difficult in times of disasters. One explanation for this challenge is the nature of disasters. Auf der Heide notes, "one of the reasons disaster response is difficult to coordinate is because disasters are different from routine, daily emergencies. The difference is more than just one of magnitude. Disasters generally cannot be adequately managed merely by mobilizing more personnel and material. Disasters may cross jurisdictional boundaries, create the need to undertake unfamiliar tasks, change the structure of responding organizations, [and] trigger the mobilization of participants that do not ordinarily respond to local emergency incidents . . . . As a consequence of these changes, the normal procedures for coordinating community emergency response may not be adapted well to the situation" (1989).

McEntire (2002) has identified additional factors that inhibited or discouraged coordination after the Fort Worth Tornado:

▲ Insufficient, incomplete, inaccurate, or an overabundance of information.
▲ Lack of communication among first responders and those in the EOC.
▲ Loss of emergency communications equipment.
▲ Language barriers among responders and victims.
▲ Controlling or domineering attitudes on the part of individuals responding to the disaster.

10.6.3 Enhancing Communication

There are several ways you can overcome the equipment and people problems associated with disaster communications. You will need to make sure that you have the right technology and equipment to enhance communication. For instance, trunk radio systems can increase channel capacity. There are also certain pieces of equipment that may link your organization to others. This is known as interoperability. **Interoperability** is the ability to communicate and operate across and with various disaster organizations. It requires not only the necessary communications equipment but a willingness to use it. The 9/11 Commission Report illustrated that the police and fire departments had at least some equipment that would have allowed interoperability. However, the organizations disagreed about who would be responsible for it. Such attitudes must be avoided at all costs in disasters.

Bill Swan, Section Emergency Coordinator (SEC) for the North Texas Section of the American Radio Relay League, provides other recommendations. He asserts that communication is most effective when information sharing is calm, courteous, correct, and concise. Here are some of his tips for communication:

▲ Do not get caught up in the excitement of the disaster.

▲ Be respectful to the others you talk to.

▲ Ensure that the information you share is as accurate as possible.

▲ Keep it short and simple.

10.6.4 Improving Coordination

Communication and coordination can both be enhanced by establishing trust within the organization and between organizations. To foster trust, Auf der Heide (1989) encourages the maintenance of formal and informal contacts between personnel within the organization and with members of different responding organizations. He also recommends the implementation of agreements regarding the division of responsibilities, response and recovery procedures, performance criteria, and resource sharing.

Coordination may be enhanced through other methods, too. In one study of response, it was observed that coordination was facilitated when there is strong leadership, a "team" orientation, experience in prior disasters, and effective EOC management (McEntire 2002). McEntire also suggests that coordination is enhanced when there is contact, communication, and cooperation among responding organizations. Networking, the relaying of information, and a willingness to collaborate with others are all positively correlated with coordination.

In addition, Drabek (2003) recommends that emergency manager employ five key strategies to coordinate disasters. These include:

1. **Core:** You may enhance coordination by clarifying agency roles before a disaster. Know what resources can be accessed for the response. Determine who should be given authority in a certain circumstance.

2. **Consequences:** Those involved in the response can promote coordination by keeping track of disaster needs and how they are being met.

3. **Customer:** Coordination can be increased when an effort is made to serve partner agencies, stakeholders, and victims of a disaster.

4. **Control:** Responders and emergency managers can improve coordination by reminding those they are working with of approved agreements, experiences from past disasters, the need to share authority, the value of

> ## FOR EXAMPLE
>
> ### "Give Me Everything You Got"
>
> According to many published reports, Louisiana Governor Blanko asked President Bush to give Louisiana "everything you've got" the night Hurricane Katrina made landfall. The Governor, however, did not specifically request the 82nd Airborne, which is what she should have done to receive the immediate assistance she was looking for. According to one of her unnamed staff members, Governor Blanko "wouldn't know the 82nd Airborne from the Harlem Boy's Choir." This is one example of how communication broke down between the state and federal government (Thomas, Evan, "How Bush Blew It," Newsweek. September 19, 2005).

departing from established procedures, and the advantages of working with emergent organizations.

5. **Cultural:** Helping other agencies understand the cultural differences of different responding agencies and view multi-agency responses critically and celebrating successes may also help organizations to coordinate.

The degree of success or failure of coordination can also be determined by two other factors (Drabek 2003). The first is the frequency of communications. The more often an organization communicates accurately with others, the better. The second factor is the breadth of coordination. This includes the number of organizations an individual, department, or agency collaborates with. Coordination is most likely to occur when organizations go out of their way to work with others.

SELF-CHECK

- What is **communication**?
- What is **coordination**?
- How is communication related to coordination?
- What are the benefits of communication and coordination?
- Why are communication and coordination difficult in disasters?
- What is **interoperability** and how can it be promoted?
- What steps can be taken to improve coordination?

10.7 Legal Concerns

Some emergency managers may not sufficiently understand disaster law because "FEMA educational materials are noticeably lacking when it comes to coverage of legal issues" (Nicholson 2003a, p. 17). However, response and recovery activities are shaped in large part by disaster law. You must be aware of the fact that lawsuits may arise from the way disasters are handled. For example, some critics of the response to the Mt. St. Helens eruption asserted that politicians and scientists drew up illogical evacuation zones near the volcano. Although some people stayed in or ignored danger zones, it is believed that the limited size of the zones on one side of the volcano was at least partially responsible for the deaths of 64 people. Should the government be held liable because of the impact of these decisions? At times, civic leaders may be taken to court for the outcome of response and recovery activities. It is therefore important that you understand disaster the law and how to protect against possible lawsuits.

10.7.1 Disasters and Law

Post-disaster operations have a close connection to the law. **Laws** are rules that are established by the government to maintain order and perform important functions in society. Laws pertaining to disasters must be understood and followed by emergency managers. Many federal laws have been passed after disasters to permit the disbursement of funds to those affected. Laws have also been established to manage response and recovery efforts.

The Congressional Act of 1803 was the first disaster law. It was established to provide relief to a New Hampshire town that was damaged by a fire. From 1803 to 1950, there were scores of disasters that received similar ad hoc decrees. In 1950, the Federal Disaster Act established permanent legislation to ensure more structured relief programs. In 1969, Hurricane Camille led to the creation of the Federal Disaster Assistance Administration in the Department of Housing and Urban Development (HUD). The Disaster Relief Act of 1970 was introduced to minimize the fragmentation of federal recovery programs. In 1974, the Disaster Relief Act of 1974 streamlined the presidential disaster declaration process. Legislation was passed again in 1979, this time to create FEMA by integrating several organizations from HUD and the Defense Department's Defense Civil Preparedness Agency. In 1988, the Robert T. Stafford Disaster Relief and Emergency Assistance Act expanded the definition of what events could be considered a disaster and specified who could receive assistance, for what purposes, and how it should be administered. There are other laws that have been passed in recent years. In 2002, the federal government passed the Homeland Security Act, which combined 22 federal agencies into the Department of Homeland Security. 9/11 also led to the creation of the National Response Plan and other measures that have had a dramatic impact on the direction of emergency management in this country.

Laws are applicable to disasters in other ways as well. For instance, there are numerous statutes that have to be followed in response to hazardous materials incidents. These include:

▲ The Comprehensive Environmental Response, Compensation and Liability Act (CERCLA)
▲ Title 29, Section 1910.1200 of the Code of Federal Regulations
▲ Federal Food, Drug, and Cosmetic Act
▲ Toxic Substances and Control Act (TOSCA)
▲ The Superfund Amendments and Reauthorization Act (SARA).
▲ The Emergency Planning and Community Right to Know Act (EPCRA)
▲ The Federal Insecticide, Fungicide, and Rodenticide Act (FIFRA)

States and local government have also passed several laws for disaster response and recovery operations. For example, states have enacted legislation to create emergency management agencies and endorse federal disaster laws and regulations. The laws are not uniform across all states, however, because of the unique disaster contexts in different parts of the country. Local jurisdictions have also established ordinances concerning disasters. Some mandate the creation and operation of emergency management offices and programs. Others discuss local disaster declarations and the management of recovery activities.

There are additional organizations that have created resolutions that may have an impact on current and future emergency management activities. For example, the National Fire Protection Association (NFPA) created NFPA 1600: Recommended Practices for Disaster Management. "**NFPA 1600** establishes a shared set of norms for disaster management, emergency management, and business-continuity programs. . . . One vital aspect of NFPA 1600 is its requirement that all emergency management and business-continuity programs comply with its relevant laws, policies, and industry standards" (Nicholson 2005b, p. 44). NFPA 1600 has been recommended or endorsed by professional entities. These include the 9/11 Commission, the National Emergency Management Association, and others.

There has also been growing recognition and support of other semilegal documents or programs. These include the Capability Assessment for Readiness (CAP) and the Emergency Management Accreditation Program (EMAP). You should ensure that you are familiar with these and any other pertinent legislation that may impact your job as an emergency manager.

As an emergency manager, you should also be aware of the possibility of lawsuits and other types of legal claims. It is true that "units of government enjoy immunity, or protection from legal liability, for many of their activities" (Nicholson 2005a, p. 12). However, liability is not unlimited. Before 1960, few states allowed civil suits against public organizations. However, this has changed over time, and governments are not fully immune from legal liability (Pine 1991).

10.7.2 Constitutional Rights

Legal claims against emergency managers may involve constitutional rights or federal statutory violations (Pine 1991). Congress passed civil rights legislation in 1871. It holds accountable public officials who deny rights established by the U.S. Constitution. "In disasters, local officials sometimes limit freedom of association, the use of public communication channels, or entry into evacuated areas, all of which pose the potential for violation of First Amendment rights" (Pine 1991, p. 300).

Other possible legal liabilities include discrimination. The Civil Rights Act of 1964 and Equal Employment Act of 1972 prohibit discrimination. Emergency managers cannot discriminate based on race, color, sex, religion, and national origin. An example of this is treating employees or disaster victims in a preferential or discriminatory manner. This may result in costly lawsuits.

10.7.3 Negligence

Negligence occurs when your actions or inactions (or those of responders) cause injuries or damage to people and their property. Negligence is the failure of emergency managers and responders to do what a reasonable and prudent person would have done under similar circumstances (Pine 1991). "For example, a state statute may require state and local agencies to prepare and keep current an emergency preparedness plan for natural, technological, or civil disasters. If a local government failed to prepare a plan and a disaster occurred, a citizen could file a suit claiming that the governmental unit had failed to carry out a statutory duty and was therefore liable for losses. In the field of emergency management, for example, a tort could involve a failure to warn citizens of a known hazardous materials release or a failure to provide adequate time for an evacuation order in a natural disaster" (Pine 1991).

Medical lawsuits are very common if victims have been misdiagnosed or treated inadequately. Lawsuits are also common if there are problems with consent, record disclosures, reporting requirements, or other issues (Hafter and Fedor 2004; Mancini and Gale 1981). Legal action may be taken against nearby jurisdictions if there have been problems with mutual aid agreement. For example, a first responder from another jurisdiction was killed when he responded to a fire in Fort Worth, Texas. A dispute arose between the cities regarding who would pay death benefits.

There are other reasons why lawsuits and prosecution might occur after disasters. These include (Williamson 2003b):

▲ Training accidents
▲ Vehicle accidents
▲ Delayed 911 dispatch
▲ Slow emergency response
▲ Failure to follow response protocols

Ignoring laws and regulations regarding the use of disaster funds can also lead to legal troubles. Lawsuits may occur if there is a failure to comply with statutes pertaining to hazardous materials record keeping and disclosure. One expert on disaster law states, "I firmly believe that liability issues are the great unplanned-for hazard faced by emergency managers" (Nicholson 2003a, p. 17). Even emergent groups could be held liable for their actions after disasters in some cases. However, most states have passed "**Good Samaritan laws**," which protect citizens who do everything they can to provide medical and other services to those affected by accidents and disasters.

10.7.4 Minimizing Liability

Since you will be involved in response and recovery operations, you should be aware of what can be done to minimize legal liability. Some measures have to be taken at the state level. "State disaster or emergency statutes often contain . . . specific immunity provisions to protect government officials engaged in critical decision-making procedures in emergencies. Some states have gone further, putting into place broad immunities shielding a variety of players (i.e., the state, political subdivisions, or local government entities) who act during an emergency response rather than just the individuals involved in decision making" (Nicholson 2005a, p. 12).

There are also things you can do to protect yourself at the local level:

▲ Develop and follow (when necessary) standard operating procedures that address various legal subjects. These topics may include employment practices and negligence.

▲ Be a proactive risk manager. Work with legal counsel in the community to discuss hypothetical scenarios. Discuss how they should be addressed.

▲ Consult with city legal staff to discuss response and recovery actions. Identify how they could conflict with citizens' rights or cause them injuries.

▲ Pursue a policy of "litigation mitigation." **Litigation mitigation** is an active effort with city attorneys to prevent legal liabilities and accept the need to spend time, effort, and money now to avoid future lawsuits (Williamson 2003b).

FOR EXAMPLE

Rhode Island Nightclub Fire

The Rhode Island Nightclub fire that killed at least 100 people was the result of at least two illegal activities. First, a rock band used pyrotechnics inside the night club. Second, flammable material was installed on the ceiling. Both of these mistakes were not prevented by the band manager, those overseeing the club, and building inspectors. Numerous lawsuits have resulted. This is one example of why it is important to have close ties to the legal counsel in your community.

SELF-CHECK

- What is a **law**?
- How do disasters influence law?
- Can first responders or emergency managers be held liable in disasters?
- What rights should emergency managers protect?
- What is **negligence** and how can it be avoided?
- What is **litigation mitigation**?

10.8 Record Keeping

Record keeping is vitally important for response and recovery operations. Accurate records help you make better decisions, and they are important for other reasons as well. During response and recovery operations, you and other organizations may need to know who is missing. You must also know how many people may be trapped or injured. Record keeping is required to track human and material resources. You will need to keep records of response and recovery activities for federal reimbursement. Lack of records can also hurt the reconstruction of the sequence of events and curtail organizational learning. The lack of records hinders preventive activities and the improvement of future post-disaster operations. Despite the importance of records, record keeping is sometimes neglected by disaster scholars and emergency management practitioners.

10.8.1 Record-Keeping Problems

There are several problems associated with record keeping and disasters. Scanlon (1996) has provided the most extensive study on the matter. He suggests:

▲ **Records do not exist before the disaster.** There may be limited or no records regarding individuals who are affected in disasters. For instance, there may be no names for people who are impacted by disasters at sporting events, outdoor concerts, and papal masses. This is also true in cases where disaster affect public transportation systems such as subways and ferries. Record keeping is lacking regarding disaster victims in libraries and museums.

▲ **Emergencies make record keeping difficult.** The initial search and rescue operations are often carried out by friends, neighbors, and co-workers. These individuals are not professional emergency personnel. They do not keep records, and they rarely tell anyone what they have witnessed before taking victims to the hospital(s).

▲ **Records are not reliable.** Subways, airlines, ferries, apartments, and public buildings often have inaccurate records of their occupants at any given time. A business or government agency that is affected by a disaster may have records of their employees but not which employees were on vacation or out ill. They probably also won't have records of those visiting their facilities. Also, hospitals that receive large numbers of victims at one time will be too overwhelmed to keep accurate and up-to-date records.

▲ **Access to records is restricted.** The buildings where the records are located may be damaged in the disaster. People may not be able to physically get to the records because the building has been condemned. Additionally, records may have restricted access due to their contents. The problems associated with secrecy may be more prevalent in the future due to homeland security concerns.

▲ **Records are lost or destroyed.** Records may be destroyed due to the damage sustained in the disaster. For example, the terrorist attacks on 9/11 completely destroyed the city EOC, and some businesses lost records if they had no electronic backups. Another example is from the Fort Worth tornado. This hazard destroyed many computers in downtown office buildings. The strong winds broke windows and sucked away corporate documents and even classified FBI files (McEntire 2002).

▲ **Records may be toxic.** Many disasters involve hazardous materials, and "it follows that documents recovered after such events will be contaminated" (Scanlon 1996, p. 275).

▲ **Record keeping fails after a disaster.** In the midst of the numerous response and recovery activities that take place after a disaster, there is often not enough time to accurately record the details of what has occurred (Hatfield 1990, p. 28, as cited by Scanlon 1996).

10.8.2 Keeping Accurate Records

Although record keeping is challenging after a disaster, the problems are not insurmountable. There are several steps that can be taken to improve record keeping after disasters. For instance, the emergency manager must recognize the importance of records. He or she should take the time to note names, contact information, activities, and expenses accurately during response and recovery operations. The following questions may also help the emergency manager keep more complete and accurate records:

▲ If an incident happens, what sorts of records would be of value?

▲ How could such records be compiled?

FOR EXAMPLE

Using Records to Solve Crimes

After 9/11, the United States became aware of the fact that Al-Qaeda and Osama Bin Laden were behind the terrorist attacks. They knew this in part thanks to a flight attendant on the first hijacked airplane. After the terrorists took over the airplane, she called the flight control tower. She told the authorities what seat the terrorist was sitting in. Using the airliner's records, the authorities could see that the seat belonged to Muhammed Atta, one of the masterminds of 9/11. Other terrorists were tracked by apartment contracts, drivers licenses, flight school documents, etc.

▲ How can such valuable records be stored safely?

▲ Who should have access to these records?

▲ What are the costs of record keeping, and is it worth it? (Scanlon 1996).

Emergency managers may obtain pertinent disaster records and vital data from a variety of sources. There are a number of ways to save information for scholars (Killian 1996). These useful documents and means of recording data include tape-recorded material (dispatch conversations and interviews), personal documents (diaries), agency and official letters (police reports, situation reports), and notes from EOC meetings and operations (after-action reports).

Putting someone in charge of records can also be helpful. If you are unable to carefully keep records in the immediate aftermath of a disaster, it is imperative that you review the response and recovery operations with others as soon as it is feasible to reconstruct incomplete notes or elaborate on details.

SELF-CHECK

- Is record keeping important to the emergency manager?
- Why is it difficult to keep complete and accurate records after disasters?
- What steps can be taken to improve record keeping?
- What sources of information can emergency managers pursue to facilitate record keeping?

SUMMARY

There are numerous challenges that you will face after disasters. The lack and dynamic nature of information in disasters make decision making problematic. Road bridges will be destroyed and traffic will be disrupted severely. Politics will enter response and recovery operations as interorganizational conflict occurs, blame is placed, and people express frustration with post-disaster activities. Numerous people will require special attention because they are the most vulnerable in disaster situations. Communication is difficult because of technological failures or human error. This leads to coordination problems among organizations. There is also the chance that you or your city might be held liable after a disaster. Records will need to be kept, but this is difficult in light of the many other activities that must be performed after a disaster occurs. Overcoming these challenges through carefully crafted operations is necessary if you are to facilitate resilience after a disaster.

KEY TERMS

Bounded rationality — The attempt to be rational is never fully achieved because of the constraints disasters present to the decision maker.

Communication — The process of relaying information that has bearing on the effectiveness of disaster response and recovery operations.

Coordination — The harmonization of activities among diverse actors in emergency management with the purpose of overcoming the challenges inherent in disasters.

Debugging — A method that includes a keen observation of the decision process to correct potential weaknesses and mistakes.

Design-preferable models — Studying the situation or problem in detail, determining the gap that exists between the goal and reality, and intervening to adapt the process to the desired outcome.

Good Samaritan laws — Statutes that protect citizens who do all they can to provide medical and other services to those affected by accidents and disasters.

Interoperability — The ability to communicate and operate across and with various disaster organizations.

Laws	Rules that are established by the government to maintain order and perform important functions in society.
Litigation mitigation	An active effort with city attorneys to prevent legal liabilities and accept the need to spend time, effort, and money now to avoid future lawsuits (Williamson 2003b).
Negligence	Actions or inactions of emergency managers and responders cause injuries or damage to people and their property.
NFPA 1600	A shared set of norms for disaster management, emergency management, and business-continuity programs.
Rational decision making	Searching for alternative solutions and selecting the one that is deemed most appropriate.
Situational awareness	A need to be vigilant of circumstances to understand the context of what is taking place.
Special populations	People who are susceptible to disasters and those who may be least able to deal with them.

ASSESS YOUR UNDERSTANDING

Go to www.wiley.com/college/McEntire to evaluate your knowledge of post-disaster problems.
Measure your learning by comparing pretest and post-test results.

Summary Questions

1. Emergency managers will not face decision making challenges after disasters. True or False?

2. Tragic choice suggests there will be drawbacks to nearly every decision made in a disaster. True or False?

3. Disasters permit bounded rationality at best. True or False?

4. Designing preferable models is similar to rational decision making. True or False?

5. Eating right and getting sufficient rest can improve decision making. True or False?

6. School busses cannot be used to evacuate people in your community. True or False?

7. Police and public works departments may play a role in traffic control. True or False?

8. Hurricane Katrina illustrated the potential for blame after a disaster. True or False?

9. Emergency managers should recognize that they may be a convenient scapegoat for politicians if post-disaster operations are ineffective. True or False?

10. Clarifying responsibilities when disasters strike will not reduce interorganizational rivalry. True or False?

11. Keeping records can help the emergency manager retain his or her job. True or False?

12. Although all people may be vulnerable to disaster, some people are more vulnerable than others. True or False?

13. Women may constitute special populations in disasters because they often have to care for children. True or False?

14. Language issues are not a concern for the emergency manager. True or False?

15. Prisoners may be considered special populations because they have to be monitored closely after a disaster. True or False?

16. One reason communication is problematic in disasters is because disasters destroy communication equipment. True or False?

17. Reminding others about the need to focus on disaster victims is one way to improve coordination. True or False?

18. Coordination implies an ability to work together to resolve mutual disaster concerns. True or False?

19. Disasters pose coordination challenges because they are dramatically different than routine emergencies. True or False?

20. Interoperability means that organizations are not capable of communicating effectively one with another. True or False?

21. Mt. St. Helens is a good example of possible lawsuits resulting from the government's handling of disasters. True or False?

22. Laws are rules that guide government behavior and the performance of tasks for the public good. True or False?

23. Disasters have no bearing on the creation of emergency management law. True or False?

24. Record keeping is vital for federal reimbursements of disaster expenses. True or False?

25. Even though you will be busy after a disaster, it is imperative that you give sufficient attention to record keeping. True or False?

26. Situation reports can help you with record keeping but tape recording communication with others will not. True or False?

27. Keeping a diary of your activities could help you remember what steps were taken to respond to a disaster. True or False?

28. Hazardous materials may limit the availability of certain records after a disaster. True or False?

29. Facing adversity implies:
    (a) Emergency managers have compressed time to make decisions.
    (b) Disasters kill some people and injure others.
    (c) First responders are tired.
    (d) No decision will be optimal.
    (e) None of the above.

30. Situational awareness:
    (a) Is closely related to tragic choice
    (b) Cannot be construed as a decision-making challenge
    (c) Implies that one is aware of what is taking place during response and recovery operations
    (d) Is a result of fuzzy gambling
    (e) Is a trait to be avoided by the emergency manager

31. Which disaster illustrated problems with insufficient fuel?
    (a) The Northridge earthquake
    (b) The Asian Tsunami
    (c) Hurricane Andrew

(d) Hurricane Rita

(e) The Fort Worth Tornado

32. Public transit authorities may be helpful after a disaster because:

(a) They deal with traffic problems on a regular basis.

(b) They provided transportation to thousands of people for special events.

(c) They operate at peak traffic periods.

(d) They are eager to help emergency managers.

(e) All of the above.

33. Interorganizational rivalry can be increased when:

(a) Organizations dispute authority over a given domain area

(b) Questions about tasks arise

(c) It is unclear who will get resources or credit

(d) All of the above

(e) a and b

34. A focusing event:

(a) Helps bring political attention to disaster issues

(b) Is a major problem for decision making

(c) Was evident in a small earthquake in Idaho

(d) Was evident in a tornado in Cincinnati

(e) Cannot be related to the strain and stress of disasters

35. Tourists may be considered special populations because:

(a) They are not poor.

(b) They can always speak the language.

(c) They are never minorities.

(d) They often lack sufficient information about local hazards.

(e) None of the above.

36. To deal effectively with special populations:

(a) It is advisable that you avoid nursing homes and prisons.

(b) It is advisable that you work closely with nonprofit organizations.

(c) It is necessary that you communicate with the fire department only.

(d) It is recommended that you coordinate with prisons but not schools.

(e) b and c

37. Communication problems result from:

(a) Damaged communication equipment

(b) People problems

(c) An understanding of who needs your information

(d) a and b

(e) A failure to recognize the negative impact of situational awareness.

38. Communication is most likely to be successful when it is:

(a) Calm

(b) Courteous

(c) Correct

(d) Concise

(e) All of the above

39. Coordination will:

(a) Limit duplication of service.

(b) Limit gaps in service.

(c) Increase the effectiveness of response

(d) Increase the effectiveness of recovery

(e) All of the above

40. Tracking needs and how they are met is an example of what type of coordination strategy?

(a) Consequences

(b) Control

(c) Cultural

(d) Customer

(e) Core

41. The standards and norms for emergency management and business continuity are contained in:

(a) IEMSA 2210

(b) IAEM 3622

(c) NFPA 1600

(d) NFPA 763

(e) UNLS 7350

42. Immunity implies:

(a) A government employee can be held liable for an action or inaction.

(b) A government employee cannot be held liable for an action or inaction.

(c) The situational awareness has led to core coordination strategy.

(d) Litigation mitigation has not succeeded.

(e) The government has made a mistake in response and recovery operations.

43. Negligence occurs when:
    (a) Something is done that a reasonable person would not do.
    (b) Something is not done that a reasonable person would do.
    (c) An action or inaction hurts others or destroys their property.
    (d) All of the above.
    (e) None of the above.

44. Emergent groups cannot be held liable in some states because of:
    (a) Interoperable immunity
    (b) Negligent immunity
    (c) Litigation mitigation
    (d) Good Samaritan laws
    (e) Rational decision making

45. Reasons why record keeping is problematic after disasters include(s):
    (a) Records are not reliable.
    (b) Records have been lost or destroyed.
    (c) Records may be hazardous.
    (d) Access to records has not been granted.
    (e) All of the above.

Review Questions

1. Disasters pose serious challenges for decision makers. Why is this the case?
2. Is it possible to make fully rational decisions in disasters? Why or why not?
3. What problems hinder decision making in disaster situations?
4. There are two major recommendations for disaster decision making. What are they?
5. Can disasters impact transportation systems? If so, how?
6. What transportation related issues are evident in disasters?
7. Are disasters political? Why or why not?
8. How can emergency managers avoid blame placement?
9. What is a special population?
10. Why are some people more prone to disasters than others?
11. Do all disaster victims have the same capabilities?
12. What can you do to help special populations after disasters?
13. What is communication, and why is it important for emergency managers?
14. How would you define coordination?
15. Are communication and coordination related to each other? Why or why not?

16. What are typical communication and coordination problems?

17. How can the barriers to communication and coordination be overcome by the emergency manager?

18. How can interoperability be promoted after disasters?

19. Do laws have a bearing on emergency management?

20. What legal issues should be taken into account by the emergency manager?

21. Who can help the emergency manager make decisions to avoid legal liability?

22. What is litigation mitigation?

23. Is record keeping important after disasters?

24. What factors make record keeping problematic for the emergency manager?

25. What are some novel ways to save information after disasters?

Applying This Chapter

1. A major hailstorm has just affected your community in Mississippi. It is unclear what neighborhoods have been affected and what needs your citizens have. How does this situation affect your decision making? What can be done to overcome such problems?

2. A terrorist attack caused a major evacuation of your city initially, and resources are needed to help affected businesses in the jurisdiction. How can you utilize transportation systems and related personnel to respond effectively?

3. Two of the departments in your community are not working together after a flood because of priority conflicts among the leaders of these organizations. In particular, the search and rescue team in the fire department is not happy with the traffic control provided by the police department. What can you do to ensure that this conflict does not hinder post-disaster operations?

4. You are the local emergency manager in a community that has a state-run school for the mentally retarded. This state is also prone to tornadoes. What concerns do you have about the individuals in this facility? What activities do you undertake during an event to care for those who are most vulnerable?

5. While working in the EOC, you notice that the different organizations are not resolving disaster problems in a coordinated fashion. What can you do to improve communication across organizations and facilitate an effective response?

6. During recovery, a question has arisen regarding the relocation of homes from the flood plain. The action would reduce community vulnerability

but is not popular among many residents. Who can you talk to in your jurisdiction to ensure your decisions are within the parameters of the law?

7. Your city's response to a winter storm is unfolding. A great deal of money is being spent on sand and chemicals to keep the roads from freezing. In addition, it is expected that drivers will be required to work on a rotating basis over the next several days. What records can you keep to track expenses?

Disasters and Politics

You are the local emergency manager in the Midwest, and the response to a flooding episode was less than perfect. The media is pointing out the failures, and city leaders are calling for your resignation. While you know you committed errors, you also know that many other organizations made mistakes as well. What do you do to protect your job and avoid alienating others who participated?

Using Politics to Your Advantage

You are the risk manager for an industrial facility that has recently experienced a chemical explosion. In the past, the CEO has been less than supportive of your efforts to keep the business safe. How can the increased interest in this disaster be used to your advantage?

Special Populations

You are an emergency manager in a city that has just experienced a major fire at a nursing home. The building has been severely damaged and cannot be inhabited. What concerns do you have about the residents? How can you evacuate patients and the elderly safely? Where could they go? What considerations should be included in your decisions?

Working with Others

You are the Chapter Manager for the American Red Cross in your community. A train has derailed and spilled chemicals near an apartment complex. What organizations and levels of government do you want to work with and why in this situation? What are the benefits of coordination? How can you improve coordination among all of the groups?

Keeping Records

You are the local emergency manager for a city that has just experienced a major plane crash. Most passengers have been killed, and their belongings have been strewn about the crash site. Survivors have been taken to several nearby hospitals. Families are calling you to get information about their loved ones who are believed to have been on the flight. The media wants to know how the event unfolded. The state is asking if they can help in any way. What types of records do you need to keep and why?

Research Paper

Collect literature on at least two disaster cases. Write a six-page paper on the challenges encountered by the emergency manager in these events. Explain what could be done differently to overcome them in the future.

11

HARNESSING TECHNOLOGY AND ORGANIZATION
Tools for Local, State, and Federal Governments

Starting Point

Go to www.wiley.com/college/McEntire to assess your knowledge of managing organization and technology.
Determine where you need to concentrate your effort.

What You'll Learn in This Chapter

▲ Importance of technology for emergency managers
▲ The benefit of decision support systems
▲ Principles of Incident Command
▲ The nature of emergency operations centers
▲ Value of mutual aid and the Standard Emergency Management System
▲ The advantages of the Emergency Management Assistance Compact
▲ Principles of the National Incident Management System and the National Response Plan

After Studying This Chapter, You'll Be Able To

▲ Apply technology in response and recovery operations
▲ Examine the usefulness of geographic information systems
▲ Use incident command in times of disaster
▲ Demonstrate how to run an Emergency Operations Center
▲ Employ mutual aid from nearby jurisdictions
▲ Analyze the merit of the Standard Emergency Management System
▲ Appraise the National Incident Management System and the National Response Plan

Goals and Outcomes

▲ Evaluate how technology is used in disaster response and recovery operations
▲ Compare different types of technological tools
▲ Manage the scene of a disaster in an effective manner
▲ Set up an EOC and work closely with others in it
▲ Organize local response operations seamlessly with nearby jurisdictions
▲ Select disaster assistance from other state governments
▲ Arrange municipal recovery in conjunction with federal disaster organizations

INTRODUCTION

Resilience is improved when you harness technology and organization after a disaster. It is imperative that you understand the importance of technological tools in response and recovery operations. Communications equipment, decision support systems, and Geographic Information System (GIS) will help you work with others, make good choices, and track resources. Although you will not be deployed to the field in most disasters, it is useful that you understand the principles and limitations of the Incident Command System. Being able to run an Emergency Operations Center is a vital skill that you must acquire. Besides these steps, you must recognize the operational characteristics of the Emergency Management Assistance Compact, the National Incident Management System, and the National Response Plan. Such measures will help you manage the disaster effectively and work closely with local, state, and federal governments.

11.1 The Importance of Technology

The role that technology plays in response and recovery cannot be overestimated. Innovations in technology are occurring rapidly, and the new technological tools will help you save more lives and improve effectiveness of post-disaster operations. A revolution has also occurred in communications, with the advent of two-way radios, cell phones, and the Internet. In addition to the availability of these new tools, technology is more easily acquired by local jurisdictions. As costs for computers, software programs, and other equipment comes down, emergency managers will be more able to use them. Not all communities have the same technology resources, however. In fact, some communities may have very few technological tools. Nonetheless, federal grants are helping many cities acquire technological improvements. Although each community does not use every tool, there are numerous examples of how you can use technology in emergency management (see Figure 11-1):

▲ Doppler Radar improves the forecasting of severe weather such as tornadoes.

▲ Reverse 911 systems warn thousands of people about impending hazards within a short amount of time.

▲ Computers are used to manage dispatch centers and assist responders in reaching the destinations of emergencies and disasters quickly.

▲ Traffic signal preemption devices use high-frequency strobe lights to change lights and allow responders to arrive at the scene of an incident without unnecessary delay.

▲ Computer programs can also be used to brief workers before they enter the site of a disaster.

▲ Detection equipment can determine the presence of weapons of mass destruction.

▲ Cardiac defibrillators help to save lives when people are in medical distress.

▲ Listening devices and extraction equipment help search and rescue teams locate and remove those crushed under disaster debris.

▲ Cell phones increase the ability of people to communicate in remote locations.

▲ Ham radios permit the sharing of information when many other communication systems fail to operate.

▲ Global positioning systems (GPS) help to plot damages and locate the position of first responders and other critical assets.

▲ Video cameras help law-enforcement agencies investigate acts of terrorism.

▲ Remote sensing provides information about the extent of disaster damages.

▲ E-mail and text messaging are other ways to communicate when information needs to be shared after a disaster in real time.

▲ Personal digital assistants (PDAs) are small portable computers that can also act as phones. They contain phone numbers and addresses, calendars, and to-do lists. These can help you contact resources and schedule activities.

It is important to keep in mind that some of this technology can be rendered useless if the power goes out. Technology can also become inoperable if phone

Figure 11-1

Technology such as computers and satellite imagery play a vital role in warning communities about impending hazards.

> **FOR EXAMPLE**
>
> **Technology and 9/11**
>
> Many technology tools were used at ground zero after 9/11. One of them was LIDAR. LIDAR is an acronym for Light Detection and Ranging. **LIDAR** is an airborne laser system that was used to detect heat and dangerous debris accumulations after the World Trade Center Towers collapsed on 9/11. It helped responders improve safety under extremely dangerous circumstances.

lines or towers are damaged. However, it is also true that "innovative technological advances are transforming the practice of emergency management" (Sutphen and Waugh 1998, p. 9). If you are to be successful, you must have knowledge and expertise in the technological realm.

SELF-CHECK

- Why is technology important for emergency managers?
- How has technology or its accessibility changed over time?
- How can technology help with warning?
- How does technology help dispatchers and responders?
- How can technology help with other post-disaster functions?

11.2 Communications Equipment

Being able to talk to co-workers and those in other agencies has always been a problem during disasters. For this reason, the Department of Homeland Security has created an Office of Interoperability and Compatibility. This office was established in response to the 9/11 report that detailed several communications problems among responders. It is working on the development of equipment to improve communications capabilities.

There are several types of equipment to assist with communications:

▲ **Transmitters** are communication instruments that convey information through radios, sirens, television stations, and cable override systems.

▲ **Receivers** are equipment devices that obtain signals from transmitters. They include stereos, pagers, police scanners, and televisions.

▲ **Transceivers** are able to both transmit and receive information. Examples of transceivers include telephones, satellites, personal digital assistants, two-way radios, citizen band radios, 800-Mhz radios, and ham radios.

These basic types of communications equipment should be familier to you as an emergency manager.

11.2.1 Trunked Radio Systems

The history of communications equipment reveals steady progress for those involved in response and recovery operations. Traditionally, emergency communications took place through transceivers. They used low-band VHF or UHF frequency. This usually required a radio tower, repeaters, and an uninterrupted power supply. In time, communications were improved by using common radio channels or relaying information through a designated dispatcher. By 1977, the Association of Public Safety Communications Officers created minimum standards for 800-/900-Mhz trunked radio systems. A **trunked radio system** is a computer-controlled network. It searches for a clear channel available to users to talk to each other (Dees 2000, p. 8). The major advantage of trunked radio systems is their ability to serve a number of users. Put differently, these systems allow a variety of "talk groups." A **talk group** is a unit with its own designated channel. Today, some radio systems have digital coding to identify the source of communication and rely on encryption in the case of high-security operations (e.g., response to terrorist attacks). Although advances like these are beneficial, many of the systems across jurisdictions do not work well with each other. Each community has equipment based on their own needs, preferences, and budgets. These are a few of the many challenges inhibiting interoperability.

11.2.2 ACU-1000

In light of the inability to communicate across departments and jurisdictions, numerous vendors invented radio bridges and other interfaces. A very valuable piece of equipment is the ACU-1000. The **ACU-1000** is a type of interface equipment that links mobile radios, cell phones, satellite technology, and regular phones in a single real-time communication system. It is now common in many EOCs. It is also common in many mobile command posts (a vehicle with EOC capabilities). During emergencies and disasters, ACU-1000 allows different radio systems to be cross-connected and routed over wide-area networks. Local, state, and federal agencies can then coordinate responses with multiple organizations. You should become familiar with this equipment as it will facilitate interoperability across departments and jurisdictions.

11.2.3 The Internet

The Internet has become a useful tool for response and recovery operations. As an emergency manager, you can use the Internet to research the unique features of specific types of hazards. The Internet allows you to read case studies to determine how other professionals in the field handled the same threats you face. The Internet may also help you to compare notes with others on the best equipment for your city's needs. For example, you can use the Internet to get opinions on which rain gauges are the most reliable.

From the Internet, you can also access vital information from research centers and government disaster-related agencies (Fischer 1998). The Internet makes a vast amount of information available to a large group of people at one time. "Internet communication has radically changed the relay of information so that in most cases the 'generals' hear the news about road closures and flood gauge readings at precisely the moment the data are first available and at the same time as the 'underlings'" (Gruntfest and Weber 1998, p. 58).

The Internet is also a great tool for citizens to use to obtain information. For example, citizens can print off instructions on what to do in case of a hurricane or tornado. Before or after a disaster, you could set up a page on your city's website to give people all kinds of information, including evacuation routes, emergency numbers, shelter options, and other recommendations. The Internet may help you video conference with other remote agencies. The Internet may also allow you to communicate with colleagues. Through e-mail you can share and receive information that could help you deal with disasters.

11.2.4 Voice over IP (VoIP) and Other Equipment

Another system, **Voice over Internet Protocol,** routes communications over the Internet. It uses a packet-switched set of lines instead of circuit-switched voice transmission lines. The possibility of communication through Voice over Internet Protocol (VoIP) has increased over the years. VoIP is used in cell, radio, and computer networks. Wireless systems also help to overcome communication problems, and they became a reality with cell and satellite systems. Of course, some equipment may be damaged or overloaded after a disaster. In addition, it should be restated that many communications problems cannot be blamed on equipment only.

FOR EXAMPLE

Equipment or People Problems?

Communications are often problematic in disasters. Equipment may be damaged, fail, or become overloaded. However, research reveals that most communications problems are the result of interpersonal or interorganizational failures rather than equipment difficulties. Repeaters did fail during the response to the 9/11 disaster. However, police and fire were unable to communicate for other reasons as well. These departments had at least some interoperable communications equipment. Disagreements arose as to who would possess it and what rules should be followed for its use. Both equipment and human error seem to have a bearing on the effectiveness of communications, but there is a tendency to downplay people problems.

SELF-CHECK

- What are the three types of communication equipment?
- How can trunked radio systems aid communications?
- What can an ACU-1000 do for interoperability?
- How can the Internet improve disaster response and recovery?

11.3 Decision Support Systems

There are several computer programs to assist those involved in disaster response operations. These are commonly known as **decision support systems**—software applications that help the emergency manager determine priorities and respond to a disaster. "Decision support systems (DSSs) are computer information systems that have evolved from existing but disparate information pathways used by decision makers. The computer allows for instantaneous links among the database, simulation models, and management tools. Other components may be part of a DSS, such as optimization of routines for resource allocation or artificial intelligence and expert systems. . . . The DSS ties together spatially and temporally based information with simulation models that depict a spatial/temporal reaction to a response and allows problem-specific information to be reported. . . . [They may include] historical data (losses, physical events, trends), current data (weather, demographics, and political information), simulation tools (environmental, economic, and socio-political models), and report tools (statistical analyses, maps)" (Mileti 1999, p. 248).

There are several types of DSS, including:

▲ **SoftRisk** http://www.softrisk.com/. SoftRisk is a software program for critical incidents and emergency management. It has a large database for resource lists and relevant contacts. The software supports call taking and the assignment of tasks and responsibilities. It helps with e-mail and fax communications. SoftRisk integrates with ArcView for spatially referenced mapping.

▲ **CoBRA** (Chemical Biological Response Aide) http://www.defensegroupinc. com/cobra/products.htm. This software is designed for incidents involving chemical, biological, radiological, nuclear, and explosive materials. It has an extensive database and checklists to help manage response operations. CoBRA tracks user activities to facilitate an after-action incident log. It also relies on various reference books such as the DOT Emergency Response Guide and DOJ Crime Scene Investigation for improved evacuations/sheltering and prosecution.

▲ **E-Team** http://www.eteam.com. E-Team facilitates the management of crises and disasters. The software enables the user to gather information. It helps the user to assess damages and notify agencies of the status of the incident. E-Team is designed to request and deploy resources. It is anticipated that E-team will soon be able to assist with the management of volunteers and donations.

▲ **EPlan** http://www.eplanonline.com. EPlan is a secure web system. It provides vital information to firefighters such as access to hazardous materials inventories. It provides access to Material Safety Data Sheet (MSDS) site maps—maps that note the location of hazardous materials. EPlan also has links to the DOT Emergency Response Guide and can help you with many other disaster functions.

▲ **Disaster Management Interoperability Services** http://www.cmi-services. org/. This program includes Internet service for improved communication among first responders. It helps facilitate awareness and coordination among local, state, and national emergency response organizations. One of the strengths is its ability to ensure security due to passwords and encryption.

▲ **CAMEO** http://www.epa.gov/ceppo/cameo/request.htm. This program was created by the EPA's Chemical Emergency Preparedness and Prevention Office with the assistance of the Atmospheric Administration Office of Response and Restoration. The entire program includes a database of over 6,000 hazardous chemicals and supports regulatory compliance on reporting chemical inventories. CAMEO is a combination of three programs. It includes:

- A chemical database
- ALOHA (Area Locations of Hazardous Atmosphere)
- MARPLOT (Mapping Applications for Response, Planning and Local Operations Tasks)

CAMEO therefore provides important response information regarding health hazards, firefighting strategies, plume modeling for evacuation, personal protective equipment, and clean up.

There are many other decision support systems. Some include SLOSH, HURRIVAC, and the Health Alert Network. SLOSH stands for Sea, Lake, and Overland Surges from Hurricanes. It is a computer model that helps you predict storm surge heights from tropical cyclones. HURRIVAC is another program that examines storm surge, but it also predicts the time it will take to evacuate an area that is expected to be affected by a hurricane. The Health Alert Network is used by hospitals and public health agencies. It is a program that tracks disease outbreaks and bed availability in medical facilities. As an emergency manager, it is your responsibility to determine what programs are available and how this software can assist you in disasters.

FOR EXAMPLE

WEBEOC and Other DSS

WebEOC is another decision support system that can be used in your emergency operations center. With a computer and modem, you are able to access information about the weather, satellite images, and maps. WEBEOC also allows you to track resources deployed by local, state, and federal governments. WEBEOC is touted as the first DSS for emergency managers. Additional information on WEBEOC can be accessed at http://www.esi911.com/esi/products/webeoc.shtml.

SELF-CHECK

- What is a decision support system?
- What are the features of SoftRisk?
- How is CoBRA different from EPlan or CAMEO?
- What does E-Team do for the manager?
- Can you think of other software that might be useful for disaster response or recovery operations?

11.4 Geographic Information Systems (GIS)

A **Geographic Information System (GIS)** is an "organized collection of computer hardware, software, geographic data, and personnel designed to efficiently capture, store, update, manipulate, analyze, and display all forms of geographically referenced information" (ESRI as cited by Dash 1997). GIS can help emergency managers determine what is at or near a certain location. GIS can also be used to show how the use of an area has changed over time as well as patterns in spatial analysis (Dash 1997). Organizing geographic information in a computer database has many applications. The information available can be very helpful to the emergency manager. For example, New York City emergency management personnel use GIS on a regular basis. They can point to a neighborhood on electronic maps. The information displayed may include the languages spoken by the population in that particular area. This information will allow authorities to tailor a warning message based on the predominant and other languages of that specific location.

Spatial analysis is important for mitigation and preparedness as well as post-disaster operations. It has been argued that "spatial data analysis is the most exciting technological development in emergency management in the past decade" (Waugh 1995). HAZUS, for example, is a powerful software program developed by the federal government. **HAZUS** is an assessment software tool that is used for analyzing potential losses from floods, hurricane winds, and earthquakes. In HAZUS, scientific and engineering information is combined with GIS. This information works together to produce estimates of hazard-related damage. Such estimates may include physical damage, economic loss, and social impacts, including the estimated shelter and medical needs of the citizens. These calculations can be made before or after a disaster occurs.

GIS programs have also been used widely in post-disaster operations, including hurricanes and oil spills (see Figure 11-2). For example, after a hurricane, GIS can show the emergency manager destroyed areas and needs for rebuilding. GIS can also illustrate what utility lines are down and where service needs to be restored. This system helps you determine what the priorities should be during response and recovery activities. For instance, "after the first shock of a catastrophic event. . . the focus of everyone even remotely connected to the disaster will be on one thing: understanding all that has happened. Of all the tasks of disaster management, it is this one at which GIS excels. Its visualization and data consolidation capabilities allow GIS to convey large amounts of information to a large number of people in a short period of time—exactly what is needed in the immediate aftermath of a disaster" (Greene 2002, p. 42).

GIS was used after Hurricane Andrew in 1992. "The initial use of GIS was in mapping damage and analyzing community demographics. . . . Later, as the potential of GIS was better understood, its use grew in areas like Public Assistance. . . . Projects included tracking (1) debris and debris removal, (2). . . damaged homes, and (3) the location of trailers used for temporary housing" (Dash 1997).

Other applications of GIS after a disaster include:

▲ Assessing the extent of floods, fires, and earthquakes
▲ Showing the path of tornadoes
▲ Plotting the location of fire stations
▲ Locating fire hydrants and other critical infrastructure (e.g., water mains)
▲ Noting the geographical need for emergency personnel
▲ Finding where the American Red Cross has open shelters.
▲ Understanding what field hospitals are in use
▲ Conveying where to go to be fed at mass disaster kitchens
▲ Conveying information about incident command posts and EOC locations
▲ Relaying how to access disaster sites or secure zones
▲ Viewing what buildings have been condemned
▲ Transmitting the location of donation sites
▲ Denoting where to go for disaster assistance

Figure 11-2

Personnel that have expertise in GIS can be a valuable asset to the local emergency manager and other agencies and departments in the joint field office.

To use GIS effectively, accurate information must be put into the computer program before a disaster occurs (Dash 1997, p. 140). Relevant disaster information must be inputted correctly and completely, which is a time-consuming process. Data can be put into a computer after a disaster occurs. But this will require that the emergency manager or other city personnel be familiar with the program and its capabilities. Fortunately, many cities have designated GIS departments today.

FOR EXAMPLE

GIS and 9/11

Prior to the terrorist attacks on the World Trade Center, New York was already developing a detailed spatial system to track parcel information and street centerlines. When the towers collapsed, GIS was modified to track the geographical changes of Manhattan (e.g., affected buildings, search and rescue grids, utility outages, and new transportation routes). The hundreds of maps that were produced identified not only the impact but resource allocation during response and recovery operations as well (Thomas et al 2002, p. 4). So many maps were produced that it was difficult to ensure that everyone had the latest information. Nevertheless, GIS was a great tool in this disaster.

11.5 Managing Disasters at the Local Level

In addition to the technological tools that help improve response and recovery operations, organizational structures will also assist you. The Incident Command System (ICS) and the EOC are two means by which you can more effectively work with other agencies at the local level. Incident command is used for every emergency or disaster. EOCs, on the other hand, are used mainly for large disasters. Mutual aid may also help jurisdictions collaborate successfully after a disaster.

11.5.1 Incident Command System

Incident command, or the incident command system (ICS), has become the most important field-level operations strategy for first responders. **ICS** is "a set of personnel, policies, procedures, facilities and equipment, integrated into a common organizational structure designed to improve emergency response operations of all types and complexities" (Irwin 1989, p. 134). The purpose of incident command is to "allow its user(s) to adopt an integrated organizational structure equal to the complexity and demands of single or multiple incidents without being hindered by jurisdictional boundaries" (Gordon 2002, p. 12). Incident command is therefore an organizational strategy for management. If implemented properly, it may facilitate a more successful field response to emergencies and disasters.

Incident command was created after firefighters had significant challenges while responding to wildfires in California in 1970. After a dry and hot summer, at least thirteen large fires were ignited in Southern California. Sixteen lives were lost as a result. More than 600,000 acres were burned. Nearly 800 structures were destroyed over a 13-day period. The fires affected property and land in local, county, state, and federal jurisdictions.

The efforts to deal with the fires were heroic. However, several interrelated shortcomings were made evident during the response. These problems were investigated by congress and the United States Forest Service. Local, state, and federal authorities also formed the Firefighting Resources of California Organized for Potential

Emergencies (FIRESCOPE) to review the incident. The final reports pointed out the problems during the response to the 1970 fires (Irwin 1989, p. 135-136; FEMA 1998, p. 1-2). They noted that more than 100 local, state, and federal agencies participated in the fire suppression. The difficulty of integrating all of these agencies into a coherent response system was recognized as these organizations did not always work together to accomplish goals. In most cases, the agencies performed their functions in isolation from others. There were four reasons for this:

▲ **Poor communications.** Supervisors could not always contact subordinates. They had difficulty reaching other agencies. This was a result of limited channel capacity on radios and different frequency usage. Unfamiliar terminology also complicated the reception and interpretation of conveyed messages.

▲ **Insufficient intelligence and prediction.** None of the responding organizations was asked to gather information about the size and movement of the fires. Information that did exist was incomplete and late. Expertise was not always available to help make decisions about the number of threatened structures, available evacuation routes, and possible shelter arrangements.

▲ **Lack of joint planning.** The responding agencies did not meet to discuss the fires and outline a coordinated strategy to deal with them. This jeopardized safety and resulted in duplication of effort and gaps in service.

▲ **Inadequate resource management.** All of the above problems resulted in overstaffing of firefighters in some areas. At the same time, there was a scarcity of personnel for other fires. Resources such as fire apparatus, bulldozers, and airplanes were lost, underutilized, or overcommitted.

The investigations revealed that response operations must be based on standard criteria. Those involved in the disaster realized that a system was needed to aid the operations of single agencies and allow them to work closely with other organizations. The new system "must be readily adaptable to new technologies that may become available to support emergency response and management. It must be able to expand from the organizational requirements of simple, daily incidents up to the needs of a major emergency. It must have basic common elements in organization, terminology, and procedures" (Irwin 1989). All of this led to the development of ICS.

11.5.2 Principles of Incident Command

ICS is based on a common organizational structure. It includes the incident commander(s) and the information, safety, and liaison officers. There are also four supporting sections under incident command. These four sections are planning, operations, logistics, and finance/administration (FEMA 1998). **Incident command** is the on-scene leadership for the disaster. Initially, this may be the first person to respond to the incident. Incident command may also be given to the person(s) with the most expertise in certain disasters or those who have extensive knowledge of certain response functions. Later on, command will often be taken over by the highest-ranking official. Command can also be shared among the leadership of several responding agencies. Whether command is given to one person or shared among many others, it has the goal of facilitating coordination.

Three officers work closely with the incident commander(s). Figure 11-3 shows standard ICS structure.

▲ The **information officer** works with the media to answer their questions about the event. He or she releases information to the public.

▲ The **safety officer** monitors the hazardous conditions of the disaster to ensure protection of responding personnel.

▲ The **liaison officer** is the point of contact with other organizations responding to the incident.

Each of these officers reports to the incident commander(s) to provide an update of the situation as it unfolds.

If needed, the incident commanders establish and work with four sections:

1. The **planning section** collects and evaluates information about the disaster. This section also defines operational priorities. The planning section disseminates information about the incident and the use of resources during response operations (e.g., the location of the fire and crews to fight it).

2. The **operations section** is responsible for implementing the strategy to respond to the incident as determined by the incident commander and the planning section. For instance, fire suppression or search and rescue may be located under operations.

3. The **logistics section** acquires and provides materials, services, and facilities to support the needs of responders as directed by the incident commander and the operations section. Seeking additional firefighters and fire engines is an example of a logistics activity.

4. The **finance/administration section** tracks costs, completes and files paperwork, and records expenses of operations and logistics. This is especially important for payment purposes, and especially if there is hope of being reimbursed by the federal government in a Presidential Declaration.

The incident command system is also based on a number of vitally important principles:

▲ **Common terminology.** Because there are so many response organizations involved in the response, common vocabulary should be used instead of "ten" codes (i.e., 10-4).

▲ **Modular organization.** Depending on the nature and scope of the disaster, ICS consists of the incident commander and one responding unit. In

Figure 11-3

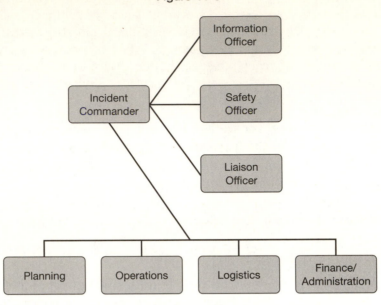

ICS structure.

other cases, ICS may be comprised of the incident commander(s), liaison officers, support sections, and additional layers as needed. For example, you may need divisions, branches, and strike teams. The system is designed to be flexible.

▲ **Integrated communications.** To accommodate each of the participating agencies, a common communications plan is used. Assigned frequencies are clearly identified.

▲ **Unity of command.** As a way to limit organizational confusion, each person reports to one commanding officer only.

▲ **A unified command structure.** When there is more than one responding organization, the command structure expands to include all major agencies. This facilitates joint decision making.

▲ **Consolidated IAPs.** The incident commander(s) and planning section identify operational goals. They produce written incident action plans to guide operations. This typically happens over recurring 12-hour periods.

▲ **A manageable span of control.** Each supervisor should manage between three and seven people. Five is the best number of people to manage.

▲ **Designated incident facilities.** All of those responding to disaster should be made aware of the location of the incident command post (ICP). They should know the locations of the following: staging areas, camps, helibases, helispots, casualty collection points, etc.

▲ **Comprehensive resource management.** Human, material, and equipment resources are always checked in. They are given assigned, available, or out-of-service status. This designation maximizes the effective use of resources.

11.5.3 Strengths and Weaknesses of Incident Command

It is vital that you are aware of the advantages and disadvantages of incident command. Strengths of incident command include:

▲ Closer contact among key decision makers

▲ An ability to adapt to both small and large events

▲ Increased safety for responders

▲ Improved information flow to the public and from other organizations

▲ A logical system of organization that addresses many important disaster functions

▲ Joint planning and operations for emergencies and disasters

▲ Enhanced communication due to common terminology

▲ More realistic expectations for management processes (e.g., span of control)

▲ Increased ability of supervisors to work with subordinates (e.g., unity of command)

▲ More efficient acquisition of resources and improved management of personnel and equipment

ICS is not without its critics, however. Neal and Phillips (1995) illustrate that the command and control approach may be too rigid for disaster situations. Dynes (1994) also shows that incident command models are often based on false assumptions about human behavior in disasters. Other weaknesses of incident command are also notable:

▲ The term "command" may imply excessive authority in multiorganizational responses. Department heads may sometimes fight over who is in charge rather than recognizing that they need to coordinate joint efforts. For this reason, it might be better to use the term "incident management" instead of "incident command."

▲ ICS loses strategic importance in larger emergencies and disasters. In widespread events, the EOC becomes more critical for effective management of response and recovery operations.

FOR EXAMPLE

ICS in Action

On September 15, 1999, a disgruntled man walked into a youth rally at a Baptist Church in Fort Worth, Texas. He opened fire, killing several of those attending the event, and then turned the gun on himself. A policeman lived across the street and was notified of the incident. The fire department showed up and sounded a second alarm, indicating the need for additional resources. As the response unfolded, the area was divided up by battalions (e.g., sectoring off the room, building, and treatment and transportation areas). A command post was also set up, and it included police officers, firefighters, and other department heads, including the ambulance company.

These departments worked closely to respond to the situation. Police were initially the first responders, and their goal was to protect civilians from the gunman. The fire department then took care of emergency needs, and the ambulance transported the wounded to nearby hospitals. Later on, the police conducted the preliminary investigation and requested the assistance of the fire department (since they had a well-trained bomb squad). The police then finished the investigation. This event illustrated how incident command principles can be applied effectively across organizations.

11.5.4 Emergency Operations Center (EOC)

According to FEMA, "the Emergency Operations Center is the central direction, control, and coordination point for emergency operations. It is the place to decide what specific information should go to persons carrying out an 'emergency service' operation" (FEMA 1981). The EOC is the facility where key decision makers gather information and assess policy options regarding the event. It supports field operations for emergency service and other disaster personnel and agencies by acquiring needed resources. EOCs are crucial for effective response and recovery operations.

There has historically been very little known about emergency operations centers in the research literature (Perry 1995, p. 37). We do know, however, that in any major disaster, the emergency manager and other key leaders are likely to open and manage the response and recovery operations from the EOC. What is more, in any disaster, multiple EOCs may be open at any given time. There is the possibility that EOCs will be opened by the affected community and nearby jurisdictions. There may be EOCs for utility companies, nonprofit organizations, and state and federal levels of government. Personnel in the field also interact with those in the EOC on a frequent basis. Therefore, it is vitally important that everyone understand what the EOC is and what it does for you in a disaster.

11.5.5 Characteristics of an EOC

According to Ronald Perry (1991), the EOC is a place, a structure, and a function. First, the EOC is a location where the disaster is managed. It is typically a permanent facility, often at a department headquarters, city hall, or another publicly owned building. There can be temporary units also. An example is an EOC that is quickly set up after a disaster in a room that has multiple purposes (e.g., a conference or training room in the county office building). Some EOCs can be taken to the scene of a disaster. They are nothing more than a mobile coordination center made out of a bus or semitrailer. For these reasons, EOC setup or organizational arrangements will vary dramatically. There is also no correct floor plan for every community. "A wide array of types and designs of emergency command and control centers exists within the United States. These range from simple, inexpensive single or adjoining rooms with several telephones and radios to multimillion-dollar, stand-alone facilities with the latest warning and communications technology" (Moore 1998, p. 2).

Regardless of significant differences, many EOCs have a large open room. This room is where most of the representatives gather to manage response and recovery activities. It has desks, chairs, computers, TVs, phones, and other communications equipment. EOCs do not usually consist of a single room only, however. EOCs often have a series or cluster of closely positioned and interconnected rooms. These rooms have various designated functions. For example, the EOC may have a separate room for key decision makers. This conference room can be used by political leaders to analyze the information from the field, declare a state emergency or disaster, and develop policy options for response and recovery operations (Moore 1998, p. 5). The EOC may also have restroom facilities, a break area, and a room to assess hazards and issue warnings.

The EOC also has a structure. This means EOC includes an organization of many different agencies that are involved in post-disaster operations. Some EOCs may have a single large table where each agency leader meets to discuss the disaster and how to respond to it. Other EOCs may have a series of individual desks for each participating agency. "In this organizational design resources are merely titled under very general disciplines, such as fire, law enforcement or police, utilities, and so on" (Moore 1998, p. 7). Many EOCs are organizing in accordance with the sections of incident command (e.g., planning, operations, logistics, and finance/administration). Other EOCs are organized according to Emergency Support Functions or ESFs. An **ESF** is an activity that must be performed in the aftermath of a disaster. This brings us to the last characteristic of EOCs.

EOCs perform several important functions in disasters. According to Quarantelli (1979), these functions include:

▲ **Information gathering**. After a disaster occurs, one of the primary functions of the EOC is to gather information. This information includes what happened, why it happened, how many people are injured/dead, what areas are affected, what resources are needed, and how to respond most effectively.

▲ **Policy making.** Public officials will meet with the emergency manager and key department leaders to identify what needs to be accomplished in the aftermath of a disaster. They will discuss what options there are for accomplishing those goals. Leaders will also discuss which alternative is most likely to remedy the situation.

▲ **Operations management.** EOCs help to meet agent- and response-generated demands. For instance, a heat wave may require that fans be given to the elderly. An earthquake will require ongoing assessments of damages. A disease outbreak will require doctors and medical treatments. All of these activities will require a great deal of logistical support.

▲ **Coordination.** Another task the EOC performs is coordination of response-generated demands. If fans are needed, the EOC may help to acquire them. If an assessment of damages is required, the EOC may organize teams for that purpose. If doctors and medicines are needed, the EOC may communicate with hospitals and special teams from local, state, and federal public health departments.

▲ **Hosting visitors.** Politicians and public servants from various levels of governments may visit the EOC to determine what is going on. They may also provide recommendations or offer assistance that can benefit response and recovery operations.

▲ **Public information.** To keep citizens apprised of the status of the disaster and what they can do to protect themselves, the EOC will communicate with the media to relay vital information.

▲ **Record keeping.** Because disaster response and recovery are costly operations that involve hundreds of personnel and equipment from numerous agencies, the EOC will track expenses and human and material resources.

11.5.6 Challenges Facing EOCs

The management of EOCs presents many problems (Scanlon 1994). One challenge is that the EOC may be rendered inoperable, as was the case on 9/11 (Building 7 caught on fire when the Twin Towers collapsed). EOCs located in the area of impact will have to be reestablished elsewhere when disaster strikes. Also, access to the EOC may be inadequately controlled. Too many individuals in the EOC can hamper, rather than help, response and recovery operations. There is high turnover in the EOC, and it isn't always clear who is managing the EOC itself.

There are other challenges associated with the EOC environment (Perry 1991, p. 210). Disasters produce a great deal of stress in EOCs. This is a result of the many tasks that have to be accomplished in disasters and significant constraints on time. There is an emotional toll after disasters because people's lives are at stake. There may also be too little or inaccurate knowledge about what is occurring as the disaster unfolds. This complicates decision making in the EOC. There will also be shifting priorities. As new information arrives in the EOC, or as incorrect or incomplete messages are clarified, the goals of response may quickly change.

During response and recovery operations, there will also be overlapping lines of authority and responsibility. The presence of numerous agencies creates organizational confusion, conflict, and competition over who has jurisdiction over geographic areas, response functions, etc. Communication problems are common in the EOC. "The concern with problems and difficulties should not obscure the fact that the concept of an EOC for disasters is an extremely valid one. In most emergencies DRC [Disaster Research Center] has studied, EOCs have functioned relatively well" (Quarantelli as cited by Scanlon 1994, p. 70).

11.5.7 Using EOCs

There are many things that can be done to overcome typical EOC problems. There are several steps that will also ensure successful response operations.

1. Have a backup location in mind for the EOC in case it is needed.
2. Control access to the EOC with guards or identification cards. Allow only essential personnel into the EOC.
3. Have people working in the EOC take frequent breaks to reduce stress.
4. Ensure everyone is familiar with more than one single function. This allows people to take breaks or go home to rest for a shift and still cover all of the important functions.
5. Be sure to communicate effectively with all of the parties involved in response and recovery operations.
6. Put someone with clear authority in charge of the EOC. "The most common management situation was to have the EOC run by the political head of the affected community, either the mayor or someone equivalent" (Scanlon 1994, p. 60). This eliminates questions of power and delegation of responsibility.

The management of EOCs can also be enhanced by ensuring equipment is operational. Communications capabilities and backup power may not work at all or adequately in a disaster. Radios and generators should be tested on a routine basis to verify operability before disaster strikes. Supplies such as paper, pencils, phones, and fax machines will also be required if EOCs are to be used effectively in a disaster.

11.5.8 Comparison of ICS and EOC

As an emergency manager, you must recognize that ICS and EOCs do not operate in isolation from one another. Both may function in the same incident, emergency, or disaster. The incident commander may also radio the EOC for additional resources. These resources may include personnel, mutual aid, barricades, sandbags, and so on. The EOC then attempts to acquire the requested items and updates incident command on their arrival. In addition, there are similarities between the ICS and EOC. Both ICS and EOC have the common goal of coordinating the response. They work together to minimize disruption, save lives, and protect property and the environment. They may also have common organizational structures. In other words, both may include people from the fire department, police department, Red Cross, and so on.

Nonetheless, there are substantial differences between ICS and EOC. First, incident command is utilized in almost every emergency or disaster. These events range from car accidents to major earthquakes. In contrast, EOCs are not used in small incidents. They are typically staffed and employed for large disasters. Second, incident command is a field level coordination point. It is concerned with operations at the scene of an emergency or disaster. EOCs are located at the headquarters level. They coordinate much larger and more complex response and recovery operations. Third, incident command generally includes emergency service personnel such as first responders. EOCs include city leadership (emergency managers, politicians, and other decision makers). Police and fire service leadership can be represented in most EOCs, however (Scanlon 1994, p. 58). Fourth, incident command generally involves a limited number of agencies. On the other hand, EOCs may include a much broader number of agencies. These agencies include representatives from parks and recreation, the engineering department, utility companies, nonprofit organizations, and so on.

Finally, incident command is concerned with tactical decisions and operations. For example, ICS deals with fire suppression at a specific location. EOCs focus on strategic issues instead. Rather than giving attention to the needs of a specific location, EOCs oversee the deployment of resources based on needs for all types of response and recovery operations. Thus, "an EOC is an effective way to achieve coordination among agencies responding to a major emergency or disaster. The absence of an EOC seems to encourage the opposite" (Scanlon 1994, p. 70).

11.5.9 Memorandums of Understanding and Mutual Aid Agreements

Memorandums of understanding (MOUs) and mutual aid agreements are other ways to gain assistance and cooperation from different agencies. Both of these documents are developed by different departments and communities to promote interagency and interjurisdictional assistance in a disaster. MOUs are less formal than mutual aid agreements. MOUs tend to be agreements that may be activated

---

FOR EXAMPLE

EOCs and Disasters

Multiple EOCs may be opened after a disaster. Hurricane Katrina provided a vivid example of this. Affected communities opened EOCs to manage response and recovery operations. Nearby, but unaffected communities, opened EOCs in order to provide mutual aid. Cities and states that received evacuees also opened EOCs in order to manage shelter operations. FEMA opened EOCs in Region VI and at national headquarters. Such EOCs interact one with another and may look at times like a complex network system.

---

if it is possible to do so. In contrast, mutual aid agreements have to be approved by the city/county attorney and the mayor/judge/commissioner. The mutual aid agreement could be legally binding. They may open up liabilities in terms of who will be responsible for injuries, fatalities, and expenses.

Despite the risks, MOUs and mutual aid agreements are beneficial to you for many reasons. MOUs and mutual aid agreements open up the possibility of acquiring much-needed resources after disasters. Communities may not be allowed to request certain types of federal disaster assistance unless they have entered into and activated mutual aid arrangements. Equipment supplied by the federal government is also based on the assumption that it will be shared with nearby communities. Mutual aid agreements improve the coordination of disaster responses because they resolve concerns about joint operations. For all of these reasons, emergency managers should consider participating in MOUs and mutual aid agreements.

SELF-CHECK

- What is **ICS** and what are the different components?
- What are the principles of incident command?
- What are the strengths and weaknesses of ICS?
- What is an **EOC**?
- EOCs have been described as a place, structure, and function. What does this mean?
- What is the relationship between ICS and EOCs?
- What is a **MOU**? What is a mutual aid agreement?

11.6 Managing Disasters at the State Level

When disasters exceed the capability of local jurisdictions, state resources may be utilized. California is one state that bases its response on the **Standard Emergency Management System (SEMS)**. SEMS is the adoption of incident command by all political jurisdictions in a given state. States may also support one another by participating in the Emergency Management Assistance Compact. The **Emergency Management Assistance Compact** is a mutual aid agreement for states.

11.6.1 Standard Emergency Management System (SEMS)

The federal government now mandates that the ICS principles be established and used everywhere. However, the Standard Emergency Management System (SEMS) was developed by California before this was a national requirement. SEMS was established after the Oakland Hills firestorm in 1991. Because of dry weather conditions and inadequate mitigation activities, a series of fires broke out in a residential area in Northern California. Within the first hour of the fire, 790 structures were destroyed. The firestorm eventually destroyed 2,449 homes as well as 437 apartment and condominiums. Numerous individuals were killed or injured by the event as well.

During the incident, firefighters had communication and coordination problems. They had difficulty communicating within their own organization and especially with mutual aid partners from other fire departments. The units that arrived from outside the area also had hoses that did not connect to Oakland's hydrant system. In response to these and other problems, Senator Dominque Petris introduced Senate Bill 1841. This proposal called for the integration of response operations among all jurisdictions in California. The bill was approved on January 1, 1993. It mandated that the California Governor's Office of Emergency Services implement a strategy to improve communication and coordination among all responding agencies. The strategy is based on ICS but has other unique features as well.

Specifically, SEMS mandates ICS as the standard for emergency and disaster operations in California. All cities must use this system while assessing damages, requesting mutual aid, and managing resources. SEMS also integrates all organizational levels involved in disaster response. These five organizational levels are:

▲ **Field Response:** First responders from local agencies
▲ **Local Government:** Subdivisions in each county
▲ **Operational Area:** County governments
▲ **Regional Levels:** Regional governments offer assistance
▲ **State Levels:** State governments offer assistance

SEMS also requires a great deal of education and awareness. First responders have therefore improved responses to disasters as a result of SEMS. It has helped to improve interoperability of organizations in California disasters such as the Northridge earthquake.

11.6.2 Emergency Management Assistance Compact (EMAC)

Because a state may not be able to respond alone, EMAC may be needed. EMAC owes its existence to one of the most devastating disasters in the early 1990s. Hurricane Andrew made landfall over Florida on August 24, 1992 and then traveled to south-central Louisiana. It was one of the most destructive hurricanes ever to hit the United States. This disaster was responsible for at least 23 deaths and $45 billion dollars in damages. Hurricane Andrew was similar to Hurricane Katrina in that there were many complaints that federal help did not arrive soon enough. After this experience, it became clear that states would also need to rely on each other for resources.

Later on several states joined together to respond to Hurricane Andrew, Congress ratified EMAC in 1996. Forty-nine states, the District of Columbia, Puerto Rico, and the Virgin Islands are now participants. Hawaii has not yet joined. States are asked to donate $1,000 as a membership fee to maintain and build system operability. The goal of EMAC is to provide quick assistance to states in need.

EMAC has proved useful and has facilitated the sharing of ferryboats, police, and other resources in disasters. In 2004, EMAC had the largest deployment of state-to-state mutual aid in history. Over a span of 85 days of response to Hurricanes Charley, Frances, Ivan, and Jeanne, EMAC deployed more that 800 state and local personnel from 38 states. The cost in personnel, equipment, and National Guard expenditures was $15 million. EMAC is very helpful but it may not be enough at times.

FOR EXAMPLE

EMAC and Hurricane Katrina

EMAC was an important part of the response to Hurricane Katrina. EMAC deployed more than 1,000 doctors, nurses, emergency medical technicians (EMTs), dentists, ambulances, and medivac helicopters. In addition, EMAC assisted in the deployment and management of other resources in the response effort. These resources included National Guard troops, law enforcement, search and rescue, hazmat teams, communications dispatchers, and satellite phones (www.emacweb.org, "Emergency Management Assistance Compact Deploying Help Across Disciplines," September 12, 2005).

SELF-CHECK

- What is **SEMS** and where was it developed?
- Why was SEMS needed after the Oakland Hills Fire?
- What are the five organizational levels of SEMS?
- What is **EMAC**?
- What are the benefits of EMAC? Can you provide an example?

11.7 Managing Disasters on a Federal Level

Unfortunately, there are many disasters that overwhelm local and even state resources. In these cases, the federal government must step in and provide assistance. Adding another layer of bureaucracy and even more agencies further complicates response and recovery operations. However, there are strategies employed at the federal level to facilitate coordination. We will discuss each one of these.

11.7.1 National Incident Management System (NIMS)

The **National Incident Management System (NIMS)** "is a comprehensive, national approach to incident management that is applicable to all jurisdictional levels and across functional disciplines" (FEMA 2004). It is similar to SEMS in that it adopts ICS as a standard. However, NIMS operates at the federal level, whereas SEMS is applicable to the state level only.

NIMS owes its existence to two sources. First, NIMS is an offspring of the National Interagency Incident Management System. This system was developed in 1980 by the Forest Service in the United States Department of Agriculture to fight fires and deal with other types of disasters. It is somewhat similar to ICS as proposed by FIRESCOPE. Second, NIMS was an outgrowth of recent unique, well-publicized, complicated, and deadly disaster incidents.

For example, the breakup of NASA's space ship, Columbia, over Texas in February 2003 presented debris collection challenges. This was due to the widespread scattering of shuttle fragments across many counties and states. But it was complicated by the overwhelming response to this event that included groups such as NASA, FEMA, police, and state forest service personnel. These groups had never been involved so closely together in any type of disaster response before.

Another event that had a bearing on NIMS was the biological terrorist attacks in 2001. The mailing of letters containing anthrax spores to various locations in Florida and Washington, DC, illustrated the:

▲ Complexity of biological terrorism
▲ Need to provide detailed information to the public

▲ Importance of improving coordination with law-enforcement and public health organizations

Nonetheless, it was really the terrorist attacks on 9/11 that underscored the need for an improved approach to disasters. The heroic efforts of first responders saved the lives of several tenants and visitors in these buildings. However, a variety of problems confronted emergency personnel. Under pressure from victims' families, a bipartisan committee was formed to review the response operations. The committee reviewed mistakes made in intelligence gathering, counter-terrorism operations, and emergency response to the terrorist attacks. After months and even years of investigation, the committee released its findings in the 9/11 Commission Report. The 9/11 Commission Report identified many interrelated weaknesses:

▲ **Communications technology.** The radio equipment, for example, could not penetrate the steel and concrete floors that separated firefighters. Also, most Port Authority police used local channels that did not work in this particular situation.

▲ **Communications procedures.** "There were no standard operating procedures covering how different [Port Authority] commands should communicate via radio during such an incident" (National Commission on Terrorist Attacks 2004, p. 282).

▲ **Information management.** Responders had inaccurate information or no information at all. For example, "The deputy fire safety director in the lobby, while immediately aware that a major incident had occurred, did not know for approximately ten minutes that a commercial jet had directly hit the building" (National Commission on Terrorist Attacks 2004, p. 286).

▲ **Interorganizational coordination.** There was a lack of communication and coordination between the Port Authority police, the firefighters, and the police. There was no unified command structure in place to deal with this event.

▲ **Public information.** People did not receive information because the public address systems were not heard. In other cases, people were given conflicting information. For instance, some people were advised to wait for further instructions, whereas others were advised to evacuate the twin towers.

▲ **Incident Management.** There was a breakdown in issuing and following orders. Many off-duty firefighters rushed to the scene and did not have radios. Others were ordered to evacuate because the other tower had crumbled to the ground. Despite this request, many refused to out of a desire to help the citizens get to safety. There were also areas of the buildings that were searched twice. This occurred because of the lack of communication and coordination.

As a result of these weaknesses, the Commission wrote that, "The lesson of 9/11 for civilians and first responders can be stated simply: in the new age of terror, they—we—are the primary targets. The losses America suffered that day demonstrated both the gravity of the terrorist threat and the commensurate need to prepare ourselves to meet it" (National Commission on Terrorist Attacks 2004, p. 323). The events of 9/11 underscored the need for and importance of national standards for disaster management (FEMA IS-700, 2004).

11.7.2 Goals of NIMS

Aware of the problems identified by the 9/11 Commission, President George W. Bush issued two Homeland Security Presidential Directives (HSPD). HSPD-5 called for standardization among responders. HSPD-8 reiterated the importance of disaster preparedness.

HSPD-5 was issued on February 28, 2003, and stressed the need to "enhance the ability of the United States to manage domestic incidents by establishing a single, comprehensive national incident management system." This Presidential Directive:

▲ Encourages the integration of local, state, and federal disaster responses
▲ Seeks to coordinate government activities with the private and nonprofit sectors
▲ Promotes information sharing with the public, the private sector, local and state authorities, and federal departments and agencies
▲ Provides for improved interoperability and compatibility among local, state, and federal governments
▲ Recommends the development of a National Response Plan

HSPD-8 was issued on December 17, 2003. It was to establish "policies to strengthen the preparedness of the United States to prevent and respond to threatened or actual domestic attacks, major disasters and other emergencies." This Directive:

▲ Requires the development of a national domestic all-hazards preparedness goal
▲ Ensures continuous efforts to prepare first responders for major events. This is mainly for terrorist attack prevention and response
▲ Describes the allocation of funds to states to strengthen capabilities
  The distribution is based on population, infrastructures, and other risk factors.
▲ Points out that the Federal government will support state and local entities in planning, interoperability, and equipment acquisition
▲ Establishes national standards for preparedness

▲ Develops a system to collect, analyze, and disseminate lessons learned, research, and best practices to improve response operations

▲ Maintains adequate teams, stockpiles, and caches in accordance with national preparedness goals

▲ Encourages active citizen participation in preparedness measures

▲ Demands periodic assessment of progress made and areas needing improvement

The National Incident Management System (NIMS) was created with the goals of these Presidential Directives in mind.

11.7.3 Principles of NIMS

NIMS has the objective of helping the nation prevent, prepare for, respond to, and recover from all types of disasters including domestic terrorist incidents. It intends to facilitate government and private entities at all levels working together to deal with disasters. NIMS is supposed to allow a flexible response regardless of cause, size, location, or complexity of a disaster. At the same time, NIMS provides a set of standardized organizational structures. It also specifies requirements for processes, procedures, and systems designed to improve interoperability (FEMA IS-700, 2004).

NIMS includes six key components:

1. **Command and management.** NIMS is based on three organizational/operational systems. The first is the **ICS.** This defines the management structure and operations at the scene of a disaster. This may include unified command, which is comprised of more than one responding agency or multiple jurisdictions. It may also incorporate area command. Area command oversees the management of multiple incidents. Each organizational structure requires ICS. The second system is the multiagency coordination systems. These define the structure and management principles for those working with or supporting incident command. Such systems facilitate logistics. They also allocate and track resources. They share information. They coordinate interagency and intergovernmental issues regarding policies, priorities, and strategies. These may be EOCs and multiagency coordination entities that take a strategic perspective. They also provide support to incident and area commanders. The third system concerns public information. This includes ways for communicating timely and accurate information to citizens. Such systems include Public Information Officers. They advise Incident Command about public information matters. It also includes Joint Information Centers. This is a system where PIOs from multiple agencies meet to provide critical information, crisis communications, and public affairs assistance.

2. **Preparedness.** Under NIMS, "preparedness is implemented through a continual cycle of planning, training, equipping, exercising, evaluating, taking action to correct and mitigate" (FEMA IS-700, 2004). Preparedness involves all levels of government. Preparedness also involves the public and nonprofit sectors. Such readiness efforts are based on standards and certification for planning, training, equipment, mutual aid, emergency assistance compacts, etc. Preparedness efforts require the involvement of "a wide variety of committees, planning groups" to create plans, integrate activities, promote interoperability, establish priorities, and improve coordination.

3. **Resource Management.** Resource management involves four primary tasks:

   - Describing, inventorying, requesting, and tracking resources
   - Activating those systems before, during, and after an incident
   - Dispatching resources before, during, and after an incident
   - Deactivating or recalling resources during or after an incident

   Resource management also operates under five key principles. It recommends advanced planning among agencies before disaster strikes, resource identification and ordering using standard processes and methods, and resource categorization based on size, capacity, capability, skill, or other characteristics. Effective resource management also requires use of agreements for resources before an incident occurs as well as effective management (implying the reliance on validated practices).

4. **Communications and information management.** NIMS recognizes that responses require effective communications. Responses also require successful information management strategies. This is facilitated by "a common operating picture that is accessible across jurisdictions and agencies" (FEMA IS-700, 2004). It is also fostered through common communication terminologies, processes, and standards.

5. **Supporting technologies.** NIMS recognizes the importance of technology but recommends:

   - Interoperability and compatibility. Systems must work together.
   - Technological support. Communication equipment and expertise is vital in response.
   - Technology standards. Common rules will enhance interoperability.
   - Broad-based requirements. All types of technology, procedures, protocols, and standards must be recognized and incorporated.
   - Strategic planning and R&D. This signifies that an agenda for technological research and development has been identified and prioritized.

6. **Ongoing management and maintenance.** To provide direction as well as routine review and refinement of NIMS, the Department of Homeland

Security established a NIMS Integration Center. Its purpose is to serve as a resource to better coordinate responses to all types of disaster incidents.

11.7.4 Strengths and Weaknesses of NIMS

NIMS has many strengths that you should consider. One of the main strengths is that it incorporates the lessons we have learned from prior disasters such as the 9/11 terrorist attacks. It also recognizes the need to include the public, private, and nonprofit sectors in response operations. NIMS has other advantages because it suggests the need to focus on all hazards, desires to address each phase of emergency management, promotes proactive measures for preparedness, and intends to improve interagency communications. NIMS also gives extra attention to resource management, recognizes the need for flexibility and standardization, is based on the Incident Command System, and updates emergency management in the United States.

NIMS also has weaknesses that you must acknowledge. NIMS illustrates an over-learning from 9/11 events. For instance, it has an evident bias toward terrorism as opposed to natural or technological disasters. NIMS also discusses government operations more than the role of the private and nonprofit sectors. NIMS also:

▲ Does not give sufficient attention to prevention activities

▲ May downplay mitigation and recovery activities

▲ Focuses too heavily on technology for improved coordination

▲ Possibly marginalizes functions other than resource management

▲ May stress standardization at the expense of flexibility

▲ Does not adequately capture a strategic perspective as it is based on the Incident Command System

▲ Reinvents the wheel rather than addressing more fundamental problems in emergency management

11.7.5 National Response Plan (NRP)

The **National Response Plan (NRP)** is a companion to NIMS. It was created as a result of HSPD-5 and finalized in December of 2004. The purpose of the NRP is to align federal agencies, capabilities, and resources into a unified, all-discipline, and all-hazards approach to disasters. The plan was jointly developed by federal, state, local, and tribal governments as well as the private sector. It creates no new authorities, but it does attempt to unify and enhance the incident management capabilities. The plan intends to enhance the resources of responding agencies and organizations. For instance, the plan uses best practices and procedures from incident management disciplines, including Homeland Security, emergency management, law enforcement, firefighting, public works, public health, and emergency medical services.

The NRP is the basis for how the federal government coordinates with state, local, and tribal governments and the private sector during incidents. It establishes protocols to help:

1. Save lives
2. Protect the health and safety of the public, responders, and recovery workers
3. Ensure national security
4. Prevent imminent threats from terrorists
5. Seoure and restore critical infrastructure
6. Conduct law enforcement investigations
7. Protect property and mitigate damages
8. Facilitate recovery of individuals, families, businesses, and governments

The NRP is activated when an "Incident of National Significance" is declared. The first use of this declaration was during Hurricane Katrina. The declaration means that the incident is a major disaster or emergency that overwhelms the resources of state and local authorities.

11.7.6 Emergency Support Functions (ESFs) in the National Response Plan

The National Response Plan also outlines fifteen Emergency Support Functions (ESFs) that must be performed after a disaster. Each ESF is a grouping of government and private sector capabilities into an organizational structure to provide support, resources, and services during response and recovery operations. The federal government's response to Incidents of National Significance is provided through the partial or full activation of ESFs. Each ESF is composed of primary and support agencies.

▲ A **primary agency** has ultimate responsibility for a particular emergency support function.
▲ A **support agency** has the role of assisting the primary agency in the fulfillment of ESFs.

These designations are made on the basis of authorities, resources, and capabilities of each federal department or agency. The fifteen ESFs are listed below.

▲ **ESF 1: Transportation.** Includes federal and civil transportation support, safety, restoration of the infrastructure, restricting movements, and an impact assessment.
▲ **ESF 2: Communications.** Comprises coordination with the telecommunications industry, repair of the infrastructure, and protection and restoration of cyber and information technology resources.

▲ **ESF 3: Public Works and Engineering.** Consists of engineering services, construction management, and repair and protection of the infrastructure.

▲ **ESF 4: Firefighting.** Incorporates firefighting activities and support to urban and rural firefighting operations.

▲ **ESF 5: Emergency Management.** Involves coordination of incident management efforts, incident action planning, resource management, and mission assignments.

▲ **ESF 6: Mass Care, Housing, and Human Services.** Includes mass care, housing, and human services.

▲ **ESF 7: Resource Support.** Covers resource support such as facility space, office equipment, and contracting services.

▲ **ESF 8: Public Health and Medical Services.** Comprises public, medical, and mental health and mortuary services.

▲ **ESF 9: Urban Search and Rescue.** Covers life-saving assistance.

▲ **ESF 10: Oil and Hazardous Material Response.** Includes hazardous material response, environmental safety, and short- and long-term recovery.

▲ **ESF 11: Agriculture and Natural Resources.** Captures nutrition assistance, animal disease, plant disease, food safety, and natural and cultural resources protection and restoration.

▲ **ESF 12: Energy.** Includes energy infrastructure assessment, repair, and restoration, energy industry utilities coordination, and energy forecast.

▲ **ESF 13: Public Safety and Security.** Consists of facility and resource security, security planning, public security support, and support to access, traffic, and crowd control.

▲ **ESF 14: Long-Term Community Recovery and Mitigation.** Covers social and economic community impact assessment, long-term recovery assistance to states, local government, and the private sector, and mitigation analysis.

▲ **ESF 15: External Affairs.** Includes media and community relations, congressional and international affairs, and emergency public information.

Not all Incidents of National Significance result in the activation of each ESFs. It is possible that an incident or disaster could be adequately addressed by DHS and other federal agencies. However, it is believed that the ESFs in the NRP will help the country identify and resolve the most pressing problems after a disaster.

11.7.7 Area Field Office (AFO)

The fulfillment of ESFs does not necessarily guarantee that the federal government responds in a successful manner. For this reason, an Area Field Office is established in the disaster-affected area. The **Area Field Office (AFO)** is like an EOC or JOC, but it coordinates the efforts of federal, state local, tribal, nongovernmental, and private-sector organizations. The AFO is a central location where response and recovery is managed at a federal level. When needed, an AFO can be open before or after a disaster. It can also be activated during an event of national significance (e.g., Olympics) for prevention and preparedness activities. The AFO is mainly for federal authorities. However, the AFO may include representatives from local and state agencies and other organizations when they visit to coordinate policy.

The AFO uses the organizational structure of NIMS for both preincident and postincident management activities. However, the AFO does not manage on-scene operations. Instead, the AFO provides support to on-scene efforts and also addresses a broader range of response and recovery concerns. The broader support operations will most likely extend beyond the incident site and encompass multiple JFOs. Additionally, threat situations or incidents that affect multiple states or communities may require separate AFOs. In these circumstances, one of the AFOs may be identified to provide strategic leadership and coordination for the overall incident management effort. The AFO that is identified as lead is usually the one that is in the most heavily impacted area (FEMA, National Response Plan, 2004).

FOR EXAMPLE

Federal Deployment for Special Events

A JFO was used in the presidential inauguration for the first time in 2005. The JFO housed dozens of officials from 50 federal, state, and local agencies in a high-tech command center. The JFO was located in northern Virginia and had 120 work stations and several giant video screens. Law enforcement and security personnel watched the cameras that monitored downtown Washington streets. They kept track of aerial surveillance flights. They checked sensors scanning for evidence of biological or chemical weapons. The JFO also commanded the Coast Guard cutters and helicopters. The JFO oversaw canine bomb-sniffing units, customs aircraft, bicycle patrols, and crowd control issues. All of the federal agencies that handled security, law enforcement, and crisis response were housed in the JFO. The federal agencies participating in the JFO were under the command of a single federal officer. The officer was Tim Koerner, the top deputy of the Secret Service. Koerner reported directly to Homeland Security Secretary Tom Ridge. The JFO and the reporting structure had the goal of improving communication and coordination among the federal agencies. Jim Rice, the FBI supervisory agent, said, "When an incident first happens, in the first 30 minutes probably about 75 percent of the information you get is wrong. Being able to look the guy in the eye that you're talking to, that eliminates a lot of problems" (Associated Press, "Security Goes High Tech for Inauguration," January 18, 2005).

SELF-CHECK

- What is **NIMS** and how is it related to ICS?
- Why did NIMS come about?
- What is **crisis management**? What is consequence management?
- What are the six components of NIMS?
- Is NIMS beneficial or detrimental for emergency management?
- What are some ESFs under the National Response Plan?
- What is an **Area Field Office** and how is it different from a JFO?

SUMMARY

Technology and organization are tools that you can use to improve response and recovery operations. Knowing what technology is available is a crucial responsibility you will have in emergency management. Understanding communication and decision support systems will help you manage post-disaster operations. Incident command can facilitate communication and coordination at the scene of an emergency or disaster. EOCs can also be utilized to harmonize response and recovery activities among a myriad of organizations. If a disaster overwhelms your jurisdiction, you may seek help from mutual aid partners or the state Emergency Management Assistance Compact. You should also be aware of NIMS and the National Response Plan if federal initiatives are to be integrated seamlessly into local and state efforts. Harnessing these tools will help you develop resilience after a disaster.

KEY TERMS

ACU-1000	A type of interface equipment that links mobile radios, cell phones, satellite technology, and regular phones in a single real-time communication system.
Area Field Office (AFO)	An office like an EOC or JFO that is responsible for coordinating the entire effort of federal, state local, tribal, nongovernmental, and private-sector organizations.
Decision support systems	Software applications that help the emergency manager determine priorities and respond to a disaster.

Emergency Management Assistance Compact (EMAC)	A mutual aid agreement for states.
Emergency Support Function (ESF)	An activity that must be performed in the aftermath of a disaster.
Finance/administration section	An organizational division under ICS that tracks costs, completes and files paperwork, and records expenses of operations and logistics.
Geographic Information Systems (GIS)	"Organized collection of computer hardware, software, geographic data, and personnel designed to efficiently capture, store, update, manipulate, analyze, and display all forms of geographically referenced information" (ESRI as cited by Dash 1997).
HAZUS	An assessment software tool that is used for analyzing potential losses from floods, hurricane winds, and earthquakes.
Incident command	The on-scene leadership for the disaster.
Incident Command System (ICS)	"A set of personnel, policies, procedures, facilities and equipment, integrated into a common organizational structure designed to improve emergency response operations of all types and complexities" (Irwin 1989, 134).
Information officer	Professional who works with the media to answer their questions about the event and release information to the public.
Liaison officer	The point of contact with other organizations responding to the incident.
Light Detection And Ranging (LIDAR)	An airborne laser system that is used to detect heat and dangerous debris accumulations.
Logistics section	An organizational division under ICS that acquires and provides materials, services, and facilities to support the needs of responders as directed by the incident commander and the operations section.
National Incident Management System (NIMS)	"A comprehensive, national approach to incident management that is applicable to all jurisdictional levels and across functional disciplines" (FEMA 2004).
Operations section	An organizational division under ICS that is responsible for implementing the strategy to

respond to the incident as determined by the incident commander and the planning section.

Planning section — An organizational division under ICS that collects and evaluates information about the disaster to determine operational priorities.

Primary agency — Department that has ultimate responsibility for a particular emergency support function.

Receivers — Equipment devices that obtain signals from transmitters. They include stereos, pagers, police scanners, and televisions.

Safety officer — Professional who monitors the hazardous conditions of the disaster to ensure protection of responding personnel.

Standard Emergency Management System (SEMS) — The adoption of incident command by all political jurisdictions in a given state.

Support agency — Department with the role of assisting the primary agency in the fulfillment of ESFs.

Talk group — A unit with its own designated channel.

Transmitters — Communication instruments that convey information through radios, sirens, television stations, and cable override systems.

Transceivers — Instruments that are able to both transmit and receive information. Examples of transceivers include telephones, satellites, personal digital assistants, two-way radios, citizen-band radios, 800-Mhz radios, and ham radios.

Trunked radio system — A computer-controlled network that searches for a clear channel for users to use to talk to each other.

ASSESSING YOUR UNDERSTANDING

Go to www.wiley.com/college/McEntire to evaluate your knowledge of managing organization and technology.
Measure your learning by comparing pretest and post-test results.

Summary Questions

1. A Doppler radar helps the emergency responders find victims trapped after a disaster. True or False?

2. A talk group is a unit with its own designated communications channel. True or False?

3. VoIP stands for Vector Organization Incident Plan. True or False?

4. E-Team helps the emergency manager request and deploy resources. True or False?

5. ICS was developed after Hurricane Andrew. True or False?

6. The logistics section acquires and provides materials for the operations section. True or False?

7. It may be advisable to change the name of incident command to incident management. True or False?

8. EOCs are places where leaders get together to discuss response priorities. True or False?

9. Controlling access to EOCs is not needed since you actually want all departments to be represented. True or False?

10. Mutual aid agreements are beneficial in that they resolve concerns about joint operations. True or False?

11. Operational area is not included as one of the five organizational levels of SEMS. True or False?

12. NIMS is similar to SEMS in that it mandates the use of ICS in disasters. True or False?

13. The first AFO was set up to deal with the shuttle disaster. True or False?

14. What device can help responders arrive at the scene of a disaster quickly?
    (a) Video cameras
    (b) Detection equipment
    (c) Traffic signal preemption devices
    (d) Remote sensing
    (e) All of the above

15. Trunked radio systems:
    (a) Get their names from vehicle trunks, where they are mounted
    (b) Do not permit communications among different organizations

(c) Cannot overcome the VoIP

(d) Search for clear channels for the user

(e) a and c

16. Internet communications:

(a) May help generals get information as quickly as underlings

(b) Are not related to VoIP

(c) Cannot overcome the ACU 1000

(d) Are used by responders who use the DOT 250

(e) None of the above

17. Decision support systems

(a) Do not allow for instantaneous links among the database

(b) Include SoftRisk but not E-Team

(c) Include GIS but not CoBRA

(d) Include Eplan only

(e) None of the above

18. GIS may assist with:

(a) The tailoring of warnings for a specific population

(b) The identification of tornado paths

(c) The identification of fire hydrants

(d) All of the above

(e) Two of the above

19. ICS and Mutual aid are geared:

(a) Specifically for local governments

(b) Specifically for state governments

(c) Specifically for the federal government

(d) Specifically for the private sector

(e) Specifically for the nonprofit sector

20. Problems leading to the creation of ICS included:

(a) Poor communications

(b) Insufficient intelligence and prediction

(c) Lack of joint planning

(d) Inadequate resource management

(e) All of the above

21. Which officer is in charge of relaying information from other organizations to the incident commander?

(a) Incident command

(b) Safety officer

(c) Liaison officer

(d) Information officer

(e) Planning officer

22. Which section would be involved in carrying out debris removal?

(a) Planning

(b) Operations

(c) Logistics

(d) Finance/administration

(e) Incident command

23. What are the strengths of ICS?

(a) Closer contact among decision makers

(b) Improved information flow to the public

(c) Enhanced communication due to common terminology

(d) More realistic expectations for managers over employees

(e) All of the above

24. Research reveals:

(a) EOCs are not valuable

(b) EOCs are extremely valuable

(c) EOCs cannot overcome the VoIP

(d) EOCs should subsume ICU-1000 statutes

(e) EOCs do not host visitors

25. ICS focuses on tactical issues, whereas EOCs:

(a) Focus on planning only

(b) Focus on field operations

(c) Focus on strategic issues

(d) Focus on small disaster issues

(e) Focus on simple disaster issues

26. NIMS includes:

(a) Command and management

(b) Preparedness

(c) Resource management

(d) Supporting technologies

(e) All of the above

27. NIMS:

(a) Suggests the need to focus on all types of hazards

(b) May downplay recovery issues

(c) Focuses too heavily on technology for effective response management

(d) a, b, and c

(e) b and c

28. AFOs:

   (a) Are not associated with the federal government

   (b) Are associated with the federal government

   (c) Are associated with the federal government only

   (d) Are not associated with the NRP

   (e) Cannot be opened for anything but a natural disaster

Review Questions

1. Do all communities have the same technological tools? Why or why not?
2. How can technology help with emergency medical care or search and rescue?
3. How is a transmitter different from a receiver?
4. Can any equipment be used to improve interoperability?
5. What are the benefits of the Internet for emergency managers?
6. What is a decision support system?
7. How can CAMEO assist with a hazardous materials response?
8. GIS has been described as "the most exciting technological development in emergency management." Why is this the case?
9. What problems were evident in the response to the 1970 fires in California?
10. What are the four sections listed under ICS?
11. How can "common terminology" help response operations?
12. Is ICS beneficial? Is it without drawbacks?
13. What are the three characteristics of EOCs?
14. What are the seven functions of EOCs Quarantelli mentions?
15. Why are mutual aid agreements helpful for response and recovery operations?
16. What is SEMS and how is it related to ICS?
17. Why did states develop EMAC?
18. Why did 9/11 lead to the creation of NIMS?
19. What is the relationship between crisis and consequence management?
20. What are the six components of NIMS?
21. What are the goals of the National Response Plan?
22. What is the difference between a primary and support agency?
23. How is an AFO different from an EOC or JFO?

Applying This Chapter

1. You are a business continuity specialist for a Fortune 500 company. The company stores data for the mortgage industry. Your role is to get the business up and running after a disaster and ensure that employees can continue to serve their clientele. What types of technology would you need to fulfill your responsibilities if a power outage disables your operations?

2. You are the emergency manager for a city that has hazardous waste transported on its interstate highways every day. One of the semitrucks carrying the waste turned over and is threatening a nearby residential area. Traffic needs to be controlled, and evacuees need to be sheltered. The media has arrived, and the Department of Transportation is seeking answers. What principles of Incident Command do you use, and why are they important?

3. A major drought has affected your community and jurisdictions in the nearby state. Farmers are losing cattle at an astonishing rate because of the heat and lack of rain. Hay and veterinarians are needed immediately or further deaths will result. How can mutual aid or EMAC be applied in this situation?

4. You work for FEMA and have just been deployed in San Jose, California. A major earthquake occurred and affected the community in almost every way imaginable. How can the ESFs from the NRP help you to respond and recover? Would a JFO be necessary? Why or why not?

5. You are the Director for Homeland Security. Terrorists have threatened an attack against the Super Bowl, and it appears that the evidence is credible. Should you set up an Area Field Office? If so, why? Who should be involved?

6. You are the emergency manager in a city that is having a parade. You are concerned about protestors or terrorist attacks because controversial groups are participating. What kind of technology do you want at your disposal to respond to the situation and why? What equipment would be useful if the situation turns violent?

7. You are the emergency manager in Washington State. In the early hours of the morning, an earthquake occurs in the central business district. There is significant damage to roads and businesses. Fires have spread throughout various neighborhoods. How do you activate the Emergency Operations Center, and who do you want involved?

YOU TRY IT

Using Technology After a Terrorist Attack

You are the emergency manager for New York City. During the afternoon rush hour, terrorists unleashed multiple bombs on four different subway systems. You are worried about the presence of dangerous chemicals and would like to apprehend the suspects. What kind of technology would you use to respond to the situation and why?

Applying Incident Command

You are the emergency manager in Kansas. You have been alerted by the National Weather Service that a tornado unexpectedly touched down in your moderately sized community. Under Incident Command, what four sections do you activate at the scene of a disaster to facilitate emergency and disaster management?

Class Presentation

Select a disaster that has occurred in the past. Prepare a 10- to 15-minute presentation on how technology or organization was used during response and recovery. Be sure to highlight successes and failures. PowerPoints or handouts are preferred.

12

DEALING WITH FUTURE DISASTERS
Prior Lessons, New Threats, and Rising Vulnerability

Starting Point

Go to www.wiley.com/college/McEntire to assess your knowledge of the preparing for future disasters.
Determine where you need to concentrate your effort.

What You'll Learn in This Chapter

▲ The different threats that face the United States
▲ The interaction of primary, associated, and secondary hazards
▲ The nature of industrial hazards
▲ How to prepare for and respond to acts of violence
▲ What events to expect after a terrorist attack
▲ New threats and insufficiently recognized hazards
▲ Reasons for rising vulnerability across the different hazards

After Studying This Chapter, You'll Be Able To

▲ Examine the complexities inherent in disasters
▲ Appraise the danger of hazmat incidents
▲ Question the similarities of mass shootings to other types of disasters
▲ Employ methods to protect evidence and first responders after a terrorist attack
▲ Demonstrate an ability to take steps to prepare for biological threats
▲ Compare and contrast the different future technological hazards
▲ Analyze additional causes of vulnerability

Goals and Outcomes

▲ Manage natural disasters effectively
▲ Perform successfully after technological disasters
▲ Assess how to collaborate with law enforcement after mass shootings
▲ Select ways to coordinate with public health officials after terrorist attacks
▲ Estimate the different biological threats that currently face the United States
▲ Plan steps to take to deal with new threats
▲ Evaluate alternative ways to reduce vulnerability

INTRODUCTION

As an emergency manager, you must not only foster resilience today. It is vital that you think critically about how to advance it in the future. You must realize that disasters are on the rise. This disturbing fact suggests that we will have to deal more effectively with the complex nature of natural disasters. It is vital that you recognize the unique challenges of technological disasters. Furthermore, you will need to understand how to deal with violent activity and take precautionary steps to protect your community after terrorist attacks. There are also new or unrecognized hazards that threaten us. These include environmental degradation, meteor strikes, disease outbreaks, and computer-related disasters. Vulnerability is also increasing around the world, and it is your job to help everyone in the community take steps to reverse it. You must have an understanding of the factors that will have a bearing on future disasters if you are to respond to and recover from them successfully.

12.1 Disasters on the Rise

There is a growing feeling among many scholars and practitioners that disasters are becoming more frequent and intense compared to the past (Quarantelli 1992). For instance, the 1980s witnessed major events such as the Mt. St. Helen's eruption, the Bhopal chemical release, the Chernobyl nuclear accident, and the Loma Prieta earthquake. In the 1990s, Hurricane Andrew, the Northridge earthquake, the bombing of the World Trade Center, the Oklahoma City bombing, and the Tokyo sarin gas release were also noteworthy events. The new millennium appears to be continuing this trend of major disasters. Catastrophes have taken their toll in recent years.

The terrorist attacks of September 11, 2001, for example, were costly in terms of physical damage, lives lost, and economic impact. These well-orchestrated events also had global implications due to the deposing of the Afghanistan government and subsequent military conflict in Iraq. During the late summer and early Fall of 2004, Florida was hit by several hurricanes and a tropical storm. This severely tested the emergency management capacity in that state and the government at the federal level. A few months later, an extremely strong earthquake occurred off of the coast of Indonesia. The quake produced a Tsunami in the Indian Ocean, which took more than 300,000 lives and cost billions in damage. This event illustrated the power of nature and lack or failure of warning systems. In 2005, Hurricane Katrina struck New Orleans and other communities of the Gulf Coast area. The wind, storm surge, and flooding resulting from breached retaining walls killed more than 1,300 people and produced billions of dollars in damages. The response by local and federal authorities was harshly criticized by citizens and politicians. The government appeared to be unable to react effectively to this major calamity.

Such events and weaknesses lead many people to wonder if disasters are on the rise. Some scholars point out that our record keeping has improved and this accounts for the disturbing trends. It has also been suggested by others that the media is better able to report disasters than in the past (e.g., the CNN effect). Other researchers point out that hazards are both more numerous and severe than they were in prior decades. Several scholars are beginning to focus on how human attitudes and activities are augmenting disasters (Mileti 1999).

While there is some disagreement if we are experiencing more earthquakes, tornadoes, and tsunamis than we did in the past, evidence does suggest that we are experiencing more flooding hazards. Flooding is occurring at rates and intensities in areas that previously were not affected by such hazards. This may be due, in part, to the extensive use of concrete and asphalt in locations that were previously undeveloped. The use of these materials in urban areas covers soil (the earth's natural sponge) and causes run-off water to flow rapidly in low-lying areas. Besides more flooding hazards, it is also true that we are entering a phase of increased hurricane activity. Some researchers believe this is a naturally occurring cycle, whereas others credit the spike to global climate change. Regardless of the cause, this could also alter the probability of both flooding and drought episodes domestically and abroad.

Apart from these hazards, there is the possibility of major disease outbreaks around the world. The increased use of hazardous materials will likely create more technological hazards in the future. With the emergence of militant terrorist groups like Al-Qaeda, terrorist incidents will continue to occur around the world. These often involve suicide bombings in places like Israel, but it is likely that they will morph into the use of weapons of mass destruction in the United States. There is also a higher probability of disease outbreaks, environmental degradation, and computer-related disasters. As an emergency manager or responder, it will be imperative that you understand how to deal with these types

FOR EXAMPLE

Terrorists and WMD

Terrorist leaders like Osama bin Laden have clearly indicated their desire to obtain weapons of mass destruction and use them against the United States. There is at least some superficial evidence that Iran is also pursuing a program to develop nuclear weapons. This, combined the with hostility of some radical Muslims and our pourous borders, creates an extremely vulnerable situation. It is an unfortunate probability that the United States will be attacked with weapons of mass destruction in the future. Emergency managers and others in homeland security must anticipate, prevent, and prepare for such contingencies.

of events. You must be aware of the new hazards and rising vulnerability that will have bearing on future disasters. Without this knowledge, you will not be able to reverse such trends or promote resilience.

SELF-CHECK

- Are disasters on the rise?
- What are the causes of more and worse disasters?
- What is the CNN effect?
- Are there more natural hazards than in the past?
- Why is it important to think critically about the future?

12.2 Understanding Natural Disasters

Natural disasters are becoming increasingly complicated, and the primary hazards that trigger them may have a close relation to other hazards.

▲ A **primary hazard** is a natural hazard agent that interacts with vulnerabilities and therefore produces a disaster.

▲ An **associated hazard** is a natural hazard agent that typically occurs at the same time as the primary hazard (e.g., hurricanes produce flooding).

▲ A **secondary hazard** is a hazard (natural, technological, or otherwise) that occurs as a result of the primary hazard.

Some associated and secondary hazards are immediate, and others are delayed. Sometimes it is difficult to distinguish between associated and secondary hazards. Examples of these hazards are listed in Table 12-1.

Primary associated and secondary hazards interact to produce complicated disaster situations.

1. A **complex or compound disaster** is an event that involves multiple variables. An earthquake with a landslide, structural collapse, and fires is an example of this.
2. A **cascading disaster** is an event that triggers additional hazards or impacts. A good example of this is 9/11. A hijacked plane hit the trade center towers. These, in turn, caught on fire and collapsed. As a result, the infrastructure and subway systems were jeopardized.
3. A **synergistic disaster** is an event where one resulting impact seems to magnify others. For instance, the loss of power or water in a disaster may limit the ability to communicate or fight fires.

Table 12-1: Primary, Associated, and Secondary Hazards

Primary Hazard	Associated Hazard(s)	Secondary Hazard(s)
Volcanic eruption	Earthquakes	Wildfires, fires, flooding, and mudslides
Earthquake	Landslides	Structural collapse, fires, chemical releases or explosions, landslides, tsunamis
Hurricane	Tornadoes and flooding	Structural collapses
Lightning strikes	Thunderstorms	Urban and rural fires
Flooding	Hurricanes, tornadoes, and other forms of severe weather	Structural collapse, mold, and diseases such as cholera and diphtheria
Winter storms (snow and ice)	Traffic accidents	Fires (as people try to keep warm) and avalanches
Tornadoes	Hurricanes, hail, flooding, and other forms of severe weather	Structural collapse
Wildfire	Thunderstorms, lightning strikes	Landslides due to loss of vegetation

4. A **na-tech disaster** occurs when a natural hazard interacts with technology to produce or magnify adverse effects (Cruz, Steinburg, and Luna 2001). A tornado that overturns a train full of hazardous materials is an example of this type of event.

Natural (and other types of) hazards may also lead to complex, cascading, synergistic, or na-tech (natural and technological hazards) disasters. Hurricane Katrina is a good example of these types of disasters. The hurricane was the initial hazard. It was associated with flooding due to the breaching of the levees. As the water settled in New Orleans, gas lines and fuel storage tanks were broken. Fires erupted as a result. Hazardous chemicals and sewage also ended up in the floodwaters, causing an environmental nightmare. The impact of the hurricane was therefore more severe than would normally be the case in most prior disasters. The nature of today's hazards and disasters necessitates that first responders and you approach response and recovery operations in a cautious and holistic manner.

12.2.1 Responding to a Natural Disaster

Every type of disaster creates common and more unusual challenges for you as an emergency manager or responder. To examine these challenges, we will review one incident and see what we can learn from it. The case that we will rely on is the East Bay Hills fire that occurred in California in 1991 (FEMA, no date).

The East Bay Hills fire was a devastating event that occurred from October 19 through October 22, 1991. The event started out as a brush fire that was reported on a hillside at 12:12 pm on October 19. The cause of the fire is unknown, but there is some speculation that it was a result of arson. In time, five alarms were sounded as firefighters tried to get control of the situation. This included 12 engine companies, two ladder companies, and other emergency resources and personnel. Several helicopters were brought in as well. Because the wind was very light that day, the firefighters were eventually able to get control of the fire and extinguish it.

Unfortunately, several flare-ups occurred throughout the night due to embers that remained hot. Most of these small fires were quickly quenched. But at 10:40 am on October 20, another major flare up occurred, and cinders were carried elsewhere by strong winds. Within a few minutes, a new fire started crowning trees on another hillside. Superheated gasses from the fire would dry out vegetation; the shrubbery and trees would then explode on fire. The fire was so hot that even the power poles would ignite far from the actual fire. When all was said and done, the fire:

▲ Covered 1,500 acres
▲ Destroyed more than 3,000 houses and 2,000 vehicles
▲ Killed 25 people and injured 150 others
▲ Left 10,000 people homeless
▲ Necessitated the evacuation of 20,000 to 30,000 people
▲ Resulted in $1.5 billion in damages and losses
▲ Was declared a presidential disaster

This disaster shows the complex interaction of systems Mileti discusses in *Disasters by Design* (1999). Natural disasters are obviously closely associated with the natural environment. The **natural environment** is the physical milieu in which many disasters occur. For instance, the East Bay Hills area is very hazard prone. There have been many fires in this area over the past 70 years. Since 1930, there have been 14 large-scale fires. In 1923, a fire destroyed 640 structures. In 1970, a fire destroyed 37 homes. In the 1980s, another fire destroyed five buildings.

Not only is the area hazard prone, but the nature of hazards has changed over time. In the 1800s, most of the wood in the East Bay Hills was consumed by citizens from the area. As a result, people imported Eucalyptus from

Australia. Monterrey Pine was also brought in from other parts of California. These trees grow rapidly and are extremely vulnerable to fires and produce flying brands and embers. Furthermore, because the West side of the hills gets more rain than the East side, the vegetation became thick and lush in this area. Complicating the matter further is the fact that the East Bay Hills experienced 5 years of drought prior to 1991. In addition, a severe winter also killed many Eucalyptus trees and underbrush. Consequently, there was lots of flammable vegetation after a long, hot summer. At this time, the Diablo or Santa Ana Winds were growing in strength (which are very common in September and October due to a high pressure system in the Great Basin and a low pressure system off the coast in the Pacific Ocean). Making matters worse, there was low humidity at the time of the fire. The terrain was also steep, making fires burn much faster than in flat areas.

The built environment exacerbated vulnerability to the natural hazard conditions. The **built environment** includes the structures, technology, and infrastructure created by humans. After the 1906 San Francisco earthquake, the East Bay Hills area began to be developed. Cities expanded dramatically again during the 1960s and 1970s. A 456-unit apartment complex was built in the area at this time. Three-hundred forty densely built condominiums were placed here as well. Homes were expensive and had multiple floor levels. Homes also had garages, decks and short bridges, mostly made of wood. Roofs included shake (wood) shingles. New roads were constructed to further development of the area. However, some neighborhoods only had one entrance/exit, and roads were narrow and included many switchbacks. Water systems installed in the area relied on electricity to pump supplies from storage tanks. Electric lines erected in the area often arc in high winds; this actually occurred in the East Bay Hills fire.

The social environment was also to blame for the impact of the disaster. The **social environment** includes the social, political, economic, cultural, and demographic activity or characteristics of the community. In the past, the grazing of animals on the hillside required the introduction of new grasses, oats, and barley. These plants were allowed to grow even when grazing ceased. People in San Francisco, Oakland, and San Jose moved to the area because they prefer the beautiful views due to the 1,300-foot elevation of the East Bay Hills.

As the area transitioned from a rural to suburban area, fire suppression was utilized as a way to protect property (thus permitting further growth of plants and trees in the area). New regulations on shingles were proposed after a fire in 1923, but these were not implemented as they were not politically popular. Similar regulations were recommended in a study in 1959, and these same regulations were suggested again in 1970. In both cases, the regulations were bypassed. After a fire in 1980, an ordinance for fire control was passed in Berkeley, but it was soon rescinded due to popular outcry. In 1982, a Blue Ribbon Committee studied the need for fire breaks, but these measures fell victim to the poor economic performance at the time. In the 1980s, the fire department lost 40% of its staff due to fiscal constraints and 10 companies were discontinued. Local and state governments did not spend money on fuel thinning and fire breaks because of limited budgets.

Adding to the problems above, some property deeds in the East Bay Hills residential neighborhoods restricted removal of trees, thereby adding fuel for future fires. In addition, people built decks connected to their homes but did not clear brush underneath. One expert observed that there was no warning of the residents about the rising dangers of the threat: "If the Oakland Hills had been part of a national park or forest, instead of a commercial neighborhood, the area would have been evacuated during the Red Flag weather conditions." Unfortunately, no one addressed the growing wild land-urban interface issues, and disaster resulted. In short, the natural, built, and social environments combined to produce a vulnerable situation.

The Oakland Hills fire also provides important lessons that you should consider when dealing with a natural disaster:

- ▲ **Be sure to finish the job.** The initial fire on October 19 was extinguished, but hot embers reignited the next day. Fire officials and firefighters should do all they can to douse hot spots and monitor potential flare ups.

- ▲ **Give extra attention to communications in disasters.** Because of the large numbers and diverse nature of responders who helped to fight this fire, communications were overwhelmed immediately in the field. In light of the large volume of calls and inadequate communications with those at the scene, the 911 center could not process calls or tell people where to go for the purpose of evacuation. It took a great deal of time to locate and utilize public information officers as the fire occurred on a Sunday.

- ▲ **Expect a chaotic and dangerous incident area, and do all you can to protect the safety of your personnel.** When police warned people to evacuate, the narrow roads became clogged as up to 5,000 people tried to leave the area. Firefighters had to protect themselves from the rapidly moving flames. Some were forced to take refuge in swimming pools when the fire jumped roads and freeways. One firefighter commented, "It's hard to get organized [to respond] and run for your life at the same time!"

- ▲ **Be sure not to repeat mistakes regarding mutual aid.** All local resources were quickly committed to the fire. Either a request for mutual aid was delayed, or the arrival of outside personnel took longer than anticipated. Besides this error, planes were restricted by strong winds, turbulent updrafts, and heavy smoke. By the time mutual aid personnel arrived at their designated location, their areas to protect were already burned. One captain reported to a command post as instructed but was then told that he was actually supposed to be elsewhere (thus delaying his contributions further). Scores of strike teams were used (some from 99 to 350 miles away). Unfortunately, some mutual aid teams did not have the right hose connectors. Oakland and San Francisco opted to maintain 3-inch lines when the rest of the state went to 2.5-inch lines. Adapters were available in a warehouse but could not be acquired quickly because the fire occurred over the weekend.

▲ **Advise the public on appropriate response activities.** Some people turned on sprinklers to protect their homes from the fire. The water remained on even if homes were burned to the ground. This caused a shortage of water and water pressure for firefighters.

▲ **Technology helped firefighters respond to the fires.** As the incident proceeded, a helicopter with an infrared monitor and a GPS system pointed firefighters to hotspots that needed to be extinguished. Because power lines were down, firefighters obtained generators to pump water out of wells to fight the raging fires.

▲ **Be sure to address victim needs.** Instead of establishing a DRC, a Community Restoration and Development Center was established in a vacant grocery store. This venue provided access to federal and state disaster assistance, city permitting, psychological and financial counseling, and other victim support services.

▲ **Be sure to consider all options in recovery.** Rather than rebuilding as quickly as possible, a great deal of planning should go into recovery operations. For instance, policy makers faced with this situation should grapple with important questions. Should the homes in this incident be rebuilt or relocated? If they are to be rebuilt, should the neighborhood be planned first? Are new restrictions needed to reduce vulnerability. What retrofit requirements should be applied to repairs? What restrictions should be put on nearby vacant land? Would it be safer to move these homes to a new area?

▲ **Take advantage of opportunities after the disaster.** A new task force on Emergency Preparedness and Community Restoration was created, and it pushed through a $50 million bond election for safety improvements. This resulted in the acquisition of new water supplies, seismic reinforcement of fire stations, the establishment of an EOC, and the purchase of a GIS system to mark natural fire breaks. The task force pushed through new (class A) roofing requirements and additional restrictions on siding, eaves, decks, and balconies. The task force could not address

FOR EXAMPLE

Complex Disasters

The Northridge earthquake is an example of a complex disaster. The earthquake occurred in an extremely hazardous area in southern California. The infrastructure, including roads and industrial facilities, was seriously impacted in the event. Many of those affected in the disaster were poor minorities who lived in vulnerable housing. Lives were lost, property was damaged, and the response was complicated due to fires resulting from broken gas lines. Language barriers among emergency management personnel and victims slowed down response and recovery operations. The natural, built, and social environments interacted to produce a complex disaster.

street issues (relating to the size of roads and cul-de-sacs). The large cost per property ($6,000 to $10,000 for each lot) made this prohibitive. However, they were able to implement more stringent parking restrictions. Such steps may reduce risk in the future.

The East Bay Hill fire is significant because the event teaches us to complete our work, ensure first-responder safety, plan for mutual aid, acquire adequate equipment for responders, utilize technology in our response operations, and think critically about recovery options and opportunities. These lessons must be incorporated into emergency management if we are to avoid a repetition of the problems in the response to the East Bay Hills fire.

SELF-CHECK

- What is the difference between a primary, associated, and secondary hazard?
- Future disasters may be described as being cascading or synergistic. What does this mean?
- Hurricane Katrina is labeled as a complex or na-tech disaster. Why?
- The East Bay Hills fire illustrated the interaction of three environments. What are they?
- What lessons do we learn from the response to the East Bay Hills fire?

12.3 Understanding Technological Disasters

While working in emergency management, you will most likely be required to respond to various types of technological hazards. Some of these hazards appear to have characteristics similar to natural hazards. For example, fires can be produced by lightning or through electrical short circuits. There can be structural failures resulting from dams that have been affected by earthquakes or buildings that collapse because they have been poorly designed and constructed. Other technological hazards and disasters may result from transportation accidents such as plane crashes or train derailments. One of the most common technological agents is associated with industrial hazards and hazardous materials.

As an emergency manager, you should be aware of the nature of industrial hazards so you can respond effectively to their consequences (Mitchell 1997). Such disasters may include fires, explosions, chemical leaks, hazardous materials spills, and other forms of environmental degradation. Industrial disasters may occur when companies convert raw materials into usable products for society. These events may happen during the extraction, processing, manufacturing, transportation, storage, use, and disposal of hazardous materials. Industrial disasters also take place at the intersection of people, place, property, and product. That is to say, humans are typically involved at a location where buildings and equipment are affected by hazardous materials. Such incidents have been classified by Mitchell (see Table 12-2).

As an emergency manager, you should recognize that no two disasters are exactly alike. However, evidence from several industrial disasters (e.g., Bhopal, Chernobyl, Challenger) reveals several similarities:

▲ **Risk is often underestimated.** CEOs, engineers, and plant operators often ignore the probability of accidents and disasters.

Table 12-2: Industrial Disasters as Classified by Mitchell (1997, p. 11)

Experience	Unsuspected Hazards (Unknown)	Improperly Managed Hazards (Mistakes)	Instrumental Hazards (War and Terrorism)
One of a kind	Ozone depletion: chlorofluorocarbons	Kyshtym: nuclear wastes	Hiroshima, Nagasaki: atomic bombs
First of a kind	DDT: pesticide	Metal fatigue: comet aircraft	World War I: poison gas
Worst of a kind	Minamata: methyl mercury biomagnification	Chernobyl: nuclear power station	Kuwait: oil well fires

▲ **Planning and design are frequently faulty.** Engineers may not consider all possible negative outcomes of technological equipment.

▲ **Operation is improper.** Maintenance may be neglected and regulations or policies are not followed.

▲ **Denial of wrong doing or the hiding of evidence is commonplace.** Corporate public relations specialists sometimes place the blame on others, and company leaders do not fully disclose everything they know about the incident.

▲ **Knowledge is lacking about hazards and the materials involved.** Employees and first responders do not fully comprehend what they are dealing with.

▲ **People are killed and health is jeopardized.** The disaster might kill people and threaten the physical well-being of others.

▲ **The environment may be adversely impacted.** The natural habitat can be degraded and rendered unusable due to an industrial hazard.

▲ **Lawsuits and fines typically result.** Victims seek compensation from the company, and the government imposes penalties to prevent recurrences.

12.3.1 Responding to HAZMAT Incidents

Because it is unlikely that all technological hazards will be completely avoided, you must respond to hazardous materials incidents in a very careful manner, as should first responders. Hazardous materials releases are probably the most common type of technological or industrial disasters, and they are extremely dangerous and even life-threatening.

There are several steps that can be taken to respond effectively:

1. **Ensure everyone has the proper background and personal protective equipment.** If firefighters, police, medical technicians, public works employees, and others do not have the proper credentials and gear, they should not be allowed to respond to the hazardous materials incident.

2. **Obtain as much information when en route and while on scene.** When the call comes in, responders can obtain information from 911 call centers and material safety data sheets (MSDS). Knowledge about the contents of containers can be gathered from employees and witnesses to the event.

3. **Approach cautiously and maintain a safe distance from the scene.** Do not rush in! Doing so could kill or injure you. Stay upwind (opposite of wind direction) and uphill from most hazardous materials.

4. **Determine what you are dealing with.** Use binoculars and look for placards to know what hazardous material has been released. The DOT

Emergency Response Guidebook (ERG) lists hazardous materials in terms of class. The ERG also has useful indexes of dangerous goods in numerical and alphabetical order. It also helps responders understand potential hazards, public safety measures, emergency response actions, and how the material reacts with water.

5. **Seek expert advice if needed.** There are thousands of types of hazardous materials, and many of them are complex and volatile. If you do not know what to do with the situation, find someone who does.

6. **Evacuate or shelter in place, and seal off the area.** Determine if it is best to evacuate people from the area or have them shelter in place. Work with the police and media to implement the decision. Use barricades and public safety officials to keep people from entering the danger zone.

7. **Be aware of the dynamic nature of the disaster scene.** One hazardous material may interact with another in complicated ways. Temperature, humidity, wind, and other variables can cause hazardous materials to react differently at any given time.

8. **Contract with remediation companies.** If needed, consult your resource lists and colleagues to seek the assistance of corporations that specialize in hazmat response and recovery. Examples include Cura Emergency Services (http://www.spillsolutions.com/Spills/Index.htm) and Hulcher Services (http://www.hulcher.com/).

FOR EXAMPLE

Haz Mat Incident on the Railways

On April 14, 1983, one of the rail cars on a train traveling through Arizona began to emit smoke. The engineer brought the train to a stop on the west side of the city of Casa Grande. Recognizing the potential for a major hazardous materials incident, emergency response personnel tried to determine what was on board. Information from the rail operator was slow in coming, so there was a great deal of confusion regarding the need to evacuate people from the nearby area. Police and fire also had difficulty communicating effectively during the response and notifying each other of potential dangers and proposed solutions. The delay in requesting assistance from the state hazardous materials coordinator further complicated the response to the incident. This case illustrates the potential for uncertainty and the need to rely on expertise for effective decision making (see Pijawka, Radwan, and Soesilo 1987).

9. **Follow all regulations for reporting and cleanup.** State and federal transportation and environmental agencies have several rules that must be followed to avoid fines or prosecution. This includes a quick time frame to notify authorities of the spill as well as cleaning up the contaminated soil and disposing of hazardous materials in an acceptable manner.

Only by following these guidelines can you reduce the risk facing personnel, rescue those affected, limit property damage, protect the environment, and avoid costly legal fees.

SELF-CHECK

- What are some examples of technological disasters?
- What are the common features of technological disasters?
- What should be done to respond effectively to a haz mat incident?
- What recovery considerations are evidence after haz mat releases?

12.4 Understanding Acts of Violence

As an emergency manager you may unfortunately be called on at times to deal with acts of violence. War among countries is the most devastating type of violence, and it results in the death of hundreds, thousands, and even millions of people. War also devastates the infrastructure of the warring parties and disrupts their economies significantly. In some countries, there may be significant bouts of civil war where internal factions vie for power. Civil wars are often characterized as complex emergencies. A **complex emergency** is a humanitarian crisis that involves an extreme amount of violence among different ethnic groups coupled with political instability, poor economic conditions, weak law enforcement capabilities, and disaster conditions of some sort (e.g., drought and famine). The genocide in Rwanda and ethnic fighting in the former Yugoslavia are visible examples of this type of activity that borders on anarchy. These incidents are especially problematic in that the warring factions disapprove of humanitarian aid sent to their enemy. Many external disaster relief providers have been killed as a result. Convoys of humanitarian aid has also been hijacked by warlords in countries with failed governments. Such situations present serious challenges for relief workers from the United Nations, the U.S. Office of Foreign Disaster Assistance, or the International Red Cross.

The United States may not have to deal with complex emergencies directly, but it is currently involved in a military campaign against insurgents in Iraq. It is also feasible that the United States could be involved in a major war if Iran obtains and threatens the use of nuclear weapons. Internal conflict could also result if the ideological gaps between political parties widens in the future or if class or ethnic strife worsens. However, the United States is most likely to be affected with mass shootings. There have been several episodes of mass shootings at the workplace or in restaurants. In the Maryland and Washington, D.C. areas, there were snipers who killed several people over a multiple-week period. Disgruntled employees or deranged individuals will enter a facility or hide in secluded areas. They will then begin to fire their weapons intentionally or randomly. Incidents of mass violence produce several injuries and deaths. Emergency medical personnel and law enforcement officials will play significant roles in the response to acts of violence. To learn how to better respond to these incidents, we will look at the events surrounding the Columbine school shootings.

12.4.1 Responding to Acts of Violence

In 1999, Columbine High School students Eric Harris and Dylan Klebold carried out a shooting rampage. These students felt they were mistreated by their peers in high school. To seek revenge, the students planned an attack involving bombs and guns. The students planted bombs in the school cafeteria and other locations in advance. Harris and Klebold then entered the school and killed 12 of their peers and one teacher. The shootings also wounded 24 others before the gunmen committed suicide. It is to date the deadliest act of violence at a school in American history.

The response to the shootings was heavily criticized even though the police and firefighters arrived only 12 minutes after the first 911 call. The most significant problem responders had was that they did not know who the perpetrators were. Any of the exiting students first responders came in contact with could have been carrying weapons discretely. Eric Harris and Dylan Klebold could have also put down their guns and blended into the crowd. Those responding to the situation also lacked information about the layout of the school. Needing this, they had to first interview some students and ask for help to draw a rough schematic of the school floor plan.

The unfolding and dangerous situation at Columbine did not allow responders to get sufficient or accurate intelligence they needed. This delayed the police and medical response for what seemed to be an eternity. Thirty minutes after the shootings began, 10 officers from three agencies assembled into teams and finally entered the building with sufficient force to do so safely. During the next 90 minutes, additional help arrived. Three SWAT teams made up of 50 officers from four jurisdictions walked through the hallways (Macko 1999). They found hundreds of students and their teachers hiding in classrooms and hallways to protect themselves. As they were discovered, the students and teachers were evacuated from the premises. Many of the students needed both protection from the assailants and medical care from paramedics.

There were many other difficulties in responding, including:

▲ **A failure to recognize warning signs.** Both Eric Harris and Dylan Klebold were in trouble with law enforcement before the Columbine massacre occurred. They both also went on websites and posted messages about murder, hate, and revenge. Eric Harris is also said to have had bombs under his bed. If the parents would have known this, the tragedy could have been prevented. School officials also should be made aware that they needed to look for antisocial behavior in Harris and Klebold.

▲ **Inaccurate information.** The SWAT teams received incomplete or incorrect information during initial moments of the event. They heard that there were eight gunmen, that there were snipers on the roof, that the killers were mingling with the students, and they were located in the classrooms (Macko 1999).

▲ **Lack of intelligence.** Because the SWAT teams were not thoroughly familiar with the school, they did not know how to operate the building's emergency systems. Alarms, strobe lights, and sprinklers added to the chaos. A SWAT team member incorrectly entered the code to turn off the alarm. In frustration, he hit the panel with the butt of his rifle, which made the system inoperable.

▲ **Lack of communication.** Distinct agencies operated on radios set at different frequencies, and vital information from outside the building did not reach the SWAT teams on the inside (Macko 1999). No one seemed able to grasp the nature of this incident.

▲ **Dangerous bombs.** The planted pipe bombs, CO_2 bombs, and propane bombs were all unstable and required careful removal since many were antipersonnel devices. SWAT members could not enter some areas until the explosives were removed and defused by bomb technicians. If the bombs had gone off, the casualties could have been much higher—perhaps in the hundreds.

▲ **Difficult choices.** During the incident, one teacher, Dave Sanders, was shot in a classroom and was bleeding to death. A student put a sign in the window that read, "1 bleeding to death." Police spotted this sign before noon and yet no one reached Sanders until after 3:00 pm. Many argue that the SWAT team should have rushed in and saved Sanders.

However, the SWAT team was being cautious since they could have been ambushed in the dangerous situation (Macko 1999).

▲ **Dangerous media coverage.** As the response unfolded, the media filmed the entire event with helicopters overhead. Their footage could have given vital information about police activities, which could have jeopardized their security.

▲ **Distribution of victims.** Hospitals had some difficulty coordinating two helicopters and 48 ambulances for the injured. Medical rescue efforts in mass emergencies are often problematic because of the large numbers of victims.

▲ **Lengthy investigation.** Because of the presence of bombs and the need for a thorough investigation into the incident, over 1,000 backpacks had to be examined. Approximately 2,000 lockers were searched as well. The search for bombs and evidence was a long and tedious process.

There are several lessons we can glean from the response to the Columbine massacre. The most important point is that you should work closely with law enforcement officials, the media, and the medical community when dealing with these types of situations. Personnel trained in **Tactical EMS** (emergency medical technicians that can use weapons) may be particularly useful in cases where there are both threats and medical needs. Careful efforts must also be taken to track down, negotiate with, or neutralize the perpetrator by force if necessary. At the same time, emergency responders must protect potential victims, treat the injured, and distribute patients to medical facilities before initiating the investigation. It is likely that you will need to help your community recovery psychologically after these disturbing incidents.

FOR EXAMPLE

Protest of the World Trade Organization

On November 29, 1999, people unhappy with the economic policies of the WTO gathered in Seattle to protest an economic summit that was being held there. Most protesters held signs and expressed their views peacefully. There were some that began to act violently by pestering police and burning vehicles. Those involved in this behavior exploited police procedures as well as the lack of equipment and personnel among law enforcement agencies. The city did not have the ability to deal with the situation effectively. This experience taught city officials about the importance of being ready to deal with protests that turn violent.

SELF-CHECK

- What is a **complex emergency?**
- Do emergency managers need to be concerned about international political conflicts?
- What are the most likely acts of violence to be committed in the United States?
- Why did first responders have difficulty after the Columbine school shooting?
- What lessons are gleaned from the mass emergency situation at Columbine?

12.5 Understanding Terrorism

As we have sadly learned from first-hand experience in this country, terrorist acts pose serious challenges to those involved in response and recovery activities. Terrorists—whether individuals, groups, or states—instill fear in others as a way to reach their aims and intentions. According to the FBI, **terrorism** is defined as "the unlawful use of force against persons or property to intimidate or coerce a government, the civilian population, or any segment thereof, in the furtherance of political or social objectives." The Department of Defense defines terrorism as "the calculated use of violence, or the threat of violence, to inculcate fear, (and is) intended to coerce or to intimidate governments or societies in the pursuit of goals that are generally political, religious or ideological."

McEntire, Robinson, and Weber (2001) note that terrorists use the drug trade, burglary, or other illegal activities to finance their operations. In other cases, terrorist activity will be sponsored by wealthy individuals, corporations, or governments. Terrorists actively recruit people who adhere to their ideology, and they use the Internet to spread their message to others. Sometimes terrorist groups like Al Qaeda set up camps and conferences where recruits are taught to raise funds, stake out targets, forge passports, use weapons, and carry out attacks. Common terrorist tactics include threats, assassinations, and suicide bombings. Terrorists also use weapons such as knives, guns, and computer viruses to carry out these attacks. They may likewise seek weapons of mass destruction (including biological, nuclear, incendiary, chemical, and explosive devices).

Terrorists select a variety of targets for maximum exposure and impact. Their preferences include:

▲ Public venues such as malls, restaurants, stores, and sporting stadiums
▲ Information and communication technology

▲ Water and electricity utilities
▲ Bus and subway systems
▲ Petroleum/chemical facilities
▲ Business districts
▲ Emergency and government services

12.5.1 Responding to Terrorist Disasters

As an emergency manager, you should be aware of the similarities and differences of terrorist attacks as compared to natural disasters. Webb (2002) has provided an excellent description of the common patterns of human behavior in both terrorist attacks and other types of disasters. Similarities among both types of events include:

1. **Very little looting, if any.** Most people have no intention of taking other people's property after a terrorist attack.
2. **Emergence of therapeutic communities.** Individuals and groups almost always help victims who are in need.
3. **Convergence of people and resources at the scene.** People come to the site of a disaster and send supplies to assist with the response and recovery operations.
4. **Adaptability of organizations.** Emergency response agencies are able to deal with difficult challenges.
5. **Reliability of emergency workers.** Police and firefighters typically overwork themselves after terrorist attacks (e.g., in New York after 9/11).
6. **People do not panic.** The evacuation of the World Trade Center was, for the most part, orderly.
7. **Certain groups are more vulnerable than others.** For example, in the 9/11 attacks, first responders were most at risk.
8. **Placement of blame and litigation.** There is always a belief that we can do more than we are doing to prevent and respond (e.g., the 9/11 Commission Report identified several steps that can be taken to reduce vulnerability to terrorism).
9. **Re-emergence of societal conflict.** President Bush has been criticized for the war on terrorism even though the response to 9/11 was seen as a success.

Despite notable similarities, you must be cognizant of possible differences which may have significant implications for post-disaster operations. In comparison to certain types of natural disasters, there may be no warning before a terrorist attack. Terrorist attacks, especially if they involve WMD, could conceivably generate a larger number of casualties than some natural disasters in the United States. For instance, an attack involving biological weapons could kill millions of people. Another area of concern is human behavior. Although there is little or no evidence to expect that humans will react differently after a terrorist attack, it is unclear if typical responses will remain the same in such disasters. The use of biological weapons may result in people questioning potential isolation practices. Victims may also have a more difficult time coping emotionally after a terrorist attack as the event was an intentional act rather than a natural hazard. In addition, citizens may not always be able to protect themselves in a terrorist attack since this might require national security, law enforcement measures, or technical medical knowledge. Evacuation may or may not be advantageous depending on the nature of the situation (e.g., an attack involving hazardous chemicals). The circumstances of the agent and weather will determine whether people should leave or shelter in place.

In addition to these complications, there are other challenges associated with terrorist disasters. Emergency services may need to communicate through secure radio channels so their operations will not be overheard by terrorists. It may be wise to stop citizen involvement in search and rescue activities as soon as possible. This is because one or more of the volunteers might be a terrorist in disguise. Even donations might not be safe as the generosity of others may include secondary devices that cause more destruction. Debris removal could be complicated as well. Debris is evidence and may be contaminated in the case of nuclear, biological, or chemical weapons. Victims may also require decontamination before medical care can be given. Environmental restoration may be impossible in the short term for certain types of attacks. For example, a dirty bomb (a conventional explosive packed with radioactive material) may spread hazardous substances in a vital commercial district. The effected area may not be habitable for months, years, or even decades. Those responding to terrorist incidents must therefore be aware of the extreme dangers associated with these types of disasters.

There are other, more specific things to consider when dealing with these situations. For instance, it is important for you to recognize that any disaster other than a natural disaster could be a terrorist attack. A structural fire may be due to arson. An explosion may be due to a bomb. A disease outbreak may be due to bioterrorism. A plane crash may be due to hijacking or bombing. The scene of a terrorist attack may be very dangerous. A terrorist incident may include one or more of six types of harm you can encounter (based on the TRACEM acronym) (FEMA 1999).

▲ **Thermal**—excessive heat from a fire
▲ **Radiological**—emission of alpha/gamma particles and gamma rays
▲ **Asphyxiative**—blood poisons or agents that displace oxygen

▲ **Chemical**—toxic materials and corrosive materials

▲ **Etiological**—biological living agents

▲ **Mechanical**—an explosive device

For this reason, it is imperative that responders look for identifiers of weapons of mass destruction before rushing onto the scene of a terrorist attack. FEMA (1999) has listed several clues that should be considered. For instance, in a biological attack, there might be unusual numbers of sick or dying people. A nuclear attack might be accompanied by the presence of Department of Transportation placards and labels. An incendiary device might produce multiple fires, odors of accelerants, and heavy burning. An incident involving dangerous chemicals might generate unusual dispersion of mists and gasses, odors and tastes, and the onset of similar symptoms in a large group of people. Attacks involving explosives may result in damage to buildings, scattered debris, and victims with shrapnel or shock-like symptoms.

The scene of a terrorist attack may also include secondary devices. There may be bombs designed to take out emergency responders. Terrorists may target police, fire, and EMS personnel in order to add to the loss of life. Terrorists may want to limit the effectiveness of first responders when they arrive at the scene. They may also attempt to create a mood of confusion and fear. There are several examples of terrorists using secondary devices. As responders showed up to a 1997 abortion clinic bombing in Atlanta, a bomb was detonated in a dumpster. In Ireland, terrorists called in a bomb threat for a public building. The bomb actually was detonated at the evacuation site. The scene of any terrorist attack is therefore a dangerous crime scene. Physical evidence will be present, and it is crucial for prosecution.

12.5.2 Protecting First Responders

You should be extremely cautious during responses to terrorist attacks. Responders should be aware at all times of the circumstances in which they find themselves. A particular concern is to ensure the scene is as secure as possible. Police may be needed to block off roads and limit access to the area. All personnel entering the site should have identification and be screened, having a justified reason for being there. Incident commanders and emergency managers may need to refuse donations if they appear suspicious or come from unknown sources. Fences may be needed to keep citizens out of the area. Patrol of the area on the ground, in the air, or by sea may be needed to detect potentially harmful terrorist activities.

According to FEMA (1999), emergency responders should take other measures to protect themselves at the scene of a terrorist attack. This can be accomplished by limiting time at the incident scene to minimize exposure to hazards, keeping a safe distance between you and the agent to also prevent or minimize exposure (e.g., stay uphill and upwind), and utilizing shielding (e.g., personal protective equipment and self-contained breathing apparatus). Waiting for hazardous materials teams to arrive (if you do not have the proper training or equipment), creating a site safety plan, and ensuring there is a safety liaison officer to monitor activities at the incident scene will also help to protect first responders.

All personnel, equipment, and victims must be decontaminated if there is an indication that weapons of mass destruction are used in the attack. The decontamination process should include hot, warm, and cold zones (see Figure 12-1).

▲ The **hot zone** is the affected (or contaminated) area.

▲ The **warm zone** is the washing (or decontamination) area.

▲ The **cold zone** is not affected and can only be accessed by clean (or decontaminated) individuals.

Zones should be set up in such a way so that wind blows toward the hot zone (see Figure 12-2). The warm zone should include tents or plastic sheeting to protect the privacy of victims as they are being decontaminated.

Figure 12-1

First responders may require decontamination after disasters. For this reason, they practice this process periodically.

Figure 12-2

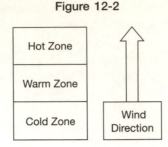

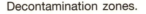

Decontamination zones.

When undertaking decontamination procedures, you will need to ensure that first responders take the following steps:

Step 1: Put on necessary personal protective equipment.

Step 2: Have responders enter the cold zone first before entering the warm and hot zones.

Step 3: Remove victims from the hot zone and transfer them to the warm zone.

Step 4: Decontaminate individuals and equipment using water, bleach or mild soap, brushes, and plastic pools (to retain the contaminated solution in the warm zone).

Step 5: Extract victims to cold zone and give proper medical care (including transportation to hospital).

Step 6: Ensure all responders are decontaminated before entering cold zone again.

Step 7: Dispose of contaminated solution and other contaminated items properly.

Once this process is completed, be sure to decontaminate all first responders and clean or properly discard all clothing, supplies, equipment, gurneys, blankets, etc. Ensure that hospitals also follow the same decontamination process before admitting patients (if this is applicable). Failing to do so may render the hospital emergency room useless after a terrorist attack.

12.5.3 Protecting Evidence

As terrorist acts are criminal acts, all evidence around the scene is important. Emergency responders should do all they can to protect evidence and collect information vital for prosecution (FEMA 1999). When and if possible, responders and officials should try to avoid disrupting the scene (e.g., leave things as they are), be aware of persons entering or leaving the scene, and record the license plate numbers of vehicles leaving the area. It would also be useful if responders jot down descriptions of people and cars, encourage witnesses to remain at the scene until investigators come (if safe to do so), and take photos of the scene when possible. Other steps include drawing a map of the scene and writing an after-action report. Ensuring the evidence is protected (e.g., through a chain of custody) and testifying in court are other activities that can improve the chances for apprehension and prosecution.

12.5.4 Relying on Other Organizations

Because terrorist events require technical knowledge and special skills, it is imperative that you know who can assist at the local, state, and federal levels. At the local level, you may request the assistance of the fire department, emergency medical services, police department, hospitals, public health officials and coroner's office (see Perry 2003). Note the organization and roles below in Table 12-3.

Table 12-3: Roles and Responsibilities of Emergency Response Organizations

Organization	Roles and Responsibilities
Fire	Isolate impact area and set up perimeter Position equipment and responders upwind, uphill, and upstream from the incident site Assess downwind hazards and implement evacuation or shelter in place decisions Identify agenda and adjust scene layout if required Respond to victim needs with appropriate PPE Decontaminate all victims, responders, and equipment as needed
EMS	Implement mass casualty triage procedures Provide medical treatment as dictated by the incident Transport victims to definitive care facilities Determine mental health impact and treat accordingly
Police	Share preliminary intelligence data with incident command and the EOC Notify and interact with the FBI Deploy law enforcement personnel, including bomb squads and tactical operations teams Assure incident security for first responders Collect and control evidence Apprehend and assume custody of suspects at the scene

(Continued)

Table 12-3: (continued)

Organization	Roles and Responsibilities
Hospitals	Implement lockdown of facility to ensure security Decontaminate and triage all arriving patients Track patients, including their symptoms, and communicate with public health officials Decide where to treat patients (internally or externally) Treat as dictated by nature of injuries
Public Health	Conduct surveillance for evidence of epidemics Identify and control agent Determine and implement protective measures for the population, including immunizations or prophylactic medicines Work with police to implement quarantines if needed
Coroners	Receive human remains Safeguard personal property Identify the deceased and notify next of kin Prepare and complete file for each decedent Photograph, fingerprint, and collect DNA specimens as appropriate Provide death certificates Coordinate and release remains for final disposition

States may also have specially trained teams to assist in the detection of weapons of mass destruction and subsequent response operations. For instance, Texas has a specially trained unit (the 6th Civil Support Team) to identify what weapons have been used and how to deal with them effectively. The 6th Civil Support Team is a specially trained National Guard unit that can be activated as needed. It has WMD detection capabilities that can help you identify what hazard agent you are dealing with (e.g., poison gas vs. radioactive material). The federal government also has similar teams to assist in terrorism response. The Center for Disease Control and Department of Homeland Security can help with WMD detection. The FBI will mobilize to protect evidence and begin investigation for prosecution purposes. Under the Metropolitan Medical Response System, the federal government may also send pharmaceutical supplies to the scene of a terrorist event. National Medical Response Teams (NMRTs) may also deploy for WMD events or provide medical standby support for National Special Security Events (NSSEs). The EPA and CDC may also have expertise to help you deal with chemical or biological attacks.

FOR EXAMPLE

Oklahoma City Bombing

After the Oklahoma City bombing in 1995, there was a swift response on the part of many different organizations. At the scene of the destroyed Murrah Federal Building, local police, fire, and medical units arrived quickly. They took care of immediate life safety issues. The state and federal governments also arrived to assist. The state law enforcement agency monitored highways to capture potential suspects. FEMA showed up with resources and personnel to help with search and rescue as well as long-term recovery operations. The Red Cross assisted with donations management. When the vast majority of bodies had been recovered, the FBI took over the scene for investigation.

Federal activities have been categorized as crisis management or consequence management.

▲ **Crisis management** is a law enforcement activity that includes intelligence gathering to prevent terrorist attacks or evidence collection for the purposes of prosecution. The FBI was designated as the lead agency for crisis management.

▲ **Consequence management** concerns typical emergency management response and recovery operations, which also take place after terrorist attacks. FEMA is in charge of consequence management.

In light of the operational problems made evident across crisis and consequence management after the 9/11 terrorist attack, the Department of Homeland Security is now downplaying the use of these terms or at least trying to minimize the distinction of these functions. They are now viewed as integrated activities that cannot be separated operationally.

SELF-CHECK

- How do terrorists operate?
- What are the likely targets for terrorists?
- Are terrorist attacks similar or different from other types of disasters?
- What are the important considerations when responding to a terrorist attack?
- How can you protect first responders after a terrorist attack? Evidence?
- Who can help you deal with terrorist attacks?

12.6 Insufficiently Recognized Hazards

Since the attacks in September 2001, the United States has been focused primarily on future acts of terrorism. As an emergency manager, you must recognize that there are other hazards that are being neglected by decision makers. These include environmental degradation, pole reversals, meteor impacts, biological threats, and computer/information technology hazards.

12.6.1 Environmental Degradation, Global Warming, and Climate Change

The earth's resources are being polluted or depleted in dramatic fashion. This can have extremely negative consequences. For instance, the dumping of toxic chemicals into rivers and the ocean may limit the supply of fresh water or food such as fish. In the next few decades, oil and petroleum products may become scarce, which may make it difficult to deliver needed products and heat homes during the winter. Such **environmental degradation** is serious and should not be ignored or downplayed. The emergency manager must be conscious of the impact of human activity on the environment.

In addition to focusing on the protection of natural resources, attention needs to be given to global warming. **Global warming** is the rise of temperatures in the earth's atmosphere. According to the National Science Academy, the temperature of the earth has risen one degree Fahrenheit within the last century (see Figure 12-3).

Figure 12-3

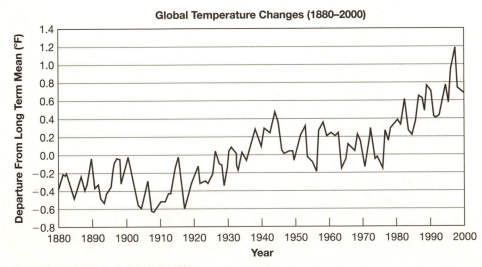

Global Temperature Changes (1880–2000)

Source: U. S. National Climatic Data Center, 2001

Accessed at http://yosemite.epa.gov/oar/globalwarming.nsf/content/climate.html on January 18, 2006.

Figure 12-4

The Greenhouse Effect

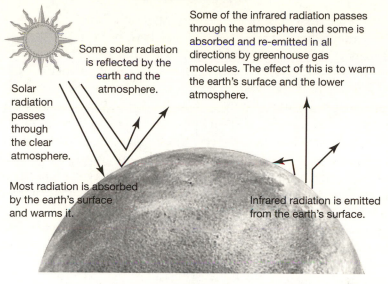

Some solar radiation is reflected by the earth and the atmosphere.

Some of the infrared radiation passes through the atmosphere and some is absorbed and re-emitted in all directions by greenhouse gas molecules. The effect of this is to warm the earth's surface and the lower atmosphere.

Solar radiation passes through the clear atmosphere.

Most radiation is absorbed by the earth's surface and warms it.

Infrared radiation is emitted from the earth's surface.

Accessed at http://yosemite.epa.gov/oar/globalwarming.nsf/content/climate.html on January 23, 2006.

The sun provides heat for our planet, but the earth also produces heat. This heat is trapped within the atmosphere by the heat-retaining greenhouse gasses. Global warming is attributed to the buildup of three such gasses: methane, carbon dioxide, and nitrous oxide. This naturally occurring process, called the greenhouse effect (see Figure 12-4), allows the earth to maintain temperatures hospitable for humans, animals, and plant life. However, scientists are concerned because the amount of greenhouse gas in the environment is increasing. The assertion is that the combustion of fossil fuel is augmenting greenhouse gasses.

Global warming has drawn concern from the scientific community for many reasons. As the earth warms, climate changes will begin to take place. **Climate change** is an alteration of the earth's temperature and weather patterns. For instance, according to the EPA, extreme rainfall across the United States has increased in recent years, while snowfall and ice accumulation in the arctic has decreased. However, scientists still do not know exactly how global warming will affect the climate. The U.S. National Assessment of Climate Change Impacts (NACCI) has issued several reports that conclude that humans will be able to adapt to their changing climate, but not without significant regional affects. Their best estimations are that warmer weather will cause an increase in evaporation. Some regions will become more arid, whereas others will see a drastic increase in rainfall. Agriculture, forestry, and land and water management may all be affected. There is also an indication that coastal areas could be flooded if the earth warms and ice caps continue to melt.

Findings about global warming are not without criticism. Some scholars argue that the earth's temperatures have always varied over time. Others assert that while temperatures on the earth's surface have been rising, the temperature in the upper level of the atmosphere has shown very little change. Moreover, scientists are still determining exactly how much human behavior, such as driving, influences global warming.

Despite these divergent findings, there are several implications for disaster scholars and you as a practitioner. Should rainfall increase drastically, the prominence of waterborne vectors may increase, leading to disease outbreaks in areas where the disease was formerly unheard of. Flood mitigation would also have to be addressed for the communities facing extreme rainfall or coastal areas affected by rising sea levels. Drought and famine would also become more prevalent issues as well.

Ambiguity and controversy surrounding global warming will make it difficult to establish mitigation and emergency management protocols. For this reason, it will be imperative that research continues to solidify trends and reduce uncertainties about climate change predictions. You should take steps to ensure that they are monitoring research data produced by reputable agencies. Moreover, it would be beneficial for you to establish relationships with these organizations to increase understanding and awareness. Prevention and precautionary actions should be implemented as recommended.

12.6.2 Pole Reversals

Another unsuspected hazard is a pole reversal. A **pole reversal** is a change in the earth's magnetic fields. Our planet is surrounded by a magnetic field that is generated by a magnet that runs through the center of the earth, called a dipole. The dipole has a north and south end, but it does not correspond with the geographic north and south. The poles of the dipole are offset approximately 11 degrees (NGDC 2006). This magnetic field is measured according to vertical intensity, horizontal intensity, and magnetic declination. The force is not uniform across the globe but varies according to location.

Scientists are closely monitoring the intensity of earth's geomagnetism. By analyzing minerals in the earth's magma and crust, geophysicists have determined the orientation and strengths of the dipole (Glatzmaier and Olson 2005). The information gathered indicates that the magnetic orientation of the dipole has repeatedly reversed itself over time. What comes into question is the frequency and time frame in which these reversals take place. Some scientists believe that a pole reversal has occurred approximately every 200 thousand years over the last 100 million years. It is also believed that the most recent reversal would have taken place 750,000 to 780,000 years ago (NGDC 2006). Other scientists refute this theory by stating that pole reversals happen much quicker. They assert reversals take place nearly 1,000 times faster than previously observed (Coe, Prevot, and Camps 1995).

Scientists do not have any conclusive evidence as to the cause or speed of pole reversals. They now know that lava flows have a connection with the magnetic fields. Researchers have used cooled lava to study the changes in direction and frequency of a reversal (NRC 2005). The theories about reversals are generally divided into two groups. The first is based on the hypothesis that intense volcanic eruptions can alter the regeneration of the earth's magnetic field (Jacobs 1994). The second theory states that reversals occur as a result of "irregular oscillations" of the earth's magnetic field (Jacobs 1984). Research is currently underway to test both theories.

In any case, evidence seems to suggest that the strength of the magnetic field is decreasing. The deterioration of Earth's magnetic field does not indicate that a reversal is imminent, however (Hoffman 1995). Scientists have stated that even with the unknown variables and conflicting timetables surrounding polarity reversal, a reversal would take at least 1,000 years (NGDC 2006). Should this occur, it is speculated that the magnetic field would weaken and produce several or different poles.

Animals that rely on magnetism for navigational purposes would be impacted by a pole reversal (NGDC 2006). Pole reversals may not produce catastrophic impact for humankind. However, technology that depends on geomagnetism would be affected. Luckily, technology can be adapted if the changes of the field are monitored and acted on. Dealing with possible pole reversals is somewhat similar to the response to global warming. Research on the phenomena must continue. Measures must also be taken to anticipate possible problems and react effectively.

12.6.3 Asteroid Strikes

Viewing meteor impact as a hazard is relatively recent. Before the 1960s, researchers did not believe that there was any threat of extraterrestrial collisions. However, this view began to change as means were developed to expose scientists to the history and effects of cratering across the earth as well as on other planets. As science progressed, researchers began to identify the presence and movement of objects that could pose a threat to our well-being (French 1998).

Everyday, foreign objects enter earth's atmosphere. Most of them burn up quickly and do not pose a threat to humans (NASA 2006). However, researchers seem to feel that a major terrestrial impact is not a matter of "if" but "when." There are several types of terrestrial impact structures (see Figure 12-6). Scientists call those structures nearest to the earth Near Earth Objects (NEO). A **NEO** is made up of mostly ice and dirt particles. Gravitational pull is attributed as the cause of NEOs entering Earth's atmosphere (NASA 2006). The measure of their proximity to earth is based on astronomical units (AU). One AU is equivalent to approximately 92,955,807.5 miles. An asteroid that comes within 0.05 AU or less of the earth is deemed a **Potentially Hazardous Asteroid (PHA).** As of February 3, 2006, 3,933 NEOs have been discovered. Of these, 748 are classified as PHAs (NASA 2006).

There are many issues surrounding meteorite impact that make it difficult to mitigate and prepare for. One expert in this area addresses three (French 1998). First, large meteorite impacts are rare. As such, it is challenging for researchers to study their effects. More vital to emergency managers, it is hard for people to comprehend the danger of an impact. With no perceived threat, those involved in emergency management must go to greater lengths to legitimize the significance of an impact. Secondly, the predicted energy a major impact would produce is greater than that produced by earthquakes or volcanoes. French (1998) points out that "the impact of an object only a few kilometers across (still smaller than many known asteroids and comets) can release more energy in seconds than the whole Earth releases (through volcanism, earthquakes, tectonic processes, and heat flow) in hundreds or thousands of years." The final issue differentiates meteoroid impact from other energy-expending disasters and their instantaneous effects. Upon impact, major energy is expended and a massive crater is formed. The striking of the earth would produce a massive crater such as the Barringer Meteor Crater in Arizona. It would also send shock waves out, causing "immediate and catastrophic changes" (French 1998). A few of the predicted repercussions could include massive earthquakes, volcanic eruptions, and tsunamis.

Scientists have created the **Torino Scale** in an attempt to predict the impact of a meteoroid strike. The Torino Scale describes the possibility of collision along with the resulting impact. Contingency planning by emergency managers becomes vital if the impact of a PHA becomes imminent. Astronomers and emergency managers need to increase their relations to devise warning and preparedness measures for the possibility of such a catastrophic occurrence (see Figure 12-5).

Figure 12-5

Asteroid	A relatively small, inactive, rocky body orbiting the Sun.
Comet	A relatively small, at times active, object whose ices can vaporize in sunlight, forming an atmosphere (coma) of dust and gas and, sometimes, a tail of dust and/or gas.
Meteoroid	A small particle from a comet or asteroid orbiting the Sun.
Meteor	The light phenomena that results when a meteoroid enters the Earth's atmosphere and vaporizes; a shooting star.
Meteorite	A meteoroid that survives its passage through the Earth's atmosphere and lands on the Earth's surface.

Types of terrestrial impact structures.
Accessed at http://neo.jpl.nasa.gov/faq/#diff.

12.6.4 Biological Threats

Because of globalization, disease can spread rapidly throughout the entire world. The ease of travel and international economic relations could easily trigger a pandemic in other nations. In other words, disease spreads at the speed and extent of travel and commercial activities. Below are a few of the biological threats that must be considered by emergency management and public health personnel.

Severe Acute Respiratory Syndrome (SARS)

Severe acute respiratory syndrome (SARS) is a viral respiratory disease caused by a corona virus (SARS-CoV). The incubation period for SARS is 2 to 14 days. During this time, it is not believed that the person is infectious. After symptoms develop the person is considered highly infectious until at least 10 days after his or her fever breaks. The symptoms of SARS are similar to the flu. Patients who contract the disease have a high fever and suffer from chills, headaches, and body aches. They usually develop a dry cough and, eventually, pneumonia (CDC 2006).

Medical personnel are still looking into the variations through which the disease is transmitted (CDC 2006). However, it is believed that SARS is spread through person-to-person contact. Individuals can contract the disease from others who are infected. Germs may be spread via droplets from a person's cough or sneeze. This may be through physical contact with bodily fluid through holding hands or kissing. Physical contact does not mean sharing the same space environment, however.

The Center for Disease Control registered the first outbreak in southern China in November 2002. SARS quickly spread and was considered a global threat in March 2003. During the 2002-2003 epidemic, 8,098 people contracted SARS, and all of them were reported to be living or traveling in Asia. Probable cases were reported in 31 countries, including Vietnam, China, Taiwan, Singapore, Canada, the United States, and Germany (Lipsitch et al 2003). Of those infected, 774 individuals died.

By July 2003, the outbreak began to temper and the World Health Organization declared the end of the epidemic (WHO 2006). Nonetheless, the CDC reports that they are monitoring several potential SARS cases throughout the world. The National Intelligence Agency concurs with a report that states that although SARS has not killed as many people as more common diseases, it is still a threat because it tends to outbreak in areas "with broad commercial links," which would accelerate the spread of the disease and exacerbate its effects worldwide (NIA 2006).

Measures taken to deal with SARS vary dramatically based on the current threat. Doctors recommend that basic hygiene measures always be followed, such as washing hands and avoiding the touching of the mouth, eyes, and nose. However, once SARS has been identified, other steps must be taken. The National Institute for Occupational Safety and Health recommends that a respirator be worn by personnel in contact with a patient (NIOSH 2006). The respirator should be rated at least a N-95. Immediate intervention should also be made to isolate any confirmed cases. This is known as a **quarantine.** Quarantines should be set up for those that are suspected to have come in contact with the disease. Lipsitch et al. makes the point that quarantine and isolation will be beneficial only as long as the number of cases present can be contained (2003). Quarantine numbers may initially be high. However, these numbers will begin to drop as individuals are either sent for treatment in isolation or confirmed healthy. Isolation will allow for treatment without spreading the disease further.

West Nile Virus (WNV)

The West Nile virus is a flavivirus that is dependent on mosquitoes as vectors. It is a seasonal disease that is more common when mosquitoes begin to breed and thrive during spring, summer, and early fall. West Nile virus affects people in different ways. There are three severe diseases caused by the virus: West Nile encephalitis, West Nile meningitis, and West Nile meningoencephalitis. These are classified as neuroinvasive because they attack the nervous system. West Nile fever is another, less-invasive reaction to the virus (CDC 2006).

As its name implies, West Nile originated in the Middle East, but it has also affected West Asia and parts of Africa. It is unknown how the virus was introduced to the United States. The Center for Disease Control (CDC) believes the disease was introduced in early 1999. In 2002, the World Health Organization tracked an outbreak of WNV across 39 states. Moreover, evidence of the virus has been found in 43 states (WHO 2002).

The most common transmission of WNV is the bite of an infected mosquito. Mosquitoes become infected when they feed on infected birds. They may then transmit the disease to other animals or humans. CDC has also tracked the transmission of the disease through blood transfusions, organ transplants, and breastfeeding. However, they note that these methods are infrequent and comprise a small proportion of WNV cases (CDC b 2006).

WNV primarily affects birds, but it is also a threat to humans, horses, and some other types of mammals (NBII 2006). In areas where the WNV is more common, birds and other affected mammals have developed the necessary antibodies to fight off the disease. In North America, where the disease is relatively new, WNV has proved particularly virulent. Of the 3,737 people were reportedly infected, 214 people have died. The disease seems to affect persons over the age of 50 years more severely, but all people are at risk.

Proper outbreak prevention and control measures require a vector monitoring system. Mosquitoes and birds must be effectually monitored for WNV. If these systems are in place, then the amount of time before human infections occur can be increased (CDC 2003). Response to WNV must include the prevention of mosquito bites. When spending time near mosquito-infested areas, it is important to apply repellent to exposed skin. People can also reduce the chances of being infected by removing standing water or other elements that may attract mosquitoes. Installing or repairing door and window screens will also prevent bites (CDC 2006c).

There is no specific treatment for WNV. At the present time there is no human inoculation available, although several laboratories are conducting pertinent research and hope to introduce a vaccine shortly (CDC e 2006). Medical care involves "intensive support therapy;" this can include hospitalization and prevention of secondary infections such as pneumonia (CDC d 2006).

Avian Influenza (Bird Flu)

Avian flu is an infection that stems from viruses commonly found in birds. The disease is frequently found in the intestines of wild birds, although it typically has no affect on undomesticated fowl. However, the viruses can be contracted by domesticated birds through excretions and secretions. Birds may come in contact with the disease by exposure to excrement in things such as dirty cages. As more virulent strains infect domestic flocks, the birds become sick and begin to die. This has serious impact on bird farms as well as bird feed producers and distributors. Outbreaks of avian flu have been reported in birds in 14 European and Asian countries. For these reasons, the USDA has an embargo in place preventing the import of birds from countries reporting the disease (CDC 2005).

Avian flu is differentiated from seasonal flu in that its viruses come from birds. There are other significant differences that must be taken into account as well. Seasonal flu comes from influenza viruses, but there are only three subtypes of seasonal flu found in humans (CDC 2006). In contrast, avian flu has 25 known subtypes, and these can combine to form a different influenza strains (CDC 2006).

Because of the many subtypes of the avian flu, it is not known exactly how the disease is contracted by humans. At this point, doctors believe that the confirmed cases all resulted from contact with infected birds or contaminated areas (CDC d 2006). Prevention measures should therefore include staying away from areas of known outbreak, limiting the handling of birds, or avoiding surfaces where birds have been present. Regardless of this admonition, avian flu has been found in humans in seven European and Asian countries. To date, there are 165 confirmed cases of humans with avian flu, of which 88 have reportedly died (WHO 2006). The disease also has serious economic consequences. As an example, economists estimate that the avian flu would cause a decrease of 29% in exports, 8% in tourism, and 2% in private consumption in Thailand alone (PECC 2005). In November 2005, the World Bank issued a statement saying that avian flu "poses one of the biggest uncertainties in the generally positive outlook for East Asian economies" (World Bank 2005). The U.S. State Department has also issued travel advisories for any American planning to spend time in one of the reported countries. They warn that in the case of a pandemic, Consular Affairs will be severely restricted in any aid they can provide (State Department 2005).

World Health officials are monitoring current outbreaks in Europe and Asia. The current fear among them is that a strain of the avian flu may mutate and make itself easily transmittable between humans. This could prove disastrous as humans have no natural immunity towards this type of virus (CDC g 2006). In addition, there is no vaccine to protect humans from the avian flu. The CDC reports that scientists have been researching the development of a vaccine since 2005 (CDC e 2005).

Patients that present themselves for treatment and display symptoms of avian flu should be questioned as to their recent travel history. If avian flu is suspected, the patient should be treated in isolation following the prescribed treatment for a SARS patient (CDC f 2004). However, because the disease is so new, the CDC is reviewing their treatment recommendations.

Hoof and Mouth Disease (HMD)

Hoof and mouth disease (also known as foot and mouth disease) is a highly infectious disease that occurs among livestock—not people. Animals such as goats, cows, sheep, and other cloven-hoofed mammals are particularly susceptible to the disease. However, camels, llamas, and alpacas have an established natural defense against HMD (Merck 2000). HMD symptoms consist of fever and blisters that develop on the hooves, in the mouth, and in some cases on the snout of the infected animal. The disease is caused by the Apthovirus. Its affects result in high mortality among young livestock (FAO 2002). The disease is very rarely transmitted to humans, and human symptoms are generally mild.

HMD can be spread through a variety of ways. The most common means of transmission is interaction of infected animals with healthy animals. An infected animal can spread the virus by breathing as well as through any excretions or secretions (Merck 2000). Nursing animals are at risk of passing the disease on to their young through their milk. The virus can survive apart from a carrier for any number of days depending on the host material. The disease has an incubation period of 2 to 14 days (Merck 2000).

The UN has declared HMD endemic throughout Africa, Asia, the Middle East, and parts of South America. Europe, North America, the Caribbean, and Pacific nations remain free from the disease, with noted exceptions that have been quickly contained (FAO 2002). The major concern with HMD around the world is its economic impact. The ease of transmission and loss of animals can severely constrict trade.

The countries in which HMD is endemic attempt to protect their animals through vaccinations. The vaccinations are not a fool-proof method, however, as they do not protect against every strain of HMD (Merck 2000). When the disease has been identified, the reaction is usually to eradicate it by killing the entire stock. Slaughtered animals should be burned or buried immediately (Merck 2000). However, James and Rushton examined alternate approaches different communities have taken in attempts to identify the most cost effective method of prevention and/or eradication (2002).

Emergency managers and public health officials have not paid much attention to this type of disease in the past. Part of this is due to the fact that it is an agricultural disease rather than a public health crisis. However, it is now becoming more important to control HMD and protect agricultural economic interests of potentially affected communities. A system should consequently be in place that will:

1. Detect and manage an outbreak
2. Prevent introduction of a foreign disease
3. Respond to and eradicate an outbreak

As with other types of diseases, success of this system depends on proper coordination among local, state, national, and international governments (Torres, David, and Bowman 2002). It is also important to note that the diseases described above are less probable than the common flu or other infections that inflict animals. They also may be less deadly than nearly eradicated diseases like the plague. However, you should be aware that these diseases may appear naturally or in conjunction with a terrorist attack. They will require close collaboration among you and medical, public health, and veterinary personnel.

One of the important steps to take after an outbreak affects humans is to request resources from the **Strategic National Stockpile.** This is a collection of antibiotics, vaccines, antiviral drugs, and other pharmaceuticals stored by the federal government. When requested, this can be sent to an affected area within 12 hours. The community will then be required to break down the supplies and transfer them to sites for treatment (points of distribution). This will require a great deal of coordination among emergency managers, public health organizations, and volunteers.

FOR EXAMPLE

Hoof and Mouth Disease

During the 2001 outbreak of hoof and mouth in the United Kingdom, more than 6.5 million animals had to be slaughtered. The country took special precautions in disposing the carcasses. Nevertheless, it became impossible for farmers to bury all of their animals, and communities were concerned about emissions let off from pyre burnings (Scudamore et al 2002). Many farmers were adversely affected by the temporary loss of their livelihoods.

12.6.5 Computer/Information Technology Hazards

Another underestimated hazard concerns computers and information technology. In his very important study on the matter, E.L. Quarantelli (1997) uncovers several social problems resulting from the information/communication revolution. The problems he discusses may have a significant impact on disaster response and recovery operations. The challenges are as follows:

▲ New computers and communications technology will undoubtedly result in information overload. The ease of communications often exceeds human capacity to absorb information.

▲ Technological advances will likely result in information that is lost or outdated. For instance, you may seek information to assist with your response operations, but these websites may be outdated or defunct.

▲ Improved technology will likely lead to the diffusion of inappropriate information. Rumors about or after disasters could spread quickly because of modern computers and today's communications equipment.

▲ Advanced computer equipment may lead to the diminution of nonverbal communication. This could hinder your ability to understand the information being relayed after a disaster.

▲ Technology may make intragroup and intergroup communication more difficult in the future. The sharing of information and coordination of actors is difficult at best in most disaster situations. Computers and communication technology could conceivably magnify this problem in the future.

▲ Today's technology is not supported by an adequate infrastructure and culture. For instance, some organizations or communities do not develop back-up systems for computerized databases. This information will most likely be lost after a disaster.

▲ Computers will produce new types of disasters that we will have to deal with in the future. For example, a small fire at a Bell Telephone switching center in Chicago caused severe disruption in the transportation, retail, and financial sectors (Quarantelli 1997, p. 103).

In addition to the problems described by Quarantelli, you should be aware of other threats relating to computers. A **computer virus** is a program that contains malicious codes. It reproduces itself and overloads the infected computer, causing it to run slowly or ineffectively. **Worms** are similar to viruses, but they are generated over many computer systems due to Internet, networks, and e-mail connections. **Hackers,** individuals that log into others' computers illegally, may also enter programs to run or disrupt them from afar. Cyber-terrorism is another threat that must be considered. **Cyber-terrorism** is the use of computers and the Internet to plan or carry out attacks.

Such problems could create additional problems or disasters for you and your communities. These threats can hinder response and recovery operations (as technology and computers become increasingly vital in emergency management today). Furthermore, hackers and cyber-terrorists may enter computers to disrupt post-disaster operations. These individuals have already managed to enter government computers on occasion to dispatch fire personnel to false calls. There is also the possibility that they could control gas lines, water mains, and other critical infrastructure remotely. The unintended negative consequences of computers and information technology must accordingly be considered by you as an emergency manager.

12.6.6 Responding to Computer/Information Technology Disasters

Because of the newness of computer and information technology problems, there are no definitive solutions for emergency managers. However, the following steps can be taken to minimize the negative impact of the information/communications revolution on your organization or community. Some of these measures may include:

1. Filtering incoming information to prevent an overload of information about disasters.
2. Ensuring information provided or received is as accurate and up-to-date as possible.
3. Halting the distribution of incorrect information, and using the media and Internet to correct false reports.
4. Attempting to be as clear as possible in nonverbal communication (e.g., when you are communicating via e-mail or text messaging).
5. Acknowledging the drawbacks of technology and creating redundant systems to prevent overreliance on computers and modern communication equipment.
6. Being aware of new types of technological disasters and understanding how these might adversely impact subsequent response operations.
7. Using antivirus software and firewalls to reduce the possibility that hackers and cyber-terrorists will enter your systems and create denial of service impacts.

By addressing the negative aspects of the computer/information revolution, you will be able to foster resilience as an emergency manager. This will require closer contact with information technology specialists in the future. It will also be imperative that you consider the need for continuity of operations (COOP) in your community. **Continuity of operations** is a goal to maintain the functioning of government in time of disasters and is somewhat similar to business continuity. It deals with computer systems as well as personnel staffing, alternate

EOC locations, and lines of succession. If the emergency management office and other government departments cannot operate after a disaster, response and recovery activities will surely be limited, delayed, or ineffective.

SELF-CHECK

- What is **environmental degradation,** and how is it related to global warming and climate change?
- What is a **pole reversal,** and what are the possible effects of one occurring?
- Are meteor impacts probable? Are they possible?
- What are the different types of biological threats facing us today?
- Has technology produced new disasters?
- What can be done to deal effectively with the new hazards that threaten us?

12.7 Increased Vulnerability

As an emergency manager, you should recognize that hazards are not the only concern regarding future disasters. As society changes, our vulnerability to disasters may increase as well. Augmented vulnerability comes from poverty, population changes, increased diversity, industrialization, improper land use and construction, and weak emergency management institutions. There are many other factors that increase our vulnerability to hazards. Interestingly, it is this vulnerability that we are most able to limit and control to reduce future disasters

12.7.1 Persistent Poverty

Poverty is a major problem around the world. In 1990, for example, 2 billion people lived on less than a dollar a day (World Bank, "Global Economic Prospects, 2004"). Today, the annual salary in East Asian countries is only $1,000. Others in developing nations live in more dire situations. Individuals finding themselves in these circumstances are living in conditions of **absolute poverty.** This means that they do not have sufficient resources to take care of basic needs such as food and shelter.

In contrast to these situations, the salaries in industrial countries are much higher. They average $20,000 or even more. Those living in the United States are very well off, and their income has increased dramatically over time. However, there are still large segments of the population that are poor. The overall poverty rate in our country is 12.7%, or 1.1 million people living at or below the poverty line.

Minorities comprise a larger share of those found in poverty. For example, 24.7% of African Americans and 21.9% of Hispanics live at or below the poverty line.

The causes for poverty are highly political, ranging from capitalist exploitation to a poor work ethic. People also view a lack of education, overspending, and addiction to vices as culprits. Regardless of the source, poverty has a bearing on disaster vulnerability. The lack of resources limits one's ability to buy safe housing and ensure personal and family preparedness. Poverty constrains choices regarding insurance and hinders effective family response activities. It is one of the many factors that makes some people more vulnerable than others.

12.7.2 Growing Population and Urbanization

Changes in population are having a huge impact on vulnerability. In 2006, the world population reached 6.5 billion people. This growth has not stopped. Population experts expect enormous population growth through the year 2050. It is anticipated that total world population will soar over 9.3 billion at the mid-point of this century. How does population growth relate to disasters? Vulnerability is increased when more people are exposed to hazards. Also, with the increased demand for water and food, droughts and famine will likely increase. When resources are scarce due to large populations, there is the possibility of conflicts over resources as well.

While the population is growing, it is also changing as well. The elderly segment of the population is much larger than in the past. In most cases, the elderly are not as able to protect themselves when earthquakes, floods, and tornados occur. Although the elderly segment is larger than in the past, the largest proportion of the population is in the age range of 15 to 24 years. Youth may be better able to protect themselves from different hazards. However, younger individuals, especially infants and children, will not have sufficient knowledge to deal with hazards. Many are particularly vulnerable if their parents are not present when a disaster occurs.

Population growth also pressures people to migrate to new areas. Many families are leaving the rural communities where their family had lived for generations and are moving to the cities to seek jobs. Many cities are located in seismically active areas or locations in the path of potential lava flows. But such urbanization has a bearing on disaster vulnerability. These areas are obviously vulnerable to major earthquakes or volcanic activity. When buildings are placed closely together, fires will also spread more quickly. Buildings that house a large number of residents or workers will also kill more people when they are damaged or collapse. Population growth and urbanization should be recognized as major concerns to you as an emergency manager.

12.7.3 Increased Diversity

Many United States cities are now quite diverse, with large representations of immigrants from all over the world. Even smaller cities are collectively home to hundreds or thousands of immigrants. This diversity is what makes the United

States the "melting pot" of the world. Such diversity may have an impact on disaster, vulnerability however. Many ethnic groups see hazards differently. Some may adopt a fatalistic attitude or fail to take any precautions for disasters (Quarantelli 1993, p. 21).

Diversity can also affect disasters in a variety of other ways (Quarantelli 1993, p. 21). The most obvious difficulty is that the different languages spoken by ethnic groups complicate warning processes. Notification must be given in several languages, but this does not guarantee that everyone will understand the recommended protective actions. Many of the immigrants do not speak or read English fluently. Language barriers also complicate the delivery of disaster relief and recovery assistance.

Furthermore, some ethnic groups may have extended friends and family in the area that they can turn to for support. However, other immigrant groups may be small and distrustful towards outsiders (Quarantelli 1993, p. 21). All things being equal, the more heterogeneous a society is, the more difficult it will be to manage disasters (Quarantelli 1993, p. 21).

12.7.4 Further Industrialization

The increased use of technology may also add to our vulnerability. In one study on the matter, Quarantelli wrote that "there are new and escalating kinds of technological accident and mishap which were almost non-existent prior to the Second World War and which will increasingly result in disasters [sic]" (1993, p. 12). Since this time, the world has become even more industrialized. There are now greater risks to nearby populations. Possible vulnerabilities are in the chemical and nuclear areas.

The widespread use of chemicals also has an impact on vulnerability. The 1984 Bhopal disaster was an example of an industrial disaster. A pesticide production plant located in India accidentally released 40 tons of methyl isocyanate (MIC). The gas rolled along the ground through the streets and killed thousands instantly. People did not know what they were dealing with and could not take necessary precaution measures. Even doctors did not know how to treat those who were affected in the incident. Although final numbers are in dispute, it is estimated that more than 15,000 people were killed in the short-term and another 15,000 died due to related illnesses over time. It is argued that an additional 200,000 to 600,000 people were injured due to the chemical release. Even though the accident occurred over 20 years ago, reports in 2004 suggest that contamination is still present. Chemicals provide many advantages for life, but they may present complications for first responders, medical care providers, emergency managers, and environmental specialists.

Nuclear material is also a concern today. Before the nuclear bomb was developed in the 1940s, we did not have to worry about such problems. Today, the manufacturing, transportation, and use of nuclear material all pose threats to people in the United States and around the world. The Three Mile Island accident illustrated the extreme difficulties associated with people's concern about nuclear material. Citizens did not trust the information provided by government officials and the evacuation was problematic. Another example involving nuclear material is the Chernobyl accident in the Ukraine. This disaster occurred in 1986 and is the worst accident in the history of nuclear power. Because the plant was not properly constructed, maintained, and operated, a plume of radioactive fallout drifted from parts of the Soviet Union all the way around the world in the Northern Hemisphere. Fifty-six people (including some children) died in the short-term. Forty-seven of these deaths were emergency responders who did not have sufficient knowledge about radioactive material. There has been debate as to the long-term effects of Chernobyl, although some scientists worry the fallout will cause cancers and lead to the early deaths of many others. There are many more nuclear power plants in operation today. More might be anticipated as fuel costs continue to rise. While most have or will have adequate safeguards, the dangerous nature of nuclear material complicates response and recovery operations for emergency managers and first responders.

12.7.5 Internationalization

The world truly is a global village. The shrinking of distance and disappearance of national borders is beneficial in that it allows for additional trade and commerce. However, globalization is not without its drawbacks. A disaster in one part of the world may adversely affect those in other countries. For instance, when an earthquake affected Japan in 1995, the computer markets in other countries were severely disrupted. The same could be said of the 9/11 disaster in New York City. It had serious implications for international financial corporations. Globalization could also increase the spread of other disasters such as infectious disease outbreaks. Travel to and from exotic places may augment the possibility of epidemics.

Internationalization also has a bearing on vulnerability to conflict-type disasters. Improved communication and media capabilities are able to relay different cultural viewpoints around the world. Unfortunately, this creates animosity among some extreme Islamic fundamentalists and others in western nations. Such clashing attitudes and values were responsible for the terrorist attacks in the United States on September 11, 2001. This, in turn, led to the war in Afghanistan and the war in Iraq. More of this conflict is possible in the future.

12.7.6 Improper Land Use and Construction

Vulnerability has also increased due to location and building decisions. At times, the most hazardous land is also the most desirable real estate. For instance, people are moving to coastal areas for the warm weather and beautiful scenery. This has a significant impact on future disasters, however. Coastal property is more vulnerable to flooding and hurricanes than other land. Not only are there homes in these areas, but there are also large hotels, casinos, restaurants, bars, and other gathering places such as clubs. People also like to live close to mountains, which can produce landslides or wildfires. In 2006, a town in the Philippines was buried due to a landslide and 1,500 people were killed. Insufficient attention is given to slope stability. Major forest fires have broken out in Arizona, New Mexico, and California in recent years. Hundreds of homes have been destroyed as a result. Location choices therefore have a significant impact on vulnerability. Unfortunately, we seem to overlook this important lesson.

Construction also plays a role in disaster vulnerability. The devastation of Hurricane Andrew was not universally felt. Neighborhoods built by certain contractors or developers faired better or worse than others. In many cases, the design of the buildings was flawed (e.g., because of too many gables). In other cases, shortcuts in building processes or materials were taken. For instance, roofs were not properly fastened to walls and the foundation. Material such as chipboard often becomes weak when exposed to excessive wind and rain. This, in addition to poor inspection practices, left many homes and businesses vulnerable to the hurricane. Ironically, our nation has yet to universally adopt more stringent building code standards.

12.7.7 Weak Emergency Management Institutions

Increased vulnerability also results from the intentional or unintentional neglect of emergency management institutions. There are several reasons why this occurs. Politicians do not always take disasters seriously. They are often more concerned about short-term priorities and choose not to see beyond the next election. Citizens do not think much about disasters until they occur, so priority is often given to other issues such as transportation systems, law enforcement, or education. Emergency management also has to compete with scores of other governmental programs, and it often fails to gain the support and resources needed to prevent or deal effectively with disasters. Other departments will sometimes ignore your requests to prepare for disasters since they have their own issues to worry about.

There are also too few emergency managers in the United States. Many cities do not have a full-time designated emergency manager. The vast majority fail to hire one emergency manager for every 25,000 people residing in their jurisdiction (as is recommended by FEMA). Emergency managers also lack adequate EOCs, equipment, and operating budgets. These problems are especially detrimental in that the work load of emergency managers has increased dramatically over the past few years due to more frequent and severe disasters, new homeland security concerns and programs, the preference of cities to obtain additional resources through grants, and increased desires to prevent disasters and mitigate their effects. The capacity of emergency management institutions has not kept pace with the expectations they are to meet.

In addition, our vulnerability is increased when politicians appoint unqualified persons to positions of great responsibility. Historically, the post of FEMA Director has been given to a colleague of the president or to someone who had supported the campaign or party of the administration. This can cause major problems for policy direction and morale in this emerging profession. This mistake is not limited to the federal level, however. The New Orleans levee board was comprised of people who were political appointees as well. After Hurricane Katrina, it was revealed that the board spent money on fountains and other projects for casinos but not for the levees as intended. As we saw with Hurricane Katrina, even the most powerful country in the world can be unprepared for a disaster when emergency management institutions are dismissed as unimportant or otherwise neglected.

12.7.8 Other Factors

Not all of the activities and changes taking place in society increase disaster vulnerability. In fact, there are several positive transformations that are reducing vulnerability. For instance, there are more democracies today than there were just 30 years ago. This is good for emergency management as this type of government is less able to cover up the causes of disasters. Politicians cannot keep information from people as was the case in the Soviet Union in the immediate aftermath of the nuclear accident of Chernobyl. The impact of 9/11 and Hurricane Katrina have also brought further support and funding to emergency management. Improved engineering practices and advances in technology facilitate mitigation and the development of better warning systems. Regional approaches to emergency management are improving the possible uses of mutual aid.

However, there are many other factors that are augmenting disaster vulnerability. Many of these have yet to be recognized. For instance:

▲ The National Flood Insurance Program (NFIP) may be augmenting vulnerability to this hazard instead of decreasing it (because NFIP allows development in flood-prone areas if certain criteria are met).

▲ The focus on terrorism at the expense of other hazards has caused our vulnerability to rise in regards to natural disasters.

▲ Increasingly complicated and intertwined infrastructure systems raise the probability of more complex disasters in the future.

▲ An overreliance on technological solutions to the disaster problem masks other, more fundamental causes of vulnerability in society.

▲ The reorganization of FEMA after 9/11 has created considerable confusion, at least initially, regarding the workings of the National Response Plan.

▲ The consolidation of dispatch centers across many cities may prohibit their capacity to answer calls in major emergency or disaster situations.

▲ The additional layers of bureaucracy under the Department of Homeland Security has increased the organizational distance between the FEMA director and the president of the United States.

▲ The overreliance of Americans on fast food may complicate people's ability to care for nutritional needs when disasters occur.

▲ People's expectations that the government should care for them in time of disaster decreases their ability to take care of their own needs and those of others.

▲ The building of new jumbo jets (holding over 500 passengers) will place extra burdens on responders, emergency medical care providers, and coroners if they are involved in crashes.

▲ Weak border control (due to corporate desires to keep wages low and the promotion of a better way of life for illegal aliens) increases the vulnerability of our nation to terrorist attacks.

▲ Further obesity in the United States may complicate rescue operations from confined spaces, lead to poor health, and increase susceptibility to various diseases.

▲ The presence of more children in day care centers today may limit the ability of such providers to ensure the well-being for children after disasters.

▲ The reduction of back stock in supermarkets may limit the presence of needed supplies before and after a disaster takes place.

FOR EXAMPLE

Is There a Doctor in the House?

The 2003 heat wave in France illustrated the deadly consequences of not assisting vulnerable populations. During France's vacation holiday, temperatures soared to record highs. The elderly could not support the excessive heat, and more than 14,000 elderly people died as a result. The deaths sparked a major public debate. Surviving friends and relatives criticized the government for not ensuring that sufficient care was given to those who passed away. The government suggested that family members did not take care of their own elderly parents. The government also blamed the doctors and family practitioners who were on vacation in August during the heat wave. In return, the doctors argued that the government did not issue an emergency recall of all physicians. One thing was not debated, however. The elderly were severely affected by the extreme temperatures.

▲ The de-emphasis of close-knit family and neighborhood relationships may hold back community recovery after disaster.

▲ Federal disaster assistance for victims and communities may subsidize risk and discourage increased attention toward mitigation.

These causes of vulnerability, along with many others not mentioned here, must be addressed if disasters are to be reduced in the future. As an emergency manager, you must develop an ability to see and correct the linkages that have bearing on the probability and impact of disasters. This skill is imperative if disaster resilience is to be promoted in the future.

SELF-CHECK

- Is poverty related to disaster vulnerability? If so, how?
- Does population growth impact urbanization? What does this mean for the emergency manager?
- Does diversity complicate disaster response and recovery operations?
- How do internationalization, land use, and construction practices impact vulnerability?
- What concerns should you have regarding the status of emergency management in the United States today?
- What are the other unrecognized causes of vulnerability? Can you think of any other factors that augment the probability of disaster?

SUMMARY

Although this chapter presents a rather bleak view of emergency management in the United States, we have gained a great deal of knowledge about how to deal with natural, technological, and conflict disasters. Nonetheless, as an emergency manager, you must recognize that disasters are becoming more frequent and intense. It is therefore imperative that you learn from prior response and recovery operations and anticipate how disasters will change in the future. You must be able to deal with all types of events and foresee new hazards that will certainly threaten us. In addition, it is vital that you understand the predominant and multiple causes of vulnerability so you can work with others to address them. Only by learning from the past and anticipating the future will you be able to promote resilience in your community.

KEY TERMS

Absolute poverty
A condition where people do not have sufficient resources to take care of basic needs such as food and shelter.

Associated hazard
A natural hazard agent that typically occurs at the same time as the primary hazard (e.g., hurricanes produce flooding).

Avian flu
An infection that stems from viruses commonly found in birds. Also know as the "Asian flu" or the "bird flu."

Built environment
The structures, technology, and infrastructure created by humans.

Cascading disaster
An event that triggers additional hazards or impacts.

Climate change
An alteration of the earth's temperature and weather patterns.

Cold zone
An area not affected that can only be accessed by clean (or decontaminated) individuals.

Continuity of operations
A goal to maintain the functioning of government in time of disasters.

Complex emergency
A humanitarian crisis that involves an extreme amount of violence among different ethnic groups coupled with political instability, poor economic conditions, weak law enforcement capabilities, and disaster conditions of some sort (e.g., drought and famine).

Complex or compound disaster
A disaster event that involves multiple variables.

Computer virus
A program that contains malicious codes.

Consequence management
Typical emergency management response and recovery operations that also take place after terrorist attacks.

Crisis management
A law enforcement activity which includes intelligence gathering to prevent terrorist attacks or evidence collection for the purposes of prosecution.

Cyber-terrorism
The use of computers and the Internet to plan or carry out attacks.

Environmental degradation
The depletion or pollution of the earth's natural resources.

Global warming	The rise of temperature of the earth's atmosphere.
Hackers	Individuals that log into other's computers illegally and run or disrupt them from afar.
Hoof and mouth disease	A highly infectious disease among livestock created by the Apthovirus. Also known as foot and mouth disease.
Hot zone	The affected (or contaminated) area.
Na-tech disaster	A disaster that occurs when a natural hazard interacts with technology to produce or magnify adverse effects.
Natural environment	The physical milieu (earth's systems) in which disasters occur.
Near-earth object (NEO)	A terrestrial impact structures made up of mostly ice and dirt particles.
Pole reversal	A change in the earth's magnetic fields.
Potentially hazardous asteroid (PHA)	An asteroid that comes within 0.05 AU or less of the earth.
Primary hazard	A natural hazard agent that interacts with vulnerabilities and therefore produces a disaster.
Quarantine	The isolation of people who have contracted a communicable disease.
Secondary hazard	A hazard (natural, technological, or otherwise) that occurs as a result of the primary hazard.
Severe acute respiratory syndrome (SARS)	A viral respiratory disease caused by a corona virus (SARS-CoV).
Social environment	The social, political, economic, and cultural activity or characteristics of the community.
Strategic national stockpile	A collection of antibiotics, vaccines, antiviral drugs, and other pharmaceuticals stored by the federal government.
Synergistic disaster	An event where one resulting impact seems to magnify others.
Tactical EMS personnel	Emergency medical technicians that are also trained to use weapons.
Terrorism	Violent acts committed by individuals or groups seeking to disrupt society, instill fear, and promote objectives that are ideological in nature.

Torino scale   A measurement tool scientists created in an attempt to predict the impact of a meteoroid strike.

Warm zone   The washing (or decontamination) area.

West Nile virus   A flavivirus that is dependent on mosquitoes as vectors.

Worms   Viruses that reproduce over many computer systems due to Internet, networks, and e-mail connections.

ASSESS YOUR UNDERSTANDING

Go to www.wiley.com/college/McEntire to evaluate your knowledge of preparing for future disasters.
Measure your learning by comparing pretest and post-test results.

Summary Questions

1. Because emergency management has improved over the years, there are less disasters today than in the past. True or False?

2. A secondary hazard occurs as a result of the primary hazard. True or False?

3. A na-tech disaster is disaster that results from a computer malfunction only. True or False?

4. The introduction of trees, the building of narrow roads, and cut backs in the fire department were some of the factors that led to the East Bay Hills fire. True or False?

5. Mutual aid teams had no problem responding to the East Bay Hills fire. True or False?

6. After the East Bay Hills fire, several improvements in emergency management were made. True or False?

7. Natural and technological hazards may share many similarities. True or False?

8. People will often deny wrongdoing or hide information after an industrial disaster. True or False?

9. If you don't know how to deal effectively with a hazardous materials incident, it is okay to respond anyway because people's lives are at stake. True or False?

10. Chemicals always react the same way—regardless of the weather. True or False?

11. Acts of violence will require close coordination between emergency medical personnel and law enforcement officials. True or False?

12. Planted bombs may complicate emergency response operations or criminal investigations. True or False?

13. Terrorists may attack with the use of knives, guns, computer viruses, or weapons of mass destruction. True or False?

14. Although the initial period after a disaster is characterized by a "therapeutic community," it is not long lasting, as conflict re-emerges during recovery activities. True or False?

15. Unusual numbers of sick or dying people may be an indicator of the use of a biological weapon. True or False?

16. Terrorists will only target civilians and not first-responders. True or False?

17. A hot zone is the place where decontamination takes place. True or False?

18. Hospitals may need to lock down their facilities after terrorist attacks in order to avoid contamination. True or False?

19. If you need assistance in dealing with terrorist attacks, the state and federal governments may have specialized teams that can help you. True or False?

20. Scientists agree on the cause and speed of pole reversals. True or False?

21. Avian flu is exactly like seasonal flu. True or False?

22. Hoof and mouth disease affects humans and not animals. True or False?

23. SARS is spread by droplets from a person's cough or sneeze. True or False?

24. Modern computer equipment may prohibit the sharing of nonverbal communication. True or False?

25. The population is only growing; it is not changing also. True or False?

26. There is no single cause of vulnerability. True or False?

27. Disasters are increasing because:
    (a) We are entering a period of more active hurricanes
    (b) Global climate change may alter episodes of rain and drought
    (c) Urbanization may lead to more flooding
    (d) a and b
    (e) a, b, and c

28. An example of a cascading disaster is:
    (a) Hurricane Iniki
    (b) The 9/11 terrorist attacks
    (c) Hurricane Andrew
    (d) The Oklahoma City bombing
    (e) The Bhopal chemical release

29. The social environment before the East Bay Hills fire:
    (a) Promoted and encouraged the development of emergency management
    (b) Discouraged development in hazard-prone areas
    (c) Agreed with all of the findings of the Blue Ribbon Committee
    (d) Opposed new regulations that could have limited the impact of the event
    (e) None of the above

30. During the response to the East Bay Hills fire:
    (a) The first responders made sure they put out all embers
    (b) There were not problems with mutual aid
    (c) Firefighters had to protect themselves by diving into a pool

(d) There was not a reliance on technology

(e) There was a failure to address all options for recovery

31. Types of technological hazards include:

(a) Electrical short circuits

(b) Dam failure

(c) Train derailments

(d) Hazardous materials releases

(e) All of the above

32. Which of the following is not often a problem in technological disasters?

(a) Emergency responders have full and complete information about what they are dealing with

(b) Lawsuits and fines typically result

(c) Risk is often underestimated

(d) Operation is improper

(e) All of the above

33. When responding to a hazmat incident, it is imperative that:

(a) Everyone is wearing personal protective equipment

(b) You approach the scene cautiously

(c) You seek expert advice if needed

(d) You be aware of the dynamic nature of the scene

(e) All of the above

34. An environmental remediation company:

(a) Is only useful in after a terrorist attack

(b) Can help you clean up after a hazardous materials incident

(c) Will never follow regulations after a hazardous materials incident

(d) Is beneficial for law enforcement agencies

(e) None of the above

35. The response to Columbine:

(a) Was regarded as a complete success

(b) Showed no problems regarding the identification of the perpetrator

(c) Illustrated the dangers of live camera footage of police operations

(d) Illustrated that the police had ample intelligence about what was taking place

(e) Did not include the planting of any dangerous bombs

36. Terrorists:

(a) Seek targets with maximum exposure

(b) Avoid the intimidation of others

(c) Do not pursue ideological goals

(d) Do not pursue social or religious goals

(e) Cannot utilize WMD

37. The T in TRACEM stands for:

(a) Terrorism

(b) Technology

(c) Trunked radio systems

(d) Thermal

(e) Temperatures

38. What is an indicator of an explosive device?

(a) Blown-out windows

(b) Dead animals and fish

(c) Mass casualties with no obvious trauma

(d) Mass casualties that are associated with unscheduled sprays

(e) None of the above

39. To enter a contamination zone, you should:

(a) Approach from the hot zone

(b) Approach from the cold zone

(c) Approach from the warm zone

(d) Bypass medical screening

(e) Bypass law enforcement personnel

40. In order to protect evidence:

(a) You must secure the scene of the crime

(b) You must avoid interaction with terrorists

(c) You must deny entry to authorized personnel

(d) b and c

(e) None of the above

41. Responsibilities of the coroner in after a terrorist attack include:

(a) Receiving human remains

(b) Identifying the deceased

(c) Notifying next of kin

(d) Providing death certificates

(e) All of the above

42. Global warming is attributed to:

(a) Natural processes

(b) Automobiles

(c) The build up of three greenhouse gasses

(d) a, b, and c

(e) b and c

43. Which type of biological disease is spread by birds?
    (a) Hoof and mouth
    (b) Avian flu
    (c) SARS
    (d) AIDS
    (e) West Nile virus

44. PHA stands for:
    (a) Prime hazard assessment
    (b) Potentially hazardous avalanche
    (c) Potentially hazardous asteroid
    (d) Perspective hazard adjustment
    (e) Probably hazard association

45. In order to prevent computer/information technology disasters, you should:
    (a) Filter incoming information to prevent information overload
    (b) Avoid up-to-date information
    (c) Avoid e-mails all of the time
    (d) Harness antitechnology firms
    (e) Rely on back-up systems only

46. Why are emergency management institutions weak?
    (a) People downplay the possibility of disaster
    (b) Politicians frequently ignore long-term issues
    (c) There are not enough emergency managers
    (d) Demands placed on emergency managers are excessive compared to their resources
    (e) All of the above

Review Questions

1. What disaster events occurred in the 1980s and 1990s that have impacted emergency management in the United States? Have events in the past 6 years given additional attention to emergency management? If so, why?

2. What are the associated and secondary hazards associated with primary hazards?

3. How did the natural, built, and social environments produce the East Bay Hills fire?

4. What are the types of industrial hazards that may occur, and what are their consequences?

5. What steps must be taken to respond effectively to hazardous materials incidents?

6. What lessons does Columbine have for first responders and emergency managers?

7. Are responses to terrorist attacks similar or different from responses to natural disasters?

8. What are the different types of harm that could be encountered at the scene of a terrorist attack?

9. How can time, distance, and shielding keep you safe after a terrorist attack?

10. What steps need to be taken to decontaminate victims effectively?

11. What other organizations can help you deal with terrorist disasters?

12. Is global warming controversial? How do you feel about the possibility of rising temperatures? How could this influence future disasters?

13. Why is it difficult to encourage people to prepare for possible meteor impacts?

14. What are the symptoms of avian flu? SARS? West Nile virus?

15. Are advances in computers and information beneficial and detrimental?

16. What are the causes of vulnerability, and how can they be corrected?

Applying This Chapter

1. You are the emergency manager for a small town in Tennessee. You have just been advised by the National Weather Service that severe thunderstorms are likely to occur in about 12 hours. What are some associated and secondary hazards that you should be concerned about? What should you be ready to do if the inclement weather produces flooding, hail, or tornadoes?

2. You are the risk manager at a chemical plant outside of Houston, Texas. You have been asked to review your company's operations with an eye on potential safety problems. What types of industrial accidents could occur and why? If an explosion took place and it emitted dangerous chemicals into the atmosphere, what should you do to respond effectively?

3. You are the emergency manager for Seattle, where there has been a terrorist attack with nerve gas. What measures should be taken to protect first responders? What can be done to help law enforcement officials obtain evidence and prosecute the guilty party?

4. As the president of the International Emergency Management Association, you have been asked to testify before congress regarding some of the new threats our nation should be aware of. What would you convey in your briefing? Can you think of any other hazards or threats that have not been identified in this chapter?

5. A wildfire has just erupted in Arizona and is moving toward a small mountain city. You are the emergency manager. Keeping the lessons of the East Bay Hills incident in mind, what steps can you take to respond effectively?

6. You are the emergency manager for Miami, Florida, and you have been assigned to review your ability to implement disaster response and recovery operations. What areas in and around Miami are vulnerable to natural disasters and why? What population segments are more vulnerable than others and why? What other factors could augment vulnerability in this area?

7. You are the emergency manager for Cleveland, Ohio. You have a son who is in high school, and he shows you a website where students express their views on a variety of subjects. Some of the students espouse affinity towards violence and how much they hate gay and lesbian groups. From an emergency management perspective, why should this concern you? What should you do to alleviate your fears?

Responding to Hazmat

You are the emergency manager in Chicago, where there has been a spill of hazardous material on a major interstate highway. The spilled product has shut down traffic and is draining into a nearby river. What measures should be taken to respond safely to this incident? What else should be done to protect the environment?

Responding to Biological Hazards

You are the emergency manager for Washington, D.C., an international city that welcomes thousands of visitors from other countries every day. What information can you give to people in a public education campaign that will prevent them from being infected with diseases such as SARS and West Nile virus?

Technological Hazards

Quarantelli asserts that computer and information technology is producing new types of disasters. What steps can you take to minimize the negative impact of the technological revolution? How could this technology help or hinder response and recovery operations?

13

PROMOTING DISASTER RESILIENCE
Preparedness, Improvisation, Professionalism, and Leadership

Starting Point

Go to www.wiley.com/college/McEntire to assess your knowledge of promoting disaster resilience.
Determine where you need to concentrate your effort.

What You'll Learn in This Chapter

- ▲ The need for preparedness
- ▲ Methods for acquiring financial resources for your program
- ▲ EOC activation and management
- ▲ The importance of hazard and vulnerability assessments
- ▲ The components of EOPs
- ▲ The benefit of training
- ▲ Types of exercises
- ▲ Ways to promote community education
- ▲ The value of improvisation
- ▲ Principles of leadership

After Studying This Chapter, You'll Be Able To

- ▲ Apply the concept of preparedness
- ▲ Understand the different types of resources available to you
- ▲ Differentiate between the EOC as a place, structure, and function
- ▲ Examine who can help you assess hazards and vulnerability
- ▲ Analyze the benefit and limitations of planning
- ▲ Comprehend the organizations that provide training
- ▲ Illustrate how to manage disaster exercises effectively
- ▲ Recognize the value of disaster education
- ▲ Explain why departing from plans and SOPs can be beneficial
- ▲ Indicate the importance of professionalism

Goals and Outcomes

- ▲ Propose ways to increase preparedness in your community
- ▲ Write grants and manage budgets
- ▲ Design and operate an EOC
- ▲ Formulate a hazard and vulnerability assessment
- ▲ Create an emergency operations plan
- ▲ Propose training programs for your community
- ▲ Design disaster exercises for your jurisdiction
- ▲ Increase readiness of the public for disasters
- ▲ Assess ways to improvise when the situation requires it
- ▲ Evaluate the benefit of professionalism and leadership in a disaster situation

INTRODUCTION

Effective response and recovery operations often result from the decisions and activities taken after disasters occur. However, it is imperative that you do not wait until after a disaster to promote resilience. There are many proactive steps you can take before and after disasters to facilitate a strong emergency management program. Creating an ordinance and a preparedness council are some of the first obligations you will have as an emergency manager. Obtaining resources from internal and external sources will help to fund your emergency management program. Establishing an EOC will help you coordinate post-disaster functions during response and recovery operations. Beyond these steps, you should assess the hazards and vulnerability in your community and write an emergency operations plan to anticipate and guide your activities after a disaster. Training can help build capabilities in first responders and among the heads of the various departments in your jurisdiction. Exercises should be held to verify understanding of the plan and to ensure equipment is operating properly. Public education will also be needed if you are to enlist the support of citizens in your community. When a disaster occurs, you can also increase resilience by adapting to the unusual circumstances that inevitably arise during response and recovery operations. Finally, professionalism and leadership skills will help you promote emergency management and make disasters a bigger priority in your jurisdiction.

13.1 Preparing Your Community

Preparedness has been described as one of the twin foundations of emergency management (Kreps 1991, p. 31). Interestingly, there is little agreement on what preparedness actually means. Some scholars see preparedness as "planning, resource identification, warning systems, training, simulations, and other pre-disaster actions taken for the sole intent of improving the safety and effectiveness of a community's response during a disaster" (Gillespie and Streeter 1987, p. 155). Others assert that preparedness has the goal of foreseeing potential disaster problems and projecting possible solutions (Kreps 1991, p. 34). An alternate perspective is that **preparedness** builds capabilities to improve the effectiveness of response and recovery operations.

Despite this disagreement about meaning, you should recognize the value of preparedness. Preparedness anticipates and develops a variety of resources for response and recovery. It identifies important functions to be performed after a disaster. Preparedness also facilitates the assignment of roles and responsibilities among organizations (Auf der Heide 1989, p. 39-41). Communication and coordination are improved when preparedness is emphasized in a serious manner (Auf der Heide 1989, p. 39). Because preparedness provides further options for first responders and emergency management personnel, it also allows for increased flexibility during response and recovery operations (Kreps 1991, p. 34). Creating an ordinance and establishing a preparedness council are some of the first steps you will take to prepare for disasters.

13.1.1 Creating an Ordinance

One of the first things you will need to do to facilitate preparedness is to develop an emergency management ordinance or law. This gives the emergency management program legitimacy and authority in your community. Such ordinances illustrate the jurisdiction's commitment to preparedness, and these laws typically include several sections:

▲ **Justification.** This illustrates why emergency management is needed.

▲ **Organization.** This denotes how the functions will be assigned among leaders and various departments.

▲ **Powers and duties.** This indicates who is in charge of emergency management in terms of approving plans or declaring local disasters.

▲ **Joint operations and mutual aid.** This permits agreements with other jurisdictions in case outside assistance is required after a disaster.

FOR EXAMPLE

Highland Village's City Ordinance

The preamble to Ordinance Number 97-761 describes the purpose of the law in the city of Highland Village, Texas: "An ordinance of the city council for the city of Highland Village, Texas, establishing a municipal emergency management program; organizing the emergency management program; providing for the offices of an emergency management director, an emergency management coordinator and an emergency management committee; requiring an oath of office; providing for duties and responsibilities: authorizing a survey of hazards, development of a plan, and ordering an emergency curfew. Providing for joint operations and mutual aid; providing for emergency override; providing for exemptions from liability; providing for restricted expenditures and contracts; providing for conflict with other provisions and with the state and federal law; providing for obstruction of authority; providing for impersonation of personnel. Prohibiting unauthorized warning and all-clear signals; providing a severability clause. Repealing in its entirety ordinance No. 87-503 of the city relating to emergency management; providing for a review; making violations punishable by fine not to exceed $2,000.00; and providing an effective date."

▲ **Expenditures and contracts.** This describes who can make purchases and for what purposes.

▲ **Relation to state and federal law.** This reiterates that the local ordinance will comply with state and federal statutes pertaining to emergency management.

▲ **Violations and penalties.** This outlines the enforcement of emergency management laws and regulations.

The ordinance sets the foundation for everything else you will do as a local emergency manager.

13.1.2 Establishing a Preparedness Council

When the legal foundation has been or is being set, you should establish a preparedness council. In other locations they will be given different names. For example, in Denton, Texas, this organization is known as the Denton Emergency Preparedness Advisory Council (DEPAC). There may even be multiple committees in each community. These organizations may be based on the hazards threatening the jurisdiction, functions to be performed, needs to be addressed, and agencies to be involved. The council may include:

▲ The mayor, city manager, and emergency manager
▲ Department leaders from the local government
▲ Representatives from public health agencies, utility providers, insurance companies, universities, the FBI, nursing home units, and so on
▲ Others from the American Red Cross, Salvation Army, churches, and nonprofit groups

The most well-known preparedness councils are Local Emergency Planning Committees (LEPCs) (Lindell 1994). LEPCs were created in the late 1980s in response to the Emergency Planning and Community Right to Know Act (SARA Title III). This law had the goal of helping communities prepare for hazardous materials releases and other disasters. Constituting agencies vary by jurisdiction but typically include the emergency manager(s) and representatives from the fire department, hospitals, environmental protection agencies, and petro-chemical facilities. These advisory councils have been studied extensively by Michael Lindell. He affirms that they have a positive impact on disaster preparedness since they reject the isolated planning undertaken by former Civil Defense directors (1994, p. 103). Other factors that facilitate LEPC preparedness and response to industrial disasters include the ability to:

▲ Acquire funding
▲ Maintain the organization

▲ Incorporate highly committed members

▲ Assess risks accurately

▲ Identify evacuation routes

▲ Develop knowledgeable hazardous materials (haz mat) teams

Such preparedness councils can do much to ready a community for disasters.

SELF-CHECK

- What is **preparedness?**
- Why is preparedness necessary?
- What is an **ordinance?**
- How can a preparedness council help you prepare your community for disaster?

13.2 Acquiring Financial Resources

Without resources, you will not be able to maintain an effective emergency management program or increase the chances for successful post-disaster operations. It is vital that you identify resources that can be obtained in a disaster and seek funding from internal and external sources. You will want to ask yourself three questions:

▲ What resources does the community have that will help response and recovery operations?

▲ What external resources can the community obtain, and how can you access them?

▲ What other needs might arise, and how will you find required resources? (McEntire and Myers 2004).

13.2.1 Resource Lists

A good way to begin to answer the above questions is to develop a resource list. A **resource list** is a database that includes human and material resources that can be deployed in a disaster. Such a list should include equipment, supplies, and services that are available on a 24-hour basis. Resource lists may also have:

▲ Names, phone numbers, fax numbers, physical addresses, e-mail addresses, and a description of the service to be provided, which can be recorded on a spreadsheet. This may include city officials, department leaders, private companies, and nonprofit organizations. It may also have information about those who can assist with vehicle towing, sand bagging, power generation, sheltering, mass care operations, etc.

▲ An inventory of government vehicles and heavy equipment
▲ Preapproved contracts with vendors and expense estimates for certain services such as debris removal

The resource list should be updated at least on an annual basis. Having a list with incorrect names, old phone numbers, and expired contractual agreements will hurt your ability to respond to disasters and recover from them effectively. Conversely, an extensive and maintained list will help you acquire resources on a moment's notice.

13.2.2 Annual Budgets

Another way to ensure the availability of resources is to seek as large a budget as possible. A **budget** is an allocation of monetary support for a given department by city or county leadership. Budgets are typically requested and approved on an annual basis. They may pay for office use, equipment, personnel, and operating costs such as phone lines and power bills. Such funding may also help to acquire computer decision support systems or upgrade warning systems. Financial support can also improve dispatch and emergency operations centers. It is important that you keep in mind the fact that budgets allocated to police, fire, and public health departments may positively influence overall community preparedness as well.

Because resources are always scarce, denials for increased funding will be common. However, you should not give up on your efforts to obtain internal funding. Persistence will pay off over time. In addition, it is recommended that you remember that the best time to ask for additional funding is immediately after a disaster. When a disaster occurs, begin conversations with authorities about how to prevent or prepare for the same type of event in the future. Be sure to take advantage of the increased interest in emergency management that disasters provide.

13.2.3 Grants

Funding can also be sought from outside agencies. Many grants are provided by the federal government. You can find grant opportunities through:

▲ Emergency management associations
▲ Emergency management newsletters or bulletins
▲ Federal agencies
▲ The state administrative agency in charge of emergency management grants

▲ Websites such as www.grants.gov

▲ The Catalog of Federal Domestic Assistance at www.crda.gov/default.htm

▲ A city or county grants manager or coordinator

Some federal grants, such as the Emergency Management Performance Grant (also known as the Emergency Management Preparedness Grants), are vital for emergency management. This grant is allocated to the states on the basis of population and with consideration given to hazard and vulnerability assessments. The state may keep some or all of the money, but most pass much of the financial assistance to local governments. Local governments are given the funds based on needs and efforts to promote disaster preparedness.

EMPG often funds the emergency manager's salary or portions thereof. In addition to funding salaries for those in emergency management, the money also pays for travel, equipment, insurance, and supplies. The money can be shared with other departments that assist in emergency management activities. Although the EMPG funding is useful, it does not pay for everything. For example, the EMPG will not pay for rent on EOCs. It will not cover expenses associated with advertising, convict labor, benefits for volunteers, or motor vehicles.

There are many other grants beside EMPG, and these help acquire equipment or fund special programs. Examples include:

1. National Urban Search and Rescue Response System
2. First Responder Counter-Terrorism Training Assistance
3. Fire Suppression Assistance
4. Pre-disaster Mitigation Grants
5. Chemical Stockpile Emergency Preparedness Program
6. State and Local All-Hazards Emergency Operations Planning
7. Interoperable Communications Equipment, Port Security Grants
8. State Homeland Security Grant Program (SHSGP)
9. Community Emergency Response Teams (CERT) Grants
10. Information Technology Evaluation Program (ITEP)

Most of these grants are available from the Office of Domestic Preparedness. However, certain grants have match requirements. For instance, many federal grants require that the local jurisdiction fund 25% of the total cost of the project in order to be eligible.

13.2.4 Applying for and Managing Grants

When applying for grants, you will first need to request an application package or download one from the Internet. At this point, you should follow all directions to complete the document as outlined. If needed, you may want to involve

FOR EXAMPLE

Local Grants

States often give grants to local governments. For example, Florida distributes grants to local governments to mitigate repetitively flooded structures. Flooding is Florida's most prevalent natural hazard. Many structures in Florida were built before flood-resistant design and construction techniques were implemented. In 2006, Florida had over $4 million dollars to distribute to local governments for mitigation. Grants can be used for prevention and not preparedness activities alone.

others in the writing of the grant. Your jurisdiction may have a full-time grant writer who can help you develop the proposal as well. Whether writing the grant alone or with others, be aware that concise, clear writing is critical. Your proposal should include the goals of the proposal, the team to be involved in the project, the work plan, deliverables, a budget, information on matching funds, performance measures, and the frequency of activity reporting.

Getting the grant isn't the end of course. It is only the beginning. If you are awarded the grant, you will need to accept the funds in a letter. You will also need to set up a grant budget, and this increasingly means setting up an account for electronic bank deposits. Be aware that funding may be given up front, in intervals, or after the activity has been performed and documented. Regardless of how this takes place, you will need to have a strong management team to accomplish the goals of the grant. You should consider hiring additional employees to complete the work of the grant contract if that is necessary. You will also need to complete the activities that you outlined in the proposal and issue regular reports. Failing to do so, or using the funds for fraudulent purposes, could lead to prison terms and fines.

SELF-CHECK

- Why is it important to have resources at your disposal in a disaster?
- What is a **resource list**?
- How can a **budget** help you develop an effective emergency management program?
- What grants are available to the emergency manager?
- What considerations should you have when applying for grants?

13.3 Establishing an Emergency Operations Center (EOC)

One of the most important resources for your community is an emergency operations center. Therefore, another important step is to build an EOC or designate the location of where one can be established after a disaster. There are several things to keep in mind while doing this:

▲ Locate the EOC in a safe area (FEMA 1995, 1-6).

▲ Have an alternate location in case the primary EOC is affected in the disaster (FEMA 1995, 1-6).

▲ Determine the best space configuration for the community EOC. For example, you will need to determine how many rooms you will need. You will also need to determine what personnel or organizations will participate.

▲ Identify and acquire the equipment and supplies that will be needed (FEMA 1995, 2-4). This may include computers, phones, fax machines, desks, tables, chairs, and so on.

▲ Address life support requirements. These include sleeping accommodations, food service, water, sanitary facilities, medical supplies, heating, and air conditioning (FEMA 1995, 3-11-12).

▲ Ensure backup power and communications (FEMA 1995, 1-6).

▲ Maintain and update EOC personnel contact list (FEMA 1995, 2-6).

▲ Clarify under what criteria the EOC will be opened. For example, will the EOC be opened for a tornado watch or warning?

Once the EOC is ready to be activated in an actual disaster, be sure that all of the personnel are familiar with the protocols and procedures. An EOC will be of no use to the emergency management personnel if they do not know how to use it.

FOR EXAMPLE

Colin County's Fusion Center

One county in north central Texas has created a fusion center that integrates many different departments and other organizations that have an interest in emergency management and homeland security. If required, this EOC may include the presence of people from various government departments as well as others from the private and nonprofit sectors. Participating stakeholders include police, fire, EMS, public health, and other agencies. The fusion center also allows the sharing of information with the military, intelligence agencies, and the department of transportation. It is novel in terms of organization and technological capabilities.

SELF-CHECK

- Why is an EOC an important resource for your community?
- Should cities and counties have a back up EOC? Why?
- What equipment and supplies are needed in EOCs?
- Are back-up power and communications necessary for EOCs?
- What else should you do to establish an EOC?

13.4 Hazard and Vulnerability Assessment

To prepare adequately, you will also need to know what types of disasters are most likely to occur in your jurisdiction. With the preparedness council and other experts, you will need to assess the threats facing the community and the capabilities for dealing with them. A **hazard and vulnerability assessment** is an evaluation of the risks facing your community along with your capability for dealing with them. These assessments should explore:

▲ All natural, technological, and civil hazards and rank them according to their predictability, speed of onset, magnitude, duration, seasonality, and so on

▲ The location of buildings, property, and critical infrastructure near hazardous areas

▲ The status of building codes and a measure of their enforcement

▲ Demographic patterns, including race/ethnicity, age, and income levels

▲ Potential impact of a disaster and expected ability to deal with needs, problems, and functions to be performed

There are many resources available to help you complete your hazard and vulnerability assessment. These resources include historical data on prior disasters, FEMA

FOR EXAMPLE

The Importance of Assessments

Most federal homeland security grants are based on terrorism threat assessments. If a community cannot illustrate that it is a possible target and that it has many vulnerabilities that need to be addressed, it will not receive funding. Conversely, if a community can illustrate hazards and vulnerabilities effectively, they may obtain money for both prevention and preparedness activities.

and state websites, and other emergency managers that work in the field. You may also want to meet with geographers, flood plain managers, and meteorologists to understand risks. Scholars and state/federal emergency management personnel can also help you determine what could happen in your community. These assessments play an important role in steering the direction of the emergency operations plan, first responder training, disaster exercises, and public education.

SELF-CHECK

- What is a **hazard and vulnerability assessment?**
- What do these assessments examine or look at?
- Are hazard and vulnerability assessments important?
- Who can help you complete a hazard and vulnerability assessment?

13.5 Writing an Emergency Operations Plan (EOP)

After the hazards and vulnerabilities have been identified, you should work with others to create the emergency operations plan (EOP). The **EOP** is a document that describes what the community will do in the aftermath of a disaster. The EOP should address all functions pertinent to response and recovery operations (McEntire and Myers 2004). EOPs should give extra attention to EOC management, interdepartmental coordination, mutual aid, and interaction with private companies, nonprofit organizations, and the involvement of different levels of government. Typical sections include:

▲ **Authority.** This section describes the legal basis of emergency management and the plan. It may cite laws, decrees, or other documents.

▲ **Purpose.** This section discusses the objectives of the plan. This part of the plan will often mention the four phases of emergency management. It may also state that the plan is an overview of who does what, where, when, how, and why.

▲ **Situation and Assumptions.** The situation part of the plan discusses what hazards the unit is faced with and the potential disruption, injuries, deaths, and damages that can result. It may also discuss how one hazard can interact with another. The assumptions section of the plan mentions things such as an ongoing presence of hazards, the unpredictability of disasters, how officials will recognize and respond to the event, difficulties that might arise, and that plan implementation may limit the loss of life, property, and the environment.

▲ **Concept of Operations.** This section discusses who will do what and how. It discusses the fact that departments will respond based on their daily activities and areas of expertise that are also similar to emergency functions. This section does not have many details.

▲ **Organization and Assignment of Responsibilities.** This part of the plan describes the roles of each responding department. It is more specific than the concept of operations section.

▲ **Direction and Control.** This portion describes the management of the entire operation. The role of the top official and those in the EOC are mentioned.

▲ **Plan Development and Maintenance.** This section describes plan revisions and who will be in charge of them. It may also state who gets copies of the plan. This section notes that each department should give input to the plan, even if you are ultimately responsible for the entire document.

The plan may include other sections as well. These possible sections include increased readiness conditions and administration and support.

The development of the EOP should be based on collective decision making. That is to say, you should work with other department leaders to write the emergency operations plan. Meetings might be held to discuss the best way to respond to and recover from disasters. Notes from these discussions can then be folded into the EOP. Drafts should be circulated to make sure that the plan addresses response and recovery operations in a logical fashion. If needed, templates can be taken from state and federal emergency management websites. However, it is imperative that you tailor your plan to the community that you serve. Each city and county has different organizational arrangements, distinct hazards, and unique vulnerabilities. Above all, remember that planning is only one part of the preparedness process. In fact, having a plan is of little benefit if you have no capabilities to implement it.

FOR EXAMPLE

Avoiding Fantasy Documents

Planning, if it is to be effective, must be based on accurate assumptions (Dynes 1994). It is imperative that emergency managers think about what they will do under worse case scenarios rather than engage in wishful thinking. The document should be seen as a part of preparedness but not the only indicator of increased readiness. Writing an EOP without building capabilities amounts to a fantasy document (Mitchell 1999). Emergency managers must not get caught up in the paper plan syndrome (Auf der Heide 1989).

SELF-CHECK

- What is an **EOP**?
- What are the typical sections of EOPs?
- Should you write the EOP alone?
- Is planning the only step you have to take to prepare for a disaster?

13.6 First Responder Training

Training is another way to prepare communities for disaster response and recovery operations. **Training** involves a review of emergency procedures as well as their application in a nonthreatening situation. Training is important as it compensates "for the limited opportunities available for acquiring actual disaster response experience" (Jackson and Paton 2002, p. 115). Examples of training include ensuring:

▲ Firefighters can don and doff appropriate bunker or hazardous materials gear

▲ Department leaders understand the incident command structure

▲ EOC personnel are familiar with their roles and responsibilities in disasters

▲ City officials know how to assess damages, declare a disaster, and seek federal disaster assistance

Training can be conducted at the local level, across multiple jurisdictions, by the state, or through FEMA and other agencies (see Figure 13-1). Public health agencies and the FBI also provide several training courses. Training should be seen as a process to maintain first responder certifications. It is another way to promote disaster resilience.

FOR EXAMPLE

The Emergency Management Institute

FEMA operates a training facility in Emmitsburg, Maryland. A series of dorms and classroom buildings are located on what used to be a former Catholic girls' school. First responders and emergency managers travel to this location and attend classes for several days and weeks at a time. Participants may learn more about incident command, EOC management, or how to deal with acts of terrorism.

Figure 13-1

FEMA has training centers like this one in Anniston, Alabama to help first responders and emergency managers prepare for disasters. Additional training courses are offered by state and regional governments.

SELF-CHECK

- What is **training**?
- How can training impact your level of preparedness?
- What type of training opportunities exist for first responders, emergency managers, and department leaders?
- Where can you learn more about training opportunities?

13.7 Disaster Exercises

Conducting disaster exercises is another way to increase the effectiveness of post-disaster operations. An **exercise** is a simulation of a crisis, emergency, or disaster that has the goal of improving response and recovery operations in an actual event. There are several reasons why exercises are beneficial. Exercises:

▲ Help all responders become familiar with the emergency operations plan.

▲ Test the plan to ensure that no functions or assignments have been overlooked.

▲ Provide an opportunity to verify the availability and utility of equipment and resources.

▲ Provide a nonthreatening or less-threatening atmosphere to hone skills and practice disaster response operations.

13.7.1 Types of Exercises

According to FEMA, there are five types of exercises.

1. An **orientation** is an informal introductory meeting. It familiarizes people with the plan and motivates active participation in response operations. It covers policies and procedures in addition to roles and responsibilities. Orientations are typically geared to new agency representatives, and they last about 1 hour in an office setting. Orientations do not involve any equipment, and they do not create stress for the participants.

2. A **drill** is a small and limited exercise to improve a single function in response and recovery operations. It typically includes first responders in the field to test their use of equipment. A drill may last 1 or 2 hours, and it may produce limited stress.

3. A **table-top** is an informal discussion of a mock emergency or disaster situation. This improves problem solving and facilitates coordination. Table-top exercises usually involve department leaders in an office or EOC setting. Table-tops are usually a few hours in duration and may or may not involve equipment. These types of exercises lead to low stress among the participants.

4. A **functional exercise** is a moderately sized drill to test a limited number of response and recovery capabilities. Functional exercises may involve one or a few agencies, and they occur at the EOC, in the field, or at both locations. These types of exercises will often test the use of equipment. They may take up to a half day and evoke a medium degree of stress among those involved.

5. A **full-scale exercise** is a very large simulation which tests nearly all response and recovery capabilities. It requires the inclusion of most organizations and incorporates dispatch, field, and EOC components. Full-scale events utilize equipment to an impressive degree, last nearly an entire day, and create a significant degree of stress since they appear to be real-life incidents.

13.7.2 Managing Exercises

Exercises do not just happen by themselves. A great deal of work goes into exercises. You will need to review the EOP and current capabilities to determine what should be exercised. You will also need to schedule the date for the exercise in advance as well as the location, equipment, and personnel. It is also imperative that you decide on the purpose, objectives, narrative, events, expected actions, messages, evaluation criteria, and enhancements for the exercise. For instance:

▲ The purpose of the exercise identifies the functions to be tested, the agencies to be involved, the type of exercise, the simulated hazard, and the location of the event.

▲ The objective of the exercise is a statement of what will be tested according to a simple, clear, achievable, and measurable standard.

▲ The narrative is an introduction of the event. It often covers where, when, and why the hazardous event takes place.

▲ The events portion of the exercise lists the problems or challenges all participants will face as they respond to the hypothetical emergency or disaster. Events may be labeled as major or minor. A major event, for example, might be an explosion resulting from an earthquake. A minor event could include a resulting fire that creates the need for emergency medical care.

▲ Expected actions list how participants might react to the problems or challenges that they encounter in the exercise.

▲ Messages describe the problems or challenges to be encountered as a result of the major and minor events. They evoke expected actions. Messages include the source of the message, the content and means of transmission, and the position of the designated recipient.

▲ Evaluation criteria may include a list of things to assess along with forms to verify compliance with emergency management policies and procedures.

▲ Enhancements are the props needed to bring realism to the exercise. For example, if you want to simulate the experience of being in a collapsed building, you will need props such as scattered debris or smoke.

Failing to include these components will limit the effectiveness of exercises.

13.7.3 Exercise Participants and Other Considerations

Participants in the exercise may include the design team, players, victims/simulators, controller, and evaluators. The design team helps to develop the purpose, objectives, narrative, events, expected actions, messages, evaluation criteria, and enhancements for the exercise. **Players** are the responders or department leaders that are evaluated in the exercise. **Victims** are simulators who provide opportunities to test the players' knowledge and skills. The **controller** runs the exercise by initiating the events and distributing messages to be acted upon. **Evaluators** determine if the players responded to the exercise effectively and in accordance to the established plan.

Exercises are not completed when they are over. They require a significant amount of follow up. Paperwork should be filled out and sent to state and federal emergency management agencies to illustrate compliance with exercise require-

---

FOR EXAMPLE

Tabletop Drills

The Office of Emergency Management (OEM) in New York City carries out a variety of drills and exercises. OEM conducts tabletops to determine the effectiveness of its plans and degree of preparedness. One such exercise, which deals with a hypothetical biological attack on New York City, involved several agencies. Participating in this drill were the commissioners of the NYPD, FDNY, and the Department of Health and Mental Hygiene. Also participating were several city and state agencies. Even the Mayor took part in this particular drill. Exercises such as this help all pertinent actors in the community prepare for disasters.

---

ments. This is important since funding may be tied to the number and type of exercises undertaken in a given year. The recommendations of after-action reports also need to be acted on to improve response and recovery operations for actual disaster events.

Strong exercise programs have the following characteristics:

▲ They are progressive, meaning that a current exercise builds on the strengths and corrects the weaknesses of prior exercises.

▲ They are programs, implying that they are carefully planned and conducted to meet goals and objectives.

▲ They involve the community, suggesting that all other organizations should participate. First responders and the emergency manager will logically be involved. Every effort should be given to get local officials, businesses, and nonprofit agencies involved as well.

SELF-CHECK

- What is an **exercise**?
- Why are exercises beneficial?
- What are the different types of exercises?
- What are the various components of exercises?
- Who are the participants in exercises?
- What makes an exercise program strong?

13.8 Public Education

Citizens may not always understand what types of hazards threaten their community. They may not know what to do in time of a disaster. For this reason, public education programs are vital if response and recovery are to be effective. **Public disaster education** can be considered a concerted effort to inform people about hazards and what to do if a disaster should occur. Public education can be directed toward individuals, school children, community groups, families, and businesses. It may describe the nature of hazards, what can be done to prepare for them, and how to react should a disaster occur. For example, public education can outline the need to store food and purchase a first aid kit. It can also tell people to rotate flashlight batteries and pay attention to weather reports. Education programs can also instruct people on how to evacuate or where it is safe to seek shelter. Disaster education materials can be obtained from FEMA or the American Red Cross. Other brochures and pamphlets can be developed by the jurisdiction and distributed at fairs, parades, sporting events, public speaking engagements, or in utility bill envelops.

For those jurisdictions that want to include the public in further proactive efforts, Community Emergency Response Teams (CERT) can be established (see Figure 13-2). **CERTs** are groups of citizens that have received detailed information

Figure 13-2

Participants involved in post-disaster operations must be made aware of the steps they should take to facilitate community recovery.

> **FOR EXAMPLE**
>
> ### Educating our Youth
>
> If emergency managers are to improve disaster response and recovery operations in the future, it is imperative that they educate children. Children often influence parents to take greater precautionary measures. They are also the best hope for implementing change. For this reason, the emergency manager should visit schools to educate youth about disasters. Girl Scouts, Boy Scouts, and church groups would also be logical candidates for disaster public education programs.

and specialized training to improve self-sufficiency in disasters. First responders will be overwhelmed in major disasters. State and federal assets may not arrive for 72 hours. Therefore, it has been decided that the public should be able to care for themselves until outside help arrives. CERTs have been created in cities around the United States. CERT members are taught about potential hazards, disaster preparedness, urban search and rescue, fire suppression, basic first aid, psychological effects of disasters, and appropriate responses to terrorist attacks. These teams require continuous education and training.

SELF-CHECK

- What is **public education**?
- Why is educating the **public** beneficial for emergency management?
- Who can help you educate the public about disasters?
- What are **CERTs** and why are they valuable after a disaster?

13.9 Improvisation, Creativity, and Flexibility

In addition to preparedness, improvisation is one of the foundations of emergency management (Kreps 1991). Improvisation, creativity, and flexibility are vitally important. **Improvisation** is adapting to an unfolding situation. This requires both creativity and flexibility.

"Considered as a noun, an improvisation is a transformation of some original model. Considered as a verb, improvisation is composing in real time that begins with embellishments of a simple model, but increasingly feeds on these embellishments themselves to move farther from the original melody and closer to a new composition. Whether treated as a noun or a verb, improvisation is guided activity whose guidance comes from elapsed patterns discovered retrospectively" (Kendra and Wachtendorf 2003, p. 126).

When the preparedness is inadequate, improvising becomes critical (Kreps 1991, p. 31). Also planning and exercises may take place in an artificial environment. Since this is the case, real-world problems create a need for creativity. Kreps (1991, p. 32) provides an excellent, but perhaps fictitious, example of improvisation, creativity, and flexibility:

> *A city is hit by a tornado. It causes major damage to homes. There are not many staff members available to perform damage assessment. The building commissioner seeks the assistance of a regional building association. To limit legal liability, the volunteers from the building association are hired immediately with a salary of $1 each. After being trained on damage assessment, the teams are divided up. They are assigned different sections of the city. The teams categorize buildings as lightly, moderately, and severely damaged. When the assessments are completed, repairs begin on the buildings with light and moderate damage. Those with heavy damage are condemned and destroyed. This quick thinking and novel approach enables the city to meet the needs of insurance claim adjustors and private contractors and helps victims be eligible for disaster assistance.*

As witnessed in this case, thinking outside the box can be extremely beneficial. During a disaster, you will have to respond to circumstances that you had never considered or trained for. You will have to be creative. Creativity is one part of improvisation (Kendra and Wachtendorf 2003, p. 126).

▲ **Creativity** can be described as the development of "new alternatives with elements that achieve fundamental objectives in ways previously unseen. Thus, a creative alternative has both elements of novelty and effectiveness," (Kendra and Wachtendorf 2003, p. 123).

▲ **Flexibility** is also closely related to improvization. Flexibility could be described as a willingness to depart from widely accepted standards and practices of doing things (thinking creatively and improvising solutions) in order to react effectively to unforeseen problems. "Under some circumstances . . . in dealing with less routine tasks, emergency organizations need to preserve an ability to respond flexibly, and, where necessary, an ability to improvise appropriate counter-measures for the special needs of an unanticipated situation which threatens to become a crisis" (Turner 1994, p. 87).

13.9.1 Case Study: Response to 9/11 Terrorist Attacks

Kendra and Wachtendorf illustrate the 9/11 terrorist attacks provide an excellent example of the importance of these principles in their study. How the reestablishment of the EOC and many other post-disaster activities required improvisation, creativity, and flexibility (Kendra and Wachtendorf 2003).

The EOC, located in Building 7 of the World Trade Center (WTC), collapsed as a result of a fire ignited by WTC Tower 1. All officials and key personnel were able to evacuate. But they lost scores of computer-equipped stations. They also lost communications equipment, video monitoring devices, and GIS capabilities. Emergency managers had no conference room or press briefing room among other things. Since there was no designated back-up facility, New York officials therefore had to respond to one of the largest disasters in U.S. history without a functioning EOC.

A training room served as the temporary EOC until a decision was made to move to pier 92. Having scheduled this pier on the Hudson River for a bioterrorism drill after September 11, the Office of Emergency Management (OEM) decided to make it the EOC for the 9/11 terrorist attacks. Desks, chairs, computers, and other office supplies were delivered within 36 hours. The American Red Cross provided hot meals. Sleeping arrangements were made with nearby hotels. Personal care items were available at the EOC. Security was tightened to protect the facility against possible attacks.

Although EOC personnel were initially scattered and disorganized, by September 15, more than 700 people were working each day in the EOC. It mirrored the old one and was fully functional. Thus, "although the EOC was destroyed, the emergency management organization was not. Rather, the organization in New York City exhibited robust, adaptive behavior, demonstrating considerable improvisation, evidence of goal-directed solution-seeking and incorporating resources from diverse sources" (Kendra and Wachtendorf 2003, p. 45).

Mapping and GIS functions were also adapted after 9/11 (Kendra and Wachtendorf 2003, p. 130). The collapse of numerous buildings at the WTC altered the cityscape. It resulted in several road closures and detours. The destruction created a need for a tracking system to monitor all of the people involved in response. The OEM developed a map creation and distribution system based on GIS. It was developed with local students and professors, technology specialists from New York, and software representatives from the ArcInfo vendor. Responders were able to request and pick up maps. These maps included the locations of command posts, warehouses, food-serving stations, and sanitation facilities. "The activities related to mapping and spatial analysis [therefore] illustrate . . . entrepreneurial creativity . . . " (Kendra and Wachtendorf 2003, p. 131).

Improvisation was also evident in the massive waterborne evacuation (Kendra and Wachtendorf 2003, p. 133). When the attacks on the WTC occurred, the government feared that additional terrorist events could take place on bridges or in tunnels. The collapse of the buildings also rendered some of the subways inoperable. Citizens and government officials recognized the need to leave the affected area and return home, but there were limited transportation systems available for this purpose. Tour boats, military vessels, passenger ferries, and private craft worked on an ad hoc basis with the Coast Guard to evacuate people from lower Manhattan. Coast Guard inspectors permitted vessels to exceed normal passenger capacities. They relied on their experience and judgment to determine the extent to which regulations could be safely loosened. Emergent self-organization, and flexibility from the Coast Guard, resulted in an impressive evacuation of 500,000 people from Manhattan. Such an evacuation may never have occurred to this extent by water before, although some might say that the Dunkirk experience in World War II came close to or exceeded it.

Creativity and flexibility were also prevalent features of the credentialing system (Kendra and Wachtendorf 2003). "Not only was the September 11th incident a high-impact disaster that produced numerous casualties, it was also a complex emergency with added ambiguous dimensions such as the ongoing terrorist threat, the criminal investigation, an ongoing process of remains recovery and identification that persisted more than six months after the attack, and a very dangerous collapse site situated within close range of an extremely densely populated urban area" (Kendra and Wachtendorf 2003, p. 134).

These facts, along with the loss of standard OEM visitor badges, suggested that a check-in procedure would be needed to allow access and maintain safety and security at the same time. At first, anyone needing to enter ground zero would be given a blue and yellow badge. Later on, white badges were issued. These were photo IDs. The badges had codes for different levels and locations of access. Other temporary badges were distributed to contractors and volunteers who needed to enter the site for a limited time only. Only a limited number of these temporary badges were issued, usually 20 at a time. Contractors found ways to skirt the system. For instance, one worker would take the badges from 19 individuals who already entered the site. He then gave them to new workers so they could also gain access. The credentialing system was an example of creativity. Emergency managers classified sensitive areas. For example, ground zero regarded to be a sensitive area. They ascertained who required access. They instituted a system for issuing and tracking badges. They improved the system over time. (Kendra and Wachtendorf 2003, p. 135) These cases of improvisation, creativity, and flexibility illustrate how response operations can be successful despite significant challenges.

FOR EXAMPLE

Departing From SOPs

Adapting to disasters is beneficial in almost every situation. It gives you flexibility to adapt to any contingency you might face. However, some standard operating procedures are created for a very specific reason—the protection of emergency workers. If emergency responders rush in to the scene of an incident without considering their own vulnerability, they may become victims of the disaster. This is sure to complicate response operations. Checking in with incident command, working with others, and taking breaks frequently are SOPs that can enhance safety (see Figure 13-3).

Figure 13-3

During flood disasters, evacuation can be improvised
with the use of fishing or other types of boats.

SELF-CHECK

- What is **improvisation**?
- Why are creativity and flexibility important after disasters?
- What lessons are learned from the response to the 9/11 terrorist attacks?
- Why is improvisation regarded to be one of the twin foundations of emergency management?

13.10 Professionalism in Emergency Management

Besides preparing communities for disaster and being willing to improvise when needed, you should develop professional characteristics to enhance your job. Up until the past two decades, emergency management was not seen as a profession. Those who had posts in civil defense and emergency management did not have training or education in emergency management. Many obtained their positions because of their understanding of war and experience in armed conflict. Even in recent times, there has been only one head of FEMA who was a professional emergency manager. His name was James Lee Witt. He served under President Clinton during much of the 1990s.

Things are now changing. Emergency management is evolving into a profession. A **profession** is an occupation that is based on scientific knowledge and is respected by the community. There are now undergraduate and graduate degrees offered in this field. There are continuing education requirements and demands for those employed in this career. Professional associations now exist. As natural, technological hazards and terrorism continue to confront the United States, emergency managers are recognized more and more for the vast knowledge and skills they have to deal with disasters.

In 1987, the well-known disaster sociologist Thomas Drabek interviewed officials and personnel from 62 cities. The responses from those interviewed reveal that successful emergency managers are regarded as professionals. They have unique individual qualities. They perform vital services. Professional emergency managers are individuals who have specialized knowledge regarding disasters and what to do about them. They understand legislation and are highly committed to their work. Those regarded to be professionals can motivate others to action. They integrate diverse organizations into the emergency management system. They can also resolve interorganizational conflict through mediation (Drabek 1987).

The unique qualities of successful emergency managers are consistent in many cases. Some of the most frequently mentioned characteristics include skills in communications, managing human resources, and maintaining a calm personality while under duress. Other qualities varied. They included technical training, military background, or an ability to work with volunteers (Drabek 1987).

According to Drabek, there are three types of activities performed by successful emergency managers. First is the ability to shift from a narrow focus on civil defense issues to a more comprehensive form of emergency management. In other words, successful emergency managers acknowledge the diversity of hazards that threaten their communities. Second, professional emergency managers are able to elevate the visibility and respect others had for the emergency management program. This means that they have gained the same recognition as other departments. Finally, successful managers are able to accomplish certain goals. For example, they are able to establish a new EOC, purchase a warning system, undertake a training program, or educate the community about disasters (Drabek 1987).

There are three additional principles associated with professionalism. The first is knowing the science of the field. To be a good emergency manager, you will need to understand the hazards threatening your jurisdiction and the functions that need to be performed when a disaster strikes. This understanding comes with education and experience. The second principle is networking with others. You will need to work with others in different agencies and at different levels of government. Collaboration is built on good communication and the fostering of a relationship of trust. You will also need to be a successful advocate. You will need to push for change. You can do this by helping to put emergency management on the political agenda. You will need to use your knowledge and networking ability to influence policy and increase funding and support for emergency management.

13.10.1 Leadership

In addition to being a professional, you also need to be a leader. Leadership and its attributes have been the focus of many scholarly studies. **Leadership** is an ability to motivate others to reach a goal or complete a task. Claire Rubin outlines the importance of leadership in emergency management in her book, *Community Recovery from a Major Natural Disaster*. Her research reveals that there are several qualities associated with good leaders in emergency management.

Rubin states that leaders are able to decide what to do when a disaster occurs. You must decide who you want to participate in the planning and implementation of recovery (Rubin 1985, p. 45). The quicker you are able to put resources to work and let people know what their tasks are, the more effective recovery operations will be. It is much easier to do this quickly if you already have a plan in place. It is also easier if you have experience in a prior disaster.

Rubin also points out that effective leaders understand governmental relationships. She states, "since the quality of intergovernmental relations is of paramount importance to efficient recovery, it is necessary to attend to the many intergovernmental activities entailed in recovery promptly and efficiently after a major disaster" (Rubin 1985, p. 46). As we witnessed from Hurricane Katrina, the local, state, and federal governments' interactions can be tense after a disaster. Recovery is most successful when local officials use their status as leaders to work closely with their governor, Congressional representatives, and other federal officials. Strong leaders know how to get resources from the state and federal governments (Rubin 1985, p. 50).

Another important attribute of strong leadership is having a vision of what the community should look like after a disaster. When officials have a vision of

---

FOR EXAMPLE

Rudy Giuliani and Leadership

After the terror attacks on September 11, 2001, New York Mayor Rudy Giuliani was widely praised for his strong leadership. Giuliani was recognized for his close oversight of rescue and recovery efforts. He coordinated the response of many different city departments. He communicated to the state and federal authorities the support that New York would need. He used the assistance not only for the World Trade center but also for citywide anti-terrorist measures and rebuilding. At the end of 2001, *Time* magazine named him as Person of the Year.

---

how the community can rebound, then it is much easier to reach those goals (Rubin 1985, p. 49). Rubin asserts, "If you view a heavily damaged area as a site for 'instant urban renewal', a broader perspective and a wider array of reconstruction options will be maintained during the recovery and planning process" (1985, p. 47). Her research reminds us that leadership is vital if you are to be an effective emergency manager.

SELF-CHECK

- What is a **profession**?
- Is emergency management a profession?
- What are the qualities of professional emergency managers?
- What is **leadership**?
- What are the characteristics of strong leaders in the field of emergency management?

SUMMARY

Disasters pose serious problems for communities. Emergency managers as well as first responders are needed to effectively respond and recover when disasters occur. For this reason, it is imperative that those working in the field understand human behavior in disasters, alternative management approaches, and the many response and recovery functions that must be performed in emergency management. In addition, it is vital that emergency managers understand the challenges disasters present as well as tools and strategies that can improve post-disaster management. However, it should be recognized that effective response and recovery operations are most likely to be facilitated when four conditions are met: the community has built capacity through preparedness, those responding to disasters are willing to improvise if needed, the emergency manager is a highly trained professional, and those working in the field possess strong leadership skills. If these steps are taken to ensure readiness, you will most likely facilitate effective response and recovery operations when disasters occur. Resilience is a very important goal to be sought by today's emergency manager. As an emergency manager, it is your responsibility to promote it.

KEY TERMS

Budget	An allocation of monetary support for a given department by city or county leadership.
Community Emergency Response Teams (CERTs)	Groups of citizens that have received detailed information and specialized training to improve self-sufficiency in disasters.
Controller	Person who runs the exercise by initiating the events and distributing messages to be acted upon.
Creativity	Finding ways to resolve problems through unanticipated means.
Drill	A small and limited exercise to improve a single function in response operations
Emergency Operations Plan (EOP)	A document that describes what the community will do in the aftermath of a disaster.
Evaluators	People who determine if the players responded to the exercise effectively and in accordance to established policies and procedures.
Exercise	A simulation of a crisis, emergency, or disaster that has the goal of improving response and recovery operations in an actual event.
Flexibility	A willingness to depart from widely accepted standards and practices of doing things (thinking creatively and improvising solutions) in order to react effectively to unforeseen problems.
Full-scale exercise	A very large simulation which tests nearly all response and recovery capabilities
Functional exercise	A moderately sized drill to test a limited number of response and recovery capabilities.

Hazard and vulnerability assessment	An evaluation of the risks facing your community along with your capability for dealing with them.
Improvisation	Adapting to an unfolding situation.
Leadership	An ability to motivate others to reach a goal or complete a task.
Orientation	An informal introductory meeting.
Players	The responders or department leaders that are evaluated in the exercise.
Preparedness	The building capabilities to improve the effectiveness of response and recovery operations.
Profession	An occupation that is based on scientific knowledge and is respected by the community.
Public disaster education	A concerted effort to inform people about hazards and what to do if a disaster should occur.
Resource list	A database that includes human and material resources that can be deployed in a disaster.
Table-top	An informal discussion of a mock emergency or disaster situation.
Training	A review of emergency procedures as well as their application in a nonthreatening situation.
Victims	Simulators who provide opportunities to test the players' knowledge and skills.

ASSESS YOUR UNDERSTANDING

Go to www.wiley.com/college/McEntire to evaluate your knowledge of promoting disaster resilience.
Measure your learning by comparing pretest and post-test results.

Summary Questions

1. Preparedness has been described as one of the twin foundations of emergency management. True or False?

2. Creating an ordinance is one of the first steps you will take to prepare your community for disasters. True or False?

3. An LEPC is an example of a preparedness council. True or False?

4. Resources needed for emergency management include budgets only. True or False?

5. A resource list should be updated at least once each year. True or False?

6. Emergency managers can find out more about grants by talking to colleagues or searching government websites. True or False?

7. There are no grants that help to improve mitigation measures. True or False?

8. Once you've been given a grant, you will not need to submit any additional paperwork. True or False?

9. Life support requirements for EOCs include food service and sanitary facilities. True or False?

10. Geographers can help you with a hazard and vulnerability assessment, but not scholars or meteorologists. True or False?

11. Direction and control address the role of the top officials in the given jurisdiction. True or False?

12. Training courses are available through the state only. True or False?

13. A full-scale exercise does not produce any stress for the participants. True or False?

14. The narrative is an introduction to a disaster exercise. True or False?

15. The controller is the person who manages the disaster exercise. True or False?

16. Citizens always know what to do when a disaster occurs. True or False?

17. Improvisation, creativity, and flexibility are closely related. True or False?

18. There was improvisation in the re-establishment of the EOC but not in mapping and GIS functions. True or False?

19. Professional emergency managers have special knowledge and skills and know what to do when a disaster occurs. True or False?

20. Leaders can use their status to obtain additional assistance for disaster recovery. True or False?

21. Preparedness may be defined as:

   (a) Planning and resource identification

   (b) Training

   (c) Foreseeing potential problems and finding solutions

   (d) Building capabilities to respond and recover

   (e) All of the above

22. Which of the following is not included in an ordinance:

   (a) Justification

   (b) Concept of operations

   (c) Powers and duties

   (d) Expenditures and contracts

   (e) Violations and penalties

23. Who is included on a preparedness council?

   (a) The mayor and city manager

   (b) Department leaders from local government

   (c) Private and nonprofit organizations

   (d) All of the above

   (e) All of the above except private organizations

24. In order to develop a resource list, you should:

   (a) Include names and contact information

   (b) Inventory equipment and vehicles

   (c) a and b

   (d) Not worry about updating the list periodically

   (e) Avoid preapproved contracts with vendors and other service providers

25. A budget is:

   (a) A function in disaster response

   (b) An allocation of monetary support given by the city leadership

   (c) A function in disaster recovery

   (d) A grant administrated by the federal government

   (e) An exercise program that is run by the controller

26. EMPG money:

   (a) Covers travel and equipment only

   (b) May pay a portion of your salary

   (c) Will fund the purchase of vehicles

   (d) Will pay for convict labor

   (e) None of the above

27. Grant proposals often include:
    (a) The goals of the grant
    (b) The team involved in the project
    (c) The work plan
    (d) Information on matching funds
    (e) All of the above

28. An EOC should:
    (a) Be located in a safe area
    (b) Have a back up location
    (c) Have a clearly identified opening procedure
    (d) a, b, and c
    (e) a and b

29. Resources to help you complete a hazard and vulnerability assessment include:
    (a) Flood plain managers only
    (b) Scholars but not emergency management colleagues
    (c) Historical data on prior disasters
    (d) All of the above
    (e) None of the above

30. Which component of a plan describes the hazards faced by the community?
    (a) Authority
    (b) Purpose
    (c) Situation and assumptions
    (d) Concept of operations
    (e) Direction and control

31. Training courses are offered:
    (a) At the local level only
    (b) Across multiple jurisdictions
    (c) By the federal government alone
    (d) By the FBI but not FEMA
    (e) None of the above

32. Which type of exercise is an informal introductory meeting?
    (a) An orientation
    (b) A drill
    (c) A table-top
    (d) A functional exercise
    (e) A full-scale exercise

33. An expected action:
    (a) Identifies what functions are to be tested
    (b) Includes a clear statement of what is to be tested
    (c) Introduces the disaster event
    (d) Lists how participants might respond to the problems they encounter
    (e) All of the above

34. Who is in charge of determining if the exercise participants are responding effectively?
    (a) The controller
    (b) The evaluators
    (c) The players
    (d) The simulators
    (e) The victims

35. Who should be educated about disasters?
    (a) Individuals
    (b) School children
    (c) Families
    (d) Businesses
    (e) All of the above

36. What is another foundation of emergency management?
    (a) Improvisation
    (b) Exercises
    (c) Grant management
    (d) Public education
    (e) Leadership

37. Professional emergency managers:
    (a) Focus on more than just one type of hazard
    (b) Gain respect from their co-workers
    (c) Can accomplish the programmatic goals
    (d) All of the above
    (e) a and b

38. Leadership may be defined as:
    (a) An ability to improvise
    (b) An ability to motivate others to a common goal
    (c) An ability to increase your proportion of the city budget
    (d) A willingness to be flexible in disasters
    (e) None of the above

Review Questions

1. What is disaster preparedness?
2. Why is preparedness important?
3. What is an ordinance?
4. How can you establish a preparedness council?
5. What resources are needed to increase your community's level of readiness?
6. How can budgets support your emergency management program?
7. What types of grants exist, and how can you apply for and manage them effectively?
8. How would you establish an EOC if you did not have one?
9. What type of information is included in a hazard and vulnerability assessment?
10. What are the various sections of an EOP?
11. How does one go about writing an EOP?
12. Why does training improve your emergency management capabilities?
13. What are the five types of exercises?
14. How can exercises be managed effectively?
15. What are the major participants in disaster exercises?
16. What can you do to educate the public about disasters?
17. What is improvisation? Creativity? Flexibility?
18. What lessons do we learn from the response to the 9/11 disaster?
19. What are the common characteristics of professional emergency managers?
20. What skills should you develop to be an effective leader after disasters?

Applying This Chapter

1. You are the emergency manager on an Indian reservation in Oklahoma. Your tribe operates several casinos that are located somewhat close to an interstate where hazardous waste is transported. What steps do you take to prepare for a hazardous materials incident?
2. You are an emergency manager in Ohio. Spring is right around the corner, and the possibility of severe weather will be increasing. What can you do to promote preparedness in your community?
3. The city manager in your community has asked you to obtain additional funding for emergency management in light of recent revenue shortfalls. Where can you learn about grants? What steps do you have to take to apply for them?

4. As a new emergency manager in Los Angeles, you have been asked to revise the city's hazard and vulnerability analysis. Where do you start? Who can help you with this task?

5. You are an emergency manager in Atlanta. A major power outage has occurred, and your EOC backup generation system is not working properly. How can you find out what is going on with the electrical grid? What options do you have to communicate with others? Why would it be necessary to improvise in this situation?

6. One of your major responsibilities as an emergency manager is to update the emergency operations plan annually. Who can you include in the process of accomplishing this assignment?

7. You work for the American Red Cross headquarters near Washington, D.C. You have been assigned to develop a training program for all of the employees and volunteers associated with this organization. What types of programs and materials could help you fulfill this goal?

8. You have just been hired as an emergency manager in Lincoln, Nebraska. Why is it important that you approach your career in a professional manner? What can you do to be regarded as a professional emergency manager?

9. As an emergency manager in Pueblo, Colorado, you are supposed to put in at least 10 hours of public education every month. Who or what organizations might benefit from your knowledge? What would you teach them?

10. Terrorists have just shot scores of people in a busy shopping mall. There are several deaths, a number of injuries, and a great deal of concern on the part of the public. Would leadership be important in this situation? How can you lead the community through the response and recovery operations in an effective manner?

Hazard and Vulnerability Assessment

You were recently appointed as the emergency manager for a small city in South Carolina. Your mayor has asked you to conduct a hazard and vulnerability assessment. What do you need to consider when performing such an assessment?

Acquiring Resources

You are the public health official in charge of preparing Pittsburg for a bioterrorism attack. You need funding for all phases of emergency management. What sources do you look to for funding? What else can you do to acquire equipment, supplies, and personnel?

Leadership

You are the emergency manager in Laguna Niguel, California. A major earthquake has just occurred, waking you up in the middle of the night. Because the earthquake has caused some minor damage in your home, you get in your car to drive to the EOC. On the way, you make a few phone calls to get a status on the situation. What other steps do you need to take to ensure all necessary functions are being completed in this disaster?

BIBLIOGRAPHY

Aguirre, Benigno E. 1988. "The Lack of Warnings Before the Saragosa Tornado." *International Journal of Mass Emergencies and Disasters* 6 (1): 65–74.

Aguirre, B., Wenger, D., Glass, T., Murillo, M., and Vigo, G. (1995). The social organization of search and rescue: evidence from the Guadalajara gasoline explosion. *International Journal of Mass Emergencies and Disasters,* 13(1), 67–92.

Associated Press. 2005. "Security Goes High Tech for Inauguration," January 18.

Auf der Heide, Erik. 1987. "The Media: Friend and Foe." Chapter 10 in *Disaster Response: Principles of Preparation and Coordination*. http://coe.dmha.org/dr/flash/htm.

Auf der Heide, Erik. 1987. "Triage," Chapter 8 in *Disaster Response: Principles and Practices for Coordination,* http://www.coe-dmha.org/dr/flash.htm.

Auf der Heide, E. (1989). The apathy factor. Chapter 2. *Disaster Response: Principles for Preparedness and Coordination*. Retrieved May 18, 2005, from http://orgmail2.coe-dmha.org/dr/flash.htm.

Auf der Heide, Erik. 1989. "The Paper Plan Syndrome." Chapter 3 in *Disaster Response: Principles of Preparation and Coordination*. http://coe.dmha.org/dr/flash.htm.

Baker, Earl J. 1990. "Evacuation Decision Making and Public Response in Hurricane Hugo in South Carolina." *Quick Response Research Report #39*. Natural Hazards Research and Applications Informaion Center, University of Colorado: Boulder, Colorado.

Barnett-Queen, Timothy and Lawrence H. Bergmann. 1989. "Counseling and Critical Incident Stress." *The Voice* (August/September): 15–18.

Barron, James. 2004. "Many Saw Free Air-Conditioner in Post-9/11 Clean-Air Program." *New York Times*. November 2. New York/Region Section. p. A1.

Bates, Frederick L. and Walter Gillis Peacock. 1989. "Long Term Recovery." *International Journal of Mass Emergencies and Disasters* 17 (3): 349–365.

Beggs, John J., Valerie A. Haines and Jeanne S. Hurlbert. 1996. "The Effects of Personal Network and Local Community Contexts on the Receipt of Formal Aid during Disaster Recovery." *International Juournal of Mass Emergencies and Disasters* 14 (1): 57–78.

Bierschenk, Ed. 2004. "Rules for Collecting Storm Waste Confusing Even to FEMA Reps." *Vero Beach Press Journal*. October 14.

Birkland, Thomas A. 1997. *After Disaster: Agenda Setting, Public Policy, and Focusing Events*. Washington D.C., Georgetown University Press.

Bolin, Robert and Lois Stanford. 1998. "The Northridge Earthquake: Community-based Approaches to Unmet Recovery Needs." *Disasters* 22 (1): 21–28.

Bowers, W.F. 1960. *Surgical Philosophy in Mass Casualty Management*. CC Thomas: Springfield, IL.

Britton, N. and Clark, G. J. (2000). From Response to Resilience: Emergency Management Reform in New Zealand. *Natural Hazards Review,* 1(3), 145–150.

Britton, Neil. 1989. Anticipating the Unexpected: Is the Bureaucracy Able to Come to the Party?" *Working Paper #1*. Disaster Management Studies Centre, Cumberland College of Health Sciences, University of Sydney: Sydney, Australia.

Britton, Neil R. 1989. "Reflections on Australian Disaster Management: A Critique of the Administration of Social Crisis." Disaster Management Studies Centre, Cumberland College of Health Science, University of Sydney: Sydney, Australia.

Britton, Neil R. 1991. "Constraint or Effectiveness in Disaster Management: The Bureaucratic Imperative Versus Organizational Mission." *Canberra Bulletin of Public Administration* 64: 54–64.

Burkhart, Ford N. 1987. "Experts and the Press Under Stress: Disaster Journalism Gets Mixed Reviews." *International Journal of Mass Emergencies and Disasters* 5 (3): 357–367.

Bush, George W. 2003. "Homeland Security Presidential Directive/ HSPD-5."http://www.whitehouse.gov/news/releases/2003/02/ 20030228-9.html

Bush, George W. 2003. "Homeland Security Presidential Directive/ HSPD-8."   http://www.whitehouse.gov/news/releases/2003/12/ 20031217-6.html

Campbell Public Affairs Institute. 2002. *Governance and Public Security*. New York: Syracuse University.

Cannon, T. (1993). "A hazard need not a disaster make: vulnerability and the causes of natural disasters." In Merriman, P. A. and Browitt, C. W. A. (Eds.), *Natural disasters: protecting vulnerability communities,* London: Thomas Telford.

CDC b. 2006. "Avian Influenza (Bird Flu)." Accessed at http://www.cdc.gov/flu/avian/index.htm on February 7, 2006.

CDC c. 2006. "Embargo of Birds from Specified Countries." Accessed at http://www.cdc.gov/flu/avian/outbreaks/embargo.htm on February 7, 2006.

CDC d. 2006. "Avian Influenza Infection in Humans." Accessed at http://www.cdc.gov/flu/avian/gen-info/avian-flu-humans.htm on

CDC e. 2006. "Avian Influenza Vaccines." Accessed at http://www.cdc.gov/flu/avian/gen-info/vaccines.htm on February 7, 2006.

CDC f. 2006. "Interim Recommendations for Infection Control in Health-Care Facilities Caring for Patients with Known or Suspected Avian Influenza." Accessed at http://www.cdc.gov/flu/avian/professional/infect-control.htm on February 7, 2006.

CDC g. 2006. "Avian Influenza: Current Situation." Accessed at http://www.cdc.gov/flu/avian/outbreaks/current.htm on February 7, 2006.

CDC 1998. "Deaths Among Children During an Outbreak of Hand, Foot, and Mouth Disease—Taiwan, Republic of China, April–July 1998." http://www.cdc.gov/mmwr/preview/mmwrhtml/00054640.htm accessed on February 6, 2006.

CDC 2005. "Quarantine Questions and Answers on the Executive Order Adding

CDC. 2006. Potentially Pandemic Influenza Viruses to the List of Quarantinable Diseases" Accessed at www.cdc.gov/ncidod/dq/qa_influenza_amendment_to_eo_13295.htm June 11,2005.

CDC, 2006. "Hand, Foot, and Mouth Disease." http://www.cdc.gov/ncidod/dvrd/revb/enterovirus/hfhf.htm accessed on January 1, 2006.

CDC. 2006. "Key Facts." Accessed at http://www.cdc.gov/flu/avian/gen-info/facts.htm on February 6, 2006.

CDC, 2003. "Epidemic/Epizootic West Nile Virus in the United States: Guidelines for Surveillance, Prevention, and Control http://www.cdc.gov/ncidod/dvbid/westnile/resources/wnv-guidelines-apr-2001.pdf

CDC, 2006. "Frequently Asked Questions About SARS." http://www.cdc.gov/ncidod/sars/faq.htm accessed January 29, 2006.

CDC, 2006. "Overview of West Nile Virus." http://www.cdc.gov/ncidod/dvbid/westnile/qa/overview.htm accessed January 31, 2006.

CDC, 2006. "Prevention." http://www.cdc.gov/ncidod/dvbid/westnile/qa/prevention.htm accessed January 31, 2006.

CDC, 2006. "Testing and Treating West Nile Virus in Humans." http://www.cdc.gov/ncidod/dvbid/westnile/qa/testing_treating.htm accessed on January 31, 2006.

CDC, 2006. "Transmission." http://www.cdc.gov/ncidod/dvbid/westnile/qa/transmission.htm

CDC, 2006. "West Nile Virus Vaccine." http://www.cdc.gov/ncidod/dvbid/westnile/qa/wnv_vaccine.htm accessed on January 31, 2006.

CERT Training Manual. http://training.fema.gov/EMIWeb/CERT/mtrls.asp.Federal Emergency Management Agency: Washington, D.C.

Champion, Howard R., William J. Sacco, Patricia S. Gainer and Susan M. Patow. 1988. "The Effect of Medical Direction on Trauma Triage." *Journal of Trauma* 28 (2): 235–239.

Coile, Russell C. 1994. "Emergency Managers Mutual Aid in California." *ASPEP Journal.* 57–62.

Coile, Russell C. 1997. "The Role of Amateur Radio in Providing Emergency Electronic Communication for Disaster Management." *Disaster Prevention and Management* 6 (3): 176–185.

Corneil, Wayne. 1989. "Firefighters Suffer Critical Incident Stress: Stress in the Aftermath of Disasters." *Emergency Preparedness Digest* 16 (1): 24–27.

Curran, Eddie. 2004. "FEMA to Pay for Mobile Cleanup, Not Baldwin." *Mobile Register.* September 19.

Daines, G. E. (1991). Planning, training and exercising. In G. J. Hoetmer and T. E. Drabek (Eds.), *Emergency management: principles and practice for local government.* Washington, D.C.: ICMA.

Dash, Nicole. 1997. "The Use of Geographic Information Systems in Disaster Research." *International Journal of Mass Emergencies and Disasters* 15 (1): 135–146.

Dees, Tim. 2000. "Information and Communications Technology for Public Safety." *IQ Service Report* 32 (1). ICMA: Washington, D.C.

DeParle, J. 1996. "Slamming the Door." *The New York Times Magazine.* 20: 52.

Department of Health and Human Services, National Disaster Medical System. 2003. "What is a Disaster Mortuary Operational Response Team?" http://www.ndms.dhhs.gov/NDMS/About_Teams/about_teams.html#dmort.

DOD. Improving Local and State Agency Response to Terrorist Incidents Involving Biological Weapons, Interim Planning Guide. 2000. Washington, D.C.: Department of Defense, 2000. www2.sbccom.army.mil/hld/downloads/bwirp/bwirp_interim_planning_guide.p

Drabek, Thomas E. (1985). "Managing the emergency response", *Public Administration Review,* 45(January), 85–92.

Drabek, T. E. (1986). *Human system responses to disaster: an inventory of sociological findings.* New York: Springer Verlag.

Drabek, T. E. (1987). "Emergent structures." In Dynes, R. Marchi, B. and Pelanda, C. (Eds.), *Sociology of Disasters: Contribution of Sociology to Disaster Research,* Milan,: Franco Angeli.

Drabek, T. E. (1991). "The evolution of emergency management." In G. J. Hoetmer & T. E. Drabek (Eds.), *Emergency management: principles and practice for local government.* Washington, D.C.: ICMA.

Drabek, T. E. and McEntire, D. A. (2002). "Emergent phenomena and the sociology of disaster: lessons, trends and opportunities from the research literature." *Disaster Prevention and Management,* 12(2), 97–112.

Drabek, Thomas E. and David A. McEntire. 2003. "Emergent Phenomena and the Sociology of Disaster: Lessons, Trends and Opportunities from the Research Literature." *Disaster Prevention and Management* 12 (2): 97–112.

Dror, Yehezkel. 1988. "Decision Making under Disaster Conditions." In Louise K. Comfort, *Managing Disaster: Strategies and Policy Perspectives.* Pp. 255–275. Duke University Press: Durham.

Dwyer, Jim and Kevin Flynn. 2005. 102 Minutes: *The Untold Story of the Fight to Survive Inside the Twin Towers.* Henry Holt: New York.

Dynes, R. (1970). *Organized Behavior in Disaster.* Lexington, MA: Lexington Books.

Dynes, R. (1988). "Cross-Cultural International Research: Sociology and disaster." *International Journal of Mass Emergencies and Disasters,* 6(2), 101–129.

Dynes, R. (1994). "Community emergency planning: false assumptions and inappropriate analogies." *International Journal of Mass Emergencies and Disasters,* 12(2), 141–158.

Dynes, R. (2003). "Finding order in disorder: continuities in the 9-11 response." *International Journal of Mass Emergencies and Disasters,* 21(3): 9–23.

Edwards-Winslow, Frances. 2002. "Changing the Emergency Management Paradigm: A Case Study of San Jose, California."

Eldar, Reuben. 1992. "The Needs of Elderly Persons in Natural Disasters: Observations and Recommendations." *Disasters* 16(4) 355–357.

Enarson, Elaine. 1999. "Women and Housing Issues in Two U.S. Disasters: Hurricane Andrew and the Red River Valley Flood." *International Journal of Mass Emergencies and Disasters* 17(1): 39–63.

Enarson, E. and B. H. Morrow. 1997. "A Gendered Perspective: The Voices of Women." In W. G. Peacock, B. H. Vorrow and H. Gladwin (eds.) *Hurricane Andrew: Ethnicity, Gender and the Sociology of Disasters*. Routledge: New York.

Environmental Protection Agency. 1995. *Planning for Disaster Debris*. EPA530-K-95-010. Office of Solid Waste: Washington, D.C.

EPA. 2006. Accessed at http://yosemite.epa.gov/oar/globalwarming.nsf/content/index.html on January18, 2006.

ESRI. 1995. "Florida Department of Environmental Protection Wins Major Distinction for Marine Spill GIS." ARC?NEWS< Spring: http://www.esri.com/headlines/arcnews/spring95articles/florida.html.

FEMA. "Introduction to Debris Operations in FEMA's Public Assistance Program." (IS-632) http://training.fema.gov/emiweb/IS/is632.asp

FEMA. 1994. "Inspection of FEMA's Debris Removal Mission," http://www.fema.gov/ig/i-01-94.shtm.

FEMA. 1997. *Debris Management Course*. Emergency Management Institute, National Emergency Training Center: Emmitsburg, Md.

FEMA. 1997. *Multi-hazard identification and risk assessment: a cornerstone of the national mitigation strategy*. Washington, D.C.: FEMA.

FEMA. 1998. *Incident Command System*. Independent Study–195. Emergency Management Institute: Emmitsburg, Maryland.

FEMA. 1999. *Public Assistance Debris Management Guide*. Washington, D.C.

FEMA. 2000. Equipment Cache List. See http://www.fema.gov/pdf/usr/tfcache2000.pdf.

FEMA. 2000. *Urban Search & Rescue Response System Operations Manual*. See http://www.fema.gov/usr/usrdocs.shtm.

FEMA. 2001. "Local Governments Should be Aware of Fraudulent Debris Contractors." http://www.fema.gov/diz00/d1354n24.shtm.

FEMA. 2001. *Urban Search & Rescue Field Operations Guide*. See http://www.fema.gov/usr/usrdocs.shtm.

FEMA. 2002. *Mass Fatalities Incident Response*, Course G386 (March).

FEMA. 2003. "Chapter 5: Light Search and Rescue." *In Community Emergency Response Teams Training Manual*. Http://training.fema.gov/EMIWeb/cert/mtrls.asp. Emergency Management Institute, Federal Emergency Management Agency: Emmitsburg, Md.

FEMA. 2003. "Debris Removal Management Issues," *OPM Circular A-102*. http://www.fema.gov/doc.ig/debrisremoval.doc.

FEMA. 2003. "Disposing of Debris and Removing Hazardous Waste." Http://www.fema.gov/regions/iii/env/debris.shtm.

FEMA. *EMI Workshop E270,* "Workshop in Emergency Management: Asking for Help."

FEMA. 1995. *An Orientation to Community Disaster Exercises.* IS-SM 120. Federal Emergency Management Agency: Emmitsburg, Md. http://training.fema.gov/EMIWeb/is/crslist.asp.

FEMA. 1996. *Guide for All-hazard Emergency Operations Planning.* SLG-101. Federal Emergency Management Agency: Emmitsburg, Md. http://training.fema.gov/EMIWeb/is/crslist.asp.

FEMA. 1997. *A Citizen's Guide to Disaster Assistance.* IS-7. FEMA: Washington, D.C.

FEMA. 1981. *Disaster Operations: A Handbook for Local Government.* Washington, D.C.

FEMA. 1995. *The EOCs Role in Community Preparedness, Response and Recovery. Independent Study* 275. Emergency Management Institute: Emmitsburg, Maryland. http://training.fema.gove/EMIWeb/IS/is275.asp.

FEMA. 1999. *The Role of Voluntary Agencies in Emergency Management.* IS-288. Federal Emergency Management Agency: Emmitsburg, Md.

FEMA. 1999. *When Disaster Strikes, Donated Goods and Volunteers May Be Needed; How You Can Help.* Washington, D.C.

FEMA. 1998. Incident Command System. *Independent Study – 195.* Emergency Management Institute: Emmitsburg.

FEMA. 2004. *National Incident Management System (NIMS), An Introduction.* IS-700. http://training.fema.gov/EMIWeb/IS/is700.asp

FEMA 2002. Myths NEED CITATION?

FEMA. 2003. "Chapter 5: Light Search and Rescue." *Community Emergency Response Teams Training Manual.* Http://training.fema.gov/EMIWeb/cert/mtrls.asp. Emergency Management Institute, Federal Emergency Management Agency: Emmitsburg, MD.

FEMA. 2004. National Response Plan, An Introduction. IS-800. http://training.fema.gov/EMIWeb/IS/is800.asp

Ferrante, Julia. 2004. "Clear Out Storm Debris By Friday." *Tampa Tribune.* October 13.

Fischer, Henry W. III. 1998. *Response to Disaster: Fact Versus Fiction and its Perpetuation: The Sociology of Disaster.* Lanham, MD.: University Press of America.

Fischer, Henry W. III. 1998. "The Role of the New Information Technologies in Emergency Mitigation, Planning, Response and Recovery." *Disaster Prevention and Management* 7 (1): 28–37.

Fothergill, Alice, Enrique G. M. Maestas, and JoAnne DeRouen Darlington. 1999. "Race, Ethnicity and Disasters in the United States: A Review of the Literature." *Disasters* 33 (2): 156–173.

Fothergill, Alice. 1996. "Gender, Risk and Disaster." *International Journal of Mass Emergencies and Disasters* 14 (1): 33–56.

French, Steven P. 1990. "The Damage Assessment Process: An Overview." pp. 17–24 in ed. Bolin, Robert. *The Loma Prieta Earthquake: Studies of Short-Term Impacts.* Program on Environment and Behavior Monograph #50, Institute of Behavioral Science, University of Colorado: Boulder, Colorado.

Gibbs, Margaret, Juliana R. Lachenmeyer, Arlene Broska and Richard Deucher. 1996. "Effects of the AVIANCA Aircrash on Disaster Workers." *International Journal of Mass Emergencies and Disasters* 14 (1): 23–32.

Gillespie, David F. and Calvin F. Streeter. 1987. "Conceptualizing and Measuring Disaster Preparedness." *International Journal of Mass Emergencies and Disasters* 5 (2): 155–176.

Godschalk, D. R. (1991). Disaster mitigation and hazard management. In G. J. Hoetmer and T. E. Drabek (Eds.), *Emergency management: principles and practice for local government.* Washington, D.C.: ICMA.

Goldon, Joseph H. and Christopher R. Adams. 2000. "The Tornado Problem: Forecast, Warning and Response." *Natural Hazards Review* 1 (2): 107–118.

Gordon McBean. 2004. "Climate Change and Extreme Weather: A Basis for Action." *Natural Hazards.* 31(1): 177–190.

Gordon, James A. 2002. *Comprehensive Emergency Management for Local Governments: Demystifying Emergency Planning.* Rothstein Associated Inc.: Brookfield, Ct.

Greene, J.D., Lindy, M.C., G.C. Gleser, A.C. Leonard, M. Korol, and C. Winget. 1990. Buffalo Creek Survivors in the Second Decade: Stability of Stress Symptoms. *American Journal of Orthopsychiatry.* 60 (1): 43–54.

Greene, R. W. 2002. *Confronting Catastrophe: A GIS Handbook.* ESRI Press: Redlands, Ca.

Gruntfest, Eve. 1998. "Internet and Emergency Management: Prospects for the Future." *International Journal of Mass Emergencies and Disasters* 16 (1): 55–72.

Hafer, Jacob L. and Victoria L. Fedor. 2004. *EMS and the Law.* Jones and Bartlett Publishers: Boston.

Hampson, Rick and Martha T. Moore. 2003. "Two Years After Sept. 11, NYC Couple to Bury Son." *USA Today.* Thursday, September 4, 1A–2A.

Handmer, John. 2006. "American Exceptionalism or Universal Lesson? The Implications of Hurricane Katrina for Australia." *Australian Journal of Emergency Management* 21 (1): 29–42.

Harbaugh, Bill. 2001. "So the Red Cross Tugged Hearts to Raise Money After the Sept. 11 Attacks; the Cause is Worthy and Donors, However Well-Intentioned, Don't Know What's Best." Oregonian, November 11. http://www.oregonlive.com/commentary/oregonian/index.ssf?/x.../10053969102097322.xm.

Harris, Vickie. 1989. "Beyond Critical Incident Stress." *The Voice* (August/September): 16–18.

Hatfield, Leonard F. 1990. *Sammy the Prince.* Hantsport: Lancelot Press.

Hooft, Peter J., Eric K. Noji and Herman P. Van De Voorde. 1989. "Fatality Management in Mass Casualty Incidents." *Forensic Science International* 40: 3–14.

http://westnilevirus.nbii.gov/diseasehome.jsp?disease=West%20Nile%20Virus&pa gemode=submit accessed January 31, 2006.

http://www.cdc.gov/flu/avian/gen-info/facts.htm on February 6, 2006.

http://www.cdc.gov/ncidod/dq/qa_influenza_amendment_to_eo_13295.htm#authority on February 7, 2006.

http://www.cdc.gov/ncidod/dvbid/westnile/qa/overview.htm accessed January

http://www.cdc.gov/ncidod/dvrd/revb/enterovirus/hfhf.htm accessed on January 1, 2006. CDC, 1998 "Deaths Among Children During an Outbreak of Hand, Foot, and Mouth Disease—Taiwan, Republic of China, April–July 1998." http://www.cdc.gov/mmwr/preview/mmwrhtml/00054640.htm accessed on February 6, 2006.

http://www.who.int/csr/don/2003_07_04/en/index.html accessed January 29,

Irwin, Robert L. 1989. "The Incident Command System (ICS)." Pp. 133–161 in Auf der Heide, Erik, *Disaster Response: Principles of Preparedness and Coordination.* CV Mosby Company: St. Louis, Mo.

James, Alma. 1992. "The Psychological Impact of Disaster and the Nature of Critical Incident Stress for Emergency Personnel." *Disaster Prevention and Management* 1 (1): 63–69.

Kendra, J. M. and Wachtendorf, T. (2003). Elements of resilience after the World Trade Center disaster: reconstituting New York City's emergency operations center. Disasters, 27(1), 37–53.

Kendra, James and Tricia Wachtendorf. 2003. "Creativity in Emergency Response to the World Trade Center Disaster." Pp. 121–146 in Monday, Jacqueline L. (ed.). *Beyond September 11th: An Account of Post-disaster Research. Program on Environment and Behavior Special Publication #39.* Institute of Behavioral Science: Natural Hazards Research and Applications Information Center: University of Colorado.

Kendra, James and Tricia Wachtendorf. 2003. "Elements of Resilience after the World Trade Center *Disaster:* Reconstituting New York City's Emergency Operations Center." *Disasters* 27 (1): 37–53.

Kendra, James M. and Tricia Wachtendorf. 2003. "Reconsidering Convergence and Converger Legitimacy in Response to the World Trade Center Disaster." Pp. 97–122 in Clarke, Lee (ed.) *Terrorism and Disaster: New Threats, New Ideas. Research in Social Problems and Public Policy.* 11. Elsevier: New York.

Kim, Susan. 1999a. "Making Disaster Donations Count." May 20, http://www.disasternews.com/howtohelp/greenbeans.shtml.

Kim, Susan. 1999b. "Needed Donations Can Change Lives." April 14, http://www.disasternews.comhowtohelp/gettingitright.shtml.

Kim, Susan. 1999c. "Unwanted Donations are 'Second Disaster.'" April 5, http://www.disasternews.com/howtohelp/inappropriate.shtml.

Kreps, Gary. 1991. "Organizing for Emergency Management." Pp. 30–54 in Drabek, Thomas and Gerard Hoetmer (eds.) *Emergency Management: Principles and Practice for Local Government.* International City Management Association: Washington, D.C.

Lindell, Michael K. and Ronald Perry. 1987. "Warning Mechanism in Emergency Response Systems." *International Journal of Mass Emergencies and Disasters.* 5 (2): 137–153.

Lindell, Michael K. 1994. "Are Local Emergency Planning Committees Effective in Developing Community Disaster Preparedness?" *International Journal of Mass Emergencies and Disasters* 12 (2): 159–182.

Lipsitch, Marc, Ted Cohen, Ben Cooper, James Robins, Stefan Ma, Lyn James, Gowri Gopalakrishna, Suok Kai Chew, Chor Chuan Tan, Matthew Samore, David Fisman, and Megan Murray, 2003. "Transmission Dynamics and Control of Severe Acute Respiratory Syndrome." *Science.* 300: 1966–1970.

Lowe, Seana and Alice Fothergil. 2003. "A Need to Help: Emergent Volunteer Behavior after September 11th." Pp. 293–314 in Monday, Jacqueline (ed.) *Beyond September 11th: An Account of Post-Disaster Research. Program on Environment and Behavior Special Publication #39.* Institute of Behavioral Science, Natural Hazards Research and Applications Information Center, University of Colorado: Boulder, Co.

Macko, Steve, "Lessons Learned from the Columbine Massacre," ERRI Emergency Services Report-EmergencyNet News Service-Friday, August 20, 1999-Vol.3–232

Mancini, Marguerite R. and Alice T. Gale. 1981. *Emergency Care and the Law.* Aspen: Rockville, MD.

Mariano, Willoughby. 2004. "Hurricane Debris Burdens Neighbors." *Orlando Sentinel.* October 9.

May, Peter. 1985. "Political Influence, Electoral Benefits and Disaster Relief." Pp. 104–128 in *Recovery from Catastrophe: Federal Disaster Relief Policy and Politics. Contributions in Political Science* 128. Greenwood Press: Westport, Connecticut.

Mayer, Thom A. 1997. "Triage: History and Horizons." *Topics in Emergency Medicine* 19 (2): 1–11.

McEntire, D. A. (1997). Reflecting on the weaknesses of the international community during the IDNDR: some implications for research and its application. Disaster Prevention and Management, 6(4), 221–233.

McEntire, D. A., Robinson, R and Weber, R. (2003). Business involvement in disasters: corporate roles, functions and interaction with the public sector. In Monday, J. (ed.), Beyond September 11th: An Account of Post-disaster Research. Special Publication #39. Boulder, Co.: Natural Hazards Research and Applications Information Center, University of Colorado.

McEntire, David A. 2002. "Coordinating Multi-Organizational Responses to Disaster: Lessons From the March 28, 2000, Fort Worth Tornado." *Disaster Prevention and Management* 11 (5): 369–379.

McEntire, David A. 2002a. "Understanding and Improving Damage Assessment." *IAEM Bulletin* (May): 9, 12.

McEntire, David A. and Amy Myers. 2004. "Preparing Communities for Disasters: Issues and Processes for Government Readiness." *Disaster Prevention and Management* 13 (2): 140–152.

McEntire, David A. and Jill Cope. 2004. "Damage Assessment After the Paso Robles (San Simeon, California) Earthquake: Lessons for Emergency Management." *Quick Response Report* 166, Natural Hazards Center, University of Colorado at Boulder. http://www.colorado.edu/hazards/qr/qr166/qr166.html.

McGlown, K. Joanne. 2004. Terrorism and Disaster Management: Preparing Healthcare Leaders for the New Reality. *ACHE Management Series.* Health Administration Press: Chicago, Il.

Mileti, D. S. 1999. Disasters by design: A reassessment of natural hazards in the United States. Washington, D.C.: Joseph Henry Press.

Mileti, Dennis. S., John H. Sorensen, and Paul W. O'Brien. 1992. "Toward an Explanation of Mass Care Shelter Use in Evacuations." *International Journal of Mass Emergencies and Disasters.* 10 (1): 25–42.

Mileti, Dennis S. and Eve Passarini. 1996. "A Social Explanation of Urban Relocation After Earthquakes." *International Journal of Mass Emergencies and Disasters* 14 (1): 97–110.

Mitchell James K. 1996. The Long Road to Recovery: Community Responses to Industrial Disaster. United Nations University Press: New York.

Mitchell, Jeffrey T. 1988a. "Stress: The History, Status and Future of Critical Incident Stress Debriefings." JEMS 13 (11): 47–52.

Mitchell, Jeffrey T. 1988b. "Stress: Development and Functions of a Critical Incident Stress Debriefing Team." JEMS 13 (12): 43–46.

Moore, William. 1999. "Developing an Emergency Operations Center. *IQ Service Report* 30 (7): ICMA: Washington, D.C.

Moskovitz, Diana. 2004. "St. Lucie County's Pockets Hit Hard By Debris Cleanup." Port St. Lucie News. October 10.

Mravcak, Agnes. 1994. "From the General to the Specifics: National Donations Management Policy." Presentation at the Donated Goods and Services Workshop, National Hurricane Conference, March 10.

National Biological Informational Infrastructure, 2006. "West Nile Virus: Overview." http://westnilevirus.nbii.gov/diseasehome.jsp?disease=West%20Nile%20Virus&pa gemode=submit accessed January 31, 2006.

National Commission on Terrorist Attacks Upon the United States. 2004. The 9/11 Commission Report. W. W. Norton: New York.

National Institute for Occupational Safety and Health, 2006. "Understanding Respiratory Protection Against SARS." http://www.cdc.gov/niosh/npptl/topics/respirators/factsheets/respsars.html accessed January 29, 2006.

National Intelligence Agency, 2006. http://www.cia.gov/nic/special_sarsthreat.html accessed January 29, 2006.

Neal, David M. 1994. "The Consequences of Excessive Unrequested Donations: The Case of Hurricane Andrew." *Disaster Management* 6 (1): 23–28.

Neal, David M. and Brenda D. Phillips. 1995. "Effective Emergency Management: Reconsidering the Bureaucratic Approach." *Disasters* 19 (4): 327–337.

NGCD, 2006. Geomagnetic Field Frequently Asked Questions." Accessed at http://www.ngdc.noaa.gov/seg/geomag/faqgeom.shtml on February 20, 2006.

Nicholson, William C. 2005. "Immunity Law: Protection for Emergency Responders." *Journal of Emergency Management* 3 (1): 12–13.

Nicholson, William C. 2003a. "Litigation Mitigation: Proactive Risk Management in the Wake of the West Warwick Club Fire." *Journal of Emergency Management* 1 (2): 14-18.

Niesse, Marie. 2004. "County Debris Removal Just 15% Complete, Official Says." Palatka Daily News. October 9.

Oaks, Sherry D. 1990. "The Damage Assessment Process: An Overview." pp. 6–16 in ed. Bolin, Robert. The Loma Prieta Earthquake: Studies of Short-Term Impacts. *Program on Environment and Behavior Monograph #50*, Institute of Behavioral Science, University of Colorado: Boulder, Colorado.

Office of the Federal Register, National Archives and Records Administration. 2001. *Code of Federal Regulations 44, Emergency Management and Assistance*. (as of October 1, 2001). U.S. Government Printing Office: Washington, D.C.

O'Halloran, Philip. 1989. "Triage: Issues and Ethics." Emergency (February): 45–47.

Oklahoma Department of Civil Emergency Management. 1996. Donations Management Case Study of the Alfred P. Murrah Federal Building Bombing, 19 April 1995 in Oklahoma City, Oklahoma, Summary and Lessons Learned.

Olson, Richard Stuart, Robert A. Olson and Vincent T. Gawronski. 1998. "Night and Day: Mitigation Policymaking in Oakland, California Before and After the Loma Prieta Disaster." *International Journal of Mass Emergencies and Disasters* 14 (1): 97–110.

Onder, James J. 1999. "Media and Law Enforcement Relations During Hostage-Taking Terrorist Incidents: A Cooperative Decision." *Responder* (January): 26–32.

Payne, Christopher F. 1994. "Handling the Press." *Disaster Prevention and Management* 3 (1): 2–32.

Payne, Christopher F. 1999. "Contingency Plan Exercises." *Disaster Prevention and Management* 8 (2): 111–117.

Peacock, W. G. (1997). Cross-national and comparative disaster research. *International Journal of Mass Emergencies and Disasters,* 15(1), 117–133.

Peacock, Walk, Betty Hearn Morrow and Hugh Gladwin (eds.). 1997. *Hurricane Andrew and the Reshaping of Miami: Ethnicity, Generate and the Socio-Political Ecology of Disasters*. University Press of Florida: Gainesville.

PECC, 2005. "Thailand, Pacific Food System Outlook 2004-05." Accessed at http://www.pecc.org/food/papers/2004-05/thailand-0405-profiles.pdf on February 7, 2006.

Peek, Lori A. and Jeannette N. Sutton. 2003. "An Exploratory Comparison of Disasters, Riots and Terrorist Acts." *Disasters* 27 (3): 319–335.

Perrow Charles. 1999. *Normal Accidents: Living With High-Risk Technologies.* Princeton University Press: New Jersey.

Perry, Ronald. 2003. "Incident Management Systems in Disaster Management." *Disaster Prevention and Management.* 12 (5): 405–453.

Perry, Ronald W. 2003. "Municipal Terrorism Management in the United States." Disaster Prevention and Management 12 (3): 190–202.

Pickett, J. H. and B. A. Block. 1991. Day-today management. In G. J. Hoetmer and T. E. Drabek (Eds.), *Emergency Management: Principles and Practice for Local Government.* Washington, D.C.: ICMA.

Pijawka David A. Essam Radwan and J. Andy Soesilo. 1988. "Emergency Response to a Hazardous-Materials Rail Incident in Casa Grande Arizona." Pp. 43–61 in Charles Michael T. and John Choon K. Kim (eds.) *Crisis Management: A Casebook.* Charles C. Thomas Publisher: Springfield Il.

Pijawka, K. D. and Radwan, A. E. (1985). The transportation of hazardous materials: risk assessment and hazard management, *Dangerous Properties of Industrial Materials Report,* (September/October), 2–11.

Pine, John. 1991. "Liability Issues." Pp. 289-310 in Drabek, T.E. and Hoetmer, G.J. *Emergency Management: Principles and Practice for Emergency Management.* ICMA: Washington, D.C.

Points of Light Foundation & Volunteer Center National Network. 2002. Preventing a Disaster Within the Disaster: The Effective Use and Management of Unaffiliated Volunteers. Points of Light Foundation & Volunteer Center National Network: Washington, D.C.

Pryor, John P. 2003. "The 2001 World Trade Center Disaster." International Journal of Disaster Medicine 1: 6–18.

Quarantelli, E. L. 1970. "The Community General Hospital: Its Immediate Problems in Disasters." *American Behavioral Scientist* 13: 381–391.

Quaranteli, E. L. and Russell R. Dynes. 1972. "When Disaster Strikes it Isn't Much Like What You've Read About." *Psychology Today* (February): 67–70.

Quarantelli, E. L. 1982. *Sheltering and Housing After Major Community Disasters: Case Studies and General Observations*. Federal Emergency Management Agency: Washington, D.C.

Quarantelli, E. L. 1983. *Delivery of Emergency Medical Services in Disasters*. New York: Irvington.

Quarantelli, E. L. 1984. "Organizational Behavior in Disasters and Implications for Disaster Planning." *Monograph* Series Vol. 1 (2). National Emergency Training Center: Emmitsburg, Maryland.

Quarantelli, E. L. 1987. "Disaster Studies: An Analysis of the Social Historical Factors Affecting the Development of Research in the Area." *International Journal of Mass Emergencies and Disasters* 5 (3): 285–310.

Quarantelli, E. L. (1989). Human behavior in the Mexico City earthquake: some implications from basic themes in survey findings. Preliminary Paper #37, Newark, De.: Disaster Research Center, University of Delaware.

Quarantelli, E. L. (1992). The environmental disasters of the future will be more and worse but the prospect is not hopeless. *Disaster Prevention and Management,* 2(1): 11–25.

Quarantelli, E. L. 1996. "Emergent Behaviors and Groups in the Crisis Time of Disasters." pp. 47–68. *In Individuality and Social Control: Essays in Honor of Tamotsu Shibutani,* edited by Kian M. Kwan. JAI Press: Greenwich, CT.

Quarantelli, E. L. 1996. "Local Mass Media Operations in Disasters in the USA." *Disaster Prevention and Management* 5 (5): 5–10.

Quarantelli E. L. 1997. "Problematical Aspects of the Information/ Communication Revolution for Disaster Planning and Research: Ten Non-Technical Issues and Questions." *Disaster Prevention and Management* 6 (2): 94–106.

Rahimi, Mansour. 1993. An Examination of Behavior and Hazards Faced by Physically Disabled People During the Loma Prieta Earthquake. *Natural Hazards.* 7: 59–82.

Rubin, Claire B. 1991. "Recovery from Disaster." pp. 224–262 in *Emergency Management: Principles and Practices for Local Government.* ICMA: Washington, D.C.

Saulny, Susan. 2002. "Credit Union Says A.T.M. Users Stole Millions After 9/11." *New York Times.* August 6. p. A1.

Scanlon, Joseph and Suzanne Alldred. 1982. Media Coverage of Disaster: The Same Old Story." In Barclay G. Jones and Miha Tomazevic., Eds. *Social and Economic Aspects of Earthquakes Ithaca: Program in Urgan and Regional Studies,* Cornell University.

Scanlon, Joseph. 1994. The Role of EOCs in Emergency Management: A Comparison of American and Canadian Experience. *International Journal of Mass Emergencies and Disasters* 12 (1): 51–75.

Scanlon, Joseph. 1996. "Not on the Record: Disaster, Records and Disaster Research." *International Journal of Mass Emergencies and Disasters.* 14 (3): 265–280.

Scanlon, Joseph. 2003. "Transportation in Emergencies: An Often Neglected Story." *Disaster Prevention and Management* 12 (5): 428–437.

Scanlon, Joseph, Suzanne Alldred, Al Farrell and Angela Prawzick. 1985. "Coping With the Media in Disasters: Some Predictable Problems." *Public Administration Review* 45 (January): 123–33.

Scanlon, Joseph. 1998. "Dealing With Mass Death After a Community Catastrophe: Handling Bodies after the 1917 Halifax Explosion." *Disaster Prevention and Management* 7 (4): 288–304.

Schneider, Saundra K. 1985. *Flirting with Disaster: Public Management in Crisis Situations.* M. E. Sharpe: New York.

Schwab, Jim. 1998. Tornado Case Study: Plainfield, Illinois. Pp. 229–234 in Swab, Jim, Kenneth C. Toppin, Charles C. Eadie, Robert E. Deyle, Richard A. Smith. *Planning for Post-Disaster Recovery and Reconstruction. American Planning Association.* Chicago, I.

Selves, Michael D. 2002. "Local Emergency Management: A Tale of Two Models." Emergency Management Institute, Federal Emergency Management Agency. Http://www.training.fema.gov/ emiweb/ edu/localEM1.html.

Shoaf, Kimberly I., Loc H. Ngyyen, Harvinder R. Sareen, Linda B. Bourque. 1998. "Injuries as a Result of California Earthquakes in the Past Decade." *Disasters* 22 (3): 218–235.

Simpson, David M. 2001. "Community Emergency Response Training (CERTS): A Recent History and Review." *Natural Hazards Review* 2 (2): 54–63.

Sorensen, John H. 2000. "Hazard Warning Systems: Review of 20 Years of Progress." *Natural Hazards Review* 1 (2): 119–125.

Sorensen, John H. and Dennis S. Mileti. 1988. "Warning and Evacuation: Answering Some Basic Questions." *Industrial Crisis Quarterly* 2: 195–209.

Stallings, Robert A. and E. L. Quarantelli. 1985. "Emergent Citizen Groups and Emergency Management." *Public Administration Review* (Special Issue): 93–100.

State Department, 2005. "Avian Flu Fact Sheet." Accessed at http:// travel.state.gov/travel/tips/health/health_1181.html on February 7, 2006.

Steinberg L. J. and A. M. Cruz. 2004. "When Natural and Technological Disasters Collide: Lessons from the Turkey Earthquake of August 17 1999." *Natural Hazards Review* 5 (2): 121–130.

Steinberg L. J. V. Basolo R. Burby J. N. Levine and A. M. Cruz. 2004. "Joint Seismic and Technological Disasters: Possible Impacts and Community Preparedness in an Urban Setting." *Natural Hazards Review* 5 (4): 159–169.

Sutphen, Sandra and William L. Waugh, Jr. 1998. "Organizational Reform and Technological Innovation in Emergency Management." *International Journal of Mass Emergencies and Disasters* 16 (1): 7–12.

Swan, Robert C. 2000. "Debris Management Planning for the 21st Century." *Natural Hazards Review* 1 (4): 222–225.

Sylves, Richard T. and William L. Waugh, Jr. 1996. *Disaster Management in the U.S. and Canada: The Politics, Policymaking, Administration and Analysis of Emergency Management.* Charles C. Thomas Publisher: Springfield, Il.

Tarcey, Brian. 2004. "The Politics of Disaster." *Harvard Magazine* (March/April).

The National Academies, 2006. "A Closer Look at Global Warming." Accessed At http://www4.nationalacademies.org/onpi/webextra. nsf/44bf87db309563a0852566f2006d63bb/ f6335bf011038bb185256a84005838c7?html accessed on January 18, 2006.

The World Bank, 2005. "Economic Impact of Avian Flu." http://web. worldbank.org/WBSITE/EXTERNAL/NEWS/0,,contentMDK: 20709923~pagePK: 64257043~piPK:437376~theSitePK:4607,00. html accessed on February 7, 2006.

The World Health Organization, 2006. "Cumulative Number of Confirmed Human Cases of Avian Influenza A/(H5N1) Reported to WHO" Accessed at http://www.who.int/csr/disease/avian_influenza/ country/cases_table_2006_02_06/en/index.html on February 7, 2006.

Thoma, Kris. 2004. "Community Works On Debris Cleanup." Pensacola News Journal. October 13.

Thomas, Deborah S. K. and Susan L. Cutter, Michael Hodgson, Mike Gutekunst and Steven Jones. 2002. "Use of Spatial Data and Geographic Technologies in Response to the September 11 Terrorist Attack." *Quick Response Report* # 153. Natural Hazards Research and Information Applications Center, University of Colorado: Boulder, Colorado.

Thomas, Evan. 2005. *Newsweek.* September 19.

Tierney, Kathleen J., Michael K. Lindell and Ronald W. Perry. 2001. *Facing the Unexpected: Disaster Preparedness and Response in the United States.* Joseph Henry Press: Washington, D.C.

Tierney, Kathleen. 2003. Disaster Beliefs and Institutional Interests: Recycling Disaster Myths in the Aftermath of 9–11. pp. 32–51 in Clarke, Lee (ed) *Terrorism and Disaster: New Threats, New Ideas. Research in Social Problems and Public Policy. Vol. 11.* New York: Elsevier.

Timmerman, P. (1981). Vulnerability, resilience and the collapse of society. Toronto: Institute of Environmental Studies.

Turner, Barry A. 1994. "Flexibility and Improvisation in Emergency Response." *Disaster Management.* Vol. 6 (2): 84–89.

U.S. Department of Health and Human Services. 2001. "Emergency Response: Disaster Medical Assistance Teams (DMATs) and Disaster Mortuary Operational Response Teams (DMORTs)." http://www.hhs.gov/new/press/2001pres/20010911c.html.

U.S. Global Change Research Program accessed at http://www.nacc.usgcrp.gov/ on January 23, 2006.

Volunteer Management Committee. (undated). Managing Spontaneous Volunteers in Times of Disaster: The Synergy of Structure and Good Intentions. Points of Light Foundation & Volunteer Center National Network: Washington, D.C.

Volunteer Management Committee. 2003. Managing Unaffiliated Volunteers: Concepts of Operations. National Voluntary Organizations Active in Disasters (NVOAD): Alexandria, Va.

Waugh William L. Jr. 1988. "The Hyatt Skywalk Disaster." pp. 115–129 in Charles Michael T. and John Choon K. Kim (eds.) *Crisis Management: A Casebook.* Charles C. Thomas Publisher: Springfield Il.

Waugh, William W. 1993. "Coordination or Control: Organizational Design and the Emergency Management Function." *Disaster Prevention and Management.* Vol. 2 (4): 17–31.

Waugh, William L. Jr. 1995. "Geographic Information Systems: The Case of Disaster Management." *Social Science Computer Review* 13 (4): 422–431.

Waugh, William L. Jr. 2000. *Living with Hazards, Dealing with Disasters: An Introduction to Emergency Management.* M. E. Sharpe: Armonk, New York.

Waugh, W. L. Jr. (2004). The all-hazards approach must be continued. *Journal of Emergency Management,* 2 (1), 11–12.

Webb, Gary R. 2002. "Sociology, Disasters, and Terrorism: Understanding the Threats of the New Millennium." *Sociological Focus* 35 (1): 87–95.

Wedel, Kenneth R. and Donald R. Baker. 1998. "After the Oklahoma City Bombing: A Case Study of the Resource Coordination Committee." *International Journal of Mass Emergencies and Disasters* 16 (3): 333–362.

Wenger, Dennis E., James D. Dykes, Thomas D. Sebok and Joan L. Neff. 1975. "It's a Matter of Myths: An Empirical Examination of Individual Insight into Disaster Response." *Mass Emergencies* 1:33–46.

World Health Organization, 2002. "West Nile Virus in the United States-Update 10." http://www.who.int/csr/don/2002_11_27/en/index.html accessed on January 31, 2006.

World Health Organization, 2006. "Update 95-SARS Chronology of a Killer." http://www.who.int/csr/don/2003_07_04/en/index.html accessed January 29, 2006.

Wright, Todd. 2004. "Massive Amount of Yard Debris Overwhelms City." *Tallahassee Democrat.* October 9.

GLOSSARY

Absolute poverty   A condition where people do not have sufficient resources to take care of basic needs such as food and shelter

ACU-1000   A type of interface equipment that links mobile radios, cell phones, satellite technology, and regular phones in a single real-time communication system.

Aerial assessment   Review of damage conducted in helicopters or planes that is especially useful when roads are blocked or flooding is widespread.

After-action report   A document that describes what went right and what adjustments you will need to make in the future.

Agent-generated demands   The needs made evident by the hazard (e.g., problems resulting from the disaster agent itself).

Aggregate debris   Trash that includes asphalt and concrete from damaged roads and bridges.

Alternate projects   Permanent projects that require abandonment of an old facility and building in a completely different area.

American Red Cross   A national member of the International Committee of the Red Cross (ICRC) and a member of the International Federation of Red Cross and Red Crescent Societies (IFRCRCS).

Area Field Office (AFO)   An office like an EOC or JFO, but it is responsible for coordinating the entire effort of federal, state, local, tribal, nongovernmental, and private-sector organizations.

Associated hazard   A natural hazard agent that typically occurs at the same time as the primary hazard (e.g., hurricanes produce flooding).

Atmospheric hazards   A hazard agent that is produced in or by the earth's atmosphere

Avian flu   An infection that stems from viruses commonly found in birds. Also know as the Asian flu or the bird flu.

Benefits   Government welfare programs that can be extended to disaster victims.

Biological hazards   Agents that spread disease or are otherwise poisonous.

Bounded rationality   The attempt to be rational is never fully achieved because of the constraints disasters present to the decision maker.

Briefing   A meeting that reviews all aspects of federal programs and requirements to give local officials an overview of the entire recovery process.

Budget   An allocation of monetary support for a given department by city or county leadership.

Built environment   The structures, technology, and infrastructure created by humans.

Bureaucratized external paternalism mode   A way of operating where an outside agency controls all decisions and recovery activities.

Bureaucratized paternalistic mode   A way of operating where a person or agency inside the community controls recovery with no victim input.

Cascading disaster   An event that triggers additional hazards or impacts.

Cash donations   Financial contributions to disaster organizations or the victims themselves.

Civil defense   An effort by government officials to prepare for nuclear war. It included the building of underground shelters and the creation of plans to evacuate targeted urban areas of strategic value.

Civil/Conflict hazards   Violent events that have the potential to produce mass casualties.

Climate change   An alteration of the earth's temperature and weather patterns.

Cold zone   An area not affected that can only be accessed by clean (or decontaminated) individuals.

Collaborative partnership mode   A way of operating that takes place when outsiders and victims work together to facilitate disaster recovery.

Collective or cooperative mode   A way of operating that is characterized by victims working together to achieve a common goal.

Communication   The process of relaying information that has bearing on the effectiveness of disaster response and recovery operations.

Community Emergency Response Teams (CERTs)   Groups of citizens that have received detailed information and specialized training to improve self-sufficiency in disasters.

Complex emergency   A humanitarian crisis that involves an extreme amount of violence among different ethnic groups coupled with political instability, poor economic conditions, weak law enforcement capabilities, and disaster conditions of some sort (e.g., drought and famine).

Complex or compound disaster   A disaster event that involves multiple variables.

Compound hazards   Multiple hazards that react to each other in chaotic fashion.

Computer hazards   A disruptive hazard associated with computer hardware and software.

Computer virus   A program that contains malicious codes.

Consequence management   Typical emergency management response and recovery operations that also take place after terrorist attacks.

Construction and demolition debris   Trash that includes wood, metal, wiring, insulation, tar or clay shingles, and other types of materials.

Continuity of operations   A goal to maintain the functioning of government in times of disasters.

Controller   Person who runs the exercise by initiating the events and distributing messages to be acted on.

Coordination   The harmonization of activities among diverse actors in emergency management with the purpose of overcoming the challenges inherent in disasters.

Creativity   Finding ways to resolve problems through unanticipated means.

Cribbing   Wood stacked under debris to stabilize it after it has been lifted by a lever.

Crisis management   A law enforcement activity which includes intelligence gathering to prevent terrorist attacks or evidence collection for the purposes of prosecution.

Critical incident stress (CIS)   Unusual work stress resulting from any trauma, crisis, or event that overwhelms available coping mechanisms of emergency service personnel.

Cyber-terrorism   The use of computers and the Internet to plan or carry out attacks.

Damage assessment   A process of identifying the extent of destruction, including individual impact as well as overall economic losses in the community.

Damage Survey Report (DSR)   A document that verifies the need and validity of the local and state requests for public assistance.

Debriefing   An extensive discussion about one's feelings regarding a traumatic stress experience such as a disaster.

Debris management   The collection, sorting, storage, transportation, and disposal or recycling of rubble, destroyed materials, and other wastes associated with a disaster. It also incorporates long-term measures to dispose of debris in an environmentally sound manner.

Debugging   A method that includes a keen observation of the decision process to correct potential weaknesses and mistakes.

Decision support systems   Software applications that help the emergency manager determine priorities and respond to a disaster.

Defusings   Short, unstructured meetings that encourage a brief discussion of the events to reduce acute stress.

Design-preferable models   Studying the situation or problem in detail, determining the gap that exists between the goal and reality, and intervening to adapt the process to the desired outcome.

Disaster declaration   A statement that the community or state cannot respond effectively without outside assistance.

Disaster housing   A government program that helps people find housing for homes that may be uninhabitable due to unsafe, unsanitary, or insecure conditions.

Disaster Medical Assistance Team (DMAT)   A group or team of medical personnel who provide emergency medical care during an extreme event.

Disaster Mortuary Team (DMORT)   A group of private citizens that are activated under the National Response Plan to deal with mass fatality incidents.

Disaster plan   A document that describes how the jurisdiction might respond to a disaster.

Disaster Recovery Center (DRC)   The location where victims go to meet with FEMA representatives and other relief providers to discuss assistance programs and application requirements.

Disasters   Deadly, destructive, and disruptive events that occur when a hazard (or multiple hazards) interact(s) with human vulnerability.

Donations management   The receipt, sorting, storing, and distribution of goods and monies for the benefit of victims during response and recovery operations.

Drill   A small and limited exercise to improve a single function in response operations.

Emergency assistance   Financial or other types of assistance to help local and state governments deal with the immediate impacts of disasters.

Emergency Management Assistance Compact (EMAC)   Similar to a local mutual aid except that it is for states.

Emergency managers   Public servants that help jurisdictions reduce the liabilities that lead to disasters. They also help build community disaster capabilities.

Emergency Operations Center (EOC)   A central location where leaders can gather information, discuss options, make decisions, disseminate policy, mobilize resources, and communicate with involved parties.

Emergency Operations Plan (EOP)   A document that describes what the community will do in the aftermath of a disaster.

Emergency Support Function (ESF)   An activity that must be performed in the aftermath of a disaster.

Emergent organizations   Groups of individuals who work together to perform common goals but do not have a formalized organization (Stallings and Quarantelli 1985, p. 84).

Environmental degradation   The depletion or pollution of the earth's natural resources.

Environmental hazards   Agents that involve the degradation of the environment, such as pollution, that pose a risk to people's health and well-being.

Established organizations   Groups that perform routine tasks with existing structures.

Evacuation   The movement of people away from potential or actual hazards for the purpose of safety.

Evaluators   People who determine if the players responded to the exercise effectively and in accordance with established policies and procedures.

Exaggeration   A simplistic overstatement about some type of phenomena.

Exercise   A simulation of a crisis, emergency, or disaster that has the goal of improving response and recovery operations in an actual event.

Expanding organizations   Groups that perform routine tasks with new structures.

Extending organizations   Groups that perform nonroutine tasks with existing structures.

Faith-based organizations   Nonprofit groups that perform some of the same functions as other nonprofits but are associated with religious organizations.

Federal Emergency Management Agency   Agency created in the late 1970s by President Jimmy Carter to help coordinate the activities of the government.

Federal government   The national political unit that is composed of many agencies and officials.

Finance/administration section   An organizational division under ICS that tracks costs, completes and files paperwork, and records expenses of operations and logistics.

First responders   Public safety personnel such as police, firefighters, and emergency medical technicians.

Flexibility   A willingness to depart from widely accepted standards and practices of doing things (thinking creatively and improvising solutions) to react effectively to unforeseen problems.

Full activation   The opening of an EOC with all pertinent actors and functions.

Full-scale exercise   A very large simulation that tests nearly all response and recovery capabilities

Functional exercise   A moderately sized drill to test a limited number of response and recovery capabilities.

Geographic Information Systems (GIS)   "Organized collection of computer hardware, software, geographic data, and personnel designed to efficiently capture, store, update, manipulate, analyze, and display all forms of geographically referenced information" (ESRI as cited by Dash 1997).

Geological hazards   Hazard agents associated with the earth's soil and rock.

Global warming   The rise of temperature of the earth's atmosphere.

Good Samaritan laws   Statutes that protect citizens who do all they can to provide medical and other services to those affected by accidents and disasters.

Grants   Gift funds that do not need to be repaid.

Hackers   Individuals that log into others' computers illegally and run or disrupt them from afar.

Hazard   A physical, technological, or intentional agent such as an earthquake, industrial explosion, or terrorist bombing.

Hazard and vulnerability assessment   An evaluation of the risks facing your community along with your capability for dealing with them.

Hazard detection   The process of identifying what hazard is about to occur or has taken place.

HAZUS   An assessment software tool that is used for analyzing potential losses from floods, hurricane winds, and earthquakes.

Hoof and mouth disease   A highly infectious disease among livestock created by the Apthovirus. Also known as foot and mouth disease.

Horizontal evacuation   The movement of people away from a hazard.

Horizontal relationships   Relationships in which parties communicate across departments and communities.

Hot zone   The affected (or contaminated) area.

Hydrologic hazards   Hazard agents that occur with the earth's water systems.

Improved projects   Assistance programs that make repairs beyond the initial design or expand the building.

Improvisation   Adapting to an unfolding situation.

Incident Command System (ICS)   "A set of personnel, policies, procedures, facilities and equipment, integrated into a common organizational structure designed to improve emergency response operations of all types and complexities" (Irwin 1989, p. 134).

Incident command   The on-scene leadership for the disaster.

Increased readiness conditions   Rating system that is sometimes based on numerical numbers (e.g., 1-4) and denote the severity of an event along with appropriate measures to be taken.

Independent beneficiary mode   A way of operating that occurs when resources are sent into the affected community.

Individual assistance (IA)   A relief program for citizens, businesses, and others affected by a disaster.

Individualistic self-help mode   A way of operating that occurs when the community provides its own labor and supplies for recovery.

Industrial hazards   Hazards produced by the extraction, creation, distribution, storage, use, and disposal of chemicals.

Information officer   Professional who works with the media to answer their questions about the event and release information to the public.

In-kind donations   Physical items such as supplies, equipment, and food.

Interoperability   The ability to communicate and operate across and with various disaster organizations.

Joint Field Office (JFO)   The location where FEMA representatives manage recovery.

Kickoff meeting   A meeting that covers federal disaster assistance programs and policies in an in-depth manner.

Large projects   Permanent assistance activities requiring payment over $48,900.

Laws   Rules that are established by the government to maintain order and perform important functions in society.

Leadership   An ability to motivate others to reach a goal or complete a task.

Levers   Long pieces of wood (e.g., 2 × 4) used to lift debris off of people.

Liaison officer   The point of contact with other organizations responding to the incident.

Light Detection And Ranging (LIDAR)   An airborne laser system that is used to detect heat and dangerous debris accumulations.

Litigation mitigation   An active effort with city attorneys to prevent legal liabilities and accept the need to spend time, effort, and money now to avoid future lawsuits (Williamson 2003b).

Loan programs   Funds loaned to individuals, families, and businesses that have sustained losses from disasters.

Local governments   City or county organizations that perform important public functions.

Logistics section   An organizational division under ICS that acquires and provides materials, services, and facilities to support the needs of responders as directed by the incident commander and the operations section.

Looting   Stealing others' personal belongings.

Lump-sum contracts   Contracts that provide payment for completion of a well-defined scope of work (when debris is concentrated) (Swan 2000, p. 224).

Martial law   The replacing of civilian authority with that of the military.

Mass fatality incident   Any situation where there are more bodies than can be handled using local resources.

Media   People and news organizations that provide information about disasters to the public.

Mercalli scale   A scale to measure earthquakes based on physical observation of damages that result from the movement of the earth's crust (e.g., broken windows, cracked walls, falling pictures).

Mitigation   Activities that attempt to prevent disasters or reduce potential for loss.

Mitigation action plan   A document that describes the vulnerabilities of the community and what should be done to correct them in the future.

Mitigation-generated demands   The desire to learn from the disaster and avoid making similar mistakes in the future.

Mutual aid   The sharing of personnel, equipment, and facilities. This occurs when local resources are inadequate to meet the needs of the disaster.

Mutually assured destruction   The use of nuclear weapons against one's enemy that invites massive retaliation and results in the annihilation of most major cities in both countries.

Myth   A false belief.

Na-tech disaster   A disaster that occurs when a natural hazard interacts with technology to produce or magnify adverse effects.

Na-Tech hazards   A combination of natural and technological hazards.

National Emergency Management Information System (NEMIS) A computer program that allows FEMA representatives to record personal information about the disaster victim as well as damages, losses, needs, etc. It is an automated system that helps to distribute relief to those in need.

National Guard   A reserve military unit operated under the direction of the governor.

National Incident Management System (NIMS)   "A comprehensive, national approach to incident management that is applicable to all jurisdictional levels and across functional disciplines" (FEMA 2004).

National Processing Service Center (NPSC)   A location that victims call to apply for government disaster assistance.

National Response Plan   A document that describes what the government will do in catastrophic disasters.

National Urban Search and Rescue Response   A system made up of 28 FEMA urban SAR Task Forces that are spread throughout the continental United States.

National Volunteer Organizations Active in Disasters (NVOAD)   An organization that brings agencies together to promote various types of assistance after disasters.

Natural environment   The physical milieu (earth's systems) in which disasters occur.

Natural hazards   Those events originating from the physical environment, typically because of radiation from the sun, heat flow within the earth, or the force of gravity

Near-earth object (NEO)   A terrestrial impact structure made up of mostly ice and dirt particles.

Needs assessment   An evaluation of what supplies or services are required in the aftermath of a disaster.

Negligence   Actions or inactions of emergency managers and responders cause injuries or damage to people and their property

NFPA 1600   A shared set of norms for disaster management, emergency management, and business-continuity programs.

Nonprofit sector   The division of society that is comprised of humanitarian, charitable religious, and voluntary organizations.

Normalcy-generated demands   The pressures to get things back to pre-disaster conditions.

Nuclear hazards   A hazard resulting from the presence of radioactive material.

Operations section   An organizational division under ICS that is responsible for implementing the strategy to respond to the incident as determined by the incident commander and the planning section.

Orientation   An informal introductory meeting.

Other assistance   Category of public assistance funds for the repair of parks, airports, and recreational facilities.

Other needs assistance   A government program that provides grants for home repair, replacement of personal property, and other disaster-related expenses for funeral, medical/dental care, and transportation.

Panic   People's inability to think clearly or their tendency to run frantically from buildings or the disaster scene.

Partial activation   The opening of an EOC with some pertinent actors and functions.

Pathogens   Organisms that spread disease and may include anthrax, smallpox, plague, hemorrhagic fever, and rickettsiae.

Permanent assistance   Financial payments or reimbursements to local and state governments for long-term rebuilding activities.

Planning section   An organizational division under ICS that collects and evaluates information about the disaster to determine operational priorities.

Players   The responders or department leaders that are evaluated in the exercise.

Pole reversal   A change in the earth's magnetic fields.

Post trauma stress disorder (PTSD)   A clinical diagnosis that signifies deep stress that is sometimes debilitating, resulting from a traumatic event.

Potentially hazardous asteroid (PHA)   An asteroid that comes within 0.05 AU or less of the earth.

Preliminary or detailed assessment   Review of damage that is performed within days or weeks after the disaster and seeks to determine the need for outside assistance.

Preparedness   Efforts to increase readiness for disaster response and recovery operations.

Preparedness   The building capabilities to improve the effectiveness of response and recovery operations.

Price gauging   The selling of goods and services at a price higher than the normal market rate.

Primary agency   Department that has ultimate responsibility for a particular emergency support function.

Primary hazard   A natural hazard agent that interacts with vulnerabilities and therefore produces a disaster.

Private sector   A part of society that includes businesses and corporations.

Profession   An occupation that is based on scientific knowledge and is respected by the community.

Professional model   The all-hazards, networking, collaborative, problem-solving, or public administration model of disaster response and recovery operations.

Protective measures   A reimbursement category that has the purpose of reducing losses or eliminating threats to life, public health, and safety.

Public assistance (PA)   A relief program for government entities.

Public buildings/equipment assistance   Funds to repair or replace buildings, supplies, and vehicles.

Public disaster education   A concerted effort to inform people about hazards and what to do if a disaster should occur.

Public Information Officers   Members of a department that have special skills in dealing with the media.

Public sector   The segment of society that is made up of government offices, departments, and agencies.

Public utility assistance   Funds for water, gas, and sewage system repairs.

Quarantine   The isolation of people who have contracted a communicable disease.

Rapid or initial assessment   Review of damage that is conducted immediately when a disaster occurs and seeks to gain a quick comprehension of deaths, injuries, victim needs, and overall scope of the disaster.

Rational decision making   Searching for alternative solutions and selecting the one that is deemed most appropriate.

Receivers   Equipment devices that obtain signals from transmitters. They include stereos, pagers, police scanners, and televisions.

Recovery   Activity to return the affected community to pre-disaster or, preferably, improved conditions.

Resilience   The ability to respond to and recover from a disaster quickly, effectively, and efficiently.

Resource list   A database that includes human and material resources that can be deployed in a disaster.

Response   Activity in the immediate aftermath of a disaster to protect life and property.

Response-generated demands   The needs that are made evident as individuals, organizations, and communities attempt to meet agent-generated demands.

Richter scale   A measurement of the registered shaking amplitudes of an earthquake.

Riots   Large disturbances where people engage in antisocial behavior.

Road systems assistance   Funds that repay expenses associated with the rebuilding or repairing of bridges, lights, and culverts.

Role or post abandonment   Not showing up to work during an emergency.

Safety officer   Professional who monitors the hazardous conditions of the disaster to ensure protection of responding personnel.

Saffir-Simpson scale I   A descriptive tool to explain the magnitude of a hurricane in terms of wind and storm surge.

Search and rescue operations   Response activities undertaken to find disaster victims and remove them from danger or confinement so they may receive urgent treatment such as hydration, basic first aid, or advanced medical care.

Secondary hazard   A hazard (natural, technological, or otherwise) that occurs as a result of the primary hazard.

Seismic hazards   Hazard agents produced by the movement of tectonic plates that float on magma.

Services   Government programs that address unique issues or needs made evident in the disaster.

Severe acute respiratory syndrome (SARS)   A viral respiratory disease caused by a corona virus (SARS-CoV).

Sheltering   The location or relocation of evacuees and others to places of refuge. A function that is frequently required in many disasters.

Shock   A period of disbelief after disaster that renders people unable to think or take care of themselves.

Situational awareness   A need to be vigilant of circumstances in order to understand the context of what is taking place.

Small projects   A type of permanent assistance that is typically paid in advance by the federal government and costs less than $48,899.

Social environment   The social, political, economic, and cultural activity or characteristics of the community.

Special populations   People who are susceptible to disasters and those who may be least able to deal with them.

Spontaneous or unaffiliated volunteers   People who engage in response and recovery efforts with no thought of payment; their efforts are directed toward the benefit of victims, first responders, emergency managers, and the community at large.

Standard Emergency Management System (SEMS)   The adoption of incident command by all political jurisdictions in a given state.

Standard operating procedures (SOPs)   Rules and guidelines to complete disaster functions effectively and efficiently.

State government   The political unit comprised of numerous cities and counties, including bureaucratic agencies and politicians.

Strategic national stockpile   A collection of antibiotics, vaccines, antiviral drugs, and other pharmaceuticals stored by the federal government.

Structural collapse hazards   Hazards that occur when gravity and poor engineering result in the failure of buildings, roads, or other construction projects.

Support agency   Department with the role of assisting the primary agency in the fulfillment of ESFs.

Syndromic surveillance   Tracking the flow of patients in a hospital or clinic to determine trends and consequences of diseases.

Synergistic disaster   An event where one resulting impact seems to magnify others.

Table-top   An informal discussion of a mock emergency or disaster situation.

Tactical EMS personnel   Emergency medical technicians that are also trained to use weapons

Talk group   A unit with its own designated channel.

Technical or engineering assessment   Review of damage that is performed days, weeks, or months after the disaster to determine the exact value of losses and requirements for rebuilding.

Technological hazards   Hazard agents related to industry, structures, hazardous materials, computers, and transportation systems.

Terrorism   The threat or use of violence to intimidate someone or a government.

Terrorism   Violent acts committed by individuals or groups seeking to disrupt society, instill fear, and promote objectives that are ideological in nature.

Time and material contracts   Agreements that are based on labor and equipment costs and are suitable for rights-of-way clearance and should not exceed 70 hours according to FEMA regulations for reimbursement (Swan 2000, p. 224).

Torino scale   A measurement tool scientists created in an attempt to predict the impact of a meteoroid strike.

Toxins   Poisons created by plants and animals.

Traditional model   The civil defense, command and control, bureaucratic, or emergency services perspective of disaster response and recovery operations.

Training   A review of emergency procedures as well as their application in a nonthreatening situation.

Transceivers   Instruments that are able to both transmit and receive information. Examples of transceivers include telephones, satellites, personal digital assistants, two-way radios, citizen-band radios, 800-Mhz radios, and ham radios.

Transmitters   Communication instruments that convey information through radios, sirens, television stations, and cable override systems.

Transportation hazards   An accident that occurs in the air, on roads or railways, or at sea.

Triage   An initial assessment and separation of victims for treatment based on the severity of their injuries.

Trunked radio system   A computer-controlled network that searches for a clear channel for users to use to talk to each other.

Unit price contracts   Agreements that are based on truck load sizes and are most common in disasters when the exact quantity of debris is unknown (Swan 2000, p. 224).

Unmet needs committee   A group of government leaders, concerned citizens, business representatives, and nonprofit organizations who join forces to help collect donations to address long-term needs of disaster victims.

Vegetative debris   Trash that includes broken tree limbs, tree stumps, brush, leaves, and yard waste.

Vertical evacuation   The movement of people from low areas to higher areas (moving from lower floors in a building to those above or the roof if there is a fire or flood).

Vertical relationships   Relationships in which there is information flow up and down chains of command.

Victims   Simulators who provide opportunities to test the players' knowledge and skills.

Volunteer management   The process of including volunteers in post-disaster operations in such a way as to harness their contributions and avoid their negative impact.

Vulnerability   Proneness to disasters or the inability of individuals, organizations, and communities to prevent them or deal with them effectively.

Walkthrough or site visit   A tour of the damaged areas by foot to determine the amount and type of disaster assistance households, businesses, and the government need.

Warm zone   The washing (or decontamination) area.

Warnings   Advanced notifications that allow people to take measures to protect themselves and their property. It indicates that the hazard is imminent, is taking place, or has occurred.

Watch   Notification that conditions are ripe for a hazard to occur.

Water control assistance   Funds for repairs to rivers, dikes, levees, and dams.

West Nile virus   A flavivirus that is dependent upon mosquitoes as vectors.

Wildfire hazards   Hazards that result from lightening strikes, which can quickly envelop hundreds of acres of forest and brush.

Windshield or drive-through assessment   An evaluation performed in a vehicle and completed without leaving the vehicle.

Worms   Viruses that reproduce over many computer systems due to Internet, networks, and e-mail connections.

PHOTO CREDITS

Figure 5-1:   NOAA News Photo/FEMA; FEMA Web site, Image Number 2711, A tornado

Figure 5-2:   U.S. Air Force photo by Staff Sgt. Nathan Gallahan; http://www.af.mil/shared/media/photodb/photos/060105-F-8220G-012.JPG, Washington weatherman, Photo by Sgt. Nathan Gallahn, U.S. Air Force

Figure 5-3:   Photo by Jocelyn Augustino/FEMA; FEMA Web site, Image Number 17429

Figure 5-4:   Photo by Ed Edahl/FEMA; FEMA Web site, Image Number 15803

Figure 5-5:   Photo by Jocelyn Augustino/FEMA; FEMA Web site, Image Number 17670

Figure 7-1:   Photo by Win Henderson/FEMA; FEMA Web site, Image Number 15540

Figure 7-2:   Photo by Andrea Booher/FEMA; FEMA Web site, Image Number 2131

Figure 7-3:   Photo by Michael Rieger/FEMA; FEMA Web site, Image Number 4018, 9/11

Figure 7-4:   Photo by Ed Edahal/FEMA; FEMA Web site, Image Number 1442

Figure 8-1:   Photo by Nicholas J. Lyman/FEMA; FEMA; Image Number 14246; www.fema.gov

Figure 8-2:   Photo by Bill Koplitz/FEMA; FEMA; Image Number 15912; www.fema.gov

Figure 8-3:   Photo by Robert Kaufman/FEMA; FEMA; Image Number 21269; www.fema.gov

Figure 10-1: Jocelyn Augustino, FEMA; Image ID: 17804, www.fema.gov

Figure 10-2: Photo by Anita Westervelt/FEMA; Image ID: 14492, www.fema.gov

Figure 11-1: Photo by Jocelyn Augustino/FEMA; FEMA, Image Number #25063; www.fema.gov; photo by Robert Kauffman

Figure 11-2: Photo by Mark Wolfe/FEMA; FEMA, Image Number #8149; www.fema.gov

Figure 13-1: Photo by Mark Wolfe/FEMA; FEMA: Image Number 14400; www.fema.gov

Figure 13-2: Photo by Robert Kaufmann/FEMA; FEMA: Image Number 20509; www.fema.gov

Figure 13-3: Photo by Jocelyn Augustino/FEMA; FEMA: Image Number 17716; www.fema.gov

INDEX